GEOFFREY HINDLEY, educated at University College, Oxford, is a lecturer and writer. He was three times an invited participant at the International Congress on Medieval Studies and has regularly lectured in Europe and America on medieval social history, European culture and the history of music. He is also the co-founder of the Society for the History of Medieval Technology and Science. His many books include *The Shaping of Europe*, *Saladin: a Biography* and *The Book of Magna Carta*. He lives in Peterborough, England.

Other titles by the same author

The Book of Magna Carta
The Royal Families of Europe
Saladin: a Biography

THE
CRUSADES

Geoffrey Hindley

CARROLL & GRAF PUBLISHERS
New York

To my wife, Diana

Carroll & Graf Publishers
An imprint of Avalon Publishing Group, Inc.
245 W. 17th Street
New York
NY 10011 5300
www.carrollandgraf.com

First published in the UK as *The Crusades*
by Constable, an imprint of Constable & Robinson Ltd 2003

This revised paperback edition published by Carroll & Graf 2004

ISBN 0-7867-1344-5

Printed and bound in the EU

Library of Congress Cataloging-in-Publication Data is available on file.

Contents

Acknowledgements

The sketch maps are based on information derived from William Miller's *The Latins in the Levant* (1908), *Westermanns Grosser Atlas zur Weltgeschichte* (1956), *The Hamlyn Historical Atlas* (1981), General Editor R.I. Moore and *The Atlas of the Crusades* (1991), edited by Jonathan Riley-Smith. The captions and notes on the maps in this book and the summary chapters introducing them have also proved a useful source for the main text.

Inevitably, Professor Riley-Smith's publications have been invaluable and my other chief debts are to the military historian of the First Crusade, John France, Norman Housley for the later crusading period and of course Sir Steven Runciman's classic *A History of the Crusades* published in the 1950s. Further sources are given in the Select Bibliography and in the Notes section. I have referred to certain specialist articles and in more than one case made use of anthology publications of articles by a single scholar, of particular use in this category was the collection on *The Crusade, Holy War and Canon Law* of James A. Brundage. Where such anthology publications follow the convention of reproducing the original article and retaining its pagination note references take the form 'IV, 65', the roman numeral denoting the item, the arabic denoting the page within the item.

My publishers suggested that a chronology of main events and lists of the principal rulers involved in the period as well as the Popes, might be of use to readers and I have been happy to comply. This book does not claim originality of research but it aims to offer a survey of an aspect of western European history familiar, at least as an idea to most people, but not, perhaps, known in much detail. It becomes clear that 'a crusade', though always proclaimed in the name of religion, could in fact be prosecuted for a mixture of motives of which the political and economic could often, perhaps generally, displace the idealistic. The British Prime Minister Harold Wilson once famously said 'Socialism is a Crusade or it is nothing.' Those of a different political persuasion would no doubt passionately object to this use of the word. But it continues to be used as a rallying cry for the most diverse causes.

Illustrations

—⋘●⋙—

Saladin wrenches the True Cross from the hands of King Guy, from Matthew Paris's *Chronica Majora* MS. 26.
Courtesy of the Master and Fellows of Corpus Christi College, Cambridge

Emperor Frederick I Barbarossa

Marienburg (Malborg, Poland)

The treaty between Richard and Nasir, from Matthew Paris's *Chronica Majora* MS. 16.
Courtesy of the Master and Fellows of Corpus Christi College, Cambridge

Seals of Blanche of Castile and Margaret of Provence

13th-century French crusaders landing at Damietta

Burning of the Templars at Paris, 1312

View of the island of Rhodes

Statue of Jan Hus
Courtesy of the Czech Tourist Authority, Prague

Medallions of the Byzantine Emperor John VIII Palaeologus and Sultan Mehmet II

The siege of Malta

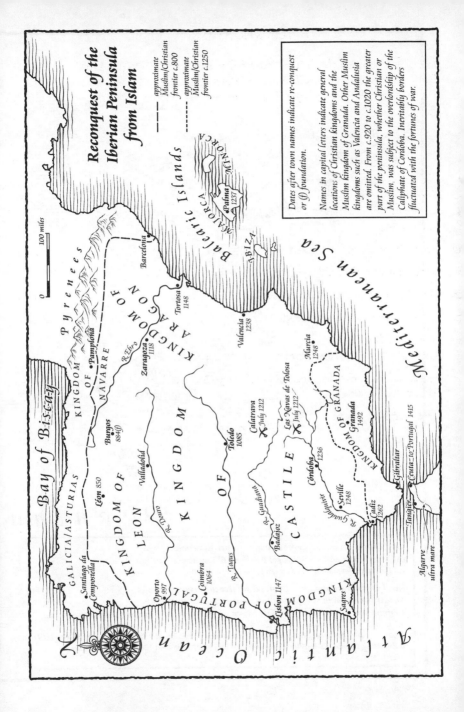

Reconquest of the Iberian Peninsula from Islam

— — — approximate Muslim/Christian frontier c.800

- - - - - approximate Muslim/Christian frontier c.1250

Dates after town names indicate re-conquest or (f) foundation.

Names in capital letters indicate general locations of Christian kingdoms and the Muslim kingdom of Granada. Other Muslim kingdoms such as Valencia and Andalusia are omitted. From c.920 to c.1020 the greater part of the peninsula, whether Christian or Muslim, was subject to the overlordship of the Caliphate of Córdoba. Inevitably borders fluctuated with the fortunes of war.

Bay of Biscay

Atlantic Ocean

Mediterranean Sea

Balearic Islands

Pyrenees

0   100 miles

GALICIA/ASTURIAS

Santiago da Compostella •

KINGDOM OF LEON

León 850
Valladolid
Burgos 884(f)

KINGDOM OF NAVARRE

Pamplona •

KINGDOM OF ARAGON

Barcelona •
Zaragoza 1118
R. Ebro
Tortosa 1148
Valencia 1238

KINGDOM OF CASTILE

Oporto 997 •
Coimbra 1064
R. Douro
R. Tagus
Badajoz
R. Guadiana
Toledo 1085
Calatrava ⚔ July 1212
Las Navas de Tolosa ⚔ July 1212
Murcia 1248

KINGDOM OF PORTUGAL

Lisbon 1147
Sagres •
Algarve ultra mare

KINGDOM OF GRANADA

Córdoba 1236
R. Guadalquivir
Seville 1248
Cádiz 1262
Granada 1492
Gibraltar
Tangier
Ceuta—to Portugal 1415

MAJORCA
Palma 1237
MINORCA
IBIZA

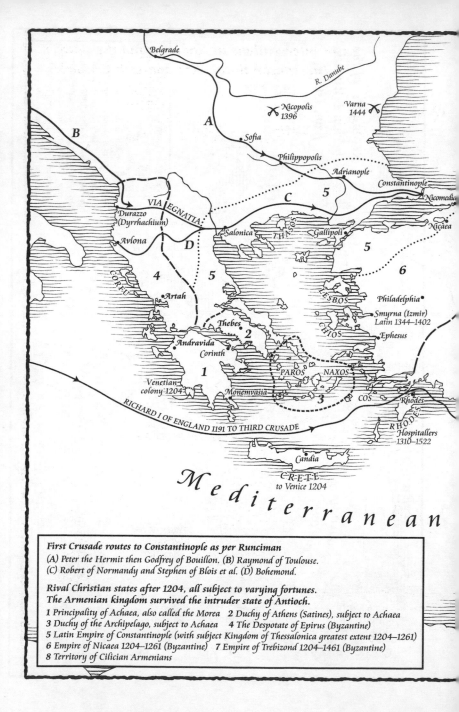

Belgrade

R. Danube

Nicopolis 1396

Varna 1444

A

Sofia

B

Philippopolis

Adrianople

Constantinople

C

5

Nicomedia

VIA EGNATIA

Durazzo (Dyrrhachium)

Salonica

THASOS

Gallipoli

5

Nicaea

Avlona

D

CORFU

4

5

LESBOS

Philadelphia

6

Artah

Smyrna (Izmir)
Latin 1344–1402

Thebes

2

CHIOS

Ephesus

Andravida
Corinth

1

PAROS

NAXOS

Venetian
colony 1204

Monemvasia

3

COS

Rhodes

RICHARD I OF ENGLAND 1191 TO THIRD CRUSADE

RHODES

Hospitallers
1310–1522

Candia

CRETE
to Venice 1204

Mediterranean

First Crusade routes to Constantinople as per Runciman

(A) Peter the Hermit then Godfrey of Bouillon. (B) Raymond of Toulouse.
(C) Robert of Normandy and Stephen of Blois et al. (D) Bohemond.

Rival Christian states after 1204, all subject to varying fortunes.
The Armenian kingdom survived the intruder state of Antioch.

1 Principality of Achaea, also called the Morea 2 Duchy of Athens (Satines), subject to Achaea
3 Duchy of the Archipelago, subject to Achaea 4 The Despotate of Epirus (Byzantine)
5 Latin Empire of Constantinople (with subject Kingdom of Thessalonica greatest extent 1204–1261)
6 Empire of Nicaea 1204–1261 (Byzantine) 7 Empire of Trebizond 1204–1461 (Byzantine)
8 Territory of Cilician Armenians

Latin interventions in Anatolia and the Eastern Mediterranean in the 12th and 13th Centuries

Black Sea

7 Trebizond

7

6

• Dorylaeum

S E L J U K S

O F

R U M

Myriocephalum

Konya (Iconium)

Heraclea 1101 •

R. Göksu

Antalya

Seleuca

KINGDOM OF CYPRUS

Famagusta

Limassol

Sea

R. Halys

Melitene •

COUNTY OF EDESSA 1120's

8

PRINCIPALITY OF ANTIOCH 1120's

Edessa •

Turbessel •

8

Alexandretta

8

Tarsus •

Antioch •

• Aleppo

R. Euphrates

St Symeon •

8

Saone •

R. Orontes

Latakia •

Tortosa •

Tripoli

• Homs

• Krak des Chevaliers

COUNTY OF TRIPOLI

Beirut •

• Baalbek

Sidon •

• Damascus

Tyre •

Acre •

Hattin ✕ 1187

Haifa •

• Tiberias

Nazareth •

• Belvoir

Caesarea •

• Ailun

Nablus •

R. Jordan

Arsuf •

Jaffa •

KINGDOM OF JERUSALEM before 1187

Ascalon •

Ramla •

• Jerusalem

• Bethlehem

Gaza •

• Kerak

Dead Sea

Damietta •

Monréal •

• Alexandria

• Mansurah

Bitter Lake

Cairo •

• Aqaba

N

0   100   200 miles

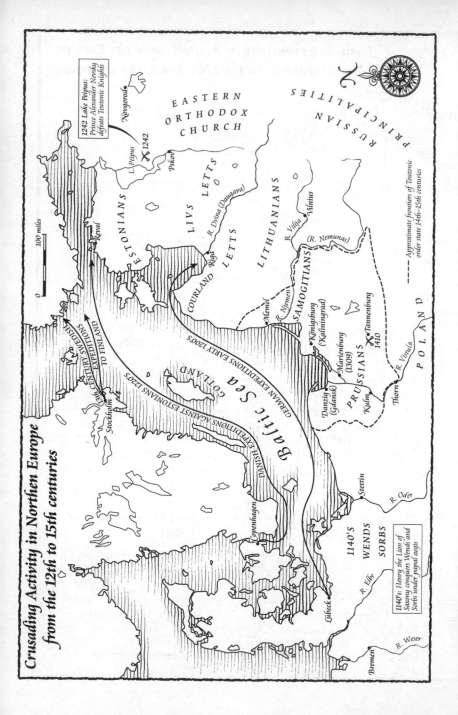

Crusading Activity in Northern Europe from the 12th to 15th centuries

1242 Lake Peipus: Prince Alexander Nevsky defeats Teutonic Knights

EASTERN ORTHODOX CHURCH

RUSSIAN PRINCIPALITIES

Novgorod

L. Peipus ✕ 1242

Pskov

ESTONIANS

LIVS

LETTS

LETTS

R. Drina (Daugava)

Reval

Riga

COURLAND

LITHUANIANS

R. Vilija

Vilnius

(R. Nemunas)

Memel

R. Niemen

SAMOGITIANS

Königsburg (Kaliningrad)

Marienburg (1309)

Tannenburg ✕ 1410

POLAND

Danzig (Gdansk)

Kulm

PRUSSIANS

Thorn

R. Vistula

GOTLAND

GERMAN EXPEDITIONS EARLY 1200's

Baltic Sea

DANISH EXPEDITIONS AGAINST ESTONIANS 1220's

13TH CENTURY SWEDES

FINNISH EXPEDITION TO FINLAND

Stockholm

Stettin

R. Oder

Copenhagen

1140's WENDS SORBS

1140's: Henry the Lion of Saxony conquers Wends and Sorbs under papal aegis

Lübeck

R. Elbe

Bremen

R. Weser

100 miles

Approximate frontiers of Teutonic order state 14th–15th centuries

Chronology of Jihad and Crusade

The Muslim world known to the crusaders stretched from Spain to Persia (though Muslim conquests had extended into northern India and beyond) and most of this territory had been acquired by conquests from former Christian rulers, notably the Byzantine Empire. Thus, both the Byzantine Emperor Alexius I and the crusaders themselves, like the rulers of Christian Spain, could claim to be recovering lands properly belonging to the Christian faith. The campaigns against the heathen peoples of Europe were justified as defensive wars against a potential threat, in the same way as the American and British governments felt justified in advocating war against Iraq in 2002.

(Capital letters denote pivotal events or key personalities)

Muslim conquests from the death of Muhammad (632) to the Turkish capture of Nicaea (1078)

635–42	Arab armies conquer Byzantine provinces from Egypt to Syria – Damascus taken (635), Antioch and Jerusalem (637), Alexandria (642).
711–32	Muslim conquest of Christian Spanish kingdoms and cities – Cordoba and Seville (711); Toledo (712); Zaragossa (714).
732	BATTLE OF TOURS/POITIERS Frankish ruler, Charles Martel ends Muslim advance in Europe.
903	Conquest of the Balearic Isles completed.
965	Arab conquest of Sicily from Byzantines.

969–73	Fatimid dynasty founds Cairo and then extends empire into Palestine.
969	Byzantine Emperor Nicephorus II recovers Antioch.
985	Antioch falls to Turks by treachery.
1012	Caliph al-Hakim destroys Church of the Holy Sepulchre.
1071	BATTLE OF MANZIKERT (Malazgirt, eastern Turkey). Sultan Alp Arslan defeats Byzantine Emperor Romanus IV.
1070s	Seljuk capture of historic Christian cities of Iconium (Konya) and Nicaea (Iznik, Turkey).

Landmarks in crusading history

1090	Visit of Count of Flanders to Constantinople prompts Emperor Alexius I to consider recruiting Western knights against the Turks.
1095	November, Council of CLERMONT. FIRST CRUSADE proclaimed by Pope URBAN II.
1096–97	Arrival of main armies at Constantinople under papal legate Bishop Adhémar of Le Puy. Military leaders: Godfrey of Bouillon, Duke of Lower Lorraine, Raymond of Toulouse, Robert of Normandy, Stephen of Blois, Hugh of Vermandois, Bohemond of Otranto. They swear loyalty to Emperor Alexius.
1097	April Capture of Nicaea. July Victory of Dorylaeum over Kilij Arslan.
1098	March Baldwin of Boulogne takes Edessa. June Capture of Antioch after an eight-month siege. Bohemond takes control of the city.
1099	15 July JERUSALEM CAPTURED.
1101–02	Lombard Crusade defeated at Amasya. Crusade of William of Aquitaine defeated at Heraclea.
1107–08	Crusade against Byzantine Empire proclaimed by Pope Paschal II in favour of Bohemond, lord of Antioch.
1107–10	Crusade of Sigurd of Norway.
1113	Knights Hospitaller given papal privilege by Pope Paschal II.
1114	Catalan Crusade against Muslim Balearic Islands.
1118–20	Knights Templar established in Jerusalem.
1119	BATTLE OF SARMADA or 'The Field of Blood' – the defeat of Roger of Antioch by Ilghazi of Aleppo.
1135	Innocent II proclaims crusade against *anti-pope Anacletus II*
1144	December ZANGI of Mosul takes EDESSA.
1145	December Pope Eugenius III proclaims a crusade.
1147–49	SECOND CRUSADE.

	Military leaders: Conrad III of Germany, Louis VII of France.
1147	October Capture of Muslim Lisbon by English and northern crusaders.
1148	July Defeat of Conrad and Louis before Damascus.
1154	Nur al-Din enters Damascus.
1169	Saladin wins control of Egypt.
1172	Saladin displaces Fatimid Caliph in Cairo.
1174	Death of Nur al-Din.
1170s	Foundation of Spanish military orders of Santiago, Avis and Alcántara.
1174–86	Saladin wins control of Damascus, Aleppo and Mosul.
1187	July BATTLE OF HATTIN.
	October JERUSALEM FALLS TO SALADIN.
1187	29 October Pope Gregory VIII proclaims a crusade.
1189–92	THIRD CRUSADE.
	Military leaders: Emperor Frederick I, Philip II Augustus King of France, Richard I King of England.
1189	May Departure of Emperor Frederick for Holy Land.
	August SIEGE OF ACRE begins.
1190	June Death of Emperor Frederick on crusade.
1191	June Richard of England takes Cyprus.
	Richard arrives at Acre.
	July ACRE CAPITULATES to crusaders.
1192	September Treaty of Jaffa between Richard I and Saladin.
1193	The death of Saladin.
1193–1230	Livonian crusades.
1202	Order of Sword Brethren founded.
1198	Foundation of Teutonic Order.
	August Pope Innocent III proclaims a crusade.
1202–1204	FOURTH CRUSADE.
	Leaders: Boniface of Montferrat, Doge Dandolo of Venice.
1204	April Crusaders' SACK OF CONSTANTINOPLE.
1208	ALBIGENSIAN CRUSADE proclaimed by Pope INNOCENT III.
1212	The Children's Crusade.
	Spanish crusade proclaimed by Pope INNOCENT III.
	BATTLE OF LAS NAVAS DE TOLOSA, Spanish and Portuguese defeat Almohads.
1213	Crusade for Holy Land proclaimed by INNOCENT III.
1216	Foundation charter of Dominican order of preachers at Toulouse.
	Missionaries against the Albigenses.

1217–29	FIFTH CRUSADE proclaimed by INNOCENT III 1213, Pope HONORIUS III, launched under Leaders Cardinal legate Pelagius, John of Brienne, king of Jerusalem; then, Emperor Frederick II.
1219	Capture of Damietta, Egypt.
1221	Crusaders capitulate at al-Mansura.
(1225	Teutonic Order established on Polish frontier with Prussia.)
1228	EMPEROR FREDERICK II finally sets out on 'Fifth Crusade' to Holy Land, though excommunicated.
1229	Feb–March Emperor Frederick agrees treaty with al-Kamil, Sultan of Egypt. Jerusalem restored to Christian rule; Frederick crowns himself 'King of Jerusalem'. (Once called the 'Sixth Crusade'.)
(1229	Teutonic Order's first campaigns against Prussians.)
1231	John of Brienne, ex-king of Jerusalem, crowned Latin Emperor of Constantinople.
1229–53	Crusades in Spain lead to Aragonese reconquest of Majorca, Ibiza and Valencia; Castilian capture of Córdoba (1236) and Seville (1248).
1237	Teutonic Order absorbs Order of the Sword Brethren.
1239	Pope Gregory IX and Emperor Frederick II at war.
1240–42	English crusade by Richard, Earl of Cornwall.
1242	BATTLE OF LAKE PEIPUS, the defeat of the Teutonic Order by St ALEXANDER NEVSKY of Novgorod, halts eastward expansion of Order.
1244	August Final loss of Jerusalem.
1248–54	First Crusade of Louis IX of France, to Egypt (once called the 'Seventh Crusade').
1249	Capture of Damietta, Egypt.
1250	Defeat of crusaders and capture of King Louis.
1250–54	Following his ransom, Louis active at Acre.
1260	Baybars becomes fourth Mamluk Sultan of Egypt.
1261	Emperor Michael VII Palaeologus expels Latins from Constantinople. Byzantine Empire restored.
1268	Antioch falls to Sultan Baybars.
1269	Second crusade of Louis IX of France.
1270	Death of Louis at Tunis.
1274	Second Council of Lyons. Byzantine envoys make formal submission of Orthodox Church to Rome – short-lived.
1285	French crusade against Peter of Aragon in support of Anjou claim to Kingdom of Sicily.

1291	FALL of ACRE to Mamluk Egypt in May. In August Franks evacuate their last territories in Palestine.
1307	Pope Clement V proclaims crusade against Constantinople.
1309	Teutonic Order moves HQ to Marienburg.
1310–11	Knights Hospitaller establish their base on Rhodes.
1312	Pope Clement V suppresses Order of Knights Templar.
1328	Pope John XXII at war against Emperor elect Ludwig IV.
1344	Crusade League takes Smyrna (Izmir). (From 1374 to 1402, held by the Hospitallers.)
1348–51	Swedish crusades against the Finns.
1365	Crusade proclaimed by Pope Urban V in support of Peter I of Cyprus, seizes and briefly holds Alexandria.
1394	Crusade to Nicopolis proclaimed by Pope Boniface IX of Rome and *anti-pope Benedict XIII of Avignon.*
1396	Bayezid I defeats army of Sigismund of Hungary and his Western allies John at BATTLE OF NICOPOLIS.
1410	BATTLE OF TANNENBERG, defeat of Teutonic Order by joint Polish-Lithuanian force.
1415	Portuguese take North African port of Ceuta.
1420	Prince Henry the Navigator of Portugal created Grand Master of the Order of Christ. His ships on voyages of discovery along the African coast bore the red cross on their sails.
1420–31	Crusades against the HUSSITES of Bohemia. Pope Martin V. Military leaders: Emperor elect Sigismund and others.
1439	At Council of Florence Orthodox Church makes short-lived submission to Rome.
1443	Pope Eugenius III proclaims crusade against Turks in defence of Constantinople.
1444	Crusade of Varna crushed by Sultan Murad II.
1452–56	Papal bulls of Nicholas V and Calixtus III sanction Portuguese conquests against 'Saracens . . . and other unbelievers inimical to Christ'.
1453	29 May CONSTANTINOPLE falls to Sultan MEHMET II 'the CONQUEROR'.
1464	Death of Pope Pius II, his proclamation of a crusade unanswered.
1492	Moorish KINGDOM of GRANADA falls to Spanish.
1523	Hospitallers quit the island of Rhodes, having capitulated to Sultan Suleyman I after a six-month siege.

1525   Albert of Hohenzollern, Grand Master of Teutonic Order in Prussia, converts to Lutheranism, dissolves the Order there and secularizes its lands as a hereditary fief in his family under the Polish crown.

1565   THE GREAT SIEGE OF MALTA Knights Hospitaller under Grand Master Valette repel the forces of Sultan Suleyman I.

1588   SPANISH ARMADA against Protestant England.

Introduction:
What's in a Name?

A crusade, or a *passagium generale*, *iter*, *voyage* or *Reise*, just some of the words used by the participants themselves, was a military expedition sponsored and blessed by the Pope or his appointed agents, against enemies of the Christian Faith. In the 400-odd years covered in this book that term was, for Western Europeans, synonymous with the Roman Catholic Church. A crusade's designated enemy was at first, and most usually, a Muslim ruler or region, but very soon crusades were launched against the heathen people of Central Europe and the Baltic region. The range widened to include heretics and schismatics deemed to threaten the authority of the Church, while more than once rival popes declared crusades against one another's supporters.

The Roman Church had an unswerving belief in itself as the vessel of divine grace in the world and the source of all divine authority, ordained by God and founded by His Son Jesus Christ on the ministry of His disciple St Peter, the first Bishop of Rome. In such a mindset it was impossible to conceive of the Roman Church as doing wrong, or of Rome admitting any rival to an equality of authority. To maintain its power and to extend the sway of Roman Catholic Christianity in the service of the Prince of Peace, even warfare was permitted – within the terms of a strict code of the Just War evolved by Church lawyers. The vast majority of Western Christians accepted these awesome claims. Many were to embark on the arduous and dangerous expeditions and all who did so were pledged by vows to the Cross, and assured of spiritual benefits in this life and the life to come.

If we take as our starting point the Council of Clermont of 1095 when Pope Urban II preached what we know as the First Crusade and, as the end of our story, the Spanish Armada against England in 1588, blessed by Pope Sixtus V and which was the last 'expedition of the Cross' on a comparable scale, we find ourselves confronted with a period of some 490 years during which hundreds of thousands of men, and many thousands of women too, embarked on hazardous military campaigns in the name of God and, as they believed, under the direct patronage of His representative upon earth. The enemy in these holy wars might be unbelievers such as the 'infidel' Muslim states in the Mediterranean lands once ruled by the Christian Roman Empire, they might be heathen Prussians or Slavs or Wends on the northern frontiers of Roman Catholic Christendom, but they might also be heretics – dissident Christians who rejected what was considered the true faith; and they might even be members of the other great community of Christendom – the Eastern Orthodox Church with its seat in the great Christian city of Constantinople sacked by crusaders in 1204.

While historians accept the word 'crusade' as a convenient term to cover the various words used by contemporaries, some question the traditional enumeration since it covers only campaigns against the Muslim world and even omits many of these. However, since the First Crusade of 1095 is accurately so called, the Second Crusade of 1148–49 is well remembered by all admirers of Eleanor of Aquitaine, the Third Crusade of the 1190s is identified for the English-speaking world with the names of Richard I, the Lionheart, and Saladin, and the Fourth Crusade of 1204 is notorious for the sacking of Constantinople, these names are universally adopted. This Introduction sets out to describe what the word 'crusade' means: the rest of the book aims to narrate the principal events of crusading history and give some idea of what the people involved supposed they were doing. The crusades and particularly those to the Holy Land were, in the words of John Riley-Smith, 'arduous, disorientating, frightening, dangerous and expensive for participants, and the continuing enthusiasm for them displayed over the centuries is not easy to explain'.[1]

The *Oxford English Dictionary*'s first record of the actual word 'crusade' in an English literary text is for the year 1757 when William

Shenstone referred to 'cowl'd zealots [who] urged the crusade'. In French too, '*croisade*', soon Englished as 'croisad', was a late comer, being a sixteenth-century adaptation from the Spanish '*cruzada*' and/ or the Italian '*cruzeta*'. From the thirteenth century on French vernacular writers spoke of '*croiseries*' or '*croisades*', in place of the more formal Latinisms (both words were adopted in English sources), officially in use. For example, men spoke of a 'general passage' (*passagium generale*), a 'journey' ('*iter*'), an 'expedition of the Cross' ('*expeditio crucis*') or quite simply of a 'pilgrimage' (Latin, '*peregrinatio*'), while the crusaders themselves were commonly known as '*crucesignati*', 'marked with the sign of the Cross'.

From the outset, pilgrimage was not, in the words of historian Marcus Bull, 'simply a simile by which to make sense of the campaign's novelty, nor as camouflage for expansionist aggression, but as the core of [such an expedition's] purpose, form and rituals'.[2] The enterprise launched by Pope Urban at Clermont was certainly a novelty, but Western Christians had been at war with the Muslim world in southern Europe for centuries. In the Iberian peninsula, conquered for Islam in the eighth century, the Spanish kingdoms had been warring with the Moorish states for more than 300 years; in Sicily Norman adventurers had been wresting the ancient Byzantine province from its Arabic rulers for the best part of 70 years. But, to follow the analysis of Bull, with Clermont three elements are brought together to create something entirely new in the wars between the religions: terminology (the vow), symbolism (the cross), and spiritual rewards (penitential remissions).[3]

The tradition of pilgrimage was well established. By AD 350 there was a regular pilgrim route from Bordeaux to Jerusalem with hospices on the way and in the 390s Etheria, a noble lady of patrician family from north-western Spain, travelled to Egypt and then on through the Sinai desert, where she marvelled at the rock from which Moses had struck water and so to Jerusalem, where she attended the Sunday dawn Eucharist at the basilica 'near the Anastasis . . . outside the doors . . . where lights are hanging for the purpose . . . and where the whole multitude assembles before cockcrow'.[4] Christian pilgrimage to the Holy Places continued after Jerusalem, then part of the Christian Roman Empire, had fallen to the armies of Islam in their century of triumphant conquest which followed the death of Muhammad in 632.

Travel lust and curiosity no doubt played a part but it would be

superficial to discount the lay participants' very real religious sentiments. As a social group, Europe's knightly class was given to acts of
practical piety as well as bloodthirsty warfare. And if we view their
endowments of local religious communities as payments of conscience
money, that is merely to admit that they were liable to the prick of
conscience. The charters speak of a powerful sense of sinfulness, 'a
concern for the spiritual welfare of kinsfolk and an appreciation that a
family's . . . living members bore some responsibility for the dead'.[5]
Christendom itself was seen as an extended family while its members
saw themselves as members of extended families inhabiting time and
eternity. Mixed motives are the common condition of all humanity but
mixed means good as well as bad. So when a man or a woman set out on
the 3,000-mile overland track to the Holy Land with a glow of religious
fervour in their heart, and on their return (should they survive) entered
a religious community, it would be stupid on our part to discount their
motivation as a mere tourist itch compounded with hunger for loot.

At first, the majority of crusaders, calling themselves Franks, came
from France, or French and Flemish Flanders. From the Second
Crusade onwards in particular, contingents of Germans, English and
Italians also contributed to a more or less important extent while
individual men and women from virtually every '*natio*' (Latin, 'birth',
'tribe') in Western Europe took part. To their Arab or Turkish opponents, for whom no doubt they all 'looked alike', all were Franks. The
crusades played a formative role in Western Christendom's development of self-identity. But the different '*nationes*' were increasingly
aware of their own distinctive traditions. Contemporaries distinguished between the bare-legged Scots, the superstitious English, the
forest-dwelling huntsmen from Wales, the hard-drinking Danes or the
Norwegians, connoisseurs of 'raw' fish. Germans were suspicious of the
French and considered them arrogant. The French of course rejoiced in
their superiority to all other peoples, though they, like the rest of
Europe, distrusted the sophisticated, street-wise, business-oriented
Italians. Everybody despised the wily, schismatic Greeks.

In the Holy Land itself, there was similar diversity of cultural and
ethnic awareness in which religion could also play its part. Arabs and
Turks tended to be mutually hostile, as the latter asserted themselves
as the new establishment in Syria. Both despised the Kurds, though
they admitted grudging respect for Saladin the Kurd. Communities of
Armenian and Syrian–Arab Christians established long before the
coming of Islam, as well as scattered communities of Jews who

antedated all, completed a complex multicultural patchwork which was to be torn and re-patterned by the incursion from the north.

In the long perspective of Christian tradition Islam was a fairly recent arrival. After all, it was only in the seventh century of the Christian era that the armies of Islam had exploded in lightning conquests of the *jihad* or 'Holy War', after the death of Muhammad in 632. Under the supreme command of the caliphs, the successors of the Prophet and, like later popes, 'Commanders of the Faithful',[6] Islam had conquered the southern Mediterranean coast from Antioch (Antakya in modern Turkey) through Syria, Egypt and North Africa to the Pyrenees from Christian kings and emperors. In the Roman Church's doctrine of the Just War, the twin rights of defence against aggression and the recovery of territory from an aggressor were central to it. Whether the military expeditions we call the crusades were inevitable may be questioned, but the evolutions of history favoured the possibility.

Whether justified or not, the First Crusade was, in administrative, logistical and military terms, an undoubted success. From the preaching of the expedition in November 1095 to the raising of the Christian standards on the walls of Jerusalem in July 1099 was a period of somewhat less than five years. In that time, forces had been mobilized in numbers hitherto unknown in the West. Military historian John France assessed William the Conqueror's force at Hastings as probably no more than 9,000 to which we may add some 5,000 sailors for the Channel crossing. In 1081, the Norman, Robert Guiscard set out to conquer the Byzantine Empire with an army of about 15,000 fighting men. As a result of Pope Urban's initiative bodies of combatants totalling some 200,000 men were brought together in four principal army groups and marched through often rugged, sometimes parched and usually hostile terrain a distance of more than 3,000 miles to a theatre of war occupied by an enemy population totalling several millions and with armies considerably larger than the effective fighting men in the crusader ranks on their arrival. They fought three great enemies: the Turks of Anatolia (Asian Turkey), the Sultanate of Baghdad, and the rulers of Egypt; won no fewer than five major engagements and took by siege three major cities and a number of lesser ones. It was, moreover, a theatre where warfare was endemic and conducted by highly professional troops and commanders according to battlefield tactics unfamiliar to Western European fighting men, techniques which had to be learned and adapted to, almost literally on the hoof. Today, when the motives of the crusaders have been the principal focus of crusade debate the military achievement is either ignored or discounted as the inevitable triumph of Western aggressiveness; but there was nothing inevitable about it.

In military technology, equipment and theory the Islamic world was every bit as advanced as its opponents and equally given to the practice of war. The Turkish horse archers introduced the Western knights to an entirely new style of fighting. Westerners did occasionally fire from the saddle but there was nothing to match the divisions of trained bowmen in a Turkish army; with arrows that could pierce chain mail, their effective range of up to 200 feet of their composite bows 'astonished' the crusaders, while their rapid fire could produce a terrifying and seemingly uninterrupted hail of missiles as they swept in to the attack and then wheeled away with breathtaking manoeuvrability. It is true that the leather or quilted undercoat worn by the men at arms afforded further protection against simple bows so that knights looking more like pin cushions continued to march and fight. In fact, battle on the march, with armed men flanking and guarding horses and baggage, became one manoeuvre for a crusader army determined to make progress even against enemy action.

Of course, the classic combat formation for the heavily armoured, professionally trained Western cavalry was the mass charge, with lances couched under the arm – the momentum was irresistible and terrified more than one Saracen force on first encounter. But the enemy soon learnt to scatter or part ranks to let the unstoppable juggernauts thunder past. More serious was the loss of horses, either from death in battle or fatigue on the immense trek to the Holy Land, which too often depleted this essential fighting resource of the crusaders. But the tough and brutal northerners, surprisingly perhaps, also proved adaptable to new conditions. In part this was encouraged by the nature of warfare in Europe of which the siege was a major factor. A successful siege required a head for organization and often the building or devising on site of specialized engines and equipment. In fact, it seems that the Western knight, used to combining the various arts of war on his home ground,[7] was mentally attuned to problem solving on site.

Most historians agree that Jerusalem was always Pope Urban's final goal for his great *passagium generale*. Certainly the average crusader would have supposed he was committing himself to an armed pilgrimage in aid of the Holy City. Though a few were motivated by crude materialism, the outlay was considerable, the hazards equally so and the chance of any substantial gain was slight for all but a very small number of exceptional individuals. But the lure was undoubtedly there as the Indulgence Decree of Clermont implicitly recognized: 'If any man set out from pure devotion not for reputation or monetary gain, to liberate the church of god at Jerusalem, his journey shall be reckoned in place of all penance.'[8] In any case, by the nature of contemporary warfare, plunder was a normal part of the reward for hard campaigning. At their first set-piece battle in Anatolia crusaders rallied to the cry: 'Stand fast all together, trusting in Christ and in the victory of the Holy Cross. Today, please god, you will all gain much booty.'[9]

The inducements and motivations for the Muslim engaged in Holy War were surprisingly similar. Strictly speaking, the word '*jihad*' meant 'striving' and this originally denoted the effort to advance Islam in one's own life by striving for religious virtue. But it soon came to mean, even during the lifetime of the Prophet, striving by warfare to defend or to extend the 'territory of the Faith' – in Arabic, '*Dar al-Islam*'. The battle zone or 'territory of war' was known as '*Dar al-Harb*'. The warriors who voluntarily took up arms in such wars were entitled to booty as their reward on this earth and immediate entry into Paradise if they fell in battle. People had always known that some went on pilgrimage 'simply to gain prestige of having been to Jerusalem'. Similar temptations were evidently felt in the Muslim world. At the siege of Malta in 1565, Christian skirmishers came upon a dead Turkish officer with a gold bracelet bearing an Arabic inscription which read: 'I did not come to Malta for riches or honour, but to save my soul.'[10] But pilgrimage was an expensive sop to one's vanity: one might have to commit up to a year's income and always there was the danger on the road, this increased with the Turkish incursions of the later eleventh century. There was safety in numbers – in 1064 some 7,000 pilgrims, drawn from all social classes, embarked on a pilgrimage to Jerusalem under the leadership of the Archbishop of Mainz and three other German bishops. Despite their numbers brigands ambushed them as they approached Jerusalem, and although they beat off the attack it was not without loss.

Thousands went out of a profound belief in God and an equally profound fear of judgement on their sins. Equally, they supposed they were entitled to such rewards as might be going on the way. After all, had not Christ himself said, though in a perhaps less bellicose context, 'the labourer is worthy of his hire.' And there were rewards aplenty in the mayhem that passed for warfare back home. According to an admirer, the future King of England, William of Normandy's favourite mode of war was unrelenting devastation to 'sow terror . . . in the land by frequent and lengthy invasions' and by inflicting an incessant toll of calamities. Vineyards, fields and estates with their houses and dwellings were systematically laid waste.[11]

Devastation and brigandage were also the foundation of the eleventh-century Norman conquests in the south of Italy. They had emigrated to the Mediterranean lands as lances for sale in the service of the warring Byzantine and Lombard princes of the region. They soon turned on their employers and so was founded the greatness of Robert Guiscard. He died in 1085, his ambitions against Constantinople unfulfilled, but his heir, Bohemond of Otranto, was adept at this kind of warfare and attracted willing recruits to his banner. In 1089 this brigand arriviste was host at Bari to Pope Urban. Gossip later said he had urged the crusade on the Pope as camouflage for him to attack Byzantium. In fact, Bohemond's kind of war, commonplace in France and a cruel oppression on the mass of the people, was probably a more compelling consideration with the Pope anxious to deflect the energies of the military caste, for whom murder and rapine were not merely a way of war but commonly a way of life. The expedition to the East proclaimed at Clermont opened up the possibility of combining warfare with a sense of righteousness.

This new departure had, in a sense, been prepared some years before, in 1089, by the visit of Robert the Frisian Count of Flanders to Constantinople on his return from a pilgrimage to Jerusalem. The Emperor Alexius I, impressed by reports of the prowess of Western cavalry, had asked his guest if he could send him a body of 500 horses. The following year he followed this up with a polite reminder and it seems the Western mounted men at arms arrived in Constantinople in 1091.[12]

1

Beginnings 632–1095

⟐

Holy War, Holy Land, Holy Father

In March 1095, in the north Italian city of Piacenza, Pope Urban II opened the first great Council of his pontificate. Aged fifty-three, born of a noble family at Chatillon-sur-Marne to the east of Paris and educated in the cathedral school of Reims, this tall handsome Cluniac monk impressed contemporaries not only by his bearded good looks but also by his capacity as a diplomat and his dedication to the prestige of the papacy at a time when that institution was contesting for the undisputed supremacy in the affairs of Western Christendom with the German emperors, successors to Charlemagne. Courteous and persuasive but of unswerveable determination, in the seven years since his accession Urban had succeeded in outmanoeuvring the powerful and charismatic Emperor Henry IV, to establish himself as the spiritual leader of the West and reassert a considerable degree of political influence. The Council over which Urban was presiding, with bishops attending from France, Italy and the German lands of the Empire, was the supreme court in Europe. As well as matters of Church administration (including a decree against clerical marriage), its business included deliberations on the scandal of the French King's adultery, and on a petition presented from Henry's Empress for redress of indignities inflicted upon her by her husband. The Pope and his advisers also considered representations made by a delegation of envoys from Constantinople, the historic city of Eastern Orthodox

Christianity, founded on the old Greek city of Byzantium by Rome's first Christian Emperor, Constantine the Great, in 330. Within two centuries Roman imperial rule in Western Europe had succumbed to barbarian incursions but in the East the successors of Constantine had continued the imperial tradition. With the coronation of the Frankish King Charlemagne as 'emperor' by Pope Leo III in 800, Western Roman Catholic Christians considered the Empire had been restored. Constantinople saw these Western emperors as pretenders to a usurped title. There was also a divergence in religious matters over the centuries. While Constantinople held to Greek, the language of the Gospels, Rome adopted Latin, the language of the imperial administration. Important doctrinal issues also came to divide Rome from the Eastern Church, which proudly flaunted the title 'Orthodox'. In return, it was viewed from Rome as schismatic in matters of doctrine, disobedient in matters of Church discipline and a rival for supreme authority in the universal Church. Pope Urban II's predecessor, Gregory VII, had envisaged a military campaign, with himself as 'general and pope', to establish papal primatial authority in Constantinople,[1] and some scholars have seen here the germ of the crusading movement. But at Piacenza in the 1090s such a plan was not an issue as the Byzantine envoys outlined the ideas of their master, Emperor Alexius I.

Embattled in centuries-long conflict against the Islamic powers on its eastern and southern frontiers, Eastern Christendom was, at this time, specifically engaged in a war with the Seljuk Turkish forces with their base at Iconium (modern Konya). The campaign was going well, Seljuk power seemed in decline and Alexius seems to have reckoned that with a major push he could recover much territory lost to the Empire over the past half century. But he needed reinforcements. Above all, he was interested in enlisting a substantial body of the heavily armoured horsemen of Europe's feudal knight service. He had been highly impressed by the military entourage of the Count of Flanders who had been his guest at Constantinople on the return journey from a pilgrimage to Jerusalem. In a tradition stretching back to Claudius in the first century, Rome's emperors had been using divisions amongst the barbarian peoples on its frontiers to its advantage, playing one off against another and, increasingly, enlisting selected tribes as favoured allies. In the eastern half of the Empire, such manipulation of barbarian rivalries became standard policy and for Alexius engaging Franks to fight Turks was a natural extension of it.

But to recruit successfully in the Roman Catholic West he wanted papal support. His envoys at Piacenza were there to appeal to the Pope to encourage westerners to help defend the Eastern Christians against the Turks.

The moment was opportune. The papacy deplored the more or less permanent state of low-level warfare between petty nobles which provided the environment of life in a society over-endowed with an underemployed knightly class short of land but high in ambition. For decades the Church's hierarchy had been in sporadic dialogue with the very highest levels of lay society in regional peacekeeping initiatives known as the Peace or Truce of God, aimed at bringing some discipline into the lawless ranks of the lesser nobility, whose vicious rivalries brutalized society, flouted the Church's teachings and often disrupted the schemes of their feudal superiors. It was a world in which an admirer of a count of Aquitaine could praise him as a man of *pietas* because he did not murder or mutilate his political opponents.[2] Unsurprisingly in such a world, peace/truce initiatives tended to be ineffective and short-lived, and had little impact on the prevailing turbulence in French feudal society. However, while the movement in favour of such initiatives may not have provided the ideological spur for the crusading spirit in Europe, from the outset the practical arrangements in mobilizing the social and military resources for a general passage or crusade were closely associated with the kind of measures deployed to set up a Peace or Truce of God. Sometimes, of course, the Church harnessed lay violence in its own interest within Christendom. In 1066, Duke William of Normandy's adventure against England had been blessed by Alexander II, angered by disciplinary irregularities in the Anglo-Saxon Church and the continent had been cleansed of thousands of ruffianly fighting men, now licensed to exercise their brutal trade in the territory of one of Europe's ancient Christian kingdoms. How much better, to use the words of Sir Steven Runciman, 'to persuade the quarrelsome knights of the West to use their arms in a distant and a holier cause'.[3]

Urban invited the Byzantine envoys to address the assembled bishops and senior clerics. Seizing the unexpected opportunity to appeal directly to the movers and shakers in the Western Church, but perhaps sensing sales resistance to the idea of Roman Catholics serving under their Orthodox emperor, they spoke of the horrors of Christians under the Infidel and the merits to be won by their co-religionists in restoring them to Christian rule. In the spring of 1095, it seems, there was no talk by these envoys of the Eastern Emperor of liberating Jerusalem. After all, it had been in Muslim hands since February 638, when the Caliph Omar received its surrender from the Christian patriarch of the city, its chief magistrate.

The Eastern Roman, or Byzantine, Empire – its capital the great city founded on the ancient Greek trading port, Byzantium, by Constantine, the first Christian emperor of Rome – had inherited all Rome's provinces along the eastern Mediterranean coast, from Egypt through Palestine and Syria towards the frontiers with Persia on the east and northwards into Anatolia, which today we call Turkey. Cities of the region shared a common cultural heritage established by the Greek conqueror, Alexander the Great. Chief among them was Alexandria, whose libraries had been the storehouses of Hellenistic literature and science. In the coastline angle formed by northern Syria and southern Anatolia stood the immensely rich and populous trading city of Antioch (Antakya), and to the east of that Edessa (Urfa), whose citizens boasted themselves the most ancient Christian community outside Rome. Finally, of course, there was Jerusalem. As the place of Christ's Crucifixion, the capital of ancient Israel was always the Holy City for Christians, but when Constantine made Christianity the religion of the Empire and, in 327, his mother St Helena announced the finding of the True Cross there, it attracted more special veneration and, soon, hordes of pilgrims.

Jerusalem had, in fact, been briefly held in non-Christian hands for a time shortly before Caliph 'Umar took it for Islam. Rome's traditional enemy on its eastern frontiers had been the empire of Persia, Zoroastrian in religion and covering modern Iran and Iraq. The Byzantine emperors inherited the conflict, with lesser powers watching the varying fortunes of the two empires as they warred across an arc from the Caucasus Mountains to northern Mesopotamia. Southwards, the superpower confrontation came to be cushioned by client tribes, supported by Byzantine or Persian subsidies according to their allegiance. Ethnically Arab, with contacts to the Bedouin in the southern deserts, both had adopted forms of Christianity and both were indebted to the Greek Hellenistic Syria. Multiculturalism was in the air. The dangerous and warlike Khosru II who became Shah of Persia in the 590s had a Christian wife, a Christian finance minister, and claimed the protection of Christian saints. Nevertheless, he ravaged the lands of the Christian Roman Empire, conquering Egypt, Antioch and in 614 making his triumphal entry into Jerusalem. By 620 Constantinople itself was under threat, the watch fires of Khosru's army clearly visible from the city's walls; but within the decade the lost territories were recovered. In a daring and decisive counter-attack the austere Emperor Heraclius drove deep into Persian territory, burning palaces and desecrating the shrines of Zoroastrianism. By 628 the discredited Khosru was dead, murdered by Zoroastrian ministers.

Byzantium triumphant paused to survey its victory; instead it was to see the dust clouds of an undreamed-of enemy host, mushrooming out of the deserts of Arabia. The ancient titans had fought themselves to a standstill; the stage of history was set for a lithe and youthful antagonist, burgeoning in the mission of an inspired man of God among the disunited and disregarded pagan Arab tribes. In the words of an Arab envoy to the Persian Shah: 'Once the Arabs were a wretched race, whom you could tread underfoot at will . . . Now, for our glory, Allah has raised up a prophet among us.'[4]

According to Peter Brown in his book *The World of Late Antiquity*, the final conflict between the Middle East's two ancient superpowers spelt disaster for the subject populations of the region. They had been mercilessly taxed, with Alexandria itself left partly deserted, while the wars had eroded the region's defensive system against the nomadic peoples of the desert – Bedouin raiders rode unopposed up to the very gates of Jerusalem.[5] The time was indeed ripe for the entry of a new player so far overlooked in the diplomacy of power politics. Already by 600 the Arab merchants of Mecca were investing heavily in trade with southern Syria and the Kingdom of Hira; their caravans traded regularly to Damascus and among them were ventures led by a certain Muhammad, business manager for a wealthy merchant's widow, Khadija.

The idea of Holy War was in the air. Heraclius had led his armies from Constantinople against Persia not only to recover the lost lands of the Christian Roman Empire, but also to recover the relic of the True Cross lost with the fall of Jerusalem. Muhammad, strong in the words of God dictated to him by the Archangel Gabriel in the recitation or Koran (Qur'an), proclaimed Allah among the polytheistic tribes of Arabia and united them in a new religion of undeviating monotheism centred upon the Kaaba at Mecca and dedicated to spreading the faith and submission to Allah – Islam – throughout the world. By the time of Muhammad's death in 632 the traditional armed rivalries between the tribes had been renounced, and the vast region of Arabia transformed into a zone of truce. But if the community of the faithful, the *Umma*, was at peace within itself, the old spirit of aggression was still alive and needed other outlets. The old inter-tribal feudal rivalries were directed outwards at the world of the Infidel. 'The conquest of the Byzantine and Persian empires was the price which others had to pay for the "pax Islamica" among the Arabs.'[6] And the conquests would go far further. In one astonishing generation of conquest and treaty – Damascus and Alexandria and other key Christian cities were yielded because the Muslim high command was willing to offer generous terms – Constantinople lost Egypt and its possessions in Palestine and Syria from Gaza to Antioch and Edessa. In 718 the great city itself survived an Arab siege only thanks to its superior naval power. In the year 732, exactly a century after Muhammad's death, when the Frankish general Charles Martel defeated an Islamic army between Poitiers and Tours near the banks of the Loire, the muezzin's call to prayer was to be heard in minarets from the Pyrenees to Kabul. But already there were divisions in the *Umma*. The Arabic language, the language of the Koran and hence of Allah, necessarily remained the 'lingua franca' of all the faithful, but the Arab establishment found itself increasingly challenged or supplanted by other races – Persians, Armenians, Jews and later Turks – in the seats of power and influence. By the time of Alexius I, Turkish immigrants from central Asia had won power in Baghdad and encroached deep into the Anatolian heartlands of the Empire; the cities of Syria like Damascus and Aleppo were in a constant state of rivalry under their own rulers (emirs and atabaks), while in the south, from their new capital city of Cairo, caliphs of the Fatimid dynasty ruled Egypt and the lands of Palestine, seizing Jerusalem in 969. They claimed descent from the Prophet's daughter Fatima and were of the Shi'ite branch of Islam, considered heretical by the main Sunnite rulers in Baghdad. The sixth Fatimid Caliph Hakim, called by his many enemies 'the Mad', abandoned a tradition of toleration to persecute Jew and Christians, and ordered the destruction of the Church of the Holy Sepulchre in Jerusalem. Far worse than this, he announced himself the reincarnation of God. In 1021 he disappeared, probably assassinated by scandalized Muslims.

The fate of the Church of the Holy Sepulchre would have angered the Caliph 'Umar. On that February day in 638, when he and his travel-stained companions entered Jerusalem as masters, they went first to revere, the Rock, on the site of the Temple of Solomon, whence his friend Muhammad, dead only six years before, had made his mystical ascent to heaven. Next they were shown the Church of the Sepulchre. The holiest of Christian shrines, it was also worthy of respect by Muslims who venerate Jesus Christ and expect his Second Coming in the Last Days.

The reign of Hakim seemed in fact an aberration in the relations between the two faiths. Over the centuries generally speaking, Christian pilgrims were allowed access to the Holy Places and Constantinople had made no attempt to recapture the city. In the 1040s, with permission from Fatimid Cairo, Byzantine construction teams had rebuilt the Church of the Holy Sepulchre. But there were Muslims in Jerusalem who thought that fraternization between Cairo and Constantinople had gone too far and, in fact, this happy state of equilibrium was already under threat as a result of events in central Asia. Nomadic Turkoman tribes, converted to Sunni Islam during the tenth century, had been intruding into the lands of the Sunni Caliphate, ruled from Baghdad and its neighbouring territories. Like most converts they were zealots for their newly found faith. The caliphs recruited them as mercenaries and then installed them as advisers and ministers. The house of Seljuk emerged as the leading dynasty and its head, invested with the grandiose title of King of the East and West, wielded supreme authority as sultan (from an Arabic word for 'ruler'), who ruled as the Caliph's deputy. These Seljuk sultans became the champions of Sunni Islam, not only against the Christian states but still more against the dissident Shi'ite Fatimid caliphs at Cairo. Having displaced the traditional political establishment within the Baghdad Caliphate they now disrupted the tentative diplomacy by which Constantinople and Islamic Cairo were attempting to stabilize the region. In 1064 the Christian Kingdom of Armenia in the Caucasus, a buffer state between Baghdad and Constantinople, was conquered. Seven years later, the Emperor Romanus IV Diogenes, led a massive army to recover the kingdom. In the spring of 1071 at Manzikert (Malazgirt, Turkey) the forces of Baghdad, led by the Seljuk Sultan, Alp Arslan, destroyed the Byzantine army and captured the Emperor.

For Christian historians, Manzikert is one of the decisive battles of the world. The Emperor had mobilized all his forces to crush the resurgent power of Baghdad under its Turkish sultans and halt their encroachments into the fertile uplands of eastern Anatolia, the

Empire's traditional power base and recruiting ground. The obliteration of the imperial army at Manzikert seemed to open the way to Turkish mastery of the region. From the point of view of the Sultan, Manzikert had secured his north-western frontier and removed the threat from the Byzantine-Fatimid alliance. For him, the unification of Islam under the orthodox tradition of Sunni rule was still the overriding priority and the Fatimid state the principal enemy. But the Byzantines' defeat opened the way to Turkish penetration into Anatolia and for adventurers further south. The year following Manzikert, a Turkish commander captured Jerusalem and occupied Fatimid Palestine down to the frontier with Egypt at Ascalon. Cairo briefly recaptured Jerusalem only to be ousted a second time. And this time the Shi'ite Muslim population was massacred, though the Christians were spared. By the end of the 1080s, western Syria and Palestine from Aleppo to the borders of Egypt had come under Seljuk Turkish rule, owing allegiance to Baghdad where the nominal authority lay with the Caliph. In fact, the effective ruler was the great Seljuk Sultan, Malik Shah and the lands of Greater Syria which concern us were just part of an imperial domain comprising in addition to Iraq and Iran lands extending northward to the Caucasus. Malik Shah's death in 1092 left these immense territories as a war zone fought over among rival members of the Seljuk dynasty while in Greater Syria the combatants were generals and former clients of the Seljuks and armies of the Fatimid caliphs in Egypt. These divisions were to favour the cause of the crusaders but this was, at first, a secondary distraction. Above the political and military turmoil of the 1090s loomed frightening prophecies concerning 'the Last Days' which were linked to the approach of the five hundredth year of the Muslim era, 500 AH (AD1106–1107). Like Christians, Muslims believed that the end of the world would be heralded by the reign of anti-Christ that would be brought to an end by Christ himself descending from heaven. He would then destroy the Cross and would then summon the peoples of the world to submit to Islam.

Since the 1060s, incursions by Turcomans, nomadic tribal Turkish forces, into the area had disrupted the pattern of life of Eastern Christians. For generations the local Muslim authorities had generally permitted the flow of Christian pilgrims to the holy sites in and around Jerusalem. Now these comparatively orderly conditions had been broken up. In 1098 Fatimid Egypt had recaptured Jerusalem from its Turkish occupiers and Fatimid garrisons held the cities. But in the countryside nomadic Bedouin and Turkish freebooters terrorized both merchants and pilgrims. Pope Urban preached a sermon urging men to help the Eastern Emperor against the Infidel. The appeal made by the Byzantine envoys had triggered an idea in the Urban's mind. Church law permitted Christians to fight in a defensive war against the enemies of the Faith, and also to recover formerly Christian lands, and Jerusalem, conquered by the armies of Islam from the Christian emperors at Constantinople, clearly fell into that category. However, the expedition which was beginning to take shape in Urban's mind was not being conceived as a relief force to support Byzantine imperial policy but as a Western military initiative under his spiritual aegis. His predecessor Gregory VII had dreamed of such a venture and may have approached Raymond of St Gilles, later Count of Toulouse; Urban retained Raymond and selected another southerner, Adhémar, Bishop of Le Puy, as the spiritual leader of his expedition.

Adhémar was accepted as the Pope's legate and deputy, but his standing among the military leaders is unclear. For contemporaries, the enigmatic figure of Peter the Hermit seems to have been as important – a tradition that endured. In the early fourteenth century we find Foulques de Villaret, Grand Master of the Knights Hospitaller, stating as accepted fact that the Bishop shared the captaincy with 'Peter the Hermit, who played almost as distinguished a role in the passage as the legate himself'.[7]

With the business of the Council concluded, Pope Urban began a slow progress through northern Italy heading for the French border en route for the Abbey of Cluny where he had been prior. Mid-August found him at Le Puy where he issued a summons to a Council to be held at Clermont (modern Clermont Ferrand, the chief city of the Auvergne) in November. From here he turned south again and by the end of August was at St Gilles, between Nîmes and Arles, a favourite residence of Count Raymond of Toulouse. No doubt the Pope met the warrior Count before heading north again, this time up the valley of the River Rhône to the great monastery of Cluny where he lodged during the last two weeks of November, involved in Church business, before going on to Clermont where the Council opened on 18 November. For nine days the participants worked on important measures of Church reform before, on 27 November, they streamed out of the city where an immense crowd was assembled. The Pope preached a sermon on the sufferings of the Christians in the East and concluded with a passionate appeal for volunteers to enlist under the sign of the Cross of Christ. The event had presumably been carefully stage-managed. Bishop Adhémar came forward first and was to be appointed the papal representative in the army or, as Urban himself expressed it: 'the leader in our place of this pilgrimage and labour'.[8] Hundreds more now surged out of the crowd to pledge themselves. Many began to mark themselves with the sign of the cross, cutting cloth from such material as came to hand and sewing it to their own garments.

Neither the colour nor the actual design of the crosses can yet have been standardized – these presumably depended upon the material available to the would-be pilgrim. We are told that some of the monks and clerics present surrendered their cloaks to be cut up by candidates seized by the spirit of the moment. Other pilgrims, in the know perhaps, seem to have come prepared. Fulcher of Chartres rhapsodizes about 'all those shining crosses, whether of silk or cloth of gold or other stuff that at the Pope's orders, as soon as they had sworn to go, the pilgrims sewed on the shoulder of their cloaks'. Later, conventions might be adopted to differentiate crusaders of different regional or national allegiances. In January 1188, when Henry II of England and Philip II took the Cross (for what we term the Third Crusade), Henry we are told 'put on the surcoat bearing a white cross borne by the English crusaders; Philip assumed the red cross surcoat of the French contingent; shortly afterwards the count of Flanders followed their example adopting a green cross for his men'.[9] As to the actual shape of the emblem, that no doubt depended on the preference of the cutter. Some might for example prefer the long-tailed cross with the crossbar high up on the shaft, like the crucifixion instrument of Calvary, others the equal-armed emblem that later became conventional.

To this visible sign would be added a still more binding commitment in the shape of a verbal oath. It was a society in which few were literate and in which solemn transactions were fixed in the memory of participants and witnesses by some symbolic act, such as the giving and receiving of a gauge. It took centuries for the written document to displace entirely the felt need for such physical symbolism. At Clermont in November 1095, caught up in a fervour of devotion, thousands of people had made a historic commitment on which their eternal souls would depend. Looking for the token that would mark that commitment, they cut crosses from the coarse cloth of the preachers' cloaks. There was apparently no further ceremony but from that point on the symbolic gesture of taking a cross became virtually standard procedure for anyone who pledged themselves. The *pere-grini* had become *crucesignati*, 'those signed with cross'; from the time of the Third Crusade onwards that became the usual term for what we call 'crusaders'[10] – a late twelfth-century English service book (now in the library of Magdalen College Oxford) includes a formula for blessing a crusader's cross as well as a formula for blessing and bestowing a pilgrim's insignia. The association of these military expeditions with the practices of pilgrimage was, from the outset, very close. Indeed, the chief emblem on the banner of the Kingdom of Jerusalem, a cross 'potent', i.e. an equal armed cross with each arm ending in a 'T' bar, seems in origin to have had the bars ending in the knob-shaped handle of a pilgrim's staff.

Men looked on their solemn vow to serve Christ and his Cross in this military pilgrimage as the equivalent of the oath of fealty taken by a feudal vassal to his lord. But from the first, there were thoughtful churchmen who disapproved of the entire venture. Although summoned to Clermont by the Pope himself, the Italian St Anselm, Archbishop of Canterbury, sent a deputy to represent him. The saint had taken the vows of a monk, a real 'knight of Christ', *miles Christi* – in his view a monk enlisting for this campaign would be yielding to an evil temptation. He even wrote to urge a knight, who was a friend of his, to abandon the worldly militia for the *militia Christi*. The actual city of Jerusalem, wrote Anselm, was no longer a vision of peace, but rather a byword for tribulation, while the heavenly Jerusalem, which is the true vision of peace, was not to be found by warriors interested in pillaging the treasures of Constantinople and Babylon (i.e. Cairo) with bloodstained hands.[11] But such saintly views were out of step with papal thinking. Soon, Rome would be looking for ways of converting the crusade vows made by those ageing knights or rich widows, who would not be of much military use, into other forms of assistance.[12] Later lawyers were to regard the vow of the crusader, made in a fervour of spontaneity, as a legally enforceable commitment and the ceremony of taking the Cross the solemn and public ratification of that vow.[13] A ruling of the First Lateran Council would specify the action to be taken against those who were known to have fixed crosses to their clothing for the *iter* to Jerusalem, but then had taken them off.[14] 'The central importance of the vow for the whole functioning of the elaborate mechanism of the Crusade could hardly be much clearer.' Soon after the fervent demonstrations of faith at Clermont, envoys arrived from Raymond of Toulouse committing him to the cause.

Four reports of Urban's sermon survive, all written after the capture of Jerusalem four years later. Hindsight was inevitably a factor but it seems clear that he emphasized the sufferings reportedly endured by the Eastern Christians under the Turks. Fulcher of Chartres, who was there, reports that the Pope made the conversion of secular warrior knights into *Christi milites*, soldiers or knights of Christ, the core of his message – those used to warring on their Christian neighbours should turn their swords against the barbarians and the Peace or Truce of God should be sworn to 'throughout all the provinces'. According to Fulcher indeed, the restoration of peace in France was the first of the Pope's achievements in his tour of the country, the second being the upholding of Church rights, while his preaching of the cause of Jerusalem came third. Robert the Monk, chronicler of the crusade, had Urban appeal to the pride of the Franks, in their past praising the military achievements of the house of Charlemagne.[15] One thing seems certain: the Pope linked the call to fight the Infidel with the merits to be won in pilgrimage to Jerusalem. Following Clermont, Urban went on an eight-month tour of southern and western France, preaching this holy war of liberation of Jerusalem and defence of the Eastern Church against the Infidel. He sent messengers to preach the Crusade in Flanders, Normandy and England, and letters to north Italian cities.

There was no doubt that, in the words of one chronicler, Urban was the 'chief author of the expedition' but, as we have seen, popular opinion attributed charismatic status to the holy man Peter the Hermit. Reputed to have visited Palestine two or three years before Clermont, it is possible he was canvassing crusading ideas before Piacenza and may even have planted the germ of the idea in Urban's mind. As would soon be proved, he had a powerful populist appeal. The Pope had allowed eight months for the great men who were to lead the *iter* or journey to mobilize their forces and set their affairs in order, and fixed August 1096 for the general departure. Popular opinion considered this overindulgent to the whims of the gentry and nobility. Within weeks of the Pope's appeal in November 1095 Peter set out from Berry in central France on a preaching tour of his own.

Heading eastwards along the valley of the Meuse through the

rolling country of Champagne and then via Lorraine into the lands of the Empire, he and his swelling band of followers reached Cologne on the Rhine in the spring of 1096. Peter had dispatched disciples to preach the message in areas bordering his main route, among them the Frenchman Walter Sans-Avoir and the German Gottschalk. Walter's name, literally 'Have Not' is a clue to the constituency most responsive to the call. In a society of endemic lawlessness and rising population, the peasant and the town poor were at the mercy of plundering by petty nobility, who were little better than brigands. Where these pillaged their own countryside and the 'great' nobles pursued self-interest on a grander scale, it seemed that the recovery of Christ's Holy Land must fall to the poor, simple and devout. Floods and epidemics followed by widespread crop failures had deepened the misery of life in much of Europe in recent years. To the landless and destitute emigration had its attractions, death in the cause of Jerusalem meant spiritual benefits in the afterlife, and to many of Peter's hearers it seemed that those who could win through to victory would find themselves in the land flowing with milk and honey promised in the Bible. When 'the People's Crusade', to give it its popular title, set out from Cologne for Constantinople after Easter 1096, it may have totalled as many as 20,000 men, women and children – entire families, sometimes entire villages had abandoned their homes to make the armed pilgrimage to the New Jerusalem, as many believed. In the ranks of these thousands of simple poor there were, inevitably, many charlatans, opportunists and petty adventurers – there were, too, numbers of knights and capable fighting men, notably from Germany, which was represented by no great lord on the general expedition.

The motley cohorts (from Flanders and France as well as Germany), fervent in their own religiosity, inspired the populations through which they passed with crusading ideas, sometimes perverted. In fact, many Rhinelanders thought the campaign against the enemies of Christ should start at home, so to speak, with war on the local Jewish communities whose ancestors, the Church taught, had been the instigators of Christ's crucifixion. For a generation and more, the target of a building hostility, this talented and prosperous group, absolved by religion from the restrictions facing Christian financiers, enjoyed special protection from the Emperor, keen to preside exclusively over the regulation and exploitation of its wealth. Rich or poor, Europe's Jews lived on sufferance as second-class citizens, dependent on the favour and protection of the feudal overlord of their region, whether emperor, king or nobleman. Some two centuries later a memorandum to Pope Clement V urging a crusading tax on Jewish goods of up to 50 per cent perfectly exemplifies the situation. While admitting that the lords in whose power the Jews lived might object to the impoverishment of their clients' taxable assets in this way, it argued they could not reasonably oppose a mulct levied in the general cause of Christendom. The sentiments of the Jews themselves were not even considered.

In the 1090s, German merchants increasingly resented Jewish involvement in overland commerce. The clergy often encouraged their admission to local business life. In the mid 1080s Bishop Rädiger of Speyer had drawn up a special charter to encourage Jews, reckoned to be familiar with the more advanced societies of the ancient world, to settle in his city, so as to 'amplify the dignity of the place a thousand times'.[16] Elsewhere they were permitted to store their money in church treasuries in times of danger. It was a concession, which angered many poor nobles and landless knights who were now finding themselves obliged to borrow money from Jews with which to equip them for the journey of the Cross. There were scattered outbursts of cruelty and harassment as crusading fervour spread, but in general the Rhineland's Jewish communities were able to buy off worse violence from the People's Crusade by the judicious payment of protection money. Expeditions on the fringes of Peter's army were to prove horribly more troublesome.

From Cologne, the route lay through Hungary where King Coloman granted them free passage on condition of no pillaging. All went peacefully until they reached the town of Semlin on the frontier River Save – there, rioting broke out leaving some 4,000 Hungarians dead, while across the river, the town of Belgrade was torched. From here to Sofia the way was punctuated by conflicts with the local Byzantine officials – at one point a pitched battle ensued in which hundreds of crusaders were killed or captured. From Sofia to Constantinople the route was trouble-free and on arrival at the capital Peter, to his grateful surprise, found an indulgent Alexius prepared to consider the sufferings of the pilgrim crusaders on their long trek sufficient punishment for any mayhem they might have provoked. Indeed, Peter was granted an audience. But while riots and major violence were averted, the westerners pilfered from the population and burgled the luxurious palaces on an almost daily basis. Early in August the crusaders were conveyed across the Bosphorus and continued their unruly progress along the coast of the Sea of Marmora, to an extensive military encampment where Alexius urged they should await the arrival of the main body of the crusade from Europe. For his part, Peter accepted the wisdom of this advice, but his lieutenants, impatient of Pope Urban's cautious schedule in Europe, insisted on pushing forward into the territory of the Seljuk Sultan Kilij Arslan, lord of Konya and Nicaea. They pillaged the Turkish countryside, killed and tortured even the Christian inhabitants and, inevitably, roused the ire of the Turks. On 21 October, while Peter was in Constantinople hoping to raise further assistance from Alexius, the army, some 20,000 strong, marched on Nicaea from their base camp, but fell into an ambush laid by the Turks. Many of the knights and men at arms fell fighting bravely – they at least had fulfilled their vows – however massacre turned to rout; fugitives poured back towards the base camp where the Turks slaughtered the children and old folk tending the cooking fires awaiting the army's return. Only 3,000 people made good an escape to a ruined fortress on the coast from where they were taken off by a Byzantine flotilla. The People's Crusade was finished; poor and simple people of Christ had failed; the Turkish Sultan turned his back in contempt on this Western rabble, confident he had the measure of the threat from Europe.

2

The First Crusade 1095–1099

Given the glow of chivalry and romance with which later generations were to surround the crusades, it comes as a surprise to find that the first, and in terms of objectives achieved the most successful, attracted neither emperor nor king. The pious adventurer Godfrey of Bouillon, Duke of Lower Lorraine, who was offered the Crown of Jerusalem by his fellow crusaders, would be honoured in the later Middle Ages along with Charlemagne, his ancestor, and King Arthur as one of the Three Worthy Men of Christendom. Yet only two of the leaders of the First Crusade were of royal blood: Robert, eldest son of William the Conqueror and his successor as Duke of Normandy, and Hugh of Vermandois, brother of Philip I, the ruling King of France. To them we may add, as a royal kinsman, Stephen of Blois, who had married the Conqueror's daughter Adela and whose letters to his wife are among the most revealing, as they are the most personal of the documents of the crusade.

The absence of the French King from the expedition is unexpected since the Pope, who had summoned up the expedition, was a Frenchman, and Raymond of Saint Gilles Count of Toulouse, the first man to take the Cross, was a vassal of France. But King Philip's eccentric views on marriage had earned him the papal ban of excommunication. Having repudiated his wife Bertha, Philip had then 'married' Bertrada, wife of Fulk Count of Anjou, while both Bertha and Fulk were still living. Accordingly, his younger brother Hugh of Vermandois, accompanied by a small force, which he seems to have financed on his own account, represented the royal house. The absence of the Emperor Henry IV was more understandable. For much of his reign he and the papacy had been involved in a titanic contest for the control of Church estates and hence Church affairs. Bishops, as well as being Church leaders, were also great landowners and the technical issue in dispute was who should invest them in their office, the spiritual or the secular power. In reality, however, it was a contest for ultimate supremacy between the two chief powers in Christendom. The new style of armed pilgrimage or Holy War against Islam was unquestionably under papal direction. It is not therefore surprising that Emperor Henry was not leading an army to it. The honour of the Empire was upheld however because Lower Lorraine (today part of France) was then within the Empire's boundaries.

The official starting date for the crusade was August 1096. As we have seen, the ill-fated expedition of Peter the Hermit had set out months before this and there were other forerunners, particularly in the lands of the Empire. The Rhineland's Jewish communities had been able to buy off the forces of Peter the Hermit, but the immunity was not to last. The Emperor Henry IV being absent in Italy, the Chief Rabbi of Mainz sent him a report of the threats and violence his Jewish protégés faced. The Emperor, we are told, 'was enraged' and sent instructions to protect the Jews to all the German bishops, his chief ministers and to Godfrey of Bouillon. Godfrey, preparing for his own crusading venture, obeyed the order but did not repulse offers of protection money lavished on him by cautious Jews doubtful of his word. But none of this was proof against the spate of ethnic cleansing about to be unleashed. Many hundreds of Jews at Neuss, Cologne, Trier, Mainz, Regensburg and many other places died at the hands of their Christian neighbours in outbreaks of communal violence, or in attacks led by crusader bands heading south in advance of the official departure date. There were protectors: bishops like Rädiger of Speyer with good reason to protect their Jewish communities; others who offered protection sometimes in exchange for handsome protection money; and still others, clerical and lay, who took huge sums – in one case as much as seven pounds of gold – and then shamefully reneged on their word.

The fiercest of all the pogroms were under the aegis of Emich, Count of Leiningen, a petty lord of the Rhineland, an established brigand with something of a military reputation and an aura enhanced by his claim to bear the sign of the cross miraculously branded on his body. He attracted other minor German and French warlords, among them William, Viscount of Melun. At Worms, we are told, some 800 people died either in their own homes or in the compound where they had sought the protection of the Bishop. A very few endured forcible baptism, many were murdered, many more died in suicide pacts. Fathers slaughtered wives and children; bridegrooms killed their betrothed. Those who survived looked upon the dead as martyrs to the faith, the victims themselves looked on their self-killing as a sacrifice acceptable to God. When a friend took a mother's child and cut its throat 'she spread her sleeves to receive the blood, according to the practice in the ancient Temple sacrificial rite.'[1]

At Mainz, in exchange for protection payments, the Bishop gave the Jews sanctuary in his palace courtyard and, with the local count, promised to protect them from the advancing forces of Emicho. The Jews sent messengers to him with presents of gold and silver bullion, but when the crusader horde reached the place the citizenry opened the gates and the cowardly Bishop, reneging on his friendship with the Jews, came to terms. Once again there was slaughter. Believing their fate to be ordained by God, few of the victims resisted and many turned their daggers and knives upon themselves. Friend killed friend; father son; mother child. For their part Count Emicho and his blood-thirsty companions, killing as they went and inspiring the blood lust of other petty 'warriors of the cross' like Volkmar, who massacred the Jews of Prague, and Gottschalk, who led the butchery at Regensburg,[2] pressed on to the Hungarian frontier. There they faced the Christian King Coloman, who had already routed their predecessors and now refused this lawless host passage through his territories. Count Emicho's forces, too, were scattered and many slain. The leaders, like William of Melun, placed their murderous swords in the service of other commanders.

Hugh of Vermandois was among the first of the official crusaders to set out, expecting the honours due to his royal lineage – he even sent a special courier ahead of him to Constantinople to request the Emperor to arrange a fitting reception. But Hugh was not to distinguish himself in action and his expedition was prone to trouble. Leaving in August for the southern Italian port of Bari, he was joined en route by a number of members of the failed expedition into Hungary. Among them was William of Melun. Nicknamed 'the Carpenter', he was renowned for his immense physical strength, but it is more than possible that he was also noted for skills in military hardware. In the warfare of the day even men of knightly class might have specialist knowledge in the construction of siege engines.[3] Yet however adept he might have been at military carpentry, William had a doubtful reputation. Ten years earlier he had joined a French expeditionary force which crossed into Spain at the request of King Alfonso VI of Leon-Castile to help him against his Muslim enemies. In fact, the French failed to make contact with the enemy and William's conduct during the episode prompted the suspicion that he had betrayed the expedition.[4]

Crossing the Adriatic from Bari to Dyrrachium in October, Hugh lost a substantial number of his men and himself had to be rescued, a bedraggled victim of the storm, by Byzantine officials. On the Emperor's orders he was treated honourably and he and his party were given a military escort along the Via Egnatia, the historic Roman road linking the Adriatic coast to Constantinople. By the time they arrived in November, rumours were reaching Godfrey of Bouillon that Hugh had travelled under arrest.

The main crusading force, which also began to move as Urban had directed in August 1096, consisted of four major contingents, each taking its own route to Constantinople, where the Emperor Alexius was directing preparations for their arrival. Godfrey of Bouillon, accompanied by his brothers, Eustace and Baldwin of Boulogne, and a kinsman, Baldwin of Le Bourg, followed, essentially, the route taken by Peter the Hermit through the lands of the Empire. The younger son of a noble house, the thirty-year-old Baldwin of Boulogne typified the crusader on the make. Originally destined for the Church, the traditional career path for landless younger sons, he had revised his plans (probably, it has been suggested, because reformers in the Church were restricting the scope for aristocratic exploitation) and made a good marriage.[5] The crusade opened up new possibilities, which he was determined to realize. Taller even than his brother Godfrey, with haughty dark eyes set either side of an imperious aquiline nose, Baldwin's dark hair and beard framed a pale, austere countenance. He affected gravity of demeanour and bore the hardships of the march unflinching. But while he dressed with monk-like simplicity,[6] he relished a good debauch. Complex and ruthless, with none of the grace and good nature of his brother Godfrey, Baldwin would be the first to take the title 'King' in Christ's city of Jerusalem.

They marched on through Hungary without incident and then into the Byzantine Balkans, crossing the Danube at Belgrade. Thence the route lay through Sofia and Adrianople (Edirne in modern Turkey) without incident. Alexius's officials arranged markets, and provisions were supplied gratis along most of the route, while imperial troops patrolled the line of march. The operation was organized with the professional efficiency to be expected of the commissariat of the imperial army. Inevitably, with such a large force marching through essentially unfriendly territory there were unruly elements and some unauthorized pillaging, but on 12 December, Godfrey's army reached the Sea of Marmora coast some forty miles short of Constantinople without serious incident. Two days before Christmas Godfrey and his army reached Constantinople where they were requested to pitch camp outside the walls.

The second main army marched under the command of the Italian-born Norman, Bohemond of Otranto – worrying news for the Emperor Alexius. Christened 'Mark', but nicknamed after a legendary local giant, Bohemond was now about forty, immensely tall, handsome and ruthless. The Norman presence in southern Italy had been established by adventurers and mercenaries, little better than gang leaders, invited to serve in their wars by the then dominant powers in the region, Lombard dukes and the Byzantine Empire. Among them, Bohemond's father, Robert Guiscard, Duke of Apulia, had made himself the dominant figure in the region. He expelled the Byzantine presence from Italy, captured the port of Bari, its last foothold, in 1071, and died in 1085 leading his second invasion of Byzantine territories across the Adriatic. He had ambitions, and he believed a right, to the succession of the Greek Empire itself. Bohemond saw himself as his father's heir – it was rumoured that he had actually pressured Pope Urban into preaching the crusade so as to give him a cloak for his plans against Byzantium.[7] He was viewed with hostile suspicion by Alexius and with animosity verging on hatred by the Emperor's daughter, Anna Comnena – though she was evidently fascinated by his blond-haired, blue-eyed good looks. Bohemond crossed from Brindisi to Avlona with a compact professional force and, joining the Via Egnatia some 100 miles from the coast, arrived at Constantinople on 9 April 1097.

The third and the largest contingent, comprising as well as fighting men a number of non-combatant pilgrims, was that assembled by Count Raymond IV of Toulouse, the man favoured by Pope Urban to lead the whole enterprise; at fifty-five he was the senior by age as well as distinction among the crusading princes and, with his cultured southern background, of them all likely to be most in tune with the sophisticated style of the Byzantine court. Adhémar, Bishop of Le Puy, the Pope's legate, travelled with Raymond, who was also accompanied by his wife and her women attendants and servants. Yet, despite its prestigious leadership Raymond's army, flanked and trailed by the pilgrims supported by his charity, caused the most trouble to the Byzantine authorities. From Provence, it marched via Genoa to Venice and thence around the head of the Adriatic, down along the Dalmatian coast to Durazzo. Its passage was marked by a number of ugly incidents with the local populations and as Raymond approached Constantinople his ill-disciplined forces came under attack from imperial troops policing the route. The Count of Toulouse, for all his urbanity, was not in a sunny mood when he reached the great city on 27 April.

Meanwhile, the fourth main army had set out from northern France in October 1096, a little after Raymond's forces had begun their march, en route for southern Italy and the Adriatic ports. At its head marched Robert of Normandy, his brother-in-law, Count Stephen of Blois, and his cousin Count Robert II of Flanders. Classed by the chroniclers with Godfrey, Bohemond and Raymond as the 'princes' of the expedition, they were a mixed group. Men said, for example, that Stephen would have preferred to stay at home had he not been ordered to follow the Cross by his wife Adela, the imperious daughter of William the Conqueror. Robert, though titular Duke of Normandy, had rendered himself effectively landless when, in September 1096, he concluded the agreement to pawn his duchy to his younger brother William II, King of England, for the immense sum of 10,000 silver marks, repayable over five years. When their father died in 1087 he had bequeathed the Crown of England to William Rufus, his second son and the duchy of Normandy to Robert his eldest. There had been desultory war between the brothers for some years. Now, Robert's sincere commitment to the crusade offered an honourable way out – and also a way to raise the necessary money. For all Normans from Rouen to Calabria, the dukedom was undoubtedly a greater dignity than the newly acquired alien kingship, its holder being the acknowledged leader of the Norman world. Conventionally pious, but notoriously lazy and comfort loving, when Duke Robert finally arrived in

Norman south Italy in December, he decided to pass the winter there assured of lavish hospitality.

Of these three leaders Robert of Flanders, whose father had made the pilgrimage to Jerusalem and as we have seen had even served for a time under Emperor Alexius, was the most complete campaigner. More forceful than the charming if indolent Duke of Normandy, and no less courageous, he was more committed to the cause than Stephen of Blois and was financially well found. While his noble companions, heeding local advice that it was too late in the season to make the crossing, lazed with the numerous ladies in their entourage in the luxuries of southern hospitality, and many poor pilgrims, demoralized by the delay, excluded from the entertainment afforded to their betters and unable to pillage in friendly country, deserted, Robert of Flanders and his men took ship at the port of Bari. As far as we know, the sea crossing and the march through the southern Balkans were uneventful and they arrived in Constantinople in April. At about this time the marshals of Duke Robert and Count Stephen were supervising the embarkation of their forces on the quayside at Brindisi, but the work was not well done. The first transport to put out to sea capsized with the loss of hundreds of lives and many horses and chests of coins, the disaster prompting further desertions. However, the rest of the army crossed to Durazzo without incident, where they were received by a Byzantine escort and arrived outside the walls of Constantinople early in May.

Surveying a new intake of ill-disciplined conscripts and recruits awaiting the ministrations of his drill sergeants, the Duke of Wellington is said to have observed: 'I don't know whether they will frighten the enemy but by God they terrify me!' As he watched the Frankish army of crusaders camped about the walls of Constantinople, did the Emperor Alexius feel very much the same? Instead of a compact and disciplined force of mailed knights and men at arms marching under the banners of imperial commanders to recover its lands from the Turk, he had conjured up an unruly host, in which battle-hardened soldiers were probably outnumbered by pilgrims and religious fanatics, and which was led by haughty princes and adventurous barons blessed by a Catholic Pope, many of whom, he guessed, were looking to carve out lordships for themselves in lands held by infidels but claimed, according to their lights, by a schismatic Orthodox emperor.

By an impressive logistical exercise Alexius had seen the Western forces – perhaps as many as 100,000 persons in all, combatants and non-combatants – through the lands of the Empire reasonably well supplied with food, and on their arrival had kept them outside the walls of the opulent city, more fabulous than anything in their former experience. The earlier arrivals had by now been transferred across the Bosphorus and were preparing for the march inland. Some of the devout would have joined the small parties admitted under escort to see the wonders of the world's great Christian metropolis and would no doubt still be talking over the treasure trove of relics and sacred sights which, more than its silks and palaces, made Constantinople the marvel of the Christian world. Others were astonished by the Emperor's generosity in gifts and coins distributed to all ranks, while the nobility had fared still better. Gift giving was the essential attribute for a leader in their feudal society and in this respect Alexius passed the test. 'Your father,' wrote Stephen of Blois to his wife Adela, the Conqueror's daughter, 'was almost nothing compared to this man.'[8] The gifts showered by Alexius upon his Western guests and allies were part of a charm offensive in a diplomatic strategy that proved for a time highly successful in bending the westerners to his purpose.

In the first place, he extracted oaths from them, which committed them to obligations that would bring real territorial advantages to the Empire. According to the Emperor's daughter, Anna Comnena, the first oath taken by Godfrey of Bouillon amounted to a pledge that he would hand over to the Emperor's representative with the army any town, fortress or territory previously part of the empire of the Romans which he conquered in the course of the crusade.[9] This seemed clear enough and would certainly apply to a place like Nicaea, some sixty miles from Constantinople and in Christian hands as recently as twenty years previously. But what about the ancient imperial province of Syria which fell to the caliphs' armies in the seventh century – what about Jerusalem itself, in Muslim hands since 638? Most historians would agree that Alexius did not for one moment imagine that the crusading army would ever get that far. Meantime, however, he was determined to bind the leaders by the strongest ties possible and, since the oath in one form or another was the most binding commitment recognized in the feudal West, he demanded oaths.

Above all he wanted an oath of vassalage from all the principals. Alexius, well informed on the conventions of the West's oath-bound feudal structure, knew that whereas he was entitled to the unquestioning obedience of all his subjects, the great feudatories of the West considered themselves bound only by oaths they pledged in person to king, emperor or other overlord. That done, they could demand that their own vassals follow them, while they themselves would not consider themselves bound by an oath made by another. The feudal vassal became his lord's 'man', that is, he was bound to the lord's service, and the vassal's men were equally bound, by their oath to him, to follow him wherever he might lead. The ceremony of vassalage was solemn and public, the vassal placing his hands in those of his lord in an act of formal homage. We are told by a Norman observer that Godfrey of Bouillon pledged such an oath to the Emperor on behalf of himself and his vassals in a great ceremony and that the other leaders present followed suit. Many were angry, suspicious and fearful, for without the Emperor's goodwill they had little hope of surviving the months that lay ahead. But, if taken seriously, the oath meant a surrender of personal freedom of action to a ruler who for the most part they heartily disliked. And yet, eventually it seems, even Bohemond and Tancred, the most recalcitrant of the leaders, fell into line.[10] True, as their 'good lord', the Emperor had his obligations to act in good faith, but who could trust this 'crafty' Greek and schismatic. The crusaders believed he was pledged to send troops and ships with the expedition, to supply it with food and other necessaries and to make good their losses in action. By and large, the Emperor seems to have held to the bargain, anxious to transform what he saw as semi-barbarian warlords into mercenary captains in the Empire's service.

As the great army embarked upon its long trek southwards, events seemed to bode well for the imperial strategy. On 6 May 1097 contingents led by Godfrey of Bouillon, with Robert of Flanders, plus a force under Tancred and followed by the remnants of the 'People's Crusade' came in sight of the city of Nicaea. In addition we should note the detachment of some 2,000 Byzantine troops under the command of Tatikios, the senior officer deputed by the Emperor to aid the army and to receive from its leaders the command of 'all the towns, districts and fortresses that they might subdue'.[11] Food was already a problem and the arrival of Bohemond's contingent with supplies a few days later was a welcome relief. By 14 May the army received major reinforcements with the arrival of Count Raymond. Actual numbers are a continuing focus of debate but if we follow the 1990s calculations of John France, military historian of the First Crusade, to whose work much of this chapter is indebted, a reasonable estimate for the Christian force now surrounding Nicaea to the north, east and south might be about 30,000. The full strength, made up with the arrival of the north French under Robert of Normandy and Stephen of Blois early in June, was probably in the region of 50,000 fighting men, plus camp followers and non-combatant pilgrims.

The lakeside city that these Western Christians were preparing to invest was an ancient bastion of the faith. It was here in the year 325 that the first General Council of the Church, convened at the Council Church in the city centre, had first drawn up a confession of the Catholic Christian faith, still known as the first Nicene creed. As late as 1075 Nicaea was still part of the Empire, but for the past twenty years had been in the hands of the Seljuk Turk, Kilij Arslan. At first a frontier outpost, it was increasingly to be seen as the northern capital of an Islamic state consolidating itself, threateningly close to Constantinople. At the beginning of May Kilij Arslan, perhaps believing that the crusader menace had been scotched by his destruction of Peter the Hermit's cohorts, was in fact several hundred miles away to the east, protecting his interests against other Seljuk rulers. But by mid month he was back in the area of Nicaea and on the 16th attacked the troops of Raymond of Toulouse on the south side of the town as they were preparing to pitch camp. Showing outstanding generalship the Count held his people together until Godfrey of Bouillon, camped along the city's eastern wall, was able to send a relief force so that together they were able to beat back the Turkish onslaught. There was as yet no overall command of the crusader host but solidarity was evidently high. It seems the Seljuk had attacked before his full force had come up but the Franks had won a 'glorious victory', as even the generally hostile Anna Comnena conceded.

While the Seljuk forces regrouped, the crusading army began the siege in earnest. They had received important help from the Byzantines both in the building of elaborate siege engines and in a flotilla of boats which, by attacking from the lake, forced the garrison resources to the defence of a stretch of the wall it had supposed secure.[12] Alexius also supplied food at least sufficient to feed the fighting men, though many non-combatants, destitute after some eighteen months on the march, were facing starvation. With the arrival of the northern French and the failure of Kilij Arslan to rally a relieving force powerful enough to scatter the besiegers, the garrison of Nicaea capitulated on 19 June. A week later, having officially handed over the city to the Emperor's representative, the crusading forces were once again heading southwards. Mindful no doubt that their initial recruitment had been for the help of the Eastern Christians against the Infidel, a number of the pilgrim soldiers stayed behind and took service with the imperial authorities in Nicaea.

The army for reasons unknown moved off in two columns, the smaller one led by Bohemond, Tancred, Robert of Normandy and Stephen of Blois and comprising perhaps some 20,000 men, and the main body estimated at 30,000 following under Godfrey of Bouillon, Raymond of Toulouse, Robert of Flanders and Hugh of Vermandois, the French King's brother. There being no agreed commander-in-chief, the princes were free to deploy as seemed best to each one. No doubt the division made the forces more manageable and may have been thought to make foraging easier – it would certainly become a subject of acrimonious arguments since it might very nearly have caused the collapse of the entire enterprise. On the morning of 1 July, by which time it had probably advanced some forty miles from Nicaea and was entering the long valley of Dorylaeum, the first army came under sustained attack from a massive force under the command of Kilij Arslan.

Was the Seljuk commander still underestimating the nature of the alien threat? With the destruction of the 'People's Crusade', he seems to have assumed he had dealt with the menace, hence his absence from Nicaea when the crusaders arrived there. Now, with a force that considerably outnumbered the enemy, he may have supposed that the army before him was the entire crusader host at his mercy; alternatively, he may have known there were two armies and calculated he had time to destroy the one before the other came into play. These were reasonable calculations that were very nearly justified by events. It seems the Christian army had been alerted the night before of the enemy presence by the vanguard scouting on ahead. Camp was pitched on a site protected on one flank by marshy ground and on its front by cavalry. But these were soon driven back and as the fighting developed those in the camp huddled like terrified sheep in a fold, 'for we were surrounded by enemies on all sides'.[13] It must indeed have been terrifying – for most of the Europeans it was the first time they had had to withstand an entire army of cavalry. The Turkish bowmen were continually charging in and swerving away, discharging volley after volley of arrows and, recalled Fulcher of Chartres when he came to write up his chronicle, 'such warfare was unknown to us.' We are told that young women among the camp followers, anticipating defeat, were prettifying themselves so as to be spared by the victors – preparing, so to say, for a fate worse than death, to avoid being killed. Other women, more practically, were bringing water up to the front line. The beleaguered force held out for some five hours against the arrow showers and in bouts of vicious hand-to-hand combat against Turkish horsemen who broke into the camp from time to time. Ralph of Caen, who was in Tancred's command, wrote later that the enemy had the advantage of numbers but that their armour helped the crusaders. The heavy mail hauberk of the Western knights offered better protection than the lighter body armour worn by their opponents against any but a direct blow from the generally lighter Turkish swords; and while a direct hit from the powerful Turkish short bow might pierce it, an arrow that came in at even a slight angle would glance off ineffectually. Even so, in a battle of attrition the larger Turkish force seemed sure to win. Pilgrim stragglers between the two were casually slaughtered, but shortly after mid-day Godfrey of Bouillon and the southern French with Bishop Adhémar of Le Puy arrived on the field, forcing the Turks to divert men to face this new threat. When a body of horse under Raymond of Toulouse succeeded in riding round to attack, the Turks, fearing encirclement and already depleted by heavy casualties, turned in flight. It was a force of nomads of diverse tribal allegiances, who no doubt preferred to evade an enemy that was in any case evidently marching away from their pasture lands.[14] Whatever the reasons for the enemy's flight, the crusaders' victory at what is known to history as the Battle of Dorylaeum was complete. In purely military terms, it was another triumph, to set against the capture of Nicaea; in terms of their mission, it fulfilled an important part of their vows. At Clermont they had been exhorted to take up arms to help the Christians of the East – Dorylaeum opened the possibility of the recovery of lands and cities recently seized in the name of Muhammad. The watchword in the heat of the battle had been: 'Stand fast together, trusting in Christ and in the victory of the Holy Cross.' Their faith as well as their valour had surely been vindicated. Now they were free to continue their march south-east towards the Holy Land.

The first objective was the ancient city of Antioch, today Antakya in south central Turkey, beyond the Tarsus mountains in the valley of the Oroutes River near the Syrian border. There were a number of possibilities and it is possible that the crusaders once again split their forces. In six weeks' marching they seem to have encountered no hostility from the Turkish forces and by mid August they were at Iconium (modern Konya). Although this was a centre of Seljuk power, it was undefended and the local, mainly Christian population welcomed the crusaders. From Konya the now reunited army pressed forward to Heraclea where an attempted ambush by the Turkish garrison was easily dealt with and the city captured. Soon after this the army divided once again, Tancred and Baldwin heading due south to coastal Cilicia along the old pilgrim route, with Antioch about 200 miles away. In fact at Tarsus on the coast, Baldwin led his forces due east, ignoring the southern road to Antioch and heading towards the upper Euphrates, capturing cities as he went. Baldwin was one of the crusaders who did set out with a personal agenda and he was very successful. Thoros, the Armenian Prince of Edessa, a considerable territory based on the modern town of Urfa in southern Turkey, sent a request to Baldwin for help against the Seljuks and adopting him as his co-ruler and heir. Following Thoros' death during an uprising, timely for Baldwin and perhaps instigated by him, Baldwin became Count of Edessa in March 1098.

The main force headed north and east across the Taurus Mountains via Caesarea (modern Kayseri) before heading south for Antioch, a distance of more than 370 miles. It is something of a mystery as to why the army should have taken this long diversion. Perhaps, as French historian Claude Cahen suggested, it was to help Byzantine policy of re-establishment in an area controlling vital east–west traffic. Tatikios, the Emperor's representative, was still with them, but there may also have been an Armenian dimension. The chosen route lay through Armenian cities recently subject to the harassment of Turkish nomadic raiders and these crusaders had friendly relations with the Christian Armenians. As the army advanced many of the cities forced out their Turkish garrisons and admitted the crusaders. They for their part were again fulfilling that part of their vows to help the Eastern Christians. Certainly, as they emerged from the mountain passes into the wide valley of the Amouk which led down to Antioch itself, they had at their backs what John France has called a 'friendly hinterland'.[15] The Arab author of the Damascus chronicle confirms that the aliens had won numerous strong points down to the approaches to Antioch itself, while crusader commentators credibly put the number at between 150 and 200. It is perhaps not surprising that the Muslim powers in the region, and particularly the Fatimid caliphs of Cairo, looked upon the crusading force as an arm of the Byzantine policy of reconquest – precisely what Alexius had conceived it as being in the first place.

The crusaders were extending their lengthening lines of communication into a hostile world, but they had the advantage of singleness of purpose. Their enemies, by contrast, were intent on the infighting resultant from generations of ethnic and political rivalries. Kilij Arslan had lost Nicaea because, during the critical week of the crusaders' attack, he had been away from the city distracted by rivalries in the Muslim world. The ruler of Antioch, which they were now approaching, though appointed by the Seljuk Sultan at Baghdad was absorbed in rivalries involving Damascus and Jerusalem, Aleppo and Mosul. But there was nothing inevitable about the crusaders' success. Their enemies were operating from their home base and they had formidable resources in manpower and equipment.

On 20 October 1097 the army reached the Iron Bridge at the bend in the Orontes River north-east of Antioch. At this point the army was on the right bank of the river while its target lay on the left bank some fifteen miles distant. The crossing had to be made here and a fort garrisoned from the city protected it. Heavy archery exchanges ended in victory for the crusaders' advance guard, led by Robert of Normandy when, following the advice of Bishop Adhémar, they adopted a 'tortoise' formation.[16] Holding their shields above their heads, overlapping the edges as best they could, to provide protection against the arrow shower, they successfully rushed the enemy positions. The tortoise had been a favourite stratagem of ancient Roman commanders, who knew it as '*testudo*', and it is quite possible that Adhémar had learnt about it from a Roman military treatise. The most famous, the *de reimilitaris* of the theorist Flavius Vegetius Renatus, was consulted throughout the Middle Ages and such works would be natural reading matter for a churchman appointed head of a military expedition.

With the Orontes crossing secured, the main crusader force arrived before the walls of Antioch the next day. The leaders were intimidated by what they saw. In a letter to his wife Stephen of Blois described it as 'a city great beyond belief, very strong and unassailable'.[17] Stephen's letters home are a valuable source of information about the expedition. Like others he was able to maintain a fairly regular correspondence, thanks to the relative speed of sea travel and the activity of Christian shipping during the campaign – there are records of ships from Genoa, Pisa, Venice, Greece and England. Standing on the east bank of the Orontes, the city had been founded in 300 BC by one of Alexander the Great's generals; in the first century BC it was incorporated into the Roman province of Syria as its capital. For some years in the mid first century AD it was used as a base by St Paul for his missionary journeys; indeed it may have been here that the name 'Christian' was first heard. St Peter visited and the cave-church at the centre of the town, the Cathedral of St Peter, may be on the site of the first Christian meetings after the death of Christ.[18] Classed as an apostolic foundation by reason of its association with both Peter and Paul, the church of Antioch ranked with Rome, Alexandria and Jerusalem as one of the patriarchates of the early Church (Constantinople was later accepted in this category). After Rome, Alexandria and Constantinople the Empire's fourth largest city and the administrative capital for all the eastern provinces, in 637 it was occupied by the forces of Caliph 'Umar. In 969 Antioch was recovered by the Byzantine Empire to become a major frontier post, but in the 1080s it once again changed hands, this time falling to the Seljuk Turks of Syria. The immense circuit of the walls with their scores of towers, at one point skirting the river bank for several hundred yards, the well-equipped garrison in its fortified citadel on the heights discouraged thoughts of taking the place by assault. The army settled down to a long blockade in the hope of forcing a capitulation or, more probably, of finding a traitor among the defenders – after all, it was treachery which had yielded the place both to the Byzantines and the Turks.

The crusaders enjoyed a certain strategic advantage. Re-establishing Christian control in the Armenian cities effectively blocked communication between the beleaguered city and the Turkish powers in Anatolia, while the Christian command of the sea made relief from that quarter unlikely too. Within six weeks of its arrival the army had constructed the barbican tower of Malregard to obstruct Turkish raiding parties from nearby Harenc, probably with supplies brought by a Genoese flotilla which had put in at St Symeon and also, it has been suggested, with help from its crews skilled in the use of spars, lashings, hoists and tackle.[19] A second structure of major value to the besiegers was a pontoon bridge connecting the east bank of the Orontes, where the crusading divisions were dug in under the walls of Antioch, to the Port St Symeon road on the west bank. In normal times, traffic from the port ran into the city over the bridge that crossed the river to the heavily fortified Bridge Gate at the point where the walls skirted the river bank. Both these structures – the tower and the bridge – demonstrate the professional capacity of the crusade leaders to improvise effective responses in the face of diverse tactical demands.

Victualling the army was a constant problem. Food for sale in the camps, often brought in from distant markets in Syria, the island of Rhodes or Cyprus, for example, was expensive. The onset of winter brought conditions of near starvation to many in the ranks, making soldiers dependent on the charity of the leaders. There were to be reports of cannibalism among the camp followers. Foraging expeditions could entail heavy losses; equally they could provide valuable military experience. At the end of December 1097 Bohemond and Robert of Flanders marched a large force up the fertile valley of the Orontes. They were surprised by a force under Duqaq of Damascus, marching to the relief of Antioch. Reports of the engagement are confused but it seems that the crusaders, at the cost of heavy losses, improvised a combination of mounted and close-order foot manoeuvres by their knights to break out of a threatened encirclement and force a drawn battle on their attackers.[20] Nevertheless, they returned virtually empty-handed and the new year saw a number of desertions. Others, like Robert of Normandy, withdrew to the comparative comfort of Laodicea (Latakya). Early in February 1098, Tatikios headed north with his detachment, some thought to return with supplies and reinforcements, but more likely to join the Byzantine forces that were campaigning in Anatolia to secure further imperial gains in the wake of the crusaders' successes there. With a haemorrhage of desertion among the ranks, and the leaders Godfrey of Bouillon and Raymond of Toulouse both weakened by illness, defeat seemed imminent.

To compound their troubles, the leaders now heard that a powerful relief army under Ridwan of Aleppo was encamped at Harenc, barely twenty-five miles distant. That night a sizeable cavalry force under the command of Bohemond, who had been elected commander-in-chief for this engagement, rode out along the Aleppo road and over the Orontes River by the Iron Bridge to lay an ambush. The details of the battle are confused in the accounts that have come down to us, but it is clear that thanks to the surprise they achieved, coupled with tight discipline in the field and the timely release of a carefully placed reserve force, the war-weary crusaders brought off a near-miraculous victory over much superior numbers. Ridwan fell back and the army was able to strengthen its grip on the besieged still further, thanks to the arrival of an English fleet at St Symeon in early March. The supplies it brought and the skills of its sailors made possible the building of a counter-fort across the river opposite the Bridge Gate to impede the forays from its garrison onto the St Symeon road. Four weeks later it was possible to establish a force under Tancred in a fortified monastery opposite the St George Gate. But the army was not numerous enough to complete the circuit and after some seven months of severe losses and the most appalling privations among the lower ranks it must have seemed that if the place were ever to fall it could only be by betrayal.

In fact it was being rumoured that one of the defenders, a commander of three of the perimeter towers, was in touch with Bohemond. Again accounts are confused. Anna Comnena would even claim that the Norman, confident in his contacts, proposed a kind of competitive siege, the city to go to the prince who achieved the breakthrough. That there might be a willing traitor was perfectly plausible. The polyglot population of the great city had been in the hands of its Turkish masters for little more than a decade. Anna and another source point the finger at the Armenian minority in Antioch; others claimed it was a Persian. Another account tells how the actual plotting was done in Greek, through an interpreter in Bohemond's forces.[21] One thing was clear: if the deed was to be done, it should be done soon. Another army of relief was on its way, under Kerbogha (Karboga), lord of Mosul, and, according to the Damascus chronicle, he had an immense force with him – the besiegers were in danger of becoming the besieged. On the night of 2/3 June 1098, with the aid of a person or persons within the walls of the city, to us unknown, Antioch fell to the crusaders – the city, that is. The victorious troops, as was common in siege warfare, ran amok, slaughtering all in their way. Hundreds of Christian citizens rose to help the crusaders but, in the night-time confusion, many of them perished alongside their Muslim neighbours. Most of the soldiers of the Turkish garrison made good their retreat back into the citadel, leaving the city and the almost equally large area of wild undeveloped land within the long perimeter walls to the crusaders. For their part, it seemed the hand of God had saved them, yet again.

As they nursed their wounded and prepared for the next ordeal, the Western army could look back on a year of barely credible success. Since leaving Constantinople they had captured the well-fortified city of Nicaea, defeated Kilij Arslan, the principal Turkish ruler of Anatolia at Dorylaeum, recovered a string of cities for Eastern Christendom, defeated another superior force under Ridwan of Aleppo, and now taken the awesome fortifications of Antioch against the odds. One may doubt divine intervention, but the dimension of the military achievement is undeniable. Campaigning in territory where warfare was endemic and the enemy hardened soldiers as ruthless as they, the crusaders had marched some 700 miles without serious defeat and were within a week's march of Jerusalem, the object of their dreams. But they were a much reduced force. Lingering death by starvation on the road, sudden death in battle, excruciating death under the gangrenous ministrations of primitive surgical procedures, and desertion by opportunists and the faint-hearted, had all taken their toll. It is likely that the force now awaiting the onset of Kerbogha numbered no more than 30,000, non-combatants included.[22]

Desertion was to continue even among the highest ranks. Notorious is the case of Stephen of Blois, chosen by his colleagues as the commander-in-chief during the siege, but always the reluctant campaigner. He chose this moment to head for home and his negative report about conditions in the city may have influenced Emperor Alexius in his decision not to go to its aid. It is with no surprise that we also find the name of William the Carpenter among the list of distinguished 'rope danglers', as they were derisively named from their supposed mode of egress down the walls of Antioch.[23] On 7 June, only days following its own desperate triumph, the Christian army was able to assess the monstrous threat it still faced, as Kerbogha's interminable cohorts debouched into the terrain it had so recently quitted. Within four days the Turk had established a camp within 500 yards of the citadel. The aim was obviously to reinforce the garrison there so that it could drive down into the city and distract the defenders. After ten days of murderous hand-to-hand fighting on two fronts, a steady leakage of deserters, and the onset of starvation among the poorest of the pilgrims, the plight of the crusaders was hapless. There had been talk of treachery and at some point it seems Bohemond had even set fire to part of the city to smoke out troublemakers.

Then on 11 June a simple priest named Stephen of Valence was admitted to the presence of Legate Adhémar to report a vision in which Christ and His Mother had promised succour to the demoralized troops. The legate welcomed the timely assurance, delivered as it was by a priest respectful of his authority. He seized the opportunity to win a pledge from the leaders not to abandon the army. (There is surely no more eloquent evidence of the evaporation of the crusaders' spirit.) Meanwhile, the rank and file had been electrified by the rantings of one of their number, the Provençal pilgrim Peter Bartholomew who charged that the prince of the Church had ignored his pastoral duties to ordinary crusaders. Only if all repented, great and small, would God favour the enterprise. If they did, he, Peter, would point the way to a physical token of divine favour. On 15 June digging beneath the paving of St Peter's Church in Antioch, at a point divined by Bartholomew, a relic was unearthed which was proclaimed as the 'Holy Lance' – the spear the Roman soldier had used to pierce the side of the crucified Jesus. The discovery of this 'precious gem' caused 'boundless rejoicing' throughout the ranks. Even at the time there were sceptics who observed the fortuitous nature of the find. Not long before, Bohemond and Adhémar had ordered the gates of the city closed, to stem the flow of deserters. Now morale soared. These soldier pilgrims who had set out for the love of Christ, to recover the land of His suffering for His faithful people, believed that God had to be on their side; here was long-awaited proof. It was hardly surprising that, in their own words, the leaders now began 'most boldly and eagerly' urging one another on to battle. The citadel still held out for Kerbogha. It was fiercely defended and very well fortified and even if they should take it, the Christian forces in Antioch would still be under sentence from the huge Turkish army encamped around its walls. Victory in battle against that army offered the only hope of salvation. The chances of success were slim – apart from anything else, the crusaders had lost almost all their horses;[24] under a divided command victory would be near impossible. On 20 June his colleagues elected Bohemond commander-in-chief. Even so, it would seem from the conflicting contemporary reports, there were attempts at a parley. A deputation to Kerbogha's camp led by Peter the Hermit is said to have made proposals ranging from simple defiance to an offer to yield the city if the Muslim commander would convert to Christianity. There may also have been talk of a kind of trial by battle between two small forces of champions drawn from each force. These faint hopes having failed, the Christian army, fortified by the comforts of religious ceremonies, steeled itself to put its fortunes to a last desperate sally. On the morning of 28 June, with the agreement of his colleagues, Bohemond ordered the attack. Kerbogha had warning of the impending breakout – the commander of the Muslim garrison had minutely observed Bohemond's preparations and was already flying a black signal flag from the tower of the citadel.

The conflict that followed may be considered the hinge battle on which turned the entire fortune of the crusade; contemporary sources certainly viewed it as such. From their detailed coverage C. Morris felt able to create a computer programme 'The battle of Antioch' for publication by the HIDES Project of Southampton University.[25] R.C. Smail's summary of the contemporary accounts, contained in his classic work *Crusading Warfare*, indicates a high degree of tactical planning and control. The army was marshalled in four divisions of which Bohemond commanded the fourth, to be held in reserve.

> As soon as the first division had passed through the gate and crossed the Orontes bridge, it was to turn into line and to march upstream with its flank on the bank of the river. The second division crossed the rear of its predecessor and turned to face the enemy in line when it was in position . . . The plan ensured that each division as it left the city changed its formation from column into line at the earliest possible moment, so that it faced the enemy ready to attack, and covered the deployment of the succeeding columns.[26]

We can get some idea of what this might have meant for the men carrying out 'the long and laborious business of deploying . . . from long columns into line of battle' in the face of the enemy, from Corelli Barnet's account of the Duke of Marlborough's deployments at the Battle of Blenheim in August 1704. Even at this late date:

> precise, standard drill movements had not yet been invented. Wheelings had to take place at the halt. Sergeants pushed and jostled their men into line, dressing the ranks with their half-pikes or 'spontoons'. To Wellington's officers a hundred years later . . . Marlborough's deployment would have appeared something of a shambles.[27]

What Wellington's drill sergeants would have thought of Bohemond's deployment we can only guess! But that such deployment could be even envisaged testifies to the level of military competence which the crusading army had reached in the year since it marched from Constantinople. In the view of John France, Bohemond was 'an exceptional commander' and 'by the end of the siege of Antioch the army was cohesive and disciplined'.[28]

The Battle of Antioch was a complete victory for the Christians. Islamic sources pointed to the divisions in the Muslim high command, but Kerbogha made some puzzling decisions. For example he had divided his army between a force on the plain outside the Bridge Gate at the Orontes crossing and his main camp some three miles away to the north. That the crusaders were permitted to leave the city and deploy, in whatever formation, was a huge bonus for Bohemond. The speed of his attack wrong-footed the enemy – when Kerbogha did arrive with his main army from base camp it was to find the divisions on the plain breaking up in flight. His own people followed suit even before they had engaged the enemy, and this despite the fact that there were probably fewer than 200 well-mounted horsemen to pursue them. An army which had been called into being because Emperor Alexius had wanted to recruit brigades of professional cavalrymen had won its greatest victory as a largely infantry army against an overwhelmingly superior Turkish force of mixed horse and foot.

Barely a month after this triumph, the army lost its leader when, on 1 August, Adhémar of Le Puy died of the plague. The nucleus of the army as a fighting force was provided by the 'princes', a vague term for the great feudatories such as Robert of Normandy, and grouped round them their household knights. Below the 'princes' were lesser men – counts, viscounts, castellans – who might have their own followings, as well as individual knights. In battle a man would fight under his own leader and with his own countrymen and neighbours. Breton crusaders tended to associate with the forces of Robert of Normandy, for they had after all been allies with the Normans thirty years before in the invasion of England. The army was in effect a federation on the move, but the moral authority of Adhémar was unquestioned and more than once his military advice had been followed. When he died quarrels developed within the leadership and it was probably at this time that ambitious individuals began to think of carving out lordships for themselves in northern Syria. The chief point of dispute was whether or not Antioch should be returned to the Emperor. The three eyewitness chroniclers of the crusade all agree that the question of the oath they had made to Alexius on the point divided the army and its leaders, above all Bohemond and Raymond.[29] The former opposed the idea, arguing that the Emperor had not come to their aid in the dark days of the siege when his help could have been critical. Raymond argued in favour; in fact he was to become a close ally of Alexius and one contemporary tells us that the Emperor gave him rich presents. The army itself simply wanted to advance on Jerusalem and complete its pilgrimage vows. Guessing that Bohemond's only interest was Antioch, they offered to recognize Raymond as sole leader of the pilgrimage if he would organize and lead the march on the Holy City. In mid January 1099, led by the Count walking barefoot, the bulk of the pilgrim army marched out for the last stage of its epic campaign. The forces of Robert of Normandy and Tancred followed almost at once; Duke Godfrey of Lorraine and Count Robert of Flanders took the road a month later; Bohemond meanwhile remained in undisputed control of Antioch.

Jerusalem was now in the hands of a Fatimid garrison. Defeat for Kerbogha outside Antioch was welcome news for the other Muslim powers in the region. With the principal Turkish player out of the reckoning the rulers of Cairo moved rapidly to recover their province of Palestine as far north as Beirut from the Turkish clans that had only recently seized it and had forced them to abandon the Holy City. To the north, Arab princes until now under the Turkish sphere of influence looked for ways of exploiting the changing political map and prepared to deal with the new Christian elements where it seemed to their advantage. We shall see in the next chapter that such wheeling and dealing would be a commonplace of the new, multicultural Syria. Now it meant that the crusading army was able to advance with little opposition through what might have been expected to be hostile territories and to replenish its stocks of food and horses. They succeeded in capturing the port of Tortosa by a ruse, an important gain both for their supply lines and for communications. Continuing southwards the army intimidated the Emir of Tripoli into paying protection money rather than risk a siege. The fact was that the cities along the route were independent and often the wealth of a place was to be found in gardens and orchards beyond the walls so that a ruler might well prefer a deal with the Infidel host to move it on through his territories, rather than risk the devastation that would follow any defiance. So the crusaders marched on unmolested past Acre to the little port of Arsuf, some fifty miles to the north-west of Jerusalem, from where they struck inland heading for the Holy City. At news of their approach the Christian population of Bethlehem sent messengers to the army begging them to liberate the place from Egyptian rule. A detachment of knights under Tancred and Baldwin of Le Bourg accordingly rode over to be welcomed into the town by jubilant processions of priests and citizens. Thus it was that when, on 7 June 1099, the great host of the warrior pilgrims finally prepared to pitch camp around the walls of the Holy City, the site of Christ's suffering and Passion, they could claim they had already liberated the city of his birth.

The army faced a daunting task. Jerusalem's walls and defences were formidable and the place was well supplied with provisions and water. The garrison's commander was highly capable, he had arranged for the poisoning of virtually all the water sources outside the city walls and had sent an urgent call to Cairo for help. And if the large garrison was not big enough to man the entire circuit of the walls, then the crusading force was in the same plight. The contingents under Robert of Flanders, Robert of Normandy and Godfrey of Bouillon invested the northern perimeter, while to the south were the forces of the southern French under Count Raymond of Toulouse. The first assault was made just five days after the army's arrival and was perhaps premature as it was repulsed by the defenders. However, with the Mediterranean summer at its hottest and given the precarious nature of their situation the leaders needed a quick victory if the pilgrimage was not to end in disaster. Part of the problem had been a shortage of artillery and siege towers and, behind this, a lack of materials. Then, the week following the failed attack, a flotilla of Christian ships, Genoese and English, put in at the port of Jaffa, apparently abandoned by its garrison. As before, a detachment of sailors bringing their technical skills and military supplies brought vital aid to the cause. In the following days, two large siege towers were constructed, out of sight of the defenders, together with scaling ladders and artillery. The assault was scheduled to start after dark on 13 July with two simultaneous attacks each led by one of the siege towers, one in the northern sector, the other in the south. All night, through a hellish landscape and deluge of arrows, missiles, liquid fire and pitch hailing down from the smoke-clouded battlements, soldiers and pilgrims, women and old men among them, sweated to fill the city moats with causeways of rubble and rubbish – here and there the charred body parts of their companions – and to drag the clumsy, creaking and swaying contraptions up to the walls. It was the tower commanded by Godfrey of Bouillon on the northern sector that, on the morning of 15 July, established the first foothold. Seeing the enemy secure a bridgehead on the ramparts, the defenders in this sector streamed back to the temple area to rally for a last stand around the al-Aqsa Mosque, but they surrendered to Tancred and flew his banner over the mosque promising to pay a large ransom in the negotiations that should follow the capture. Meantime, blood-crazed crusaders were streaming over the walls and through the streets of the northern part of the city slaughtering every living thing that crossed their path. No banner was going to save lives in this shambles, while the Jewish population of the city were cut down – man, woman and child – where they stood hoping for sanctuary in their chief syna-gogue. They can have had little hope. Months before, news of the pogroms in the Rhineland had reached the city and most of its Jewish community had sided with the Muslim defenders, fearful of their fate should the place fall to the Christians. Now that fate was upon them. On the southern walls the defenders led by the garrison commander held off the attackers until, realizing that the city was lost, he and his bodyguard made a successful retreat to the citadel known as the Tower of David. They made a formal capitulation to Count Raymond, agreeing to surrender the fortress and pay a large ransom in exchange for their liberty. The agreement was honoured – the Count saw them out of the city under escort and allowed them to join the Muslim garrison at the port of Ascalon.

It is doubtful whether any other of the inhabitants of Jerusalem on that dreadful day survived. The native Christians had been expelled from the city before the siege began; they were lucky, for in the mayhem of sacking they too no doubt would have perished. The slaughter lasted the best part of two days. When it was over, the crusade leaders went in solemn procession to the Church of the Holy Sepulchre to give thanks to God, and the day after chose Godfrey of Bouillon from among their number to head the new crusader King-dom of Jerusalem. There was surely much to give thanks for. More than once over the years it had seemed that the army had survived only thanks to divine intervention. Even so some blenched at the butchery that had sealed their victory. Pope Urban had died two weeks after the fall of the Holy City but well before the news could reach Rome. When reports did reach the West many churchmen expressed horrified dismay. Accounts of the shocking events reverber-ated through Muslim Syria. When, in the year 1100, Ascalon itself was thinking of surrendering to the Christian army, consolidating the conquests in Palestine, it stipulated that Count Raymond alone receive the capitulation. Godfrey of Bouillon, in his capacity as leader of the Christian community, refused to agree to this condition, no doubt out of jealousy of Raymond. The city withdrew its offer and successfully held out. Thus, for the next fifty years, the major port of southern Palestine remained Egypt's advance naval base in its wars with the new intruder states.

3

Life and Politics
in a Multicultural World

While accepting the rule, Godfrey of Bouillon's modesty forbade him from accepting the title 'King of Jerusalem' in the land of Christ's life and suffering. Instead he adopted the title *Advocatus Sancti Sepulchri*, 'Defender of the Holy Sepulchre'. There were those who would have said he did well to be modest; brave in battle, he was a weak personality. Raymond, who had expected the election, was inevitably alienated, but Godfrey's poor handling of them angered other leaders. The treaties he was able to strike with the Muslim rulers of Ascalon, Acre and Caesarea won the infant state breathing space, but his decision to recognize supremacy of Daimbert, the new Latin Patriarch of Jerusalem, was a hostage to the future in terms of Church–State relations. Arriving in Jerusalem early in 1100, Archbishop Daimbert of Pisa had ousted the first Latin Patriarch as illegally elected, and had taken his place. For a time, following the death of Godfrey in July, he was in absolute control of the city. However, his ambitions were rudely terminated when Godfrey's brother Baldwin, Count of Edessa, marched south with an army at his back and forced the Patriarch to crown him king in December. Within twelve months Daimbert had been expelled from the city in his turn, on a charge of embezzlement, and relieved of his title.

Baldwin had impressed his authority on the Kingdom's divided nobility with a successful show of strength against the Fatimids of

Egypt. He consolidated the position and captured all the coastal cities except Ascalon and Tyre by 1112; he also laid the groundwork of the Kingdom's institutions. Palestine was culturally and ethnically diverse with religious divides between Christian and Muslim, Roman Catholic and Orthodox, but also the ancient Christian Churches antedating the Muslim conquest. There were diverse legal traditions; the Kingdom was merely first among equals of four Christian states – the Principality of Antioch, the County of Edessa and, from 1102, the County of Tripoli being the others. The Italian merchant cities, without whose maritime assistance it is doubtful the coastal conquests would have been possible, secured residential and trading quarters with extraterritorial legal status; in the countryside Muslim villagers were permitted to appeal to their own traditions; and finally this new Latin state was home to two entirely new and increasingly powerful organizations of military monks, the Knights Templar and Knights Hospitaller, answerable only to the Pope but pledged to fight with the armies of the Kingdom. This was multiculturalism to startle even a twenty-first-century observer. This chapter attempts some description of its life and politics in its extraordinary context as an intruder state in an alien environment.

The arrival of the crusading army in Syria had been shocking not only in military terms: it had confused all the political assumptions of the region. The march on Antioch was at first misinterpreted by the Fatimid regime in Cairo and other Muslim rulers in the region. They assumed that the Franks were merely the agents of imperial policy aiming to restore Byzantine power to its position before the recent Turkish successes, and that with this achieved they would withdraw so that the normal military and diplomatic exchanges might be resumed. In generations of rivalry with Byzantium, spheres of interest seemed to have been established. True, in 1085 Antioch had come to the Turks through Christian treachery, while more recently a Turkish clan had seized Jerusalem from its Fatimid garrison. But these were essentially border disputes – between Baghdad and Constantinople in the one case and between Cairo and Turkish adventurers on the other. Jerusalem had been a Muslim city for more than four centuries. Thus when Cairo proposed a deal to the crusaders advancing on Antioch to leave northern Palestine a Christian sphere of interest while it moved back to its ancient centres in the south, this seemed to make perfectly good sense in terms of the map of Syria before the coming of the Turks. The impetus of the *jihad* of the seventh and eighth centuries, which had brought the armies of the prophet from Arabia to the walls of Constantinople, was hardly a memory, and the religious fanaticism of the crusading army at first provoked no matching response. Least of all did any of the Turkish and Arab rulers of the cities of Syria imagine that the Franks intended a permanent settlement to be extended into the central power bases of Muslim Syria. An old imam of Damascus was wiser. Reflecting after the fall of Antioch, he warned that no one city-state in Syria was going to be strong enough to hold back the advance of these infidels; and even if the Muslims of Syria managed to unite in the common cause that might not be sufficient, in which case the Muslims of neighbouring territories would be duty bound in religion to join the struggle. His prescience would be confirmed by events, but it would be a generation and more before the message got home.

And the threat from the north was not over. As the year 1100 dawned there could have been few communities in Europe that did not know of the triumphs won by Western Catholicism over Islam in the land of Christ's life and Passion. With the Holy City under a Latin cleric as patriarch, and new states under Roman Catholic rulers, Christendom was entering a new age of the world. But if that new age were to be sustained, warrior pilgrims would be needed to reinforce the armies of the faithful and populate the newly won territories with true Christians. The need was for settlers and soldiers and the Church's hierarchy had not abandoned the papal project launched at Clermont back in 1095, once the armies of 1096 were assembled and on the road. Papal letters and legatine missions maintained the momentum.[1] The stay-at-homes heard marvellous tales of hardships heroically overcome, of divine miracles, of holy relics to be found – and of fortunes to be made.

Since Jerusalem was now in Christian hands, the element of pilgrimage was no doubt to the fore. In September 1100, a huge company of pilgrims set out from Lombardy under Archbishop Anselm of Milan and three minor noblemen. Thousands of priests, women and children and a swarm of out-of-work labourers and artisans, as well as petty criminals on the lookout for loot, accompanied a comparatively small body of fighting men. Travelling through Austria and Hungary and via Belgrade they arrived outside Constantinople in March 1101. The Emperor Alexius received the Archbishop with courteous hospitality, even though the crusaders had by this time been pillaging the countryside, and ferried the 'army' across into Anatolia. Count Raymond of Toulouse was also a guest of Alexius at this time, discussing ways the Franks in Syria might cooperate with Constantinople to consolidate the gains made by the crusaders, though men would later charge he was there to receive his orders. Reluctantly, the Lombards agreed to accept his leadership and, together with a force of Byzantine mercenaries under Raymond's command, to consolidate Christian gains in Anatolia, on a plan agreed with Alexius' advice. The joint force moved on to encamp under the walls of Nicomedia (Izmit, Turkey). Here they were joined by the expedition led by Stephen of Blois. He, too, it was said, was acting under orders, though in his case, said the gossips, from a wife determined he should clear his reputation from the charge of cowardice levied when he deserted the First Crusade at Antioch. It was still held against him.

A council was called to debate the next objective from Nicomedia. Many wanted to take the most direct route possible for Palestine, avoiding as far as possible the Seljuk forces. For an expedition of armed pilgrims en route to help the Holy Land it seemed common sense. Stephen advocated it, but he was a known coward. Raymond recommended a route that would consolidate the Christian presence in Anatolia while provoking the Turks as little as possible; but he was reckoned an emperor's man. The Lombard contingent wanted to liberate the Italian-born Bohemond, Prince of Antioch, presently a prisoner of the Danishmend Turks of northern Anatolia. Since it constituted the great bulk of the pilgrims and since the Archbishop of Milan supported the proposal, it was decided to head eastwards towards Ankara and beyond for the remote Turkish fortress where Bohemond was being held. And so the army, harassed by skirmishers, marched ever eastward into lands laid waste by the retreating Turks. At length, in the vicinity of the historic town of Amasya (Amasya province, northern Turkey), they were faced by an army of Turkish clans united in a common cause against the intruders. And they were utterly routed. The Lombards fled while the Byzantine mercenaries withdrew rather than face pointless massacre. Four-fifths of the army fell or were captured and sold, with such camp followers as survived, into slavery. Most of the leaders, headed by Raymond of Toulouse, managed to extricate themselves and were back in Constantinople by the autumn. Alexius was understandably furious. The rank and file crusaders absurdly enough accused him of colluding with the Turks in planning an ambush. The crusading enterprise was humiliated and the fragile amity between Latins and Greeks cracked. Worse was soon to follow.

In November 1100, at the Council of Poitiers, another crusade had been proclaimed in Aquitaine under the aegis of two papal legates. It reminded a bystander of the impression made on him at Limoges back in 1095 when he saw Pope Urban preaching the first crusade at Christmas in the cathedral there. On that occasion Duke William IX of Aquitaine and Count of Poitiers had been among the great and the good to take the Cross. Yet more than five years later he still had to fulfil his vow. Part of the explanation may be found in a classic dynastic dispute over land rights; the kind of thing which had led the popes to promise the Church's protection to the territories and interests of crusaders and their families.

Remembered today for his poetry as the first troubadour, Duke William came from a long line of powerful, aristocratic dynasts. Lord of Aquitaine, he also had ambitions in neighbouring Toulouse and indeed, years back, had gained an annulment of his first marriage so as to marry Philippa, daughter and heiress of the last count who died on pilgrimage in the Holy Land. This count was the older brother of Raymond of St Gilles, already known to us as the chief lay leader of the First Crusade. Before the Count left for his pilgrimage he appointed Raymond regent of Toulouse in his absence. But when, in 1093, news came of his death Raymond, ignoring the claims of Philippa and her husband took – some said usurped – the county. Then, in 1096, he too marched off at the head of a crusade, consigning his rights in Toulouse to his own son, Bertrand. Duke William however remained in France, biding his time. Two years later, he occupied Toulouse, against the opposition not only of the young Bertrand but also of the Church, which promised protection to absent crusaders of their lands and families. Duke William now decided to make good his vow to the Cross. He left Philippa as his regent in Poitiers and was joined on crusade by other French and German lords, chief among them Hugh of Vermandois who had deserted the First Crusade at Antioch and was anxious to fulfil his vows of pilgrimage to Jerusalem.

The joint force reached Constantinople in June 1101. After some five weeks' delay they marched off along the road towards Iconium. Progress was slow, supplies short and Iconium abandoned. Early in September, leading his broken-spirited and starving people on through villages and orchards pillaged of their supplies and stripped of their produce by the enemy, Duke William reached the town of

Heraclea, nestling by its river in the summer-scorched boulder lands of southern Anatolia. Not for the first or last time the shimmer of water cut through the parched reins of an army's discipline. As the huge rabble of horsemen and foot soldiers plunged and stumbled over one another for the river bank, flashes of sun on steel joined the glinting of the water among the bushes and osier thickets – the Turks had sprung their carefully laid ambush. Dazed and skidding to steady themselves, weapons slipping in sweaty hands or kicked clear by skittering hooves, the pilgrim army sweltered in the entrails and body parts of a butcher's shambles, as the Turkish swordsmen warmed to their work. Duke William, accompanied by a groom, was among the few knights to cut a way out of the mêlée. From the comparative safety of a mountain gully he sat his horse and looked back, weeping for the slaughter of his followers and fellow crusaders.

But much more than a battle had been lost. With their comprehensive victories over the Christians at Amasya and Heraclea, the Turks erased their humiliation at Dorylaeum, the first miracle victory of the Crusade. The Lombard Crusade, Stephen of Blois, William IX, Troubadour of Aquitaine, and the leaders of the other ill-judged initiatives of this year of losers, had seriously damaged the health of the Christian cause in Palestine. William made his way back to Tarsus where he found the dying Hugh of Vermandois, lamenting his unfulfilled vows to Jerusalem. For his part William returned to Europe.

Meantime, the Muslim rulers of Palestine did deals with the incomers where it suited their purposes, rather than campaign to expel or destroy the infidel intruders on ideological grounds. Damascus would settle a boundary dispute with the King of Jerusalem with the greatest amicability – and to the disadvantage only of the peasants of each side. In 1107 Muslim Aleppo, in alliance with Christian Antioch, defeated the combined armies of Muslim Mosul and the Christian Prince Baldwin of Edessa. As a gesture of good faith to his Christian ally, Ridwan of Aleppo even had a cross affixed to the minaret of the city's principal mosque. Such inter-faith alliances were testimony to an admirable multiculturalism of self-interest. Pious minds on both sides, however, were shocked. Ali ibn Takir al-Sulami of Damascus sought to shame princes into action, urging them to unite in a *jihad* to exterminate the Franks and recover the lost territories. In the spring of 1105, in the mosque of a Damascus suburb, he gave a public reading from his *Kitab al-Jihad 'Book of the Jihad: A call to the Holy War, the Duty to Wage it and Its Rules'*. 'Publication' was completed with a reading of the rest of the work in the great Ummayyad mosque in the city. Al-Sulami accused the princes of cowardice in the face of their conquerors. The tide of pro-*jihad* feeling surged in the 1110s as devout Muslims began to charge that some of the princes were collaborating with the Franks so as to keep themselves in power. At the end of that decade, Ilghazi, the new lord of Aleppo, found himself a champion of the Holy War, almost despite himself. He would have been happy to placate his powerful neighbour, Roger, Prince of Antioch, so as to extend his territory at the expense of his smaller Muslim neighbours. But in June 1119 a rash expedition by Roger precipitated a confrontation in broken country some fifteen miles west of Aleppo. Ilghazi, awaiting the arrival of allied forces from Damascus, found his hand forced, of all people, by his Turkoman mercenaries. As the army waited, the '*qadi*' Abu 'l Fadl, wearing his lawyer's turban but brandishing a lance, rode out in front of the troopers. At first they were incredulous at being harangued by a scholar but by the end of his passionate evocation of the duties and merits of the *jihad* warrior, according to Kamal al-Din, the contemporary historian of Aleppo, these hardened professionals wept with emotion and rode into battle. The Franks would call the engagement the Field of Blood; there were virtually no survivors among the Christians. 'The fugitives were hunted down and tortured and massacred among the vineyards . . . till Ilghazi put a stop to it, not wishing the populace of Aleppo to miss all the sport. The remainder . . . were tortured to death in its streets.'[2] Roger of Antioch had been felled at the foot of the great jewelled cross which had served as his standard. Antioch now lay virtually defenceless expecting the triumphant army hourly, but Ilghazi wasted his triumph in celebrations. Two months later, he was checked by the army of King Baldwin II of Jerusalem, but though both sides claimed victory Ilghazi left the field in good order and with a large train of prisoners, so that for the second time in two months the Aleppans could relish the street theatre of Christians being massacred. Even captives of noble blood were mown down so that valuable ransoms were squandered. Strategically indecisive, this campaign nevertheless boosted Muslim morale considerably.

Naturally, in the crusader states, the minority Frankish Roman Catholics were the ruling group – only they could participate in the feudal courts – but their Muslim and Jewish subjects enjoyed judicial autonomy in religious cases which continued to be dealt with by their *qadis* and rabbis, while the Courts of the Syrians, reporting ultimately to the royal government but administering their own customary laws, handled secular cases. The establishment operated under a modified feudal system (described in more detail in Chapter Six), by which land was held by vassals in exchange for military service obligations. For example, the lordship of Tyre, part of the royal domain, owed the service of twenty-eight fully equipped knights direct to the Crown. In the twelfth century the settler states were the County of Edessa, the Principality of Antioch, the County of Tripoli, and the Kingdom of Jerusalem of which the rulers of Galilee and Oultrejourdain (Transjordan) and a number of other lordships were technically part. The counties, Principality and even the frontier lordships of the Kingdom had considerable independence of action when it came to their dealings with their Muslim neighbours and, as we shall see, exercised it to the full.

Native Christian or Muslim peasants made up the majority rural population though there were some villages where the new Western landlords attempted to establish Catholic settlements. Typical of these were villages bequeathed to the canons of the Holy Sepulchre by Godfrey of Bouillon in the region between Sephorie (al Saffuriyah), Jericho and Bethlehem. The pioneers were tempted out mostly from southern France, though a few came from Italy and as far afield as Spain, with highly favourable terms by which house plot rents were paid in kind to canons' bailiffs. Archaeology has unearthed presses and vats which show oil and wine to be preferred products. Following Saladin's campaigns, these settlements were of course abandoned.[3]

Ancient traditions complicated society and religion within the new Christian states. Today's communities of Arab Christians in Israel and Palestine, such as those of Bethlehem, are among the earliest in the world. Before the explosion of Islam in the seventh century, there had been scattered Arab communities of Arab Christians belonging to the ancient Jacobite Church of Syria. Under Arab rule the population had been allowed freedom of worship on payment of the standard poll tax or *jizyah* levied on *dhimmis* (non-Muslims but peoples of the Book like Jews and Christians). Many found the intolerant single-mindedness of the new Latin regimes a harsh change from the arrangements under the pragmatic Islamic rule. Although Orthodox rites were permitted, they were not encouraged, while the arrogance of the Roman Catholic hierarchy was bitterly unwelcome. Latin and Orthodox alike considered Jacobite doctrines on the divine nature of Christ heretical, while the language of the Church's liturgy was ancient Syriac. The other chief local churches were the Armenian and the Maronite Christians (who held that Christ had had a dual human and divine nature governed by a single divine will), which survive to this day. To their former Muslim rulers their beliefs as Christians, like the Roman Catholics, were all equally misguided and therefore a matter of indifference, not censure or possible persecution. All were potential fifth columnists should the Franks ever find themselves under threat.

Christian pilgrims from Europe recruited to the ranks of the Kingdom's armies reckoned with the risk of violent death; many more met with it on the road. Outside the walled cities bandits and contingents of Muslim marauders were constantly on the lookout for wayfarers foolish enough not to join a merchant caravan with its escort of mercenaries or wait for an organized pilgrim party with armed men in its number. Victims' bodies rarely received Christian burial from other travellers and skeletons picked bare by carrion birds were left to whiten where they lay. In the 1090s, even before the Christian conquest of Jerusalem, a group of philanthropic knights had opened a medical centre for sick pilgrims at the hospital of St John. Now, sometime probably in 1118, a French knight, Hugh de Payens, with eight of his companions, approached King Baldwin for help with plans they had to offer protection to pilgrims en route for Jerusalem. They came from the elite stratum of their society, being proud, promiscuous and privileged, but their association was to be modelled on the vows of a monastic order – poverty, chastity and absolute obedience to the master. This new order, the Poor Knights of Christ and the Temple of Solomon, or the Knights Templar, was pledged to the profession of arms in service of the servants of the Prince of Peace.

The paradox occurred even to some contemporaries. But others saw that if Holy War as such could be justified then an institution that channelled the violence of the military class to its dedicated service did make sense. Bernard of Clairvaux, himself a nobleman who had turned monk, and related to one of the founding group, wrote the Order's Rule. What they needed from King Baldwin was premises where they could establish themselves. He assigned them what had, up till then, been the royal palace in the complex of the al-Aqsa Mosque, known to the Christian conquerors as the Templum Salomis (Temple of Solomon), as he was moving to a new custom-built palace. This 'temple' required only a few minor adjustments for conversion to Christian use; for example, the construction of an altar and the replacement of the crescent on the dome with a cross. The Templars also made extensions to east and west and partly reconstructed a range of subterranean vaults to the east to serve as stables.[4]

The Order, which acknowledged only the Pope as its superior, was under the command of a Grand Master, but no function was so vital as that of the Marshal, responsible for the all-important horses. It was he who supervised their purchase; he who assigned each brother his mount or mounts. Senior officers might be allowed four warhorses plus a riding horse such as palfrey or mule mounts, but it was the Marshal who had to authorize any replacements, and who had to be convinced that an animal had become temperamental, liable to pull to left or right or rear skittishly. A fighting horse was trained to use its hooves but only under command. There were knights who preferred mares or geldings but Ann Hyland in her enthralling book *The Medieval Warhorse* finds that stallions were also used since there are records of muzzles in the equipment inventories and stallions are liable to fight one another with their teeth.

After a successful engagement any booty and above all quadruped prizes had to be consigned to the Marshal's caravan. It was he, too, who had the last say as to what was and what was not acceptable by way of horse furniture. No silver embellishments were permitted on metal tack, Turkish saddles could be used for comfort on the march but had to be covered with black or white leather, as they tended to be flamboyant. Even hunting, that knightly diversion par excellence, was strictly forbidden. Puritanical discipline was part of the rationale – a Templar was expected to practise self-mortification, though forbidden to fast and required to eat meat – but military discipline was the overriding consideration. Without his horse a mounted man at arms was only half a soldier. Neglect of equipment or horse could sentence the offender to taking his meals on the stone-flagged floor of the refectory set apart from his colleagues, or even being flogged. One could almost say that the stables rated with the chapel as the centre of Templar devotion: to miss prayers was heinous, but an appointment with the farrier to shoe a horse was a valid excuse.

Only the knights were subject to the strictest provisions of the rule and only they could wear its distinctive white robe blazoned with the red cross. There were three other classes – sergeants, chaplains and servants – and other, non-military activities. From the beginning, thanks largely to the campaigning of St Bernard, the Templars were recipients of large donations and endowments in land in Europe as well as Palestine. Prosperous estates, administered from convents or 'preceptories', were run by and for the Order, and the profits from farms, mills, vineyards, market dues and all the diverse revenues available to a medieval manorial lord were deposited in strong-rooms and used to fund the purchase of weapons, siege equipment and other military supplies, or were forwarded under well-armed escorts to Jerusalem.

It was a network that was to develop into a prototype of an international bank. The convents with their trustworthy guardians were ideal places of deposit for money, jewels and documents, whether merely for safekeeping, or as credit centres for the transfer of goods, and soon monetary payments from one place to another. Indeed, some individuals ran what amounted to current accounts, the convent regularly receiving their revenues and making payments on their behalf. For much of the thirteenth century the Temple in Paris acted as a treasury for the French kings; and many nobles, including several of Louis IX's brothers, had accounts with the Temple there.[5] In Outremer itself they even did business with wealthy Arabs; indeed the Templars' wealth soon led them into banking activities to rival the Italian merchant houses. As moneylenders they were advancing money as early as the 1130s, and in the later thirteenth century they were regularly making loans to the Aragonese Crown. In the thirteenth century borrowing became a regular feature of European government financing, rulers regularly anticipating revenues, which they used as security for short-term loans. Both the Italian merchant bankers and the religious orders, for the Hospitallers also developed a banking service, were tempted to borrow in order to meet royal demands for money, rather than lose royal favour and custom. Paper instruments could arrange the transfer of funds paid into one preceptory and drawn on another, without the need to transport bullion across bandit-infested roads in Europe as well as the Near East. Thus pious if timid relations could fund a warlike kinsman in the fight against the Saracens. They probably had business interests in Jerusalem itself – capital 'Ts' carved on buildings in one of the city's markets have prompted Adrian Boas, archaeologist of the Holy City, to whom this chapter is much indebted, to suggest that the Order had shares in some of the shops there.[6]

Jerusalem was divided into various quarters. To the north-west, the Patriarch's Quarter, centred upon the Church of the Holy Sepulchre (the Byzantine replacement of the building destroyed by the Sultan al-

Hakim) and the nearby Patriarch's Palace, was subject to the administrative jurisdiction of his court, the *curia patriarchae*. One of the first actions by the victorious crusading army had been the expulsion of the Orthodox Patriarch and his replacement by a Roman Catholic cleric. We have already seen his fate and that of his successor Daimbert of Pisa. While subsequent patriarchs retained full spiritual authority, their administrative and legal authority was limited to this quarter. However, the Church of the Holy Sepulchre as it survived down to the start of the twenty-first century is the result of a major rebuild carried through under their aegis and consecrated on 15 July 1149, the fiftieth anniversary of the crusaders' capture of the city.[7]

To the south lay the Hospitallers' quarter with, at its heart, the great hospice and infirmary to which the work was dedicated. Considered by visitors to Jerusalem to be a marvel, incredibly beautiful, 'and abundantly supplied with rooms and beds and other material for the use of poor and sick people',[8] it was said to be able to accommodate 2,000 in-patients each with a spacious bed fitted with its own coverlet and sheets, and it was staffed with four doctors, well qualified by the standards of the day. The Hospital of St John of Jerusalem had been founded in the late eleventh century as a philanthropic body for the medical care of pilgrims. Its members would become known as the Knights of St John and by 1130 had assumed, in addition to the medical work, a military role. By the end of the twelfth century castles and walled towns built or garrisoned by them were to be found all over Frankish Syria. They numbered some of the finest examples of military architecture – for example Belvoir, overlooking the River Jordan to the south of Lake Tiberias and completed in 1168, has been identified as the first example of the 'concentric' type of castle, while Krak des Chevaliers, developed from 1142, is the most famous of all the crusader castles. Like the Templars they received immense endowments in property in Europe which was divided for administrative purposes into provinces or 'priories' such as the Priory of England (which also covered Scotland and Wales), with its headquarters in Clerkenwell, London – the crypt of the twelfth-century church there is still to be seen – the Priory of Ireland, the Priory of Castile, the Priory of Auvergne, the Priory of Bohemia and so forth. Each provincial head or prior reported up to the Grand Master of the Order in Jerusalem and had under his authority the numerous 'commanderies'. The Hospitallers' quarter at Acre, with its hospice and infirmary, large refectory and spacious halls seems, from excavations in the 1990s, to have been even more elaborate with vaulted undercrofts or cellarage space, a ramped stairway leading to their flat roofs and the upper level surrounded by colonnaded cloisters. One of the strongest and best-fortified buildings at Acre, and indeed the last one to hold out in the siege of 1291, was the Temple, heart of the Templars' quarter. Thus, during the Frankish period, Acre was one of the great bastions of the military orders but it remained, of course, one of the Mediterranean's great mercantile entrepots in the Middle Ages. The visitor entering Acre from the port side had first to pass through the customs house – the way lay through an iron gate into the Court of the Chain. This was not only the place where dues were levied but also the seat of the marine court merchant.

During the reign of Baldwin I the Kingdom acquired the major coastal cities, Jaffa and Haifa having already fallen in 1099. In 1101 Caesarea capitulated as did neighbouring Arsuf, with the aid of a Genoese fleet. Acre (modern Akko) was taken in May 1104, again Genoese help being decisive. The city's reward was a large commercial quarter containing not only a covered street market but a number of palatial mansions – though whether the close proximity of the house of the soap makers was considered an unmixed convenience may be doubted. As at Antioch, where they had won their first commercial district in the Middle East from Bohemond, the Genoese enjoyed extraterritorial jurisdiction. According to historian John France: 'The decision to send a fleet to the aid of the First Crusade was virtually the foundation of the greatness of Genoa.'[9] At Acre, both Pisa and Venice soon negotiated for similar autonomous districts, as did the merchants of Marseille. Where the aristocracy could hope to gain land from crusading, Europe's growing commercial class made major and lasting extensions to their trading horizons. Sidon and Beirut fell in 1110, but Tyre was a special case. Accessible from the landward side only by a causeway and through carefully maintained defences, it was able to repel sieges in 1102 and 1111 and only fell, in 1124, thanks to the aid of the Venetian fleet. Ascalon, the last major coastal city to fall to the Kingdom of Jerusalem, held out until 1153.

At the time of the conquest the population of Palestine presented a fairly homogeneous aspect, native Christians dressed much like their Muslim neighbours and used Arabic as the daily vernacular, while the Orthodox Church used Greek as the language of liturgy. Archaeological digs as well as literary sources show the trades and industries common in the Western towns – such as abattoirs, bakeries, coin mints, tanners etc. But there were oddities – for example one might find a baker sharing the same furnace heat source as a public baths, while soap making was more common within the city walls than in comparable European cities. And of course distinctly exotic trades such as sugar refineries, generally sited outside the walls were quite common, though they were unknown in Europe. Markets were of course an integral part of city life but in Outremer covered street markets, roofed in with handsome stone vaulting, were much more common. One visitor noted that there were occasional high windows to let in the light; though in Jerusalem's Malquissinat (street of bad cooking), apparently dedicated to takeaway cookhouses serving the needs of pilgrims, holes pierced in the vaulting at intervals would also have helped release smoke and cooking smells.

The rural population seem to have been segregated according to religion, Eastern Christians, Muslims and Franks having their own villages and with no known instances of mixed Muslim and Frankish villages. The Muslim villages had to hand over a substantial proportion of their crops at harvest time to make payments for pasture rights and pay a tithe or dime to the Church; the military orders could also receive tithes. By and large, Frankish villages came to depend for security on towns or castles. Where there were planned new villages, or *villeneuves*, the settler was not the serf but the *liber homo* (freeman). The Church of the Holy Sepulchre held numerous properties around Jerusalem where settlers could acquire plots on agreeing to the payment of a land tax. Some villagers produced wine (stone treading vats have been excavated in the houses) for church use, for sale in the towns or even for export.[10] A grange or manor house, sometimes having a fortified tower, was the principal secular building. Large, vaulted storerooms found in such manor houses were the equivalent of tithe barns in the West. Archaeologists suggest that in the early years the newcomers seemed fairly confident of their security. Before the Franks' arrival traditional villages had their houses grouped around an open area, with the community's service buildings such as barns in the centre, guarded against attack by marauders with outer houses abutting one another to form, in effect, a defensive wall. Excavations and studies by Boas revealed that a typical Frankish village plan comprised an 'axial road' – the village street in effect – lined by two rows of houses on long narrow plots. Such an arrangement made it easy to parcel out the land among settlers and it was also difficult to defend against attackers.

The newcomers encountered, to them, a virtually unheard-of product. The cultivation of sugar cane and the refining of sugar were established in the Near East before the crusader period. Under Frankish rule the Italian merchant fleets opened up the virtually unlimited Western market for this product, and large tracts of land in well-watered regions were given over to cane growing. Notable was the land around Tyre and Acre, in the coastal region, and inland along the Jordan valley. Archaeological excavations at the royal sugar mills on Cyprus, where new plantations were developed and the Frankish sugar industry moved after the expulsion of the Franks from Palestine in 1291, give some idea of the process. The complex comprised a large storage area, a grinding hall filled day and night by the grumbling roar of two water-powered mills fed by an aqueduct, and a refinery hall with its eight ovens and its furnace rooms to the south. The harvested cane was cut into short lengths which were further chopped and crushed to a pulp ready to be boiled down in great bronze vats to a syrup, the process being repeated if required to achieve different finenesses of product. This syrup was poured into ceramic hoppers and left to drip into conical moulds where it crystallized into the characteristic sugarloaf shapes ready for sale or export.[11] Most ordinary consumer needs seem to have been supplied by non-Franks. The bulk of ceramic cooking utensils and tableware, often in lively red or brown geometric designs on a biscuit-coloured background, were produced by local artisans, whether Muslim or Syrian Christians – the so-called 'Port St Symeon Ware' produced by native potters, a glazed polychrome pottery, often carried Christian motifs along with its incised decoration. More up-market wares were imported from Fatimid Egypt or Syria, noted for high-quality glazed vessels with designs in blue and black, while the Frankish upper class in the crusader states must have been among the very first Europeans to see true oriental porcelain. From the late twelfth century imports of majolica-like ware also came from Cyprus. We are told that 'the dyeing industry and glass manufacture appear to have been the province of Jews',[12] Tyre was reputed for its range of beautiful, transparent glass vases and there were quality Jewish glassmakers active in Antioch. In addition to such specialist wares, glass seems to have been much more common on the tables of Outremer than in contemporary Europe. Archaeologists have recovered bottles, goblets and beakers of distinctive designs and in comparative profusion. Ironwork produced in the crusader states includes a number of fine pieces of body armour

– notably the exquisite chain mail, now in the collection of the Convent of St Anne, Jerusalem and the delicate mid-twelfth-century grille or screen of looped spiral work now in the Islamic Museum, Temple Mount, Jerusalem. Possibly commissioned by Queen Melisende, it was designed as a protective screen to guard the Rock in the Dome of the Rock, which was converted as a church, from the predations of pilgrims and is of far finer craftsmanship than anything of the same period to have survived in Europe.

For pilgrims from Europe the land of Outremer was a place of culture shock. During a long and slow journey he or she would have grown used to the idea of foreign customs in foreign places, but the Catholic inhabitants of the crusader states were not foreigners in the ordinary sense. The vast majority spoke French, indeed most were second or even first generation Frenchmen; the gentry observed the feudal conventions of lordship and the oath of allegiance. They seemed to be good Catholics so to speak, and yet they were prepared to live cheek by jowl with other faiths, even infidels – they even accepted the Holy Land might have sacred associations for other faiths. Near Nablus were to be seen the well where Christ conversed with the Samaritan woman and also, some twenty-five miles down the road towards Jerusalem, according to Muslim tradition, the site of the pit where his brothers threw Joseph after stripping off the coat of many colours.[13] But then, the al-Aqsa complex had been turned over to the Order of the Temple and converted for Christian worship, except for one of the porches, which was retained for Muslim worshippers who were regularly to be seen at the appointed times of prayer making their devotions in the direction of Mecca, that is southwards.

Usamah, Prince of Shaizar, diplomat and traveller, with many friends among the Christian communities, and author of a volume of urbane memoirs, recalls how one day a newly arrived Frankish pilgrim interrupted him at his devotions there. Horrified by his first sight of an infidel practising his abominable creed, 'this devil of a man, his face changing colour and his limbs trembling', rushed over and swung Usamah round to face the east, crying out: 'This is the way thou shouldest pray.' He was hauled off by a couple of highly embarrassed Templars but returned to the attack as soon as their backs were turned. Clearly he was determined that, if he had any say in the matter, at least one Muslim should learn the right way to pray. This time he was thrown out of the building and the Templars explained to their friend that the man had only recently arrived from Europe. No doubt the man felt it was necessary to be wary of contamination of the faith.

There was said to be a holy image in Damascus that healed Jews, Christians and Muslims indiscriminately; while Muslim and Christian together made their devotions at a spring where it was said that Mary had washed the clothes of the infant Jesus, and where the palm tree had bent to bring its dates within her reach. In a country where the Divine could be so ecumenical, sectarian purity had to be in some danger.

For some visitors, the real shock was the luxury of the Eastern lifestyle. Knights and noblemen who could boast descent from the greatest families in Christendom were to be seen wearing the outlandish *burnous* or the turban and riding into battle, their armour covered by a long surcoat and their helmet by a flapping *kefieh*. To newcomers such commonsense precautions against the torrid heat of an Eastern battlefield verged on fraternization with the enemy. And as we know, fraternization was not exceptional. The intruder population never fully assimilated with the indigenous peoples but moves towards rapprochement verging on assimilation began very early. As early as the 1120s, in the words of a royal chaplain, many felt themselves to have become 'true Easterners'. Romans and Franks had been 'transformed into Galileans or Palestinians, the native of Reims or Chartres into a citizen of Tyre or Antioch'.[14]

Life for a villager in the new kind of settlements opened prospects unknown to a European serf. Life in the towns for gentlemen of middling rank and the mostly Italian merchant class offered luxury indeed. They covered their houses in mosaic and marble, often overlaid with carpets, while rich damask hangings adorned the walls. Furniture had decorative inlays; meals were served on silver – even gold – plate; elegant cutlery included the new-fangled eating fork, for many first encountered in Byzantium; there was regularly laundered bed linen and the ultimate luxury of fresh water brought on tap through the great aqueducts built by the ancient Romans; all these made possible a way of life that northerners tended to find alien and suspect. Wealth and comfort seemed to be much more widely spread than in Europe, brought about by the trade in exotic commodities passing from the Muslim hinterland to the ports on the coast.

The Italians – Genoese, Venetians, Pisans, Amalfitans – and French merchants from Marseille had their business in every city of importance. They had little interest in religion, or so it seemed. The cutthroat competition for monopoly in the Eastern trade between Venice and Genoa meant that a merchant from either city would help a Muslim sooner than his Christian competitor. Indeed, trade brought Christian and Muslim together like nothing else could. For the fact was that despite their despicable religious beliefs, the Christians had brought a heavy increase in the throughput of commodities to Palestine's coastal cities, had developed the new manufactures and had established markets in Europe for them, building a prompt and efficient merchandizing operation to link the two. Interpreters were needed and Franks as well as Greeks and Muslims did the work. A few noblemen learnt Arabic and some even would develop an intelligent interest in Arabic literature.

On any objective assessment, the Franks represented the backward culture, though most would have ridiculed the notion. Usamah of Shaizar recalled how a Frankish friend of his, due to return home shortly, offered to take his son with him for a visit. With such an opportunity, the boy could learn wisdom and chivalry from true knights and return home a wise man. Always the well-mannered gentleman, Usamah urbanely replied that though he personally could wish for nothing better his own mother, the boy's grandmother, had made him promise to send the boy to her. Sympathetic, but convinced, his European friend sadly agreed that he must not disobey the wishes of his mother.

Usamah privately thought his friend must have taken leave of his senses to make such a suggestion; as far as he was concerned the Franks and their ways were among the mysteries of creation understood only by the Author of All Things. His was the majority opinion in Islam. Muslim chroniclers display little interest in the crusader states and even less in their countries of origin. While they have a good deal to say about the high civilizations of the Orient, and are anxious to analyse the origins and motives of the Mongols, their prevailing attitude towards the Christians is contempt. 'The Franks (May Allah render them helpless!) possess none of the virtues of men except courage.'[15] Some Western observers admitted as much. In the early days a German writer described most of the knights who joined the crusades as brigands. Still later a German traveller considered the Latins worse than all the other inhabitants when it came to tourist rip-offs (though perhaps it should be noted that most of them would be of French extraction!). It was a general complaint among ordinary pilgrims that Christians overseas exploited their fellow Catholics shamelessly. No story to their discredit was too bad to be believed. In Jerusalem, it was said, there was barely a man, whether rich or poor, who would not offer you his daughter, his sister, even his wife for money.

Strangely, the treatment of unbelievers, whether Jewish or Muslim, was tolerant by contemporary European standards. It is true that while they could visit Jerusalem, both groups were banned from taking up residence in the city. But the situation for Jews in the crusader states was generally more civilized than that of their co-religionists in Europe. They were not subject to the fear of the pogrom and were not required to wear distinguishing emblems such as badges on their garments, or characteristic headgear. Visitors from the Catholic West were no doubt taken aback by such 'liberal' arrangements.

Thousands visited the Holy Places each year and some stayed on for a year or two to serve in the armies of the Kingdom, an important source of manpower, while a small number even decided to make a new life in the Holy Land. Many more returned home, proud to have made the pilgrimage, happy to be back among familiar surroundings and also, no doubt, delighted to have a fund of bizarre or scandalous yarns to keep the neighbours impressed. The Latin populations of the towns and villages of Outremer, always in desperate need of new settlers, never succeeded in improving the abysmal ratio between their numbers and those of the native population.

4

The Second Crusade:
Disaster on the Road to Damascus

On Christmas Eve 1144 Zangi Imad al-Din, lord of Mosul and Aleppo, captured the crusader city of Edessa. The dreadful and bloody sack that followed amply avenged the crusaders' atrocities in Jerusalem some forty years earlier. Even more serious were the strategic implications. Since its capture by Baldwin of Boulogne in 1098 from its former Armenian ruler, the city and its territory, encompassing some 10,000 square miles of what is now southern Turkey, had provided a vital buffer state on the crusaders' northern frontier, as well as a source of regular harassment to the Muslim rulers of Aleppo and Mosul. In Islam, Zangi's triumph was greeted with jubilation from Baghdad to North Africa. Whenever he should die, wrote the eulogists, for this one deed the ruler of Mosul would be admitted at once to the joys of Paradise. In fact Zangi died two years later, murdered by a servant he had insulted; but his son Nur al-Din recovered the city and secured the conquest of the County.

The Franks of Syria were numbed by the news. King Fulk I had allied with the Emperor at Constantinople against the looming threat posed by this Zangi and in 1140 had allied even with the Muslim ruler of Damascus to help save the city being absorbed by Mosul. But King Fulk had recently died and his widow Queen Melisende, after deliberation with the ruler of Antioch and others, sent an embassy to Rome – though it did not arrive until late in 1145. When the news had reached Europe reactions ranged from horror at the bloodthirsty sack to concern as to the future of the Christian cause in the East. For decades men had warned that without continuing aid from Europe, the entire Holy Land would again be lost to Islam. There had been various expeditions over the years; now in December 1145, Pope Eugenius III issued a general appeal to Christendom and especially to the King of France to mobilize in the cause of the Cross. The pious young King Louis VII, his father's second son, who before the death of his older brother had been brought up among monks, may already have been preparing plans for an expedition. He was in deeply penitential mood following a bloodthirsty punitive campaign he had waged against the insubordinate Count of Champagne. Thousands of people had perished, murdered or burnt alive in churches on his orders. Such was the way of kings. Louis was extremely unusual in feeling guilt, a pilgrimage to the embattled Holy Land would be a fitting penance. Even so, he only went public with his plans at his winter court held at Bourges at Christmas 1145, twelve months after the catastrophe in the East. Response to the King's appeal was muted. Abbot Suger of St Denis, Louis' chief minister, was actually against the idea. Thanks to his shrewd stewardship the royal finances were uncharacteristically sound and war was guaranteed to drain them. The King convened an assembly to meet at Vézélay the following Easter. Meantime, he and Pope Eugenius III approached the most famous man in Europe for help in firing up enthusiasm for the expedition.

The aristocratic-born Cistercian monk, Bernard of Clairvaux, abbot there since the age of twenty-five and mentor of the young monk who was now Pope Eugenius, had been a dominant voice in continental affairs for more than a decade. To be canonized saint just twenty years after his death, he was the 'typical ascetic: tall, skeletally thin, with transparent skin and white hair'.[1] A theologian and controversialist, he had intervened decisively in the resolution of a papal schism; he had secured the papal condemnation of the brilliant philosopher and theologian Peter Abelard as a heretic; and he was an inspired preacher. News that this famous man was to preach the cause of the Cross in the presence of the King attracted huge crowds to Vézélay on the appointed day, 31 March 1146. In anticipation, a preacher's podium was erected on a wooden stage set up in a field outside the town and stacks of cloth strips were at hand, ready to be made up into crosses for those expected to take pilgrim vows. A cross emblem specially blessed by the Pope had also been received for presentation to the King. Bernard began with a solemn reading of the papal bull, with its appeal to aid the Holy Land and its promise of absolution of sins. There followed an impassioned sermon on the dangers threatening the land of Christ's Passion. We do not know the words, but we do know that King Louis, weeping tears of emotion and penitence, prostrated himself before the Abbot who, having raised him to his feet, solemnly attached the Pope's cross to the shoulder of his cloak. The stage-managed event continued with many of the courtiers taking the Cross in full view of the crowds.

The Queen and her ladies followed the gentlemen of the court. At this time Queen Eleanor of France, daughter and heiress of William X, Duke of Aquitaine and Poitiers and granddaughter of the troubadour Duke, William IX, was aged about twenty-five, and was reputed to be the most beautiful woman in Europe. On her marriage to Louis ten years earlier, she had brought with her territories in the south and south-west of France that more than doubled the area directly subject to the royal house. She was the patroness of the troubadours in the tradition of her poet grandfather, the toast of many a courtly admirer, and rumoured to have less and less time for her 'monkish' husband, just a year her senior. The capricious, hot-blooded, southern beauty hardly fitted conventional models of domestic docility. According to a twelfth-century report, when she and her female entourage, among them Sybille, Countess of Flanders and half-sister of the King of Jerusalem, had pledged themselves to the pilgrimage at the feet of St Bernard, they retired to accoutre themselves 'as Amazons'. Then, led by Eleanor on her white horse and shod with gilded sandals, her auburn red hair bedecked with exotic plumes, they cantered out among the crowds brandishing swords and banners and distributing white distaffs to reluctant cavaliers and hesitant pilgrims. There is a tantalizing glimpse of how the ladies might have been dressed from a book written some years later and probably dedicated to her. In his *Roman de Troie*, Benoît de Sainte Maure imagines Penthesilea, Queen of the Amazons, dressed in a hauberk whiter than snow upon the frost, a helmet with circlet and nosepiece studded with precious stones, mounted on a spirited Spanish grey covered with a white silk cloth hung about with little tinkling golden bells, and with a shield whiter than snow and with a pure gold boss bordered with gems. She and her companions each carried a white shield with golden boss, and bore a pennant on a steel-tipped lance while the ladies' hair flowed out in golden tresses over their hauberks.[2]

During St Bernard's sermon, hundreds from the congregation had surged forward, demanding to be given crosses and the flow of clamouring applicants continued. As dusk darkened into night Bernard, who had given up his outer robe to supplement the depleted stocks of material for pilgrim crosses, and a group of helpers were still stitching the holy emblem onto the garments of devotees.

Bernard followed his triumph at Vézélay with a preaching tour though Burgundy, Lorraine and Flanders. In his own words 'villages and towns were deserted', everywhere there were 'widows whose husbands are still alive'.[3] Other monks were spreading the word in the German lands of the Empire, notably Bernard's Cistercian 'disciple' Raoul (Radulf in German). In Flanders Bernard got an urgent message from the Archbishop of Cologne to cross into Germany not only to preach the Cross but also to restrain his follower. As in the build-up to the First Crusade, Jewish communities were being targeted by mobs urged on by fanatics like this Radulf who called upon them to take vengeance on Christ's enemies in their own neighbourhood before going to war against the Saracens. To liturgist Rabbi Ephraim, who was for many years head of the Rabbinic court at Bonn and recorded the events, the name 'Radulf' carried a terrible resonance, for 'radof' is the Hebrew word for 'persecute'. The Rabbi thought Bernard was a decent priest sent by God in response to the prayers of the Jewish communities, and without his intervention none would have survived. For his part, we are told that Bernard proclaimed that Radulf was wrong to call for the annihilation of the Jews and, furthermore, that anyone who took a Jew's life could be said to harm Jesus Himself. In the previous century, Pope Alexander II (1061–73), in a letter to the Spanish bishops, had enunciated the bleak official rationale for humanitarian treatment of Jews. It was wrong to kill them, ran the argument, because God in his mercy had been saved by God's mercy to expiate the crime of their ancestors' 'deicide' in penitence and subjugation.[4]

Some Jews were saved, many more died horribly at Christian hands, while still others, refusing baptism with the bitter, accursed water of the font, killed themselves in suicide pacts. Apparently, they comforted themselves with the tragic and theologically questionable consolation that to die in this manner for their faith was a sacrifice acceptable to God. Some were fortunate. The wealthy Jewish community in Cologne itself paid the prince-bishop handsomely to move into the fortress of Wolkenburg, though the castellan had to be given a separate bribe before he moved out. Ephraim, then thirteen years old, was among the refugees who weathered the pogrom here. There were other cases where a friendly noble or churchman accepted money in exchange for protection, though often too the money was taken and the Jews cynically betrayed to the lynch mob. The sufferings of the Jews in Germany seem to have been particularly severe. In France, King Louis VII cancelled interest payments to Jewish money-lenders for those who took the Cross, and no doubt many French Jews found it advisable to pay protection money to the local Mr Big, although Ephraim heard of no cases of murder or forcible conversion.

In Germany, Bernard persuaded hundreds of lay people, particularly among the poor, to take crusading vows. His message had to be transmitted by German interpreters, but fervour for the pilgrimage to what for many was the semi-mystical world of Jerusalem may have been encouraged also by the near-famine conditions at home following a disastrous crop failure. These people, in the bitter words of the anonymous author of the Würzburg chronicle, the *Annales Herbipolenses*, 'driven by want and suffering from hardship at home, were ready to fight not only against the enemies of the Cross of Christ but even their fellow Christians, if this seemed to offer a chance of plunder'. In fact, they were heading for catastrophe either way. This Second Crusade was to end in defeat and humiliation for almost all concerned. When it was all over, the monk of Würzburg considered that the whole enterprise had been directly inspired by the Devil. A few may have been motivated 'by the love of Divine Majesty' but many more merely simulated religious zeal as they hurried off to join the army for utterly discreditable reasons. Some travelled out of idle curiosity or a love of novelty, or simply to find out about strange lands; while others were fleeing their creditors, or had criminal prosecutions hanging over them.[5]

At first, Bernard had little success with the German King, Conrad of Hohenstaufen, whose official title 'King of the Romans' betrayed his principal policy objective in the Mediterranean area, namely to win coronation as emperor by the Pope and to force Roger of Sicily to recognize his supremacy. The first man to bear the title King of Sicily, Roger, with ambitious plans for consolidating his power in southern Italy and determined to maintain his kingdom's independence, was supporting Conrad's Bavarian rival. However, the King agreed that Bernard could plead his cause at the Diet to be held at Speyer that

Christmas (1146). Preaching on Christmas Day the saint, speaking as if in the words of Christ himself, and before the whole congregation in the great cathedral, directly accused the King of ingratitude in failing to fight for Christ who had done so much for him. Whether shamed by the charismatic preacher, or reflecting that it would win the Pope's approval, Conrad took the Cross. Paradoxically, Pope Eugenius may not have been pleased at the news of German participation. Agitation in Rome against papal rule there had forced him into exile and he seems to have been hoping for German support to restore him. So, Bernard's preaching may have diverted the German King from his own preferred line of policy and lost rather than gained him favour with the Pope. It also meant that what Eugenius had conceived as a purely French expedition had been opened to the dangers of a divided command.

In fact, although the expedition was to be led by the kings of France and Germany, St Bernard's appeal to 'the mighty soldiers' of Christendom found many willing hearers in England too. The barons of its alien aristocracy, divided in loyalties and self-interest between the chivalrous King Stephen and the haughty Matilda, daughter of the old king, Henry I, and widow of the German Emperor Henry V, had been embattled in sporadic faction fighting which had lasted for close on a decade and was beginning to seem endless. To some, the prospect of a conflict, which should bring honour in this world and at the worst would mean assured bliss in the world to come, seemed an honourable alternative. In addition, of course, crusaders' lands and property enjoyed the protection of the Church. So a number of England's Norman baronage took the Cross for the Holy Land and with them Roger Clinton, the Bishop of Chester. For the native English commons and citizenry, subject to the systematic oppression of their Norman–French lords in normal times, and in this terrible reign harried and plundered by ruthless and rapacious warlords, the chance of an escape with the blessing of the Church offered prospects of travel, personal honour and possible gain. In fact, where the venture of the nobles under their royal and imperial commanders faltered ignominiously in the sands of military incompetence and diplomatic stupidity, the expedition of the men of Norfolk and Suffolk under their constable, Hervey de Glanville, the men of Kent under Simon of Dover, the London contingent under their leader Master Andrew and the men of Southampton headed by the brothers William and Ralph

This 13th-century window from Cologne Cathedral depicts St George, patron of Christian warriors. He was seen fighting for the crusaders at Antioch in 1098; Emperor Frederick I appointed St George's Day 1189 as the launch date for the German campaign in the Third Crusade and in 1241 Earl Richard of Cornwall negotiated the return of crusader prisoners in Egypt for St George's Day. According to the 13th-century *Golden Legend*, George slew the dragon. But the cult of St George was being honoured at Lydda as early as the 6th-century.

This view inside the Dome of the Rock, shows the rocky outcrop sacred to Jews and Muslims alike. The building, dating from the 680's and built as a shrine is situated on Temple Mount. Its proportions and exquisite dome give the building a breathtaking aesthetic presence.

The kneeling crusader is a famous image in crusading history. This line drawing depicts the crusaders' idealized view of themselves as warriors of God in the service of His Sacred Cross.

A section of the walls of Antioch as they appeared in 1890. The fortifications enclosed a large area of open ground beyond the built up area of the city proper. Principally the work of Roman and Byzantine military architects, the massive masonry provided a formidable obstacle for attackers.

From a 13th-century guidebook to the Holy Land, the map shows a diagrammatic plan of Jerusalem. Although the perfect circle of the walls depicts an idealized image befitting the Holy City, centre of the world, and the plan is certainly not to scale, the relative positions of the sites within the city would have provided the user with a reliable aid to orientation.

The underground stables of the Knights Templar in the area of the 'Temple of Solomon', Jerusalem.

The ivory back cover for the Psalter of Queen Melisende (1130s), commissioned by her husband, King Fulk. It depicts the acts of mercy cited by Jesus in his parable of the Last Judgement (Matthew 25 vv. 31-40). The front cover depicts scenes from the life of King David, supposed author of the Psalms, and the second King of Israel. Melisende, noted for her own patronage of the arts, was involved in the rebuilding of the Church of the Holy Sepulchre, completed in the 1140's.

An old street of Jerusalem photographed in the early 20th-century, but looking much as it must have done at the time of the crusades.

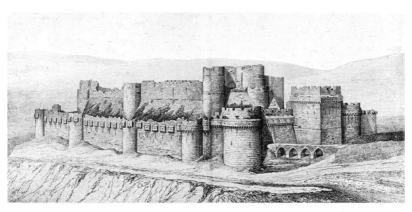

Krak des Chevaliers or 'Castle of the Knights'; the most famous of the crusader castles, it stands on the borders between modern Lebanon and Syria. Originally the Muslim 'Castle of the Kurds', it was taken over by the Knights Hospitaller in 1142. A major building programme produced a fortress which could hold a garrison of some 2,000 men. Effectively impregnable, it capitulated to the Mamluk Sultan Baybars in 1271.

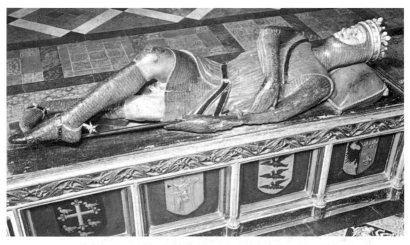

This tomb effigy of Robert, Duke of Normandy in Gloucester Cathedral follows the convention of crossed legs to commemorate service in the wars of the Cross. To raise money for his expedition, Robert had pawned Normandy to his younger brother King William II of England for 10,000 marks. But William refused to honour the deal and the next king, the youngest brother Henry I, defeated Robert's attempt to recover the Duchy, took him prisoner to England and held him under house arrest until his death.

One of two grain barns at Cressing Temple, Essex, England, this majestic piece of carpentry was originally erected in the 13th-century for an English convent of the Knights Templar, which owned various farms in the neighbourhood. Following the Order's dissolution in the 1310s, their properties were assigned to the Hospitallers.

The nave of the crypt of St John's Church, Clerkenwell, the London home of the Knights Hospitaller. The church was the venue for the assembly, convened by King Henry II in 1185 to debate the proposal made to Henry by Heraclius, Patriarch of Jerusalem, that he assume the overlordship of the Kingdom of Jerusalem.

The battlefield of the Horns of Hattin, so-called from the two low hills seen in the background, site of the great victory by Saladin over the army of the Kingdom of Jerusalem in July 1187.

Veal, accompanied by a smaller contingent of French, Germans, Flemings and Frisians, actually won a notable success.

Taking the long sea route round Brittany and the Iberian peninsula en route for the Mediterranean in June they were forced by bad weather to harbour on the Portuguese coast at Oporto. Bordered on the east by the kingdom of Leon and Castile, which claimed suzerainty over it, and on the south by the Moorish ruler of Lisbon on the Tagus River, Portugal under its Count Afonso Henriques was fighting for the status of an independent kingdom against its Christian neighbours, and to extend its territories against its Muslim neighbours. While the English contingent at first objected that they had made their vows of pilgrimage to Jerusalem, the others eagerly accepted the arguments of the Bishop of Oporto that they could fulfil their vows by fighting the Infidel on the Tagus without going on to the Holy Land, and could moreover expect immediate rewards in land and plunder. Eventually, persuaded by de Glanville, the English also agreed and the fleet was deployed along with Portuguese land forces in an amphibious assault on Lisbon. Following the conventions, before laying siege to the place the northerners sent a herald to make a formal demand for surrender. The response of the Moorish commander was a scornful and searching rejection of the kind of high-sounding principles claimed by the champions of Holy War: 'By calling your ambition zeal for righteousness, you misrepresent vices as virtues . . . It is . . . but ambition of the mind that drives you on.'[6]

By this time, the German army, led by King Conrad and the kings of Bohemia and Poland, who recognized his suzerainty, was heading south through Hungary for the Balkans and Constantinople. It was large – contemporaries spoke of a million men, modern estimates of 20,000. It was also cosmopolitan and plagued with disputes among the French-speaking contingent from Lorraine, Czechs, Slavs and Germans, and rivalries between their leaders. In his mid fifties, temperamental and indecisive, Conrad may have been helped in the management of this unruly host by his nephew and heir, Frederick, Duke of Swabia. Twenty-five, with a flaming red beard ('*Barbarossa*', in Italian), tall and imperious in manner, for him the expedition must have provided experience for the crusade he was to lead forty years later as Emperor. King Geza of Hungary was about Frederick's age and the crusaders received friendly treatment while in his realm. Before they crossed into Bulgaria, then a province of the Byzantine Empire, King Conrad pledged his oath to an embassy sent by the

Emperor Manuel that he came in peace and would do nothing injurious to the Emperor or his empire. In form the oath was suspiciously close to the one taken by a feudal vassal in the West and one may imagine that Duke Frederick would have seen it as a slight on German honour. In fact, the ill-disciplined army, pillaging the countryside and refusing payment to the peasantry for supplies they considered rightfully theirs as soldiers of Christ in a land of schismatics, was soon subject to the humiliation of a Byzantine military escort to shepherd them through the surly and hostile countryside. Even so, rioting and arson broke out along the route and, at Byzantine insistence, Conrad had to punish the ringleaders. Worse was to follow. When bandits murdered a German nobleman beneath the walls of a monastery near Adrianople, modern Edirne, Duke Frederick torched the monastery and slaughtered its inmates. Despite Emperor Manuel's request that the army cross into Anatolia by the Dardanelles, Conrad pushed on and arrived outside the walls of Constantinople in the second week of September.

The French had set out about a month after the Germans. On 8 June, in a black pilgrim's tunic with red cross, Louis had entered the abbey church of St Denis hung with banners and illuminated by thousands of candles. In the presence of the Pope he committed the Kingdom to the care of Abbot Suger. Then, to the cheers of the congregation, Eugenius gave his blessing and the traditional pilgrim's staff and wallet.[7] They arrived at Constantinople early in October. Some advance units arriving ahead of the main body had caught up with the Germans outside the walls of the great city. There was immediate friction which did not last long, for Emperor Manuel was keen to help the Germans cross the straits into Anatolia, but long before they even reached the Holy Land the two main bodies of crusaders were on bad terms.

At the other end of Europe, after four months of hard fighting against the determined defenders of Lisbon, the huge crusading enterprise, preached by Europe's most charismatic churchman, led by the monarchs of its two greatest powers and disposing of greater resources than had ever been so far assembled in defence of the Holy Land, made its first and only gain under the military leadership of lesser nobles and minor churchmen, in the name of the Count of Portugal. The English priest Gilbert of Hastings became the first Bishop of Lisbon, and while many of his compatriots continued their interrupted pilgrimage to Jerusalem, most of the northern contingent accepted the hospitality of the Portuguese and began a new life under southern skies.

On 15 October the Germans were at Nicaea, ready for the next great stage of their pilgrimage. Ignoring Manuel's advice to take the long coast road they headed south-east across the Anatolian peninsula, as had the first crusaders forty years earlier. It was, of course, more direct – but it also led dangerously close to the frontier between Byzantine lands and the hostile territory of the Seljuks of Rum. It seems the Germans did not take the most elementary reconnaissance and scouting precautions. Ten days later they had reached the region round about Dorylaeum, scene of the First Crusade's first famous victory; the army broke the line of march to rest the horses and refresh the thirsty and exhausted infantry. At this moment, the Seljuk army, whose scouts had been monitoring the Germans' progress, attacked. The result was a massacre. We are told that nine-tenths of Conrad's soldiers were killed or captured; that over the coming weeks the looted contents of camp and baggage train were choking bazaars as far afield as Persia; and that King Conrad, Duke Frederick and a handful of survivors barely made it back to Nicaea. Perhaps the reports are exaggerated, for the German crusaders rallied and joined the French along the safer more westerly route, while a body of non-combatant pilgrims continued on overland through the nominally Byzantine territory under the leadership of Bishop Otto von Freising to the port of Antalya, though suffering severely from deprivation of food and water and harassment from Turkish bandits.

At Ephesus King Conrad fell seriously ill. When the news reached Constantinople, Emperor Manuel sent transport to bring the King back to the capital where he personally supervised his treatment. Given the state of Western European medical knowledge and practice at the time this may have been a lucky break for Conrad. At all events he recovered well enough to take ship under Byzantine convoy for Acre, landing in mid April.

Meantime, the French had struck inland from Ephesus through what was, after all, Byzantine territory. As December merged into January, they too came under heavy attack from marauding Seljuk forces and Queen Eleanor and her ladies, no longer the galloping Amazons of Vézélay, were carried in litters through the inhospitable mountainous landscape. At long last, descending to the coastal plain where the Turkish nuisance abated somewhat, the weary and battle-scarred pilgrim force reached the modest port of Antalya. King Louis, deciding that the hazards of a sea voyage were preferable to the torments of the march, asked that shipping be supplied. Food was scarce, prices high and ships difficult to muster. Enough were assembled to carry the King, his household and a small force of cavalry on to the port of Antioch at St Symeon, where he arrived in mid March 1148. Like their King, the French remnant cursed Byzantine incompetence and treachery, even more so when the Turks attacked the demoralized army in a daring raid down from their mountain retreats. The remainder of the German and French forces, having made their way by ad hoc shipping or via dangerous overland routes, would finally reach Antioch, horribly reduced in numbers, weeks later. In a letter to Abbot Suger, King Louis admitted French mistakes had contributed to their plight but chiefly he blamed Emperor Manuel. And it was true that the Emperor had agreed a truce with the Seljuk lord of Konya back in the spring of 1147.

As to the royal party and the squadron of horse which had found passage with it, on arrival at St Symeon they were welcomed by Raymond Prince of Antioch and his household and escorted up to the city with jubilation. As King of France, Louis was recognized as their supreme lord by the Franks of Outremer; as uncle of the beautiful Queen of France Raymond had a family interest; while as the ruler of a state under constant threat from Muslim Aleppo he hoped for reinforcement from the French cavalry. While Queen Eleanor and her ladies revelled in the sumptuous Eastern hospitality of the Antiochene court and many of Louis' knights eagerly joined Raymond in a show of strength up to the walls of Aleppo, King Louis puzzled over what he should do – commit himself to an all-out campaign against Aleppo, as Raymond was urging; or consult first with the other Frankish rulers, all of whom were begging for his help. Above all, as its exiled ruler Count Joscelin argued, the recovery of Edessa should be the first priority – was not the city's fall the reason for Louis being in Palestine at all? Yet, strategically, the modern tendency is to agree with Raymond of Antioch. Nur al-Din of Aleppo was the great power in Muslim Syria at this time. So fearful was the ruler of Damascus of Aleppo's ambitions that he was making overtures for Christian allies. A decisive strike against Nur al-Din would not only benefit Antioch but relieve pressure points all along the Muslim–Christian frontier.

Raymond had an enthusiastic advocate in the person of his niece, Queen Eleanor. Her quick intelligence immediately grasped the military situation as explained by Prince Raymond and she argued his case passionately with the King. She was also no doubt enchanted with the luxurious and sophisticated lifestyle at the court of Antioch – years later rumours surfaced of an incestuous affair between the darkly handsome Prince and his beautiful relative. At the time, King Louis was certainly jealous of the older man. But he also held that his pilgrim's vow bound him to go on first to Jerusalem, and when a deputation, headed by the Patriarch, arrived with a formal request from Queen Melisende that he attend her and King Conrad in the capital, Louis made his preparations to leave Antioch. The Queen retorted that she at least would remain and would petition Rome for a divorce. We are told that 'in reply Louis dragged his wife by force from her uncle's palace and set out with all his troops for Jerusalem.'[8]

Eleanor's threat was a time bomb. By Aquitaine's law women, unusually, could inherit and administer property in their own right, while by his will, Eleanor's father had specified that the Duchy should not be integrated into the royal demesne but should remain independent and be inherited by Eleanor's heirs alone. When, five years later, the marriage was annulled Eleanor parted from her husband and her huge inheritance parted from the Crown of France. Within months of the divorce she married Henry II, Count of Anjou and Maine and Duke of Normandy, and two years later, when he became King of England, Eleanor's vast territories in south-western France, stretching from the Loire to the Pyrenees, became part of the Angevin empire, passing to Eleanor's heirs from her marriage to Henry. Bordeaux and its region would remain under the English Crown for three centuries. The rift between the French royal couple begun at the court of Antioch opened a chasm that would engulf England and France in generations of warfare – the Hundred Years War may be seen as a long-term consequence of the animosities of Antioch.

The immediate consequence was that Prince Raymond, furious at Louis' refusal to march against Aleppo, refused to take part in the campaign that followed. Count Raymond of Tripoli and Joscelin of Edessa were also absent from the great council convened at Acre on St John's Day, 24 June 1148. Presiding were Queen Melisende and her warlike and popular son, King Baldwin III, just seventeen years old and eager to avenge the Kingdom's recent defeats, at the same time optimistic now that the Kingdom had help from the largest European army seen in the Holy Land for fifty years. Besides King Louis of France and Conrad the German King, there was present

Conrad's half-brother Bishop Otto of Freising, his nephew Duke Frederick of Swabia, the Bishop of Metz, the Count of Flanders and many other luminaries of the Latin West.

Unfortunately, these great men understood nothing of the subtleties of local politics – their uncomplicated creed was to fight the Infidel wherever he might be found. Since the recovery of Edessa, the most logical objective for this crusade, had been abandoned, an understanding with the ruler of Damascus made the most sense. He would have welcomed alliance, even with Christians, against the threat of Nur al-Din in Aleppo, and since Nur al-Din's Aleppo was also the principal emerging threat to the Kingdom, there were strong arguments in favour of an understanding. But there were local lords with ambitious designs on the Emir's rich and fertile territories while the newcomers from Europe found it difficult to square an alliance with a Muslim with their crusader vows. In any case, for the religious warriors from Europe, the road to Damascus, where St Paul had met with his vision of the risen Christ, but under Muslim rule for half a millennium, was surely the one to take. And so the decision was taken to attack the city of Emir Unur, whose only wish was friendship.

A month following the council of war at Acre, the Christian forces, comprising the army of Jerusalem under King Baldwin and the crusader armies under Louis and Conrad, were deploying below the gardens and orchards to the south of Damascus. By the evening of Saturday, 24 July they had pushed the main Damascene army behind the city walls before clearing the orchards of guerrillas and sharpshooters. The fall of the city seemed imminent. The Emir had sent appeals to Nur al-Din for assistance but the citizens were building barricades in their streets, doubtful that the reinforcements would arrive in time. However, the crusaders had not been able to encircle the city so that when the first relief contingents from Aleppo did arrive, unexpectedly early, they were able to march unopposed in through the north gate. Now it was the Christian turn to fall back as Damascenes and Aleppans counter-attacked. Soon there were Muslim skirmishers established once more in the orchards so recently cleared. On the Monday evening a council of war decided to redeploy the army on the plains to the east of the city. The decision was a tactical disaster; some in the crusader camp said it had been taken on advice from local lords bribed by the Emir. The camp was certainly freed up from harassment by lone snipers but the enemy could now mobilize raiding parties against the Christian lines under the cover of the trees, while the forces in the city could make similar sorties.

While the European pilgrim soldiers muttered about treason, the local baronage protested that their interest was to be betrayed when the city was won by its being handed over to the Count of Flanders. In less than a week, the great army poised for the annexation of Syria's second richest city to the Christian cause had become a band of divided factions under threat of destruction. For now it was learnt that the main army of Aleppo, under the command of Nur al-Din himself, was marching south. The faction which had all along opposed the attack warned that Nur al-Din's price for rescuing Damascus would be outright lordship of the city – a dire consolidation of the Muslim threat against the states of Outremer. Without local support and with no hope of reinforcement, Louis and Conrad capitulated in council. On Wednesday morning lookouts on the walls of Damascus, who five days earlier had raised the alarm of the Christian army's approach, sent jubilant reports to the Emir's palace that the enemy was once again on the march, but this time southwards back towards Galilee.

The retreat, undertaken it seemed at the mere mention of the name of Nur al-Din, was a humiliation almost worse than defeat for the once feared Christian warriors. It fired a fresh surge of enthusiasm for the *jihad* in the Muslim world. The heroic deeds of the Damascenes would be recounted for generations to come. Among them was an aged lawyer marching with the infantry. The commander urged him to retire: 'Your age, Sir, excuses you from this battle. I and my men will concern ourselves with the defence of Islam.' But the *qadi* refused: 'I have offered myself for sale and God has bought me. I have not sought an annulment of the contract.' The allusion is to the words of the Koran: 'God has bought the Faithful, both them and their possessions and has given them Paradise in exchange.' And so the old man 'went on to fight the Franks and was killed not far from the walls of the city'.[9]

Following the debacle, most of the crusaders prepared to return home – despite military defeat and indeed humiliation, they had fulfilled their pilgrimage vows. A few chose to stay in the Holy Land in the hope of making their fortune. As a younger son of the Count of Gien, for example, Reynald of Chatillon-sur-Loing had no prospects of a landed inheritance back in France and took service with King Baldwin. King Louis also lingered on, despite letters from Abbot Suger begging that he return to Paris. It may be that, being genuinely devout, the King wished to spend Easter in the Holy Land; at any rate he did not embark for Europe until late June 1149, taking passage in a ship of his new ally, King Roger of Sicily.

Louis had by now convinced himself that the root cause of the crusade's failure had been obstruction, even hostility, from the Byzantines. After all, Manuel had made that alliance with the Seljuk Turks. From Constantinople, what seemed like betrayal of Christendom to Roman Catholic Europe, looked like sound political calculation in the ancient Roman tradition. Two years before, when the Emperor was encamped before the Seljuks' capital, Konya, with every chance of success, news had reached him that King Roger's Sicilian army had captured the Byzantine island of Corfu and raided and plundered into Greece as far as Corinth. Most observers believed that Roman Catholic Roger's aim was the conquest of Orthodox Manuel's empire. Hardly surprising, then, if the Emperor made a temporary settlement of his differences with his Muslim enemy to free his hands in fending off the more serious threat from his Christian co-religionist. Now, in July 1149, as King Louis of France broke his homeward journey as a guest at the court of King Roger in Calabria, it was learnt that the two monarchs were discussing a new crusade, with Constantinople as its first objective!

Heading homewards in October, Louis and Eleanor were entertained by Pope Eugenius at his palace south of Rome. The Pope refused to listen to Eleanor's arguments for an annulment of the marriage (indeed he presided over a reconciliation, urging that they restore love between them and providing the venue, a spacious double bed in a luxuriously appointed guest room where Louis made 'almost puerile' demonstrations of his passion). He also withheld his blessing on Louis' plans for a Catholic crusade against the Orthodox East. A month later the royal pair arrived in Paris. Loyal demonstrations of welcome were organized; a medal was struck to commemorate the crusade showing the King in a victorious pose; and Bernard of Clairvaux was persuaded to give his support to the proposed new crusade. More level heads laid the blame for the Damascus fiasco on Louis and others muttered that Queen Eleanor's participation had blighted the entire enterprise. But St Bernard, perplexed in the extreme that God had not crowned his expedition with success, enthusiastically seized on the theory of Byzantine perfidy as the explanation. It is hard to believe that Louis' proposed mission of 'divine vengeance on the guilty Empire'[10] would ever have become practical politics; indeed

Louis would soon be facing mountainous problems at home without risking renewed humiliation abroad. As it was, the plans never got beyond the stage of rhetoric. Despite Bernard's fulminations Conrad of Germany, whose cooperation would have been essential, refused to be persuaded yet again against his interests. He was now allied with the Emperor Manuel against his old enemy Roger of Sicily and was not about to put that policy in jeopardy.

Unlike King Louis, Conrad had quitted Palestine within weeks of the army's withdrawal from Damascus sailing from Acre for Thessalonica early in September. There, to his delight, he found an imperial deputation of welcome with an invitation to pass Christmas as the Emperor's guest at Constantinople. He remembered with pleasure Manuel's hospitality and solicitude during his sickness at the start of the year. Many in the German army, notably the King's young nephew Frederick, nursed bitter thoughts against the Byzantines whom they held responsible for the disaster near Dorylaeum. Conrad, perhaps, recognized that he too had been at fault in not following Manuel's advice as to the best route; moreover, during his previous visit to the imperial court, it had been agreed that his brother Henry of Austria should marry the Emperor's niece Theodora. At all events, Conrad delayed his homeward journey to share the exotic celebrations of an Orthodox Christmas at the imperial court. To the commiseration of her friends, Theodora was duly wedded to the semi-barbarian from the north – favourite oath 'so help me, God' – during the festivities. The union sealed the alliance between German king and Greek emperor and the two potentates agreed a joint campaign against Roger of Sicily. On his return to Germany in 1149, it seemed Conrad had salvaged something from the wreck of the adventure Bernard of Clairvaux had lured him into, though he would never achieve coronation as emperor and may have reflected that apart from the fulfilment of a pilgrimage vow to Jerusalem, much time had been wasted. Around 11 November Louis and Eleanor returned to Paris, after an absence of nearly two and half years, on the eve of the feast of St Martin. Two medals were struck to commemorate the crusade, one of which was embossed with a relief showing Louis standing victorious in a chariot!

5

Turk and Kurd: Heroes of Islam

The capture of Edessa put *jihad* on the political map. It also helped sharpen the focus. From general exhortation to expel the Infidel from the lands of Syria, more and more the call came for the liberation of Jerusalem. According to the French scholar Emmanuel Sivan, the first mention of Jerusalem in a *jihad* context is to be found in 1144, the very year in which Edessa fell. Sivan even argued that Muslim propagandists consciously boosted the cult of Jerusalem in response to its central importance for Christians. But Jerusalem had long had many claims to veneration by Muslims: first as the city of David and Solomon, revered by Muslims as well as Jews and Christians; second as central to the stories of the Old Testament prophets and of Jesus Christ, all of them revered as forerunners of Muhammad. Jerusalem was the first *qibla*, or direction of prayer, designated for believers by the Prophet, and when it was displaced in that honour by Mecca, it was still venerated as the second most holy place upon earth for believers. Many believed that Jerusalem would be the site of the Last Judgement, though others, it must be said, claimed that this was based on an apocryphal tradition 'invented by the people of Syria', and that Allah would resurrect the dead wherever it should please him. Others went still further, claiming that the locals would fabricate any tradition that would attract pilgrims. However, no Muslim has ever doubted that it was from the Rock in Jerusalem that the Prophet had made his mystic ascent into heaven. And this alone made its occupation by the Infidel intolerable.

But even the capture of Edessa did not signal the immediate all-out drive against the Christians that ardent devotees looked for. Zangi was succeeded at Aleppo by his younger son Nur al-Din, whose first action was to secure his father's conquest in Edessa and who was determined to become undisputed master of Muslim Syria. As fine a soldier as his father, Nur al-Din reduced the principality of Antioch to a coastal strip, defeating and killing its Prince Raymond at the Battle of Inabin in 1149, the Prince's silver-encrusted skull being dispatched to Baghdad. Yet this triumph was not followed up with an attack on the Christian city but rather with a dragged-out three-year manoeuvre to overthrow the ruler of Muslim Damascus.

At about this time, an anonymous author, apparently Aleppo based, introduced a discussion on the *jihad* into a treatise on princely virtues. While alluding to the *jihad* for self-mastery and progress in personal religion, he argues that it is a prime duty of a Muslim ruler to make holy war on the Infidel, whether on the offensive to extend the territory of the faith, *Dar al-Islam*, or by campaigns of reconquest to expel unbelievers from former Muslim lands. The parallel with Christian justifications for crusading is striking, as are the author's comments on the obligations of a married would-be holy warrior to consider the well-being of his wife during his absence and to make provision for her in case of his death on campaign. Again like Christian apologists, he extols warfare against heretics, considering their offence to be more heinous than that of unbelievers who have never received instruction in the true faith. Above all the Aleppan anonymous, probably a Persian expatriate, laments the fact that in his time Infidel princes are able to prosper while Muslim leaders war against each other. There seems little doubt that criticism of Nur al-Din is implied.

It would have been justified. When he died thirty years later, Christian princes still ruled at Antioch and Tripoli; the great fortress of Krak les Chevaliers still held the armies of Islam at bay; in the south, the castles of Krak in Moab and Montréale still plundered the rich caravans which led up from the Red Sea port of Aqaba to Damascus; and, above all Jerusalem, al-Quds, was still held by unbelievers, its sacred al-Aqsa Mosque defiled by their rites.

The fiasco of the Second Crusade strengthened Nur al-Din's hand, for it was common knowledge that the Christian army had retreated at the news of his approach. Over the next six years agents trumpeted his successes through the city and protested that all their master desired was an alliance against the Franks so that Jerusalem could be freed. When a new regime in Damascus agreed a yearly tribute to the King of Jerusalem in exchange for his friendship, the Muslim world was scandalized. Nur al-Din moved against it; it was a bloodless triumph. Aleppan propaganda had described the Damascus–Jerusalem entente as the one remaining bar to the defeat of the Franks. And yet Nur al-Din's first act was to reaffirm the truce and then to pay a further instalment of the tribute money.

In 1164, following the rout of the Christian forces at the Battle of Artah, Nur al-Din had Bohemond, Prince of Antioch, Raymond Count of Tripoli, Hugh of Lusignan and regent of the Kingdom led in chains to Aleppo and yet, despite the entreaties of his council, held his hand. The city's skeleton garrison prepared for the coup de grace; its capture would have been a triumph to match Edessa. But the Destroyer of the Infidels and Polytheists had signed a treaty with Constantinople only the year before and Emperor Manuel regarded Antioch as Byzantine territory. Better to leave the city under a weakened Latin regime than provoke an ally. Instead Nur al-Din directed his power against the heretic Fatimid caliphs who ruled the rich and strategically important land of Egypt. He was continually in need of manpower and used the rhetoric of the *jihad* to intimidate lesser rulers into compliance. There were those who criticized Nur al-Din for his failure to drive out the Christians – some even accused him of hypocrisy. But he was noted as a just ruler, a brave soldier, a man of personal piety and a charitable patron building *madrassahs* (colleges), hospitals and mosques.

In any case, at this time under two highly capable kings the Christian state was on the offensive. In 1153 Baldwin III captured the port of Ascalon from the Fatimid caliphs at Cairo and for a time in the late 1160s Amalric seemed poised to conquer Egypt itself. Nur al-Din took advantage of these expeditions south to raid into the Kingdom but for him, and certainly for the caliphs at Baghdad, the priority was the overthrow the heretical Fatimids. In January 1167 a well-found force took the road south from Damascus under the aegis of Baghdad, which had elevated the expedition to Holy War, commanded by Nur al-Din's favourite general, Shirkuh the Kurd, with his nephew Salah al-Din Yusuf, aged about thirty, or Saladin, as he has always been known in the Christian world.

A liaison officer in the personal entourage of Nur al-Din since the age of eighteen, there was nothing to mark him out except perhaps his exceptional skill at polo, a fascination with theological debate and his polished skills as a courtier. The difficult and highly dangerous sport of polo enjoyed the same kind of status in the horse-dominated society of the Muslim courts as the tournament was coming to do in feudal Europe. The *tchogandar* or polo master was a highly respected official and to be invited, like Saladin, to play with Nur al-Din's team was a high sign of favour. A shortish figure of a man, keen and alert, with black eyes, black hair and his round face coming to a trim black beard, Saladin excelled in all the elements of *adab*, a gentleman's traditional education, Koranic studies, Arabic grammar, rhetoric and poetry, and may also have had links with the Sufi tradition of Arab mysticism. Known to his intimates as the perfect companion, this complex and fascinating man was an affable conversationalist and delighted in all the elegance and social refinements summed up in the untranslatable Arabic word *zarf* 'well acquainted with the genealogies and martial triumphs of the old families, a master of all traditional lore; and with the pedigrees of the great Arab horses at his finger-tips'.[1] In the realm of public affairs, however, he had yet to prove himself.

Shirkuh's campaign had problems from the start. The Egyptian government had won the alliance of King Amalric I of Jerusalem and his barons to come to its help, with the promise of a large subsidy and the persuasive argument that if Nur al-Din, master of Syria, should add Egypt to his empire, the plight of Christian Jerusalem would be dire. Fully mobilized, the army of the Kingdom was a formidable fighting force and Shirkuh took a route through Sinai to avoid any encounter with it. However, there was no evading the wicked south wind, the *simoom* (the evil or polluted one). A few days' march from the isthmus at Suez, his army was struck by a tearing sandstorm, which caused several hundred casualties. When he reached the Nile Shirkuh seems to have taken evasive action again rather than seek out the enemy, as if the combined force of Egyptians and Franks was larger than his weakened army could face. He even proposed alliance with the Egyptian Vizier, chief minister of the very heretical regime he had come to depose. The Vizier rejected the proposal scornfully. He was content with his Frankish allies – what he did not say was that they were in any case virtually in control of Cairo. King Amalric, intent on securing the best bargain he could for his support, insisted on a personal interview with the Caliph himself. A remarkable encounter sealed the deal – indeed one of the more remarkable encounters in medieval history. To the horror of the Egyptian courtiers the infidel barbarian, King Amalric of Jerusalem, was admitted to the sacred presence of the cloistered Caliph and at his brazen insistence granted the unprecedented favour of a handshake with ungloved hands.

A battle between the Syrian army and the Frankish–Egyptian allies now seemed imminent. In fact, weeks of manoeuvring followed. Shirkuh wanted to extricate his forces from an unwanted encounter. Amalric too was hesitant – why fight if the Syrians wanted to withdraw? He was certain of his money since his army could if needs be turn on the Egyptians. But Shirkuh's council, Saladin among them, decided that honour demand they stand and fight; their opponents had reached the same conclusion. According to one account St Bernard had appeared to Amalric in a dream accusing him of cowardice.

The long-delayed battled ended in victory for the Syrian army. Using a standard Turkish battle tactic, Shirkuh deputed Saladin to lead a feigned retreat to lure the Frankish horse away from its allies, so that he could scatter the divided enemy. King Amalric barely escaped with his life. Shirkuh took Alexandria and then turned back south for a plundering raid, leaving his nephew in charge of the defence of the great city. But Amalric now rallied his forces and laid siege to Alexandria forcing Shirkuh to hurry back with the main force. Saladin successfully held Alexandria and it was he who negotiated the terms which allowed Amalric to extricate himself from Egypt with honour, and Shirkuh to return to Damascus with his self-esteem intact and 50,000 dinars into the bargain. Negotiations had merged into fraternization, and according to tradition Humphrey of Toron knighted the Muslim general – Saladin, 'the chivalrous infidel', makes his first appearance in the European folk memory.

With the overthrow of the Vizier at Cairo the kaleidoscope of Middle Eastern politics shifted once again and this time Nur al-Din, by invitation from the Caliph at Cairo, intervened with help against renewed invasion by King Amalric. Again Shirkuh commanded the Syrian army and in January 1169 he entered Cairo as the Deliverer of the Muslims. The same month the Caliph appointed him his new vizier, notifying Nur al-Din at Damascus that henceforward his lieutenant would command the Egyptian military. Far from being pleased, Nur al-Din was furious and suspicious. Only two years before, Shirkuh had argued him into a campaign to depose the heretic Caliph at Cairo, but now that he had won control of the city, he was accepting the appointment as his chief minister. Then, in March, Shirkuh died. The Caliph needed a new vizier and the Syrian army in Egypt needed a new commander. Saladin emerged holding both appointments, thanks to intrigue at the court and the victory of the Kurdish army faction in the army over the pro Nur al-Din faction. Nur al-Din, who had been involved in neither decision, rescinded all Saladin's holdings and appointments in Syria. Although Saladin had Nur al-Din's name introduced to Friday Prayers in Cairo, he never again enjoyed his full trust.

Saladin faced a critical dilemma. If he met the insistent demands of his Sunnite overlord in Damascus and deposed his Shi'ite master the Caliph in Cairo, he removed the only title to his own authority in Egypt. In the summer of 1170, Saladin's father Ayyub joined him. For years the close confidant of Nur al-Din, he had been allowed to join his son, probably to keep him in line. In fact, Saladin continued to strengthen his own position, introducing important reforms in the Egyptian army and tightening his grip on the administration. Nur al-Din now sent a direct command that the Fatimid regime be over-turned forthwith, threatening to march to Cairo in person if it was not. On Friday, 10 September the Caliph of Baghdad was named in the prayers in Cairo's chief mosque. Two days later the Fatimid Caliph died but Saladin remained head of government. In the following two years, Egyptian forces recovered Fatimid territories in North Africa and in the Yemen. Victories here gave it control of pilgrimage routes to Mecca and boosted Saladin's reputation as champion of Islam. In 1174 he successfully routed a conspiracy against his regime which had hoped to enlist King Amalric and King William II of Sicily. But Amalric died in July, shortly before his planned intervention and the Sicilian fleet's attempt on Alexandria was driven off.

Two months earlier Nur al-Din had been brought to his sick bed with an acute infection of the throat. A suppurating ulcer made his breathing painful and brought on a fever; he died on 15 May. He had been a good Muslim and a great and just ruler. His reputation, won in earlier days as the terror of the infidels, and his austere piety won the respect of his subjects, while his firm and shrewd management of men and events had brought decades of orderly and stable govern-ment to an area that had been divided for generations. His name was honoured in Baghdad, his nephew ruled in Mosul, he himself was lord of Aleppo and Damascus and their dependencies, while in the south the resurgent power of Egypt had, through the intervention of his lieutenant, been brought back into the family of Orthodox Islam. Thanks to him the great prize of Muslim unity had come nearer to achievement than ever before and the days of the Infidel appeared to be numbered.

But the old rivalries were not far below the surface. Within days of the great King's death it seemed that the succession of his eleven-year-old heir, declared in Damascus, was to be contested in Aleppo and Mosul. One thing united the Turkish ruling class of the three cities: that the heritage of their great master and their ancestor Zangi, his father, should not pass to a mere Kurd. Their divisions were not proof against Saladin's singleness of purpose. By April the following year he was master of central and southern Syria, as well as Egypt. In May an official delegation arrived from Baghdad itself with the diplomas, the honorific robes and the black banners of the Abbasid court, in confirmation of his royal title in Damascus and Egypt. Soon after, the Cairo mint issued coins bearing the proud inscription 'al Malik al Nasir Yusuf ibn-Ayyub, ala gaya' – 'The King, Bringer of Victory, Yusuf son of Ayyub, Lift high the banner!' By the end of 1176 Aleppo had conceded his supremacy in Damascus and Egypt.

In November 1177 Saladin marched north against Jerusalem. The Templar garrison at Gaza watched as he marched on past. At Ascalon, the young King Baldwin IV of Jerusalem, 'the Leper', with a force of 500 knights, held himself in readiness for the inevitable siege, but Saladin left a small force to contain the city and continued confidently on to the Holy City. The heroic young King, having sent word to the Templars at Gaza to come up and join him, and broke through the containing force; together the Christian knights thundered up the road to Ibelin and there turned inland towards Jerusalem and the Muslim army marching without Saladin's usual care for security. In the ravines below the fortress of Montgisard the Christian force took the scattered enemy completely by surprise; whole detachments were slaughtered where they stood; thousands of others fled in terror; in headlong flight southwards they abandoned camp, booty, prisoners and even their weapons. Saladin, who the day before had held the fate of the Kingdom in his hand, barely escaped with his life.

Two years later Saladin avenged this reverse with a victory near the castle of Beaufort in which hundreds of noble Christian prisoners included the Grand Master of the Temple. Huge ransoms were paid in the months ahead, but the Templar disdainfully refused the offer of an exchange with the comment that there was not a man in Islam that could find a man to match him. He died in a Damascus prison a year later.

In 1180, Baldwin proposed a two-year truce and the offer was agreed. Fire-eaters on both sides chafed in irritation and soon Saladin was heading north once more – Raynald of Chatillon, lord of the castle of al-Karak had broken the truce. We last saw Raynald, a landless younger son with no prospects at home, deciding to stay on in Palestine after the Second Crusade. Bigoted in religion, insensitive to diplomacy, land hungry and brutal, he was young, well built and a brave soldier; his marriage to Constance of Antioch raised him to the top rank of society in Outremer. In a brilliant campaign against the Armenians he took the port of Alexandretta and handed it over to the Order of the Temple – it was the beginning of a friendship that would have momentous consequences. But four years later, loaded down with booty after a raid into the territory of Nur al-Din, he was ambushed. A prisoner in Aleppo for the next sixteen years, he won his freedom in a prisoner exchange in 1175. Now in his fifties, his first wife having died, Raynald quickly found himself a rich new partner, heiress of the frontier province of Oultrejourdaine (Transjordan) and the great castle of al-Karak which glowered over the caravan and pilgrim routes from Damascus to Mecca. In the summer of 1181 he plundered his first caravan. Saladin demanded compensation from King Baldwin, and when Raynald refused the royal command, Saladin sold a convoy of pilgrims, driven by bad weather into Damietta, into slavery. In 1182 the lord of Karak, like a picador tormenting a bull, mounted an audacious raid deep into Egyptian territory to the head of the Gulf of Aqaba and then, with considerable élan, raided the ports which served Mecca and Medina, sinking a pilgrim ship. The Egyptian fleet dealt with the marauders, but if Raynald's expedition was futile in military terms, it hurt Saladin's prestige. From this point on he developed a hatred for Raynald the trucebreaker, more intense than any he ever held for any other man. The following year, however, Saladin finally made himself master of Aleppo; the threat he posed to the Christian states was manifest.

As Saladin consolidated his authority in the Muslim world, Baldwin IV, 'the Leper', succeeded King Amalric. The young successor of Amalric I proved a worthy opponent. Yet courageous and capable though he was, Baldwin was certain to die young thanks to the dread disease he had been born with. The ceremonial coronation of his six-year-old nephew as Baldwin V in November 1183 convinced nobody as a long-term solution of the Kingdom's problems – a mature, able-bodied ruler was needed. The boy's guardian, Raymond III, Count of Tripoli, and by virtue of his marriage to its heiress Eschiva, Princess of Galilee, had jealous rivals. The Latin throne of Jerusalem had been established by an election. To Heraclius, Patriarch of Jerusalem, Henry II, King of England, head of the house of Anjou and a cousin of King Baldwin the Leper's cousin and the most powerful ruler in Western Europe, seemed the obvious choice for the next reign. He journeyed to England and at the great Abbey of Reading, on 29 January 1185, he laid before the King the keys to the city of Jerusalem, the keys to the Tower of David, and the keys to the Church of the Holy Sepulchre, and finally, the banner of the Kingdom.[2] King of England, lord of Ireland, by right of his father Geoffrey of Normandy, his grandfather Fulk of Anjou (King of Jerusalem as Fulk I) and his wife Eleanor of Aquitaine, overlord of half the territories of France and acknowledged also as their overlord by William, King of Scotland and by the princes of Wales, at fifty-two Henry was Europe's most powerful potentate and most capable administrator and legislator. Despite his 'stocky frame with a pronounced tendency to corpulence, his barrel chest and strong brawny arms', Henry was a man of restless energy and charismatic presence. His friend and courtier Gerald of Wales described him as a man 'of reddish, freckled complexion with large round head, grey eyes which glowed fiercely . . . a fiery countenance and harsh, cracked voice. His neck thrust forward from his shoulders'[3] as if in an attitude of permanent enquiry, he was a versatile linguist and a connoisseur of the new learning the West was then acquiring through its contacts with the high culture of Islam. As a young prince he had been a pupil of the English scholar Adelard of Bath who had travelled the Arab world from Toledo to Syria and whose Latin translation of Euclid from Arabic remained the standard version in the West for four centuries.[4]

This then was the great ruler whom Heraclius hoped to tempt to become champion of Christ's Holy Land against its Muslim enemies.[5] Henry trod warily. He summoned a council of all those who owed him homage, including William, King of Scots, to attend on him on 10 March at the house of the Knights of St John of Jerusalem in London's Clerkenwell to discuss the matter. The unanimous view was that the King should devote himself to governing his own domains rather than get involved in Eastern affairs.[6] Apparently, a number of his counsellors took the Cross at the hands of the Patriarch but they urged Henry himself only to go if the French King could be involved in a joint venture. In fact the two monarchs promised men and money, but Heraclius, who had been looking for Henry's full personal commitment, departed disappointed.[7]

In the spring of 1187, Saladin prepared a final assault against the intruder kingdom whose destruction had been the objective of his life's work. According to Kamal al-Din, he 'wrote to all the provinces to call them to arms in the Holy War'. To many he had to promise bounties to persuade them to answer the summons to the *jihad*. The rulers of Mosul and Edessa and many others joined the muster, south of Damascus, which Saladin had left in the capable hands of his seventeen-year-old son and heir, al-Afdal. A large contingent from Egypt was promised. Al-Afdal's instructions were to dispatch the incoming detachments on harrying raids in Christian territories and particularly to probe the situation in Galilee where Raymond of Tripoli, lord of the principality, was still on terms of alliance with Saladin. Massive forces were involved. Saladin saw that the overriding objective was the destruction of the main army in the field. If this could be achieved the Christian cities and fortresses, deprived of any hope of relief, would surrender with little resistance. However, experience suggested that the Franks were virtually indestructible unless taken by surprise or at some other disadvantage. Larger forces were necessary but sheer size alone would not guarantee success, for they would have to be handled with cunning and psychological finesse. Saladin already had an important advantage as his dealings with Count Raymond had produced suspicion and recrimination in the Christian ranks. King Guy had already summoned the army of the Kingdom to meet him at Nazareth with a view to forcing Raymond's submission. With King Guy his declared enemy and the Muslim Sultan apparently his only friend, Raymond's position was at least ambiguous. It became near impossible when an envoy arrived from al-Afdal requesting, as from one friend to another, a safe passage through his lands of Galilee for a force of some 7,000 horsemen. The destination was not disclosed nor the objective discussed. In fact, according to Ibn al-Athir, al-Afdal was aiming to penetrate into the hinterland of Acre and Raymond can hardly have failed to make a similar deduction. If he collaborated in such a project Raymond would surely confirm the accusations of treachery already levelled at him in the Christian camp. Yet he could not afford to abandon the Saladin connection while still under threat from King Guy, so he proposed a compromise. Al-Afdal's force could go through on condition that they crossed the Jordan after dawn, harmed neither towns nor peasant and returned by the same ford before nightfall. The fact that al-Afdal was content with these terms would seem to confirm that the objective was diplomatic as much as military – a probe by Saladin of his allies' commitment to their arrangement. But there was a practical result also because al-Afdal's staff were able to reconnoitre the terrain well into Christian territory between Tiberias and Sephorie (ar-Saffuriyah), with the splendid watering facilities at the Springs of Gesson being the traditional assembly point for the Frankish cavalry when faced with invasion in the north of the Kingdom.

As they rested their horses there, al-Afdal's reconnaissance force were astonished to find themselves under surprise attack from a handful of Christian knights. To prevent any breach of the truce by his own people, Count Raymond had dispatched couriers across the principality with news of the coming Saracen incursion. Unknown to him, the news had come to the ears of the bellicose Gerard de Ridfort, Grand Master of the Templars, the day before. Together with Balian of Ibelin and Roger des Moulins, Grand Master of the Hospitallers, he was heading a mission to Tiberias with orders from King Guy to look for reconciliation with the Prince of Galilee. Count Raymond had known nothing of this change of heart. Had he done so events might have turned out very differently. Gerard was not a man to let infidels ride unmolested through Christian territory and the night before he had summoned all the Templars in the area to rally to his banner. Now, accompanied by about 150 horse, and by des Moulins, who had been shamed by taunts of cowardice to join in the folly, he was riding out in search of the foe. The Muslim and his men could hardly believe their luck for just three of the Christian knights survived this medieval Charge of the Light Brigade – inevitably Gerard was among them. The head of Grand Master Roger was among those adorning the lances of the returning Saracen troopers. The main army greeted the news of the triumph with jubilation but Saladin had more pressing business. News had come through that Raynald of Chatillon was moving to plunder a caravan escorting Saladin's sister, her son and a party of returning pilgrims moving up the Mecca road, before turning to intercept the Egyptian army so vital to Saladin's deployment. Intimidated by Saladin's show of force, Raynald turned away from his prey – whereupon Saladin systematically ravaged his territories and then moved back northwards. In June he set up his standard, some twenty miles nearer the Christian frontier than his main army.

His enemies were closing their ranks. Shocked by the disaster at ar-Saffuriyah, Raymond had come to terms with the King and was now with the army; it was the biggest in living memory. But the army still mustering to the standard of Saladin was even greater. In June he held a general review. No doubt for many of the commanders present the most important business was the handover of the bounties Saladin had had to promise them to be present. But there was a detailed military briefing, to maximize the coherence among the diverse contingents. At last on Friday, 26 June Saladin moved out of al-Ashtara towards the ford over the Jordan just south of the Sea of Galilee (Lake Tiberias), his army raising a 'second sky of dust' with swords and iron-tipped lances glinting through like stars. He wanted news of the Franks movements and five days later found he had forced them to take the field. They were making camp at ar-Saffuriyah, which was an ideal defensive position; now they had to be lured into the open. On 1 July Saladin crossed the Jordan. His main force was sent on a few miles to a position where they could monitor the movements of the Franks and block the route to Tiberias, the principal town of Raymond as Prince of Galilee and held for him by his wife, the Countess Eschiva. The bulk of its forces were under Raymond with King Guy and the army of the Kingdom. As a major city, defended by the wife of one of the principal men of the Kingdom, it was the logical target to lure the Christian commanders from their secure defensive position. Saladin rode with a hand-picked force to attack the place. The city fell but Eschiva retired with the garrison to hold out in the citadel and got a message through to the King asking for a relief force. Saladin's campaign was barely forty-eight hours old and already the bird seemed ready to come to the lure.

With warm medicinal springs known in Roman times, and beautiful lakeside views, Tiberias, a favourite resort city of modern Israel, lies about fifteen miles due east of ar-Saffuriyah, though the most level road, curving to the north, stretched the distance to some twenty miles, the limit of a day's march. This road lay across an arid upland plain and then descended to the lake about a mile to the north of the town. An alternative route bent to the south-east, again the distance being about twenty miles and this road, though not so good, was well watered; but with Saladin's main force straddled across it it was a hard option. If they were to relieve Tiberias, the Christians would have to face a long day's march under enemy action across waterless uplands in the heat of a Syrian midsummer. By the capture of Tiberias, by the placing of his forces, and by the blocking of the few wells and springs along the northern road, Saladin had done all in his power to force on the Christian army that all-important mistake.

The council of war that would decide the fate of Christian Jerusalem began early in the evening of 2 July. The arguments against the relief of Tiberias were roughly as follows. Saladin could not destroy the army in its strong and well-supplied position at ar-Saffuriyah, whereas if it were to venture onto a long march on the exposed and waterless plateau it would be inviting almost certain destruction. Inaction would keep the army in being and since the Muslim forces usually returned to their diverse home bases at the end of a campaigning season the loss of Tiberias could reasonably be seen as only a short-term matter. If the army were lost then so too would be the whole Kingdom. Raymond of all people was the most passionate advocate of military prudence – he would rather, he said, lose his city, even his loved ones, than lose the land of Christ's Sufferings to the Infidel. The sense of the council was with him and King Guy decided upon caution. As midnight approached, the meeting broke up and council members said their goodnights. But two, Gerard of Ridfort and Raynald of Chatillon, lingered for a private word with the King. They had arguments to put too, which Saladin must have been relying on. In any case, they were intemperate hotheads burning to avenge the humiliation they had suffered at his hands.

Ridfort charged that Raymond was a secret traitor – had he not been in collusion with Saladin only weeks earlier? If the King, commanding the biggest army the Kingdom had yet put in the field, should refuse battle on the advice of a traitor, warned Grand Master Gerard, then the continuing loyalty of the Order of the Temple could not be counted upon. It was a clinching argument. As dawn broke on Friday, 3 July, reports came to Saladin that the enemy was on the move. He turned to his secretary, jubilant. His earlier judgement had been accurate: 'If this army could be destroyed, the kingdom would be open to conquest.'

Now it was crucial that the Christian army reach the shores of Lake Tiberias before nightfall. The morning began blazing hot and dry, within two hours of leaving the trees and gardens of ar-Saffuriyah they 'were suffering greatly from thirst'. A thick dust cloud, stirred up by their own labouring feet, choked parched throats and caked on sweaty skin sweltering in quilted gambeson (under tunic) and mail hauberk. Soon they were beset by the Saracen horse archers cantering up from Kafr Sabt. The orders were to concentrate the almost un- broken arrow stream on the rearguard provided by Ridfort and his Templars. Such a battle on the move had become a classic of crusad- ing warfare in the Holy Land. So long as the well-armoured knights and men at arms could make steady progress to their objective they could generally win through with 'acceptable' losses, but it was essen- tial the column maintain its integrity. Saladin's tactic forced the rear- guard to lag and encouraged the main army to hasten its pace in the hope of reaching shelter and water, so that the column was in danger of breaking. Grand Master Ridfort sent an imperious message up to King Guy in the van to call a halt for the night and the army made camp a mile or two from a low twin-peaked hill known locally as the Horns of Hattin. The Franks had covered barely ten miles.

Surrounded by the misery of their wounded and dying they had no rest from the insistent chanting of the il-allah – 'God is great; there is no God but God' – from every quarter of the enemy camp. 'The Faithful could smell victory in the air,' recalled Ibn al-Athir. And meanwhile the Sultan was making his placements. When the sun rose again on the morning of Saturday, 4 July, the Christians found themselves surrounded so closely that 'not an ant could have escaped'. The battle opened with a charge led by Saladin himself, followed by archery fire. Tormented beyond bearing, the infantry broke their ranks in a futile scramble towards the distant shimmering waters of Lake Tiberias. A Muslim soldier torched the grass, and choking, gasping and stumbling they were cut down or taken prisoner. The horsemen were little better off. King Guy, it seems, ordered Raymond to open a way through the enemy ranks for the rest of the army, but the Muslim line opened to let the knights thunder through ineffec- tually and at once reformed. Looking back up the hill Raymond could see that the army was in a helpless plight; he and his men rode away to Tripoli, followed inevitably by the suspicion of treason. Meanwhile Saladin's army wheeled about its prey in an ever-tightening diameter as the King and a party of a few hundred, rallying round the relic of the True Cross, prepared for a last heroic stand. A dramatic illustra- tion from the thirteenth century shows Saladin himself wrestling the relic from the King's grasp – a poetic fiction, but the Cross did pass into Muslim hands that day and, according to one tradition, was buried on Saladin's orders under the threshold of the great mosque in

Damascus so that the Faithful should tread it under foot as they went to prayers.

Despite the slaughter that had gone before, the last phase of the battle was tense for Saladin. Guy raised his red tent as a rallying point on the low hillside and mobilized a furious but businesslike assault on the Muslim ranks immediately in front of Saladin. Whether devious, indecisive, honourable or untrustworthy, all crusader knights knew how to fight. Guy, Gerard and Raynald now showed the battlefield qualities that had so often saved the Kingdom from disaster and had always forced Saladin to treat his enemies with respect, so that 'he seemed distraught, tugging at his beard.' The historian Ibn al-Athur noted that al-Afdal, by his father's side in this his first battle, recalled how the furious charge was forced back and how he shouted in triumph. ' "Hold your peace," growled the Sultan, "we have not beaten them until that tent falls." As he spoke, the tent fell indeed and, dismounting from his horse, Saladin prostrated himself and gave thanks to God, weeping tears of joy.' The anecdote is revealing. These last charges were a bid for a last-moment victory and not mere gestures of would-be martyrs. All professional soldiers knew, Saladin as well as any, that a motley force like the one he was commanding might break even in the moment of victory if the commander-in-chief could be overthrown.

It was late afternoon. The final desperate hope had failed. The True Cross had fallen into the hands of the Infidel. All vigour and fighting spirit was drained and the King and his companions, 'stumbling like drunken men', were led before Saladin in fetters. King Guy and Raynald of Chatillon were ordered to sit. Saladin, for once losing control of his temper, furiously denounced Raynald as an oath breaker. The prisoner's contemptuous reply that he had merely been following the custom of princes brought Saladin to the peak of his rage. King Guy was trembling violently, perhaps with fear but more probably in delayed shock from the catastrophe he had brought on Christendom. He appealed for a drink and Saladin ordered that snow-cooled water be brought. When he had drunk his fill, Guy passed the beaker to Raynald. Immediately Saladin's temper flared dangerously: let the Count be told that he, the Sultan, had not authorized the gesture. By the sacrosanct Arab laws of hospitality an offer of food or drink extended the protection of the host to the guest who received it. Returning to the prisoners later that evening, Saladin commanded Raynald to step forward. Once again he harangued him for his oath breaking and as a truce breaker and then and there felled him with a blow, which caught him on the shoulder. A guard struck off the head and the corpse was dragged out by the heels. This time the King and his companions were afraid. Uneasily they accepted the Sultan's comment delivered through an interpreter that he had twice sworn to kill that man if he should ever fall into his power. The other noble captives, even the Grand Master of the Temple, were to be spared.

Not so the rank and file Templars and Hospitallers. Crack troops, fanatical to the cause, they were the most feared soldiers in the Christian army. Moreover by the terms of their rule no Templar funds could be used to pay ransom for captured knights. Cold-bloodedly and uncharacteristically Saladin ordered a mass killing. Seated on a dais before the whole army he presided over a horrible ceremony that Gerard de Ridfort was also obliged to witness. Scholars, Sufis and holy men who had flocked enthusiastically to the army in response to the call to *jihad* and had begged the honour, were each assigned a victim and given a sword. To the jeers and encouragement of the army these inexpert swordsmen lopped and hacked away until their allotted head fell to the ground.

The next day, Sunday, Saladin received the surrender of the citadel at Tiberias, sending the Countess Eschiva under safe conduct to Tripoli. Before the end of that week Acre was in his hands, surrendered by Joscelin de Courtenay, seneschal of the Kingdom, on condition the lives of the citizens be spared. As they marched through the gates, led by the prosperous merchant community with its household possessions, Saladin was celebrating Friday prayers, the first in Acre in more than eighty years. For the next two days the army was rewarded with the plunder of the port's warehouses which were crammed with stocks of silks and metals, jewels and arms. The Sultan's commanders were already fanning out across the Kingdom taking the submission of towns and castles, mostly without a fight and always with honourable terms to the garrisons and populations. His clemency enhanced Saladin's reputation for chivalry among his Christian enemies; it also encouraged the rapid collapse of the crusader establishment. With virtually the whole Kingdom in his hands after two months of campaigning, early in September he entered Ascalon (Ashqelon in modern Israel), the great port of southern Palestine. There he received a deputation from Jerusalem, which he had summoned to discuss terms of surrender. A capital without a kingdom, the nearest sizeable Christian force the demoralized defenders of the city of Tyre more than a hundred miles distant, and with a population of Orthodox Syrian Christians resentful at Roman Catholic domination and a potential Fifth Column, the city's position was hopeless. But for Saladin, as for its defenders, Jerusalem was more than a prize of war. In his words, it was 'God's abode' and he had no wish 'to lay siege to the house of God or to put it to the assault'. The Christian envoys saw things differently. 'Our honour lies here,' they replied, 'for here is the place of our Saviour's crucifixion . . . We shall die in the defence of our Lord's sepulchre, for how could we do otherwise?' Saladin, who had offered generous terms to obtain the city 'in peace and amity', now swore a solemn oath to take the place by the sword.

Christian Jerusalem held out for some ten days. In the final hours, the churches were filled with penitents seeking forgiveness for their sins; priests made solemn procession through the streets; mothers shaved their daughters' heads hoping to make them so ugly they would be ignored in the pillage and rape all assumed would follow the inevitable fall. The Sultan had taken a formal oath; sack was the penalty for a city that refused the call to surrender; and many on both sides had heard tell of the atrocities that had followed the Christian capture of the city eighty-eight years earlier. Among the defenders, newly dubbed knights were eager for a last glorious sortie to sell their lives dearly and win martyrs' crowns for themselves. Patriarch Heraclius persuaded them to reconsider, for while they might enter Paradise their wives and children would surely be slaughtered, brutalized or enslaved. The knights relented.

Saladin now hesitated to break the terms of his oath, but his emirs could see disadvantages in revenge. In the mayhem of a sack much wealth would be destroyed and much looted by the common soldiery; better by far an orderly transfer of ransom money supervised, of course, by them. And the Christian commander Balian of Ibelin offered a clinching argument. The garrison had been led to believe that terms would be agreed – if they were now refused, Saladin could expect to walk into a charnel house. The city's more than 5,000 Muslim prisoners and slaves would be slaughtered; the Christians would 'burn our wealth and our possessions'; they would destroy the Rock and the al-Aqsa Mosque; then they would sally out to sell their lives as dearly as possible.

Saladin's inclination was in any case always towards mercy. But there was the question of his oath. According to his religious advisers this could be honoured if the enemy made a formal surrender at discretion, by convention considered an equivalent of conquest by the sword. Reasonable terms of ransom were agreed and, once the formal fighting had stopped, not a single Christian was harmed; forty days were allowed for the raising of ransom money and the evacuation of the city. Each man was to be ransomed at ten gold pieces, each woman at five and each child at a single gold piece. People could leave the city with as much of their personal belongings as they could carry. Anyone who at the end of the allotted time had failed to raise the money would be sold into slavery – the normal fate of enemy civilians who survived hostilities. Seven thousand poor, unable to pay their own way, were ransomed for a sum of 30,000 bezants, raised incidentally from the balance of treasure given to the Hospitallers by Henry II of England in penance for the murder of St Thomas a Beckett. But there were thousands still unaccounted for. Many grumbled that the wealth of the Church should be sold to meet the payment. Instead, to the fury of the Muslims and many Christians too, Patriarch Heraclius, while he paid the capitation tax for himself and his servants, left the city accompanied by pack animals and porters carrying off the Church plate and a vast hoard of his own wealth. A thousand able-bodied poor were liberated as a gift to Saladin's brother while the Sultan ordered the release of all the old and infirm. Later he was to make compensation payments out of his own resources to Christian widows dispossessed by the loss of their husbands' lands. 'Such was the charity of the Sultan towards the poor,' commented a Christian chronicler.

In this huge population movement, people smugglers were operating scams of every kind. To clear the city gates one had to present a receipt if one had already paid the exit tax, or buy a receipt from the official at the gate if not. Of course, many ended up paying twice, or received their clearance docket while their payment went into the official's own pocket. Others were smuggled out 'free' disguised as Muslims and then blackmailed with threats of disclosure. But this kind of thing was petty cash. The great men had much more profitable lines. No doubt many Franks lost money and possessions but it was a far cry from the butchers' shambles which had been Jerusalem 1099.

By now Saladin was turning his attention to cleansing the city and the Holy Places of Islam of all traces of Christian defilement. Refugees turning back for a last look could see the workmen taking down the golden cross atop the Dome of the Rock; the Rock itself had been sheathed in marble and built over with a Christian chapel and on the place where the Prophet's foot was believed to have rested before his miraculous ascent into heaven, stood a shrine embellished with marble to honour it as a place where Christ had stood before the crucifixion. On Saladin's orders, all this was cleared away and the sacred site was once again open to the gaze of believers. The al-Aqsa Mosque was obscured by living quarters, a granary and even a latrine erected during the time of the Templars. These structures were demolished and the interior richly carpeted and adorned with magnificent lamp chandeliers and illuminated texts from the Koran hung around the walls. On the Sultan's orders too, an exquisitely carved pulpit commissioned for the Mosque of 'Umar, by Nur al-Din, when he was planning to conquer Jerusalem was brought from Aleppo and finally installed. At length, everything was deemed fitting for the resumption of Muslim worship and on Friday, 9 October, prayers were celebrated at the al-Aqsa Mosque – to be followed by a sermon from the chief *qadi* of Aleppo. It combined veneration of the holy city with a eulogy of the son of Ayyub who, with God's help, had restored it to Islam.

The *qadi*'s words must have grated on ears loyal to the memory of the Turkish hero Zangi and his son Nur al-Din. People like Ibn al-Athir could never truly forgive this Kurdish upstart for outshining his predecessors. Yet even he could not deny the fact and, however reluctantly, concluded his account with a most generous tribute. 'After only 'Umar, no-one achieved this noble act of conquest but only Saladin, which is sufficient title to glory and honour.'[8] For it remained a fact that while Nur al-Din had commissioned the pulpit for the Mosque of 'Umar it was his lieutenant who had made possible its installation by expelling the Infidel from the site. By now the news was ringing round Islamic Syria. On the day of the city's capitulation scribes and clerks in Saladin's chancery had worked into the small hours writing dispatches to every corner of the world. Before he turned in for the night the Sultan's personal secretary had drawn up no fewer than seventy to various emirs and city governors. When the news reached Baghdad, the populace broke out in jubilation and the Caliph was to send the victorious hero of Islam rich gifts and signs of his favour. When the news reached the West, by contrast, reactions, in high places at least, were a blend of pious dismay and circumspect commitment.

6

Women and an Alternative Feudalism

The general differences between the world of Outremer and conditions in Europe were marked, but there was much that seemed familiar. To us, it is obvious that the expulsion of the Christian intruder states was only a matter of time – the time it took for their Muslim enemies to find a leader to unite them. To the average inhabitant of Frankish Syria in the twelfth century it was not obvious at all. God himself had delivered the country into their hands. Knowing nothing about the politics of the land before their arrival they could reasonably assume that the divided rule of city by city and the rivalries of the various potentates was a permanent feature. Even those who knew of the claims to universal authority made by the Caliph at Baghdad could hardly imagine a future in which a sultan of Egypt would invoke that authority to unite rival Sunnite princes against the Christians. Similar large claims were made on behalf of the German emperors who, as the self-styled heirs of Rome, liked to assert lordship even over the kings of France and England. In any case, most of the crusading lords were descended from families technically subordinate to the King of France and so were quite familiar with the idea of a ruler with extensive theoretical authority but little practical power. The counts of Flanders or of Toulouse and the dukes of Aquitaine all owed feudal allegiance to Paris but had traditionally operated as petty sovereigns in their own localities. Their cousins who settled overseas found that the world beyond the frontiers of Christendom seemed to be run on much the same lines. Just as Christian kings and magnates were regularly at war so, it turned out, were the rulers of Damascus and of Aleppo. As we have seen, the newcomers were not long in adapting to the local conditions, allying themselves with Muslim as well as Christian neighbours as it suited their advantage.

At the apex of the Kingdom stood the sovereign, either king or queen, because since women could inherit in their own right a king's daughter could become queen regnant, and while the man who married her would be acknowledged head of the government, his title as 'King of Jerusalem' was by courtesy of his position as her spouse. The Crown controlled the most prosperous and prestigious territories which, in addition to Nablus and Jerusalem, included the ports of Tyre and Acre – their streets choked by all sorts and conditions of men and Muslim and Christian merchants from all parts. The royal administration was conducted through such officials as a seneschal, from whom descended the network of command to the *rais* or mayors of the native villages, chamberlain in charge of finances, chancellor and castellans of the royal castles. Then there were royal officials, viscounts and dispensators to whom reported the burgess courts governing the affairs of Western freemen in the towns with their bailiffs' courts of the chain, market courts, and a Catholic *rais* presiding over Syrian native courts. In addition there were special courts for Western colonists in the villages. Subject to the sovereign were the lordships of tenants in chief such as the lords of Caesarea or Beirut, or the princes of Galilee. His chief officers were the Seneschal of the Kingdom, who presided over the high court of the Kingdom when the sovereign was absent, and the head of the military establishment, the Constable. The High Court of the Kingdom attended by the King's own vassals had much greater importance than any such judicial body in a European feudal state and, as we have seen, Muslim and Jewish subjects had their own religious courts. In a real sense it was a multicultural society, and not everybody appreciated the consequences. In 1171 a general assembly, or '*parlement*', protested violently when King Amalric I announced his intention of going to Constantinople to seek alliance with the schismatic Byzantine Emperor Manuel, rather than to a European court. The status accorded to women in Outremer could produce still more unexpected diversions from European convention.

'There are few other periods of history in which women have played so prominent a part.' So, in 1908, wrote William Miller of the crusader period, in his book *The Latins in the Levant,* dealing with the Latin states set up in the Byzantine Balkans in the wake of the Fourth Crusade of 1204. His judgement hardly needed revision, in Europe at least, until the second half of the twentieth century. The explanation he considered was simple enough – that the 'Salic law', forbidding the succession of women, did not hold in these new feudal principalities. The same was true of the Kingdom of Jerusalem and its baronies, where the acceptance of female succession produced periods of royal government under a queen regnant, or of baronial administration by a noblewoman in her own right. Contemporaries, fully aware of the anomalies produced in feudal conventions by the female succession, would surely have agreed with Miller that 'this participation of the weaker sex in the government of a purely military community, while adding immensely to the romance of the subject, had disastrous effects upon the fortunes of the Latin orient.' Some of the military and political consequences, whether disastrous or not, have been touched on; this chapter is concerned with the unusual feudal structures of the Kingdom of Jerusalem and the decidedly unusual position which women occupied in crusading society when compared with the role traditionally allotted to them in the medieval world.[1]

This is not the place to debate the technicalities of the 'Salic law', supposedly dating from the time of the Salian Franks in the sixth century. But the principle that women could not succeed in their own right to the 'lordship' of the family lands was a convention observed almost without exception all over Europe. One place where the exception proved the rule was Aquitaine and there it wreaked havoc as we have seen in the marriages of Eleanor of Aquitaine. In the lands of Outremer it did not obtain, a fact which affected women's attitudes at all levels of society. Western women, and particularly noblewomen, were a source of wonderment verging on dismay to both Greek and Muslim. Recording a contemporary's recollection of the Frankish army's entry into Constantinople at the time of the Second Crusade, the Byzantine historian Nicetas Choniates tells us that women were seen riding mounted in the ranks of the knights and men at arms – not like the ladies of the East in closed litters, not even on modest pacing horses or palfreys, but on fine warhorses, 'boldly sitting their saddles astride after the manner of men . . . dressed in armour just like men'. In fact, with their 'warlike looks' and the pennants streaming from their steel-tipped lances, 'they behaved in a more masculine fashion than even the Amazons.'[2] Whether these great ladies actually rode with the front line into battle is not so clear.

Ibn al-Athir records that during the fighting at the seige of Acre Saladin's people found to their astonishment that among the prisoners were three women who had ridden into battle on horseback wearing coats of mail, cuirasses and helmets and who were only recognized as women when stripped of their armour. The Muslim commentators praised them for man-like endurance despite their 'feminine weakness'. Then there was the case of the woman archer dressed in a green mantle, who did great damage among the Muslim ranks before she was finally killed. Her bow was taken to the Sultan as a notable curiosity. Unfortunately, Frankish sources give no clue to who these warlike ladies were.[3] Gervaise of Canterbury says that before she retired into the monastery-convent of Fontevraud, Isabella of Anjou rode armed to war, but it is not clear that she wielded a weapon in anger. The Dowager Margravine Ida of Austria, reputedly a great beauty as a young woman, had joined William IX, the troubadour Duke of Aquitaine on his doomed expedition of 1101. Whether she was merely in quest of the thrills to be had from pious play acting, we do not know. We do know she did not return and was probably killed – though rumour reported a sighting of her in a Turkish harem.

Harem life would have seemed an outrage, just as would life in the women's quarters of a Byzantine noble household. Western noble-women suffered severe legal disabilities, they were subject to their husband as a servant to her master and they had to submit to beatings at his will. But they were not confined to the house. A Muslim tourist to the Christian states was startled to find that Frankish women walked openly in the streets with their husbands and if they happened to meet a friend, male or female, the husband would stand patiently by while they had their chat. In one case, the conversation dragged on so long that the Frank left his wife with the man, while he went about his business. There were even instances of men taking their wives into the public baths. This might have raised eyebrows in northern Europe too, but the Frankish population of Outremer had a large proportion of southern Europeans in its ethnic mix – the *langue d'oc* of Provence was the official language of Antioch, while merchants from Marseille as well as from Genoa, Venice or Pisa had their own enclaves in the major trading ports of the Kingdom and life tended to be more relaxed in the south.

In the afternoon of the second day of Boccaccio's *Decameron*,

Dineo, the young gallant responsible for the last narrative of the day, tells the old tale of Bartolomea, the feisty young wife of Messer Ricciardo di Chinzia, a learned and rich but less than virile judge, who was abducted by the sea rover Paganino da Mare and carried off to his palace in Monaco. Then accessible only from the seaward side it was a notable haunt of pirates and fast living. 'Long before they reached Monaco, Bartolomea had forgotten all about the Judge . . . for, unlike him, her new master knew how to work and beat her wool . . . and could do it three times and then stand up erect again like a club.'[4] This and more she explained with great relish to Ricciardo when he came to demand she return to Pisa. But Paganino scored not only by the quality but also the regularity of his performance. According to the calendar kept by Ricciardo: 'man and wife should abstain from carnal embraces . . . out of reverence for the saints . . . for vigils of the Apostles and for a thousand other reasons', leaving barely one day a month when sex was allowed. Bartolomea refused point blank to return to the conjugal bed. She preferred to live with Paganino, 'for as long as their legs would carry them to work together and enjoy themselves without regard to saints' days or vigils or lent'.

Writing in the 1340s, Boccaccio heralds the new humanist spirit of the Renaissance. But in Bartolomea and Paganino he depicts a reality as old as humanity and as vibrant in the world of the crusaders as at any other time. If proof were needed it is amply confirmed by the long and lubricious passage devoted by 'Imad al-Din to describing the charms of a shipload of "three hundred lovely Frankish women"' who arrived at the siege of Acre in aid of the war effort. Each of these 'licentious harlots . . . bold and ardent . . . with beautiful bottoms . . . and fleshy thighs . . . swaying like saplings . . . wearing a cross at the breast . . . [and] set up in a pavilion erected for her use . . . dedicated as a holy offering what they kept between their thighs . . . brought their silver anklets up to touch their golden ear-rings and were willingly spread out in the carpet of amorous sport . . . permitted territory [even] for forbidden acts'.[5] The sinner and his or indeed her sins were always in rude health. Pious churchmen deplored the facts, though they were not alone nor the most extreme in their disapproval. They at least accepted the sex act and procreation as God's means of populating His earth. Fanatics among the Cathar heretics were so disgusted by sex that they refused to eat any form of animal protein, it being the product of copulation and hence in the domain of the Evil One. Ricciardo's legalist calendar was pretty close to some penitential handbooks which required sexual abstinence 'throughout Lent and Advent, on Sundays, feast days, the vigils of major feasts, the week before Pentecost and, according to some who certainly had Messer Ricciardo's vote, all Wednesdays, Fridays and Saturdays throughout the year'.[6] The fact that King Louis VII of France observed such religious proprieties in his dealings with his wife Eleanor incensed her.

Evidently, puritanism had deep roots in Christendom; among the crusaders it was reckoned a practical virtue with military advantages. Pope Urban seems to have conceived the expedition to the Holy Land as an exclusively male enterprise, while contemporary records – letters, chronicles and poetic accounts – describe the tearful partings of husbands and wives. But in fact there were women in the first crusading expeditions and among them were wives.

Traditional Church teaching respected the rights of both marriage partners. Ivo of Chartres, who was writing his influential treatise on Church law, the *Decretum*, at about the time of the First Crusade, quoted from St Augustine of Hippo to argue that no married person was entitled to make a binding vow which might infringe the rights of his or her spouse to sexual intercourse, without first obtaining the freely given consent of the spouse. That the application of this Augustinian teaching on the marriage vow to crusaders was taken seriously by the Church was confirmed by Ivo himself, not merely a legal theorist but also a bishop. Contacted by a nobleman who had taken the vow to join the expedition to the Holy Land, he wrote earnestly warning him that the fulfilment of this vow must take second place to his obligations to his wife. Pope Urban, too, was anxious that would-be crusaders should not seize on the holy adventure to the hurt of their partners. In September 1096, writing to the citizens of Bologna to recruit volunteers for the 'general passage overseas', he made the proviso that young married men must first gain the consent of their wives, before setting out.[7]

It was an age when the Church was the guardian and arbiter of public morality and men like Ivo of Chartres took their duty seriously. One might suppose that, at a time when the Pope was urging the knight service of Christendom to follow the Cross to war against the Infidel, a churchman of all people would urge a warrior to disregard the opposition of his wife. In fact, Bishop Ivo tells his nobleman friend that if his partner refuses her consent, then he must renounce his warlike intentions. Even if the couple agreed on the husband's fulfilment of his vow, the wife would pay her share of the price of his piety by being denied her legitimate sexual satisfaction. If he went without her consent and as a result she lapsed into the sin of adultery, then he would be responsible as the one who had created the circumstances which encouraged this outcome. Of course, whatever joint decision spouses might have come to in the fever of crusading enthusiasm, some husbands were going to return to find wives who had taken lovers. In such cases, Ivo, a man of true Christian charity, urged his fellow clerics that judgement on the moral responsibilities of the parties should be left to God while the husband should either take back his wife or, if determined to live in separation from her, live in chastity.[8] Women could turn to various legal opinions. Probably the most generous ruling was the opinion of the distinguished canon lawyer Hostiensis, who countenanced remarriage if there was a reasonable presumption that the husband was dead, that is if most people in the community believed him to have died on campaign. In fact, the Church's lawyers were reasonable in their approach to the question. If there was any doubt as to the death of the crusader his wife was barred from a second marriage. But a thirteenth-century Spanish canonist allowed an absence of five years as a legally acceptable basis for presumption of death and most of his contemporaries permitted a woman to remarry if the commander of the expedition was willing to swear to the man's death on campaign.

Traditional teaching on the status of crusaders' wives seemed to be challenged by a ruling of Pope Innocent III in September 1201. From the first, women had occasionally accompanied their husbands in the crusading army, but the Church preferred that women, especially rich women, should redeem their vows by monetary payment to the cause. In the summer of 1200, however, Pope Innocent gave official sanction to women who wished to accompany their husbands to do so. A wife's refusal to consent to her husband's taking the vow to the Cross on the grounds of loss of conjugal rights would seem less reasonable if she had official Church approval to accompany him. Innocent was dedicated to the recovery of Jerusalem at a time when European enthusiasm for the war against the Infidel was flagging and recruitment was difficult. The new ruling does not seem to have increased numbers to any great extent, for barely a year later the Pope dispensed with the traditional right of the wife to withhold her consent. Henceforward, a man might freely take and fulfil the crusade vow, irrespective of his wife's wishes in the matter. The Pope needed recruits;

marriage vows should no longer be an obstacle. In order to maximize response to the call for assistance in preserving the Christian presence in the Holy Land, Innocent was prepared to overrule what earlier Church lawyers had considered to be a natural right of married women, deriving from the nature of the marriage contract itself.[9] The legal commentators were never happy with the implications of Pope Innocent's pronouncement. It must be considered a most extraordinary (*specialissimum*) concession in favour of the Holy Land, wrote one; another mused that the traditional parity of partners in the marriage vows could only be maintained if the ruling were interpreted to allow wives also to take crusader vows without their husband's consent. Then there was the question of morality. Could a man take the crusader's vow against his wife's wishes if he had reason to think she might be unfaithful in his absence? Back in the 1090s, Ivo of Chartres would have held him responsible for his wife's adultery in such circumstances. Debating the issue in the Easter university term of 1271, no less an authority than St Thomas Aquinas argued that while the husband might have the technical legal right to take the vow, to do so would be morally reprehensible. In other words, one of the Church's supreme theologians and lawyers rejected on moral grounds a ruling which one of its most powerful popes had made on expedient political grounds.

Women who accompanied their menfolk on the crusade, or those who went out to join them must have noticed important differences between the status they enjoyed and that of their stay-at-home sisters. Much of the early legal archive of the Kingdom of Jerusalem was lost when Saladin recovered the city for Islam in 1187, and with it much detail concerning women's legal standing in the fluid social structure of that European world 'oversea'. Yet thirteenth-century writers record tantalizing glimpses of the early days. It seems, for example, that at first even women of noble family were allowed to marry as they pleased.[10] But, while such a permissive attitude may square with our ideas of what might be expected in an essentially frontier society, it was condemned by traditionalist commentators both in Europe and in Palestine and could cause real problems for the feudal order. It seems that intermarriage with the local population, whether Muslim, Jewish or Eastern Christians, Syrian, Armenian or Saracen, was common in the early years at most levels of society. Where landholding was linked with military service and particularly in a society where military service was a condition of the survival of the state, aristocratic heiresses who followed their heart rather than their duty might cause real problems of security – a handsome minstrel or wealthy young merchant was no substitute in the armed levy of the Kingdom for a knight expert in the arduous profession of mounted armed combat.

And yet, although the crusader states were set in an ethnically and religiously hostile environment, the law of the Kingdom of Jerusalem was much more liberal in its attitude towards women landholders than traditional feudal law. It was not uncommon to find great ladies managing large landed estates that they had acquired in their own right by purchase, which would be a very unusual state of affairs in Europe. Where a woman held title to land by the rights of a widow, or as an heiress through the death of her father, she could only be required to marry if the estate was a fief carrying an obligation of military services from the fief holder, services that a woman could not discharge. However, in this case marriage, and also in the case of widows remarriage, was virtually obligatory – a woman who refused could legally be deprived of her fief. Church opinion was generally against second marriages, even for widows, but in the crusader states military requirements took priority, although there might be exceptions. According to one legal opinion, a woman over the age of sixty could not be obliged to marry. Not only would such compulsion be 'contrary to God's will and to the dictates of reason', it would be out of line with the regulations for male fief holders 'in the usage and custom of the Kingdom of Jerusalem and of Cyprus'. They were excused military service after the age of sixty so the women should receive the same concession. 'Thus,' comments James Brundage, 'the ladies of the Latin kingdom, in the view of one of the kingdom's most eminent jurists, constituted a branch of the kingdom's army.'[11]

In standard feudal practice, the liege lord of an heiress as her guardian at law often pressured her into marriage because would-be suitors to the lady's hand and fortune expected to pay for the privilege of marrying her. The laws of the Kingdom of Jerusalem set limits to the lord's rights. He could not require a woman vassal to marry if her fief was not subject to military obligations, and even if it were and she had to agree to marriage, she was not entirely at the mercy of his arbitrary whim. It was up to him to nominate no fewer than three candidates for her to chose between, each suitable to her rank and social station. Given the hierarchical nature of medieval society, and the central place of marriage in the social and economic structure, the lord's rights were a factor even where a lady of a non-military fief wished to marry of her own free will. She needed his permission. Here again, the laws of the Kingdom offered her some protection, although such permission could not be withheld indefinitely or unreasonably.

The courts of the crusader states made a distinction between marriage law governing the aristocracy and aristocratic ladies, and the law governing bourgeois marriage.[12] A great heiress might find her choice of husband debated by a Parlement whose members, in addition to nobles and senior churchmen, might include officials of the military orders and even prominent townsmen – in the embattled society of Outremer the qualities of the new man in the power elite could affect everybody. The basic text for town law and society, the *Assises de la cour des bourgeois*, sets the tone by observing that a good marriage is not only 'most pleasing to God but highly profitable to man'. There are regulations for marriage between free persons and those of unfree or freed status, and disapproval of marriage between Christians and heretics.[13] But there is also provision to allow a husband to make his wife a monthly allowance for household expenses, with the rather surprising proviso that if he did so the agreement would be a quasi contractual obligation on him and his agent. The liberal provisions for child care in the *Assises de la cour des bourgeois* go back to Roman law via a version of the laws of Justinian translated into Provençale, with obligations on fathers to provide child support should they separate from their wives, and even for contributions to the maintenance of illegitimate children. Wives also enjoyed greater protection for their dowry against a wastefully extravagant husband than did their sisters in Europe, and widows enjoyed rights of revenue from the estate of their dead husband, as opposed to modest, once-and-for-all claims against the estate at the time of his death, more commonly accorded to a widow in Europe.

But husbands too enjoyed certain unusual rights. Notably, a man could sue for a separation on grounds of *sevitia* or *odium*, roughly equivalent in modern terms to mental cruelty or incompatibility. If the court accepted his plea then he could have a 'separation from bed and board' – *a thoro et mensa* – though in this case he had to restore her dowry to her or, if she had decided to enter a life of religion, to her convent. According to the *Assises de la cour des bourgeois*, wives as well as husbands could claim for separation on compassionate grounds, and the code appears more liberal than anything in contemporary Europe. However, this was not true in the rules governing marriageable age. Whereas Church law set surprisingly low limits – twelve for girls, fourteen for boys – the laws of Outremer differed from European practice, setting thirteen as the age for both sexes.[14]

Melisende, the older daughter of King Baldwin II, revealed something of the scope available to women in this alternative feudal world. In 1129 she had married Fulk of Anjou, as his second wife. When her father died two years later Fulk and their infant son Baldwin were crowned co-rulers. But both father and son derived their title from her and she had no wish to be excluded from power. The champion of her cause was also rumoured to be her lover and while he was forced to submit, was the victim of an assassination attempt and died soon afterwards. The Queen retained a role as partner in her husband's government and when he died in 1143 continued to direct the Kingdom's affairs as her son's regent for another seven years.

Melisende's success is in stark contrast to the failure of Matilda of England, her kinswoman by marriage, who had married Fulk's son Geoffrey 'Plantagenet' as her second husband. The daughter of King Henry I of England and his designated heir, she was in addition widow of an emperor, Henry V, and supported by a considerable party of the Anglo–Norman baronage. Yet in more than a decade of civil war she never established herself as queen regnant, and was never crowned. There were, to be sure, personality failings that helped to account for Matilda's forced withdrawal from the English scene. Her arrogance towards these provincial islanders, derived from a decade of the deference expected to a German empress, did not find much favour even with her Norman baronial supporters, and none at all with the powerful English merchant oligarchy that controlled the all-important great city of London. Not even the queen of William the Conqueror had required their forbears to kiss her slippered feet, an honour that Matilda demanded. And of course a woman ruling in her own right ran counter to all traditions of northern feudalism. But it was tradition only and the fact remained that King Henry had required all his courtiers to swear an oath of fealty to his daughter as queen designate. Her amiable but dilatory rival and cousin, Count Stephen of Blois, won the first vital round in a contest Matilda was not even aware had begun with one gesture of quite uncharacteristic decisiveness. Within days of the old King's death he crossed the Channel, seized the treasury of the Kingdom housed at Winchester and was crowned king before the year was out. In the twenty years of civil war and unrest that followed he never lost the respect accorded a sovereign and she never gained it.

Queen Melisende of Jerusalem by contrast, though for a time opposing the authority of her husband with the help of her reputed lover, never lost a say in the affairs of her kingdom. For it was the law not custom that gave her the hereditary right to the Crown so that Fulk had to issue his writs 'by the assent of his wife Melisende'.[15] King Fulk, perhaps in love with, perhaps in awe of his wife, was also a worthy ruler of the Kingdom. Overriding Latin prejudice, he formed an alliance with the Byzantine Emperor Manuel I Comnenus. In the late autumn of 1143, the royal couple, long reconciled, were out for a day's hunting. Unexpectedly game was started from the covers and the King, impulsively galloping in pursuit, was thrown by his horse and horribly injured; he died three days later. The Queen grieved but the mourning period was short. She assumed full control of the government as regent for her thirteen-year-old son Baldwin III and on Christmas Day the Patriarch of Jerusalem crowned the two joint rulers. Melisende continued to exercise power well after Baldwin attained the legal age of majority. For a time, mother and son ran rival administrations, hers operating from her stronghold in Jerusalem's Tower of David, and in the end the young King had to force his mother's submission by laying siege to her.

Women in the Norman Kingdom of Sicily, even of the highest rank, could find themselves suffering more conventional treatment. In 1177 King William II married Joan, daughter of King Henry II of England. The marriage was childless and William died in November 1189. There were two contestants to the succession: Tancred, descended through an illegitimate line from King Roger II, King of Sicily, and the Emperor Henry VI who claimed the Crown by right of his marriage to Constance, King Roger's daughter. The Pope, dismayed by the possibility that Emperor Henry and his wife Constance might produce a son and that in this case the Crown of Sicily and southern Italy would be joined to the German imperial power in the north, gripping the papal states as in the jaws of a vice, supported Tancred as did most popular opinion, which was against a German succession from simple national sentiment. Crowned king early in 1190, Tancred imprisoned the widowed Queen Joan, Richard I's youngest sister (seemingly the only person for whom he had any affection), refusing to restore her dower lands, by tradition a widow's right, and to pay over a legacy that King William had promised to Richard. When he arrived in Sicily en route for the Third Crusade, Richard was a man with a grievance. Never a man to be lightly crossed, he raised havoc in the island kingdom and forced Tancred to meet his financial demands and to release his sister. In return he agreed to support Tancred against the Emperor. Although a queen, Joan had suffered the kind of humiliations to which women were especially prone in her world. However, sailing on with her brother's expedition to the Holy Land, she would in due course, find herself facing a startlingly unconventional affront to her self esteem as a Christian woman.

7

Loss of Jerusalem and the Third Crusade
1187–1192

⸺⸱⸺

Jerusalem fell to Saladin on 2 October 1187. The news reached the West some three weeks later and, it is said, the shock killed the elderly Pope Urban III. If so it was the final reverse in a troubled pontificate. The year before Henry, son and later heir of Emperor Frederick Barbarossa, had married Constance, heiress to the Kingdom of Sicily. The union threatened Rome with encirclement to north and south by its traditional enemy, when Henry in due course succeeded his illustrious father. In a recent clash over an ecclesiastical appointment the great Emperor had debarred the papal legate from entering the Empire and Urban was preparing his excommunication when he died. On 29 October, his short-lived successor Pope Gregory VIII issued a formal pronouncement in aid of the Holy Land and so initiated what we know as the Third Crusade.

In the English-speaking world it is associated with the names of Richard I, King of England, the Lionheart, and Saladin, Sultan of Egypt, Islam's chivalrous hero. In France the honours would no doubt go to the French King, Philip II Augustus, first of the royals actually to reach the theatre of war, but that would not be until March 1191. In 1189 fleets from Flanders, England and Pisa had already left for Palestine, while the year before that a fleet sent by King William II of Sicily had rendered vital assistance to the Christian forces still holding out in the remaining foothold ports of Antioch, Tripoli and

121

Tyre. But in the early years the news that Saladin himself most dreaded was about the intentions and preparations by Barbarossa ('Red Beard'), the charismatic German Emperor. A man in his mid sixties, his venerable, tall, ramrod figure, stylish if now somewhat grizzled beard and superb horsemanship made Frederick the model of the chivalric ideal of the cult of King Arthur, increasingly fashionable with the younger generation of European knights.

Crowned emperor in 1155, two years later he had inaugurated the term *Sacrum Imperium*, 'Holy Empire', and then in 1165 arranged for the canonization of Charlemagne by his own anti-pope.[1] In that year too Frederick had discussed with Henry II of England the possibility of a joint expedition to Palestine.[2] Frederick saw aid for the Holy Land as a natural function of his Holy Empire. Christ had been both king and priest, his kingly office in secular affairs devolving to the Holy Empire, his priestly office to the popes. A letter from Pope Gregory reporting the fall of Jerusalem and urging that rulers should be aflame with the Holy Spirit to recover it, only reinforced his intentions. Throughout his life, according to historian Peter Munz, Frederick had believed that 'the ultimate . . . task of the Emperor of Christendom was to protect the Church and defend the holy places in Palestine against the infidels.'[3]

With his exalted view of the imperial office Frederick must have been impressed by the semi-mystical ideas about history and the end of time current among contemporary churchmen, such as the historical writer Bishop Otto of Freising, and mystics like Hildegard of Bingen. Many believed that the last age of the world was at hand and that it would be inaugurated when the last emperor laid his crown, sceptre and empire upon the altar of the temple in Jerusalem, his work as defender of the Church discharged. There would then follow the predestined reign of the Antichrist when all the forces of evil emerged in triumph – to be struck down by Jesus Christ Himself in his Second Coming. We know that the *Ludus de Antichristo*, a compelling stage presentation of this theme, was performed in Frederick's presence early in his reign.[4] Hildegard had a vision of the severed demon head of the Antichrist upon the knees of the naked and bleeding figure of the Church. Otto saw the events of his time leading up to the Emperor Frederick's reign as a preparation for the expedition to the Holy City.[5]

Early in December 1187, Frederick was holding his court in the imperial city of Strassburg (now Strasbourg in France). With his permission Bishop Henry addressed the assembled knights and noble-men with an appeal to take the Cross. It was observed that the Emperor had tears in his eyes as the Bishop, in passionate sermon imagery, compared Christ to a feudal lord insulted by enemies while his liegemen stood by. A number in the audience begged to be allowed to pledge their oath. Frederick, wanting to be sure of the level of pious commitment among his nobles, announced a special 'Court of Jesus Christ' to convene at Mainz at Pentecost the following year. As every good Christian knew, Pentecost was the occasion when, after the Resurrection, the Holy Ghost descended from heaven upon the heads of the disciples and inspired them to go out into the world and make their witness to the Risen Lord. No day in the Church calendar could be more propitious for an appeal for warrior pilgrims to pledge themselves to the cause of the True Faith and the True Cross, shamefully fallen into infidel hands.

Saladin learnt about these developments in Europe in January 1188 from a Byzantine embassy attending his court at Acre. They worried him a great deal more than the remnants of the Frankish forces in Palestine, reduced to a few isolated coastal strongholds, succoured by a fleet sent by William II of Sicily, chief among them Antioch, Tripoli and Tyre. This last, held by Conrad of Montferrat, was the refuge of many Frankish leaders released by Saladin, after his triumph.

In April 1189 King Guy appeared before the gates of Tyre, demanding that Conrad surrender the place to him. It looked as though the Franks were bent on all-out civil war, so it is hardly surprising if Saladin was not much worried about the place as a threat to him. In a letter to his brother he wrote that thanks to the grace of Allah Tyre had turned from being a fortress protecting its inhabitants to being a prison confining them as men enjoying a kind of liberty for the time being.[6] Perhaps he should have taken rather more notice when a Pisan force, which had sailed to the aid of Conrad, transferred its allegiance to King Guy. In August Guy, abandoning his siege, prepared to march against Acre itself with the Pisan and Sicilian fleets keeping pace with the army along the coast. The King, pilloried for the disastrous defeat at Hattin, was in need of a success, but to attack Acre was a desperate gamble. In its favour was the motley nature and divided command of the Muslim forces. Saladin reckoned he could destroy the Christian force on the march. But his emirs advised waiting until it reached the plain of Acre and he unwisely followed their advice. In his early fifties he was terminally exhausted after years of almost unbroken campaigning and under doctors' orders for a chronic stomach complaint. As always, he was handicapped by the uneven quality of his contingents and the need to conciliate the conflicting ambitions of their commanders. Despite his political ascendancy, on the battlefield he was always commander of a coalition. Furthermore, his lenient treatment of the defeated Franks angered many of his reluctant allies.

Thus, in the last days of August Guy was able to establish himself outside the walls of Acre. In addition he was reinforced by some fifty ships that had sailed from North Sea ports with a force of several thousand Danes and Frisians on board, 'men of large limbs . . . and fervent devotion'.[7] It was not an encirclement so that when Saladin arrived a few days later and deployed his motley forces along the Christian line, he was besieging the besiegers, so to speak. For most of September there was desultory fighting between garrison and Franks, and Franks and the Turkish relieving force. The weather was kind and an almost tournament atmosphere developed. Knights and emirs and the soldiery of both sides got to know one another so well that the battle might be halted for an hour or so while they exchanged news and views. A mock battle was even arranged between two boys from the city and two from the besieging army. One of the Muslim boys threw his opponent to the ground and claimed him as a prisoner; a Christian knight solemnly ransomed him for two dinars. Soon after this Saladin's commander at the northern end of the lines succeeded in forcing a breach through the Christian defences so that Saladin and his entourage were able to enter Acre and survey the battle positions from its walls. As he looked out over the plain towards where his own camp was being set up in the hills, he realized that the comparatively small Christian force sandwiched between the walls of the city and his own lines could have been defeated then and there.

In Germany Pentecost 1188 was duly celebrated at Mainz by the great men of the Empire. When the day arrived, in deference to the Divine Spirit whose presence must surely be present, the Emperor refused to preside over the assembly. With the rest of the congregation he listened in sombre silence as Cardinal Henry of Albano read out a letter from the Pope describing the plight of the Holy Land; but like all the knights in the congregation, the Emperor came alive with fervour as Bishop Godfrey of Würzburg expounded to his listeners God's offer of redemption through military service. That day, it was said, some 13,000 men took the Cross, among them bishops, princes, counts and noblemen and thousands of lesser knights; at their head the Emperor in person and his eldest son Frederick, Duke of Swabia. Together the huge concourse sang the *laetare Jerusalem*, 'Rejoice, Oh Jerusalem!'. It is clear from the tone of the chroniclers' reports that '*Der Hoftag Jesu Christi in Mainz*' ('The Day of Christ's Court in Mainz') was among the most inspiring occasions of the medieval Empire. Preparations for the great military pilgrimage were expected to take the best part of a twelve month and departure day was set for 23 April 1189 – the Feast Day of St George, the Roman officer who had been martyred for refusing to acknowledge the divinity of the Caesars, holding true to his faith in the divinity of Christ, and the patron saint of soldiers.

Frederick's preparations were impressively thorough. Participants had to show adequate means of support, discipline was strictly enforced and even sexual chastity was enjoined. An effort was made to exclude the unruly non-combatants and camp followers who were the scourge of medieval armies. At Vienna, the Emperor ordered that some 500 petty criminals and other troublemakers be sent packing. By contrast, critical observers of the cynical recruiting methods in Wales on behalf of King Henry II of England reckoned that to swell the numbers scores of murderers and robbers were knowingly accepted – eagerly embracing the crusader's right to indulgence, to opt for freedom with the army and the risk of death in battle rather than the certainty of prison and death on the gallows.[8] The reputation of the imperial army's qualities went before it. Reports reached Saladin that nobles guilty of ill-treating their men were liable to execution on the Emperor's orders and that even the troopers were willing to endure harsh deprivations in tribute to the fate of the Holy Sepulchre. Hardy, and apparently dedicated to its cause, it was also a huge force. People said that it took three days to pass any given point, and modern calculations estimate it at more than 100,000.[9]

Small wonder then that Saladin took the looming threat in the north extremely seriously. He has been criticized for not completing the expulsion of the Franks from Palestine and particularly for leaving Conrad of Montferrat in possession of the port of Tyre. But perched at the end of its peninsula the place was virtually impregnable from the mainland; and while its sea link with Europe opened useful propaganda possibilities – Conrad sent out pleas for help illustrated with a painting depicting an Arab's horse defecating in the Holy Places at Jerusalem[10] – it was the only city left in the Kingdom. In any case, historically the westerners had overwhelmingly favoured the overland route and, as Saladin well knew, Barbarossa was in negotiations with the Byzantine Emperor Isaac to give him and his army free passage through his territories.

Although it had missed its scheduled departure date of 23 April by a few weeks, the imperial army that set out from Ratisbon (Regensburg) in May 1189 was probably the best trained and best equipped yet known to the crusades.[11] Comments in contemporary Muslim sources reveal dismay in the Islamic world while Saladin himself hoped to exploit shared diplomatic interests with Constantinople to block the German advance into Anatolia. His envoys had been at Constantinople for some months hoping to do a deal with Isaac who wanted a guarantee of Orthodox control of the Church in Palestine from the new Muslim master of Jerusalem, offering in exchange imperial protection to the Muslim community in Constantinople. As a gesture of goodwill, he invited Saladin to dispatch a ship carrying a *minbar* (pulpit) as a gift to his co-religionists in the Orthodox capital. But a Genoese squadron captured the vessel and the news of the Sultan's gift was taken in triumph to Tyre and the proof of the Greeks' perfidious dealings with the arch enemy was reported to Catholic Europe in letters from Conrad of Montferrat.

Over the centuries, the Byzantine emperors had dealt with their neighbours by force or by diplomacy as circumstances required. The Muslim presence was for them far more immediate and of far longer standing than the comparatively recent incursion of the Latin West, and the religious allegiance of Christian for Christian was in any case muddied by the difference between Orthodox and Roman Catholic. Frederick's imperial title was in the eyes of East Rome a usurped one and his intentions not entirely trustworthy. For a time, in October 1189, Greek–German relations erupted in open conflict in the Balkans and Isaac's intelligence service must surely have briefed him about those elements in the German army urging the outright conquest of the Greek Empire. But reason prevailed and Isaac provided the transport to carry Frederick's army across the Hellespont near Gallipoli. On 28 March 1190, to the sound of trumpets, the German Emperor set foot upon the soil of Asia Minor.

At one stage Frederick had been hoping for an easy passage across Anatolia. The Seljuk ruler in the area, no friend of Saladin, had even sent an embassy to Frederick at Nuremberg to make diplomatic soundings back in 1188, but times had changed since then and the old man's sons seem to have come to terms with Saladin. It is surely not surprising – the great Kurd, the champion of orthodox Sunni Islam, was not only lord of Egypt and Syria, and liberator of Jerusalem, he was the favoured son in religion of the Caliph of Baghdad. So the imperial army had a fight on its hands. It was in poor shape; the long trek from Ratisbon had taken its toll and now, forced to feed itself by plundering the country, it was continually harassed. By the time it reached the Seljuk capital of Konya, according to one twentieth-century German historian, the once mighty force had been reduced to half its numbers. But, strengthened as many believed by the sword of God, on 17 May they won a complete and famous victory and for the best part of a week restocked their supplies in Konya, replaced some of their fallen horses and recuperated their strength. At the end of the month the army stood on the frontier of the Christian principality of Armenia. Food and supplies were sent out to them; there was talk of a forthcoming ceremony in the city of Seleucia at which the Western Emperor was to raise the Armenian Prince to the dignity of king. But it was not to be. On 10 June, as Frederick rested in the valley of the River Saleph (modern Göksu)[12] while his army assembled for the last stretch to Seleucia, and oppressed by the heat of the day, he seems to have decided on a quick, refreshing bathe and taken a chill. There are other versions – maybe he drowned. But certain it is that the great Emperor died after immersion in the river at a point where the water 'was not even up to his waist'. To all intents and purposes the German threat was over.

For Saladin and all the Muslim faithful it was the deliverance of Allah, and many Germans thought that God had turned against their cause. We are told that some killed themselves in despair while others renounced the Christian faith and converted to the heathen.[13] Churchmen and devout laymen were horrified to think that the Emperor's soul could be in spiritual jeopardy as he had died without the last rites of the Church. One pious chronicler alleged that Frederick had in fact absolved himself with a last invocation to Christ that He bless the water in which he was drowning as the water of a second baptism which should regenerate his soul. The devout fiction is embodied in a famous manuscript illustration in the *Book to the Honour of the Caesars* now in the City Library of Bern. This shows the drowned Emperor beneath the waves of the river while a winged angel rising from the water holds a baby wrapped as if for baptism, and offers it up to the hand of God emerging from the orb of heaven.

Barely one hundred miles from the former Christian frontiers they had come to restore, much of the army turned homewards. A contingent continued on to Antioch where they buried the hastily mummified body with due solemnities. From there, Frederick of Swabia led a contingent on to Acre to join the siege lines there, arriving in October.

Given Conrad III's association with the disastrous Second Crusade and the tragic death of the great Emperor Frederick Barbarossa, their compatriots' record as crusaders in the Middle East was long a sensitive issue with German historians. According to a German Renaissance humanist Godfrey of Bouillon led a German army, for another, the failure of the Third Crusade to recapture Jerusalem was simple to explain since only Barbarossa could have defeated Saladin.[14]

But the cause of the Holy Land was everywhere and inevitably enmeshed in politics. When in January 1188, Philip II, King of France and Henry II, King of England, overlord of Wales and lord of Ireland and half France took the Cross they almost at once exercised the option this gave them to levy a tax to finance their expedition. Their subjects were furious and Philip was obliged to withdraw the impost. Henry, on the other hand, monarch of a land which since Anglo-Saxon times had been subject to nationwide taxes, was able to insist on the levy with rigour. In fact the King was sincere in his intentions – this crusading or 'Saladin' tithe was to be collected by local clergy on assessments by the local representatives of the Templars and Hospitallers. But Henry's subjects did not trust his motives and assumed the manoeuvre was simply to raise money for the royal coffers.

When Baldwin, Henry's Archbishop of Canterbury, having taken his crusading vows set out to preach the crusade in the west of England and Wales in February 1188, he too had a private agenda. With the sanction of Rome, Canterbury claimed metropolitan primacy over the Church in Wales, but Welsh churchmen, led by the canons of St David's Cathedral, rejected that claim. They petitioned the dominant local prince, yr Arglwydd Rhys ap Gruffydd ap Rhys, the Lord Rhys of Deheubarth, to obstruct Baldwin's progress and so maintain the independence of the Welsh see.[15] But Rhys valued the title of 'Justiciar' in south Wales, conferred upon him by the English King, and the powers it brought with it. As a good Christian he did not mean to impede Baldwin's mission for Christendom; as a realist in power politics he was not about to affront his mighty royal neighbour who had taken crusader vows; as a man he proved a stay-at-home, because, so said the gossips, his masculine weakness yielded to the feminine charms of Gwenillian, his wife.

Rhys accorded the Archbishop of Canterbury a sumptuous welcome. Baldwin toured all Wales, both north and south, and celebrated Mass as of right at the high altar of all four cathedrals in the province. In addition, he recruited some 3,000 men to the army of the Cross – against the protests of their wives. In at least one place the women tried to stop their menfolk going off to the war by 'snatching away their travelling cloaks'. In fact, quipped the court jester to the Lord Rhys, had the missionaries been able to speak the Welsh language many thousand more men would have answered the call.

Gerald of Barry, or Gerald of Wales, known to history by his Latin name Giraldus Cambrensis, and Baldwin's chief assistant on the preaching tour, would probably have disputed this. Archdeacon of Brecknock and educated at the University of Paris, this talented and colourful man came of an Anglo-Norman aristocratic family and descended through his maternal grandmother from the Norman–Welsh princes of south Wales. Proud in his family's share in the Norman–Welsh invasion of Ireland, he despised what he considered the 'slave-born' English – at that time the underclass in their own country, and vaunted himself a patriotic Welshman. 'No other people than this Welsh race, nor any other language shall answer in the Day of Judgement before the Supreme Judge for this corner of the earth,' he wrote in his account of the mission. As we have seen, there was a respectable body of contemporary opinion, including the Emperor himself, who thought it possible that Judgement Day was not impossibly remote. One hopes that Gerald was practising his Welsh for, as he candidly admits, it was so weak that he had to deliver his call to the Cross in Latin or French. Despite this, again according to Gerald, he spoke to such good effect in Dyfed 'that the majority of the young men and knighthood took the Cross . . . [while] the common people, though they could understand neither language, flocked forward to receive the sign of the Cross'.[16]

Once Richard became king on the death of his father in October 1189, the English exchequer had only one assignment – to raise money to finance the crusade. If he could have found a buyer, he once famously said, he would have sold London itself – and no one doubted that he meant it. An important source of income would be England's Jewish community, under royal protection; that is to say, exclusively reserved for royal exploitation. But the crusading fervour unleashed a surge of anti-semitism. To the King's intense anger his coronation feast was shamefully defiled when the mob at the gates of the banqueting hall seeing, as they thought, a party of wealthy Jews being admitted, ran amok, slaughtered many and then rampaged through the Jewish quarter burning and looting as they went. In fact Richard had ordered no Jews or women be admitted to the hall and none were. A massacre was hardly the way to celebrate a coronation; worse still the destruction of Jewish wealth was a loss to the exchequer. The King ordained special measures for the peace and safety of his Jewish subjects.[17]

Almost as soon as he had left England, from January to March 1190, a wave of pogroms swept the country. At Lynn in Norfolk the perpetrators were mostly young crusaders who plundered their victims and took ship from the port. Elsewhere, such as Stamford in Lincolnshire, the culprits seem to have been the local 'pillars of society', gentry and knights. Apart from anger against these 'enemies of Christ', plundering the Jews was one way of recouping the taxation they had had to pay out towards the crusade.[18]

Many other towns were affected but nowhere so fearfully as York. There one of the wealthiest members of the 500-strong Jewish community had built a house the chronicler William of Newburgh compared to a royal palace. The place was sacked, the family killed and the mob soon ruled the streets. Those Jews who could fled to the castle where the warden, given the royal orders, might be expected to protect them. But the refugees barricaded themselves in a tower and refused to admit him – to find themselves besieged by the sheriff's men and the rioters. After several days, on the night of 16 March, they killed their wives and children, set fire to the tower, and then killed themselves. Incandescent with rage that his exchequer should have been defrauded and his orders flouted, Richard sent a minister to punish the offenders.[19]

As far as his crusading intentions went, Richard, King of England, Lord of Aquitaine, Duke of Normandy and Count of Anjou, called the Lionheart, may have been, in the words of Sir Steven Runciman: 'a bad king, a bad son, a bad husband, and a bad father', but he was not a hypocrite. There is no reason to question the sincerity of his intentions to recover the city of Christ's Passion for Christendom. That he failed to do so was more a consequence of the geographical and political realities of the time than of any military inadequacies in the King himself. For, whatever his other failings, Richard was also, to cite Sir Steven again, a superb soldier. His undoubted courage on the battlefield merited his soubriquet of 'the Lionhearted'; the great fortress, Château Gaillard in Normandy, is an enduring testament to his brilliance as a military architect and his conduct of the campaign in Palestine showed his qualities as a strategist.

When he finally arrived there in June 1191, the Christian presence was limited to the port enclave of Tyre and the battle lines besieging the great city of Acre. These had been the focus for various crusaders from Europe such as Henry of Champagne and Louis of Thuringia who arrived in 1190, and Leopold of Austria in 1191. When he withdrew two years later, the standard of the Cross floated not only over Acre itself but also over strongholds and towns along a coastal strip southward. Jerusalem remained to the Infidel but, largely thanks to Richard, for close on a century the Christian cause had a bridgehead of territory from which its recovery was at least theoretically possible.

But even before he reached Palestine Richard had won an important territory for Catholic Christendom with his capture of Cyprus from the Byzantine Empire. On 24 April 1191, ships of Richard's en route from Rhodes for the coast of Palestine ran before a storm into Cypriot waters. Seeking shelter they were in fact wrecked by the tempestuous weather. Going ashore in the hope of rescue, the mariners and passengers were thrown into prison by the local ruler, Isaac Comnenos. A week later the ship carrying the King's sister and his fiancée, Berengaria of Navarra, came to anchor in the harbour of Limassol, and on 6 May Richard sailed in with the rest of the fleet. Using the inhospitable treatment meted out to the shipwreck refugees as a pretext, the King ordered an attack on Limassol, which fell to his forces the same day. According to a Greek source leading citizens welcomed the invaders. At any rate the unpopular Isaac came to terms with Richard, agreeing to contribute to the crusader's war chest and even, so said some, to join the campaign. The Greek must have considered it a pledge given under duress because, as soon as he and his entourage were clear of Richard's camp, he renounced the treaty and ordered the King of England to quit Cyprus. It was a risky defiance. Already, in his dealings with the Byzantine strongholds in Sicily and southern Italy Richard had proved a ruthless antagonist. Reports had long been circulating in the West of the treaty which Emperor Isaac Angelos had made with Saladin. During his brief stay in southern Italy Richard had captured a number of Byzantine strong-holds in a furious whirlwind campaign which had earned him the Greek nickname of λεοσ, 'the Lion', his first such tribute, but in this case for the ferocity of his campaigning rather than for his personal courage. Now, 'the Lion' turned his attention on the perfidious Greek and in another *Blitzkrieg* lasting just four weeks forced an abject surrender on Isaac at Kantara, the sole condition being that the Cypriot despot should not be put in iron chains. Richard blithely agreed. The huge booty he had already won provided a sufficient surplus of gold and silver to chain a prisoner in a style more befitting a prince. In fact, the proceeds of the campaign enabled Richard to feed his forces and pay them handsomely in silver, distribute largesse to his new liegeman, the refugee King of Jerusalem, Guy de Lusignan, and restock his war chest in anticipation of the coming campaign in Palestine. In fact, Guy and other leaders had come to Limassol some weeks before to swear fealty to the English King but also to plead with him to hasten on to Acre, where the French King, Philip II, was already entrenching his forces. Richard had no intention of quitting Cyprus until he was certain of the subjection of the entire island. The capitulation of Isaac Comnenos gave him his cue. Appointing Robert of Thornham as his 'justiciar' or chief deputy, on 5 June he set sail with his main force for the port of Tyre and then Acre. Comnenos may have been unpopular with the Cypriots – he was said to have golden images to himself erected in the island's churches while the Greek historian Nicetas Choniates denounced him as 'an implacable butcher' – but a Roman Catholic regime was still more so. The Latin chronicler Eracles considered Richard to have been the instrument of divine providence in establishing the rule of the Roman obedience in this ancient home of Orthodoxy.[20]

Soon after Richard's departure Thornham had to suppress an insur-rection and when the Templars offered to buy the place Richard was happy to surrender his conquest for some 40,000 golden dinars and, in addition, free up the troops of the occupying force for service in the Holy Land. But within months the Templars found managing the unruly Cypriots more trouble than it was worth – with King Richard's agreement they sold the place on to Guy de Lusignan. Richard may well have had Cyprus in his sights long before the storms drove his advance squadron into the shelter of Limassol Bay. Like most west-erners, he distrusted the Greeks, and Greek governors of Cyprus had been less than cooperative with earlier crusading fleets. Cape St

Andreas, the island's most easterly point, was barely a day's sail from the Syrian coast and a friendly Cyprus would be a major asset for the Latin West in future designs for the recovery of the Holy Land.

After Richard's conquest, the place never returned to Byzantine control. The execution of Richard's designs assured a Latin foothold in the eastern Mediterranean even after their expulsion from Palestine. In the view of the American scholar Richard Brundage, in his article 'Richard the Lion-heart and Byzantium', 'Richard thus made it possible to prolong the Holy War for nearly two centuries after the final fall of Acre.'[21] And we know from a comment by his secretary Baha al-Din that Saladin was greatly put out by Richard's conquest of the island since his own alliance with Constantinople had had as one of its objectives the prevention of just such a union of Cypriot and Frankish interests. As for Isaac Comnenos, Richard handed him over to the custody of the Knights Hospitallers in their fortress of Margat while the despot's daughter entered a kind of house arrest in the entourage of Richard's Queen, Berengaria.

Saladin had in fact been anticipating Richard's arrival in Palestine with a degree of trepidation. An English advance guard had already arrived at Acre under Baldwin, Archbishop of Canterbury. His intelligence service, much better informed about the Christian world than his predecessors, briefed him that while the King of France was to be the Christian supremo in the coming conflict, and that Richard technically ranked below him (Richard owed Philip feudal homage for his duchies of Normandy and Aquitaine), he was one of their 'mightiest princes . . . that his wealth, reputation and valour were greater' and that he had a 'burning passion for war'. For weeks past Frankish officers dealing with the Muslim camp had been bragging that once the King of England arrived they would begin the real and final siege of Acre. On Saturday, 13 jumada in the Muslim calendar, or to follow the account of *The Itinerary of King Richard*, on 8 June 'in Pentecost week' in the Christian calendar, 'the desired of all nations' arrived at the siege lines of Acre. The King of France and 'all the chiefs and mighty men' of the army went out to welcome him 'with joy and exultation'. He had a fleet of twenty-five ships full of men at arms and equipment; trumpets brayed along the shore and that night bonfires blazed between the tents of the Christian camp.

The following day Richard was confined to bed but, though sick, he was soon directing the design, placement and construction of more siege engines. One, which lobbed its stone missiles into the very heart of the city, was said to have killed twelve men with a single shot. The defenders had to service their artillery, man the walls, clear the fosse and crew the ships in the harbour with reduced forces on a twenty-four-hour basis, while their enemy, fighting in shifts, kept up a continuous offensive. And now, the walls the Franks had built around their own army against Saladin's relieving force had been perfected to be almost impregnable.

On 4 July a swimmer from the city got through to Saladin's camp with a message from the defenders. If nothing concrete was done to relieve the pressure, the city would be offered to the Franks in exchange for the lives of the garrison. The garrison commanders, two of Saladin's most trusted friends, opened negotiations. Over the next few days, apart from contingents of Kurds who launched repeated attacks on the Christian trenches, morale in Saladin's camp plummeted. The crusaders carried on negotiations with the city and the army simultaneously. Emissaries from Richard, who visited the camp during lulls in the fighting, reported back on the mood there – while also taking the opportunity to buy fresh fruit from market traders.

On 12 July the city negotiators, dealing with Conrad of Tyre, agreed sensational terms. In return for their lives, the lives of the citizens, and those of the garrison, the commanders yielded the city and its contents, the ships in its harbour, several hundred prisoners, the True Cross and, in addition to all this, a ransom of 200,000 dinars; some 3,000 of the defenders were to be held as hostages to ensure the terms were met. Conrad collected a cool 4,000 gold pieces for handling the transaction. The first Saladin heard of the terms was a notification of the done deal sent by dispatch swimmer; he is said to have wept in fury and frustration. The True Cross, for him an idolaters' bauble, was to his enemies a treasure almost beyond price and was, in any case, in his keeping; the immense ransom would beggar his already over-taxed war chest; while the surrender of the fleet seemed quite gratuitous.

The victorious kings proceeded to install themselves in the city – King Philip in the former mansion of the Templars, its outer bastion washed by the sea at the tip of the peninsula; King Richard in the former royal palace near the north wall of the city. Not all, however, was sweetness and light. Duke Leopold V of Austria, who had recently arrived from Venice to captain the rump of the German crusaders left leaderless by the death of Frederick of Swabia in January, and who saw himself as the deputy for the late great Emperor and Lord of

Christendom, Frederick Barbarossa, claimed equal standing with the King of France and certainly with the French Duke and Count who called himself King of England. He ordered his standard planted next to Richard's on the ramparts. Within hours it had been wrenched from its socle and hurled down into the fosse. A flame-haired, deep-chested and athletic six-footer, Richard was reputedly descended from Melusine the Devil's daughter. Like all his family, he was dangerously hot-tempered and that day he made an enemy for life – the immediate result was the departure of the Austrian contingent from the crusading army.

Negotiations with Saladin were still in progress. Eventually he ratified the agreement made in his name and on 11 August delivered the first of three ransom instalments plus a group of the stipulated prisoners. But Richard was less interested in a complete ransom payment than the balance of military advantage. Calculating that the Turkish defenders were too numerous to be guarded and too valuable as soldiers to be restored to the enemy, on the pretext of suspecting Saladin's good faith, on 20 August he had 2,700 of the hostages systematically beheaded on the plains outside the city, by willing fanatics from his own army. It was a barbarity which more than matched the ceremonial killing of the Templars on Saladin's orders years before and reminds us that for his contemporaries, the 'Lion' in Richard's name signified the man's ferocity as much as his courage in battle.

Two days after the massacre of the Turkish prisoners, Richard led the army out of Acre on the coast road heading south for Jaffa (Tel-Aviv Yafo). It was the best part of sixty miles, at the height of the Mediterranean summer and with eight river crossings. For two weeks the Christians marched doggedly on in three divisions parallel to the sea, the fleet with its supplies coasting down on their right, a massive Muslim force tracking them from the vantage of the low range of hills on their left. They made barely five miles a day in what was the classic crusader battle manoeuvre: engaging the enemy on the march. The outer left-hand column of foot, relying on its shields and heavy armour, and the heavy felt jerkins beneath it, took the weight of the daily Muslim attacks and was periodically refreshed by contingents changing stations from the protected right-hand coastal column marching with the baggage train. In the centre the cavalry, Templars in the van, Hospitallers in the rear, their horses sheltered from Turkish arrows, guarded the 'standard' – a wagon with a tower mounted on it from which floated a great banner. The rearguard took the brunt of the action fending off attack after attack, sometimes having to regroup desperately so as not to lose touch with the army. The crusaders' detachments of crossbows took a heavy toll but there were not enough of them. To the angry admiration of their enemies at 'the patience displayed by these people' the army kept formation. The ranks held firm thanks to one man. Richard the Ferocious or Courageous, the 'Lionheart', also maintained the tightest discipline, barking orders to hold the line, or charging almost alone, his immense sword flailing to beat back any Turkish squadron that threatened to breach it.

On 30 August the crusaders reached Caesarea and a week later they were at the port of Arsuf (Arsur). Here the coastal plain widened to give additional manoeuvrability to the Turkish horsemen and here the running action blew up into a major battle. Over the blaring trumpets and clatter of kettledrums (Turkish, *nakrs*), over a tumult of rattles, gongs and cymbals, rang out the battle cries of Turks, Arabs, Bedouin and Blacks. Saladin, oblivious to the arrow shower and accompanied by two pages leading reserve horses, rode slowly along the front line, urging his men on to break the enemy formation. The Christian knights began to falter; at battle pitch after weeks of holding station and swallowing their pride they begged King Richard permission for the charge – in fact all along the line scattered groups were already breaking through the wall of infantry. It came a minute or two before Richard's ideal timing but, seeing he could no longer restrain the knights he gathered and led the charge with a vast momentum that shattered the Muslim ranks and sent the enemy troopers flying for their lives. Saladin was left to rally his forces to prevent a rout.

The Christians had not won a crushing victory – though they were free now to proceed to Jaffa – but Saladin had suffered a great moral defeat. On the Horns of Hattin he had destroyed a Christian army and after weeks of planning and manoeuvring had forced it into a position of multiple disadvantage. Arsuf suggested that without such preparation the defeat of a crusading army – well armed, well disciplined, professionally led – was beyond the resources at his disposal. Intimidated by Richard's triumph and perhaps fearful of the fate of the defenders at Acre, the people of Jaffa opened their gates. With Jaffa once more Christian, Jerusalem itself now seemed in danger. Saladin fell back prepared to block Richard's road to the city.

But now there was a hiatus. Secure behind the walls of Jaffa, the army was recuperating, and 'lovely Frankish women' were once more in demand. Saladin had looked on in dismay at Richard's easy capture of the place. What if Ascalon should fall? The Christians might use it for an offensive against Egypt, so he took advantage of the lull in hostilities to dismantle the fortifications. His brother's capture of Ascalon had been one of the proudest moments of the 1187 campaign – to destroy it was a bitter admission of weakness, and was also a grim vindication of Richard's brutality at Acre. He could find no one willing to garrison the place – for fear of what happened to Acre.

It seemed Richard held the initiative, but he too had problems. With Philip of France back in Europe he was worried about the security of his own vast French dominions, even though in theory they were protected by the immunity extended to crusaders. And there were doubts about the army. Many had drifted back to Acre, where the living was good; many more looked upon themselves as pilgrims pledged to fight their way through to the Holy City, visit its shrines and then be free to return home. This was not a formula for long-term reconquest. In the middle of October Richard opened negotiations with Saladin's brother al-Adil whom he looked upon as a 'brother and friend'. As an initial bargaining position he demanded Jerusalem and all the lands between the coast and the River Jordan; also the actual handing over of the True Cross. Compromise was obviously expected – it was a startling one. The essential condition was nothing less than a marriage between King Richard's sister Joanna, Dowager Queen of Sicily, and al-Adil himself. It was proposed they would rule jointly from Jerusalem and with the exception of the lands held by the Knights Templar, she was to receive the homage of all the lands in Palestine under Richard's control; al-Adil was to be made lord of all the lands in Palestine presently held by Saladin. The Sultan gave his consent to this astounding line of diplomacy, confident that Richard would never consent, but he was quite wrong. Richard's only worry was that the Pope would not give his consent, and if he did not, then Richard would be happy for one of his nieces to take his sister's place as bride. His sister seems to have objected forcibly to marrying an infidel – and one must wonder whether Saladin would ever have allowed a brother of his to marry an unbeliever. The bizarre project came to nothing but the Sultan was also approached with a treasonable proposal from Conrad of Montferrat, lord of Tyre. He was proposing to betray Acre to Saladin's forces if he was guaranteed the lordship of Sidon and Beirut. But with winter advancing, Saladin had to release the Eastern contingents of his army to return to their homes. He retired upon Jerusalem. Torrential rains and churning mud seemed to make serious campaigning impossible. Even so, the crusaders made camp within twelve miles of the walls. In the first week of January 1192 the hills around the Holy City were lashed by storms that snapped the crusaders' tent poles and turned the roads into mud trenches. With the object of their pilgrimage so close the morale of the Christian troops was as high as ever it had been.

A week later, Saladin's scouts reported that the army was trudging back down the road to Ramlah. The decision to withdraw had stretched Richard's authority almost to breaking point. Militarily it was unarguable. Even if the army had taken Jerusalem, it would have melted away as the pilgrims fulfilled their vows, leaving the city to be retaken by the Muslims. Now, bitter and resentful, through driving hail and snow, over quagmires and swamps that dragged down men and horses, those same pilgrim troopers were marching away, under orders, beaten without a battle. The bulk of the French contingent went off angrily to Jaffa to live at their ease, others to Acre, others to take service with Conrad at Tyre. Now was the time for Saladin to strike, but the weather made campaigning impossible. It was not only conditions underfoot. Saladin's principal arm was his archers – rain like this would soon have slackened their bowstrings. He could only wait in the hope that the weather would improve until the contingents on seasonal leave should return. It is a telling tribute to the Kurdish hero's reputation among his enemies that there were Christians who attributed his inaction to his chivalry.

Events did not stand still. Richard, determined to be active in the cause of the Holy Land, marched to Ascalon, ruined and undefendable as it was. His men could barely enter the place for the piles of broken masonry and rubble left by Saladin's labourers. But four months later, by May 1192, the fortifications were once more in place and Ascalon once more a defensible Christian garrison town. Yet it did Richard little good. The French contingent led by the Duke of Burgundy was still sulking, while the Pisans had taken over Acre in the name of King Guy and were being besieged by the combined forces of their rivals the Genoans, allied with Conrad at Tyre. The crusaders and the Franks of Outremer were doing Saladin's work for him and the cause of Jerusalem languished.

Richard was increasingly anxious to negotiate terms with his Christians and with Saladin that would release him with honour from his obligations in the Holy Land. He was hearing disquieting reports of conflicts between his ministers in England and his ambitious brother Prince John. On Palm Sunday, 29 March, at a ceremony of much splendour, he girded al-Adil's son with the belt of knighthood. Saladin was offering to restore many Christian lands as well as finally to hand over the True Cross. Jerusalem itself would remain in Muslim hands but Western pilgrims would be allowed access to the Holy Places and Latin priests were to have the guardianship of them.

The following month Richard met in council to settle the dispute over the Crown of Jerusalem. He had favoured Guy of Lusignan, husband of the dead Queen Sibylla but when the council voted unanimously for Conrad of Montferrat, husband of Queen Isabella, the King of England gave his agreement. However on 28 April 1192 Conrad was killed by two Assassins acting on the orders of Sinan, 'the Old Man of the Mountains', from his mountain castle at Masyaf. Rumour soon fingered Richard as having 'commissioned' a contract killing from Sinan. But since the Assassin leader had his own reasons and since Richard made no attempt to force Guy of Lusignan's claim to the Kingdom, it seems unlikely he was involved. In fact, when Conrad's widow Queen Isabella married Henry of Champagne within a week of his death, Richard recognized him as king. Richard had postponed his return home and in mid May, advancing from Ascalon down the coast to the important fortress town of Darum, he seized the place. From there, he once again marched on Jerusalem and camped his army outside the walls.

The army were to enjoy one final success. News came that a large caravan was making its way up from Egypt and approaching the Holy City. Saladin's secretary tells us that King Richard himself reconnoitred the ground, disguised as an Arab. The result was a surprise attack and plunder which included hundreds of horses and camels. Saladin now resigned himself to a new siege. He sent out parties to poison the wells and water courses, and convened a council of war to prepare for an attack. Instead, news came that the enemy had broken camp. Nothing had happened to alter the realities – Jerusalem could not be held even if captured – so Richard accepted a decision by the army leaders to abandon the attempt. On Sunday, 5 July he ordered the retreat and Saladin, with his emirs, rode out to watch their enemy trudging disconsolately away southwards. Richard, bent on an early embarkation, now heard that Saladin had attacked Jaffa. The exhausted messenger had not completed his report before the King was rallying his forces in a U-turn decision and on 31 July a fleet of galleys was seen off the coast at Jaffa. Meanwhile Saladin had seized the city and forced the garrison to retire to the citadel. Seeing the Muslim banners on the walls of the city, Richard reconsidered. A soldier from the garrison swam over to the King's ship and told him the place was still being held, while negotiating terms of surrender. Waiting no longer and still wearing his sailor's deck shoes, the King plunged into the sea followed by some eighty knights. From the fortifications the negotiators watched nonplussed as they cleared the harbour of Kurdish and Turkish troops and by evening Jaffa once more seemed to be a Christian city. But his enemy was weak and Saladin refused to concede the position. As dawn broke on Wednesday, 5 August, a Genoese sentry in Richard's camp heard the sound of horses and the chink of armour beyond the lines. Still dragging on their armour and reaching for their swords, fifty-four knights led by Richard dashed to the perimeter, defended by a low palisade of sharpened tent pegs, and were quickly joined by some 2,000 Italian crossbowmen. The knights, shields on arms, stood in pairs, their lances pointing towards the oncoming horsemen, while behind them stood the archers. The crossbow fire was withering and the lance wall held – Saladin with his 7,000 horse could not break through into the camp; the city too was held. Yet again Saladin fell back, resigned, on Jerusalem, but this time Richard had no plans for a siege. Negotiations were opened at Ramlah. Richard had to concede Ascalon but the coastal territory from Acre down to and including Jaffa was to remain in Christian hands. For his army, the most valuable concession by Saladin was to allow all who wanted to make the pilgrimage to the Holy Places. During the weeks that followed, hundreds of crusaders seized the opportunity – including, to Richard's irritation, the French who had refused their help at the retaking of Jaffa, but who Saladin declined to exclude. As to Richard himself, he rejected all the appeals of his advisers, among them Hubert Walter, Bishop of Salisbury to visit the sacred shrines, since it had pleased God to deny him the reconquest of the place for Christendom. One feels that Richard was rather put out by the Almighty, but the Bishop had no such scruples. Indeed he accepted an invitation by Saladin to a private conference where they had a long conversation in which the Sultan enquired after the nature of the English King and the Bishop was shown the True Cross. Finally,

Saladin invited Walter to name a favour. The prelate asked for time to think and returned the next day to request that Latin priests be allowed to conduct Roman Catholic rites at the Holy Sepulchre. We are told that he had been shocked to find the Christian rituals only half celebrated after the barbarous Syrian fashion. Saladin was no doubt happy to agree – he knew full well of the tensions between the various Christian Churches and would be content if the Christian cause remain divided even in its holiest shrines.

Richard sailed from Palestine in October, his journey home bound to be hazardous. He could hardly expect a safe passage through France to Normandy – King Philip had abandoned the crusade ahead of his rival precisely with the intention of driving him from his French lands and making trouble for him in every way possible. The eastern route, to England, lay through the lands of the Empire to a North Sea crossing. But Emperor Henry VI was furious that Richard had recognized Tancred as King of Sicily by the Treaty of Messina, while Leopold of Austria's vendetta against the Lionheart was notorious. Only simpletons supposed that these high and mighty princes would observe the immunity which Richard could claim as a returning crusader.

When his ship was wrecked by a storm in the Adriatic he decided on the German alternative. He and his entourage donned the shapeless robes and cowls of monks. They made good progress through the alpine passes but Richard was immensely tall and his entourage could not break the habit of deference. A giant monk treated by his companions as a seigneur alerted the suspicions of a Tyrolean innkeeper. The man sent word to Duke Leopold and the King was seized and incarcerated. Besides slighting the ducal standard, Richard had humiliated one of Leopold's kinsmen – Isaac Comnenos, driven from Cyprus by the arrogant King, was related to his mother's family. In fact, Leopold had to sell his ransom right to his imperial overlord but, with the rest of Christendom, could sit back to the spectacle of the Champion of the Faith being recycled as a trading commodity by the Holy Roman Emperor. The haggle stretched over months, Prince John and Philip of France both manoeuvring to delay Richard's release. The terms were finally set at 150,000 silver marks and a ceremony of homage in which the King recognized the imperial overlordship of England. Still beautiful and imperious, a veteran crusader and

England's queen mother, the seventy-year-old Eleanor of Aquitaine accompanied the bullion convoy conveying the first massive instalment to Cologne and conducted her son back to London. Astounded by the wealth of the city, the imperial knights who provided the honour escort declared that had their master been better informed the price would have been double.

8

The Fourth Crusade:
The Latin Conquest of Constantinople
and the Scandal of Christendom

In August 1198 the thirty-six-year-old Pope Innocent III, elected the previous January, was preparing the ground for a new crusade. Few popes have come to the tiara with such unquestioned authority, in part because of the unstable situation in Rome but principally because of his towering personal abilities – the cardinals had chosen him after just two ballots on the very day of his predecessor's death. His decision to sponsor a campaign in aid of Jerusalem, which even the combined efforts of the kings of England and France and the Emperor had failed to liberate, augured well; and the time was opportune for a papal initiative. The centuries-old dream of a union of the Eastern and Western Churches under Rome might once more be open for discussion. Alexius III, the cruel and insecure Byzantine Emperor who had three years earlier ousted his brother Isaac II Angelus, blinding him and throwing him into prison along with his young son also called Alexius, was said to be prepared to consider the union of the Churches in his search for allies abroad to buttress his position at home.[1] In the West there was a temporary power vacuum on the international scene. Rivalry between Richard I of England and Philip II of France was compounded by the prospect of civil war in the Empire where technically the succession lay with a four-year-old

143

boy, Frederick of Hohenstaufen, King of Sicily and heir to Emperor Henry VI.

In a brief six-year reign, Henry, whose wife was heiress to the Norman Kingdom of Sicily, had won virtually total control of Italy, including the papal territories, and had opened the prospect of seizing the Byzantine Empire from the faltering and faction-ridden court at Constantinople. The idea of the two empires, East and West, united under the German Crown (a secular equivalent of the union of the Churches under Rome), had been mooted as serious politics by Henry's father, Frederick I Barbarossa. In a letter to the Byzantine Emperor Manuel I in 1176, following the latter's crushing defeat by the Seljuk Turks at the Battle of Myriocephalon, he had claimed not only that he derived his power from the 'glorious Roman emperors', but also that it was his duty to rule 'the Greek kingdom'. His son Henry died of malaria at Messina in September 1197 in the midst of preparations for a crusade which most informed people in the West supposed was aimed as much at Constantinople as well as Jerusalem, although the targets had not been declared.

With Henry's death, the international conjuncture was once again fluid. The German princes, ignoring the rights of Henry's child heir, Frederick of Sicily, lined up between two rivals for the German kingship. One group elected his uncle, Philip of Hohenstaufen, Duke of Swabia; the other elected Otto, Duke of Brunswick (also, incidentally, Earl of York – he was a nephew of Richard I of England). Both of these men aimed to receive coronation at the hands of the Pope, which would create them emperor. But Pope Innocent deeply feared Hohenstaufen's ambitions. A union of the crowns of Sicily and the Empire would threaten the papal territories in central Italy like a vice. He was also suspicious of Philip's involvement in Byzantine affairs through his wife Irene, daughter of ex-Emperor Isaac II Angelus. At first, he favoured Otto for the Empire, on certain conditions. Meanwhile, Innocent's realization that the Hohenstaufen family's ideas for a crusade had mixed motives was a further factor in his own decision to initiate the expedition.

Like many others, Innocent believed that the Third Crusade's failure before Jerusalem had been the outcome of princely rivalries and he wanted any new venture systematically planned and directed from Rome. But if he wanted control he also wanted manpower. He wrote to Europe's sovereigns, hoping to shame them into support:

Where is your God, say our enemies, 'we have violated your sanctuaries . . . we have taken the cradle of your superstition . . . we have shattered the lances of France, frustrated the efforts of the English and the vigour of the Germans . . . all that is left is for us to exterminate the remnant of the defenders you have left in our land and then drive you from your own lands.'[2]

Of all Europe's Roman Catholic monarchs only the King of Hungary took the Cross, though he was shortly to rue the decision.

In less emotive, more practical terms, Innocent also wrote to the Patriarch of Jerusalem, now resident in Acre, asking him to provide a survey of the state of affairs in the Levant and particularly the strengths and weaknesses of the Muslim states. He was already probing the commitment of Emperor Alexius III in the matter of Church union. They made an almost melodramatic contrast. The Western pontiff, convinced in his every action of being the agent of God's purpose on earth; the Emperor, unpopular, cruel and devious, aware perhaps of the historic dignity of his office but motivated only by self-interest. Addressing Innocent as one of 'the only two world powers: the single Roman Church and the single Empire', he had urged that they must unite against any increase in the power of the 'western emperor, our rival'. But as the correspondence continued Alexius was to argue that the imperial power was higher than the spiritual, while in a fit of pique the Pope at one point even threatened to support the deposed Isaac II, even though this would have meant favouring Philip of Swabia and his wife Irene.[3]

Such diplomatic speculations were probably never much more than that. But in 1199, the Pope announced an important practical measure, with the first levy on clerical incomes. A new kind of tax, this would form a precedent for all future papal income tax. Pope Innocent, no doubt wary of the kind of high-flown oratory of the great churchmen like St Bernard, who had led the propaganda campaign in the Second and Third Crusades, and advised, it seems, by a senior member of the University of Paris, also innovated in the area of public relations, authorizing a simple clergyman as the lead preacher for the forthcoming expedition. Fulk, 'a man of saintly character' and priest of the parish of Neuilly, between Paris and Lagny-sur-Marne, was already admired in the Île de France and its surrounding region for his simple evangelical eloquence in the *langue d'oeil* vernacular of northern France. This was also calculated to please Pope Innocent, already exercised by the growing threat of the Cathar heresy in southern France (see Chapter 9). Fulk called upon would-be crusaders for personal moral regeneration, but also took practical steps to raise considerable sums for charity, to assist poorer participants. Apparently his mission was followed by that of a cardinal legate, one Pietro da Capua, who had himself taken the Cross: 'to proclaim on his Holiness's behalf an indulgence framed as follows: All those who take the Cross and remain for one year in the service of God in the army shall obtain remission of any sins they have committed, provided they have confessed them . . . [on account of this indulgence] were moved to take the Cross.'[4]

In November of that year, at a great tournament held at the castle of Ecry in Champagne the host, Count Thibaut (Theobald) III of Champagne, took the Cross. He was just twenty-two years old, and the brother of the young, handsome and wealthy Henry of Champagne whom Queen Isabella of Jerusalem had chosen as her third husband in succession to the ill-fated Conrad of Montferrat, murdered in a revenge killing by the Assassins some years before. Count Louis of Blois, also in his twenties, took the Cross too. They were to be followed by numerous nobles 'of the highest rank', among them Simon de Montfort and Count Baldwin of Flanders, a man from a family with a long tradition of crusading, as well as men of the second rank such as Geoffrey of Villehardouin, the Marshal of Champagne. Geoffrey was to keep a detailed chronicle, obviously written with inside knowledge of the leaders' deliberations, and a prime source for our knowledge of the expedition.

After indecisive meetings at Soissons and Compiègne in 1200 the barons appointed six deputies, among them Villehardouin, to plan the expedition with full powers on their behalf. The expedition was to take the sea route and the deputies were dispatched to Venice to negotiate terms for transporting the army. It was a fateful decision. Along with Genoa and Pisa, then a coastal port before the silting up of the Arno estuary, the Venetian Republic was one of the Big Three commercial powers in the eastern Mediterranean. It already had a string of trading dependencies along the Adriatic coast, flourishing trade links with the Muslim world and, like its rivals, privileged concessions in Constantinople and other Byzantine cities. It also had a grudge. Back in the 1170s the Emperor Manuel had on the flimsiest of pretexts ordered the arrest of all Venetian merchants within his domains and the confiscation of their goods. The city's war fleet, sent to exact reprisals, had to break off hostilities because of an epidemic among the crews[5] and although, over the years, relations had been to some extent normalized, the city's precarious dependency on the arbitrary goodwill of the emperors rankled. And, in practical terms, Venice seems to have been demanding arrears in compensation and a return to the monopoly position it once enjoyed in Byzantine territory. Among the Venetian envoys who had been involved in the troubles one, Enrico Dandolo, was now head of the Republic's affairs.

It seems to have been at Venice as well that the organizing committee not only negotiated the shipping contract for the expedition, but also decided upon its immediate objective. Cairo (called 'Babylon' by the crusaders), it was agreed, should first be captured 'because from there the Turks could be more easily crushed than from any other part of their territory'.[6] Theorists had discussed the pros and cons of such strategy for some years. Before he left Palestine, Richard the Lionheart is said to have advised that Egypt was the key to the 'Saracen empire'. Egypt was certainly the chief Muslim power in the eastern Mediterranean; if it could be conquered the Muslim powers in Palestine, lacking support from the south, would, it was reasoned, have to capitulate. If Egypt were not taken, any Christian reconquests in the Holy Land would be under constant threat. However, while Cairo made good sense as a strategic target, the mass of the army had taken its vows with the pilgrimage to Jerusalem in mind. So the leaders kept the real destination 'a closely guarded secret: to the public at large it was merely announced that we were going oversea'.[7]

The ordinary pilgrim was not the only one who would object to this change of plan. Venice, as we have seen, had its own interests at stake in Egypt. In fact, it would be alleged soon after the debacle of the crusade, that the Venetians had already had dealings with the Egyptian Sultan al-Adil, before the crusaders arrived. By the terms of a secret treaty contracted between the Sultan and Venetian envoys in Cairo in May 1202, in exchange for their assurance that they would divert any planned attack on his territory, he apparently guaranteed them their own autonomous trading quarter in Alexandria and other privileges. From the start, then, there were conspiracy theorists who argued that the diversion of the crusaders to their attack on Constantinople was the fruit of a conspiracy between Venice and the Egyptian Sultan, agreed after the Franks had negotiated the terms of their transport with the Republic but before they arrived there in October 1202.

When, in the 1860s, the German historian Carl Hopf claimed to have found the very document of this treaty, dated 13 May 1202, that is some four months before the first crusaders arrived at Venice, the theory of the 'Great Betrayal' seemed to have moved from the province of rhetoric to that of proven historical fact. But the crucial document was no new discovery, rather it was a known but undated manuscript which Hopf had propelled into a new significance by attributing to it, on faulty evidence, the damning date. Further research in unimpeachable Arabic sources revealed beyond question that in May 1202 al-Adil was not conducting diplomacy in Egypt but rather was on military campaign in Syria. But while it does not prove collusion the document embodies the undoubted fact that Venetian interests lay in persuading the crusaders, if at all possible, not to attack Egypt. Events were to conspire in their favour and they were quick to exploit accidents as well as 'create facts' that furthered their objective without the need to do actual dirty deals with the Infidel. The terms of the shipping contract indicated that from the start the Venetians and the crusaders, the crusade leaders and the pilgrim soldiers had different agendas. Since the Venetians and their leader Doge Dandolo were the only party with a clear-sighted understanding of their self-interest and the singleness of purpose to realize it, they were the party that emerged successful.

At this time the Venetian Doge had real power. Already in his eighties when he came to office in June 1192, Dandolo was hale and hearty and in full possession of his considerable mental faculties, though visually handicapped to the point of blindness 'because of an old injury to his head', according to Villehardouin, who came to be a friend. Dandolo could look back on twenty years of service to the state, including missions to the Venetian quarter in Constantinople and, as ambassador, the Kingdom of Sicily. In April 1201, he proposed a contract whereby Venice would build shipping to transport a cavalry force comprising 4,500 knights and 9,000 men at arms, plus 20,000 infantry. The global fee of 85,000 marks was also to include nine months' supplies and fodder for men and horses. In addition, 'for the love of God', the Republic would supply fifty additional armed galleys on condition that it receive half of everything that was won either by land or sea. This business contract also entailed an association formed 'to act for the service of God and Christendom' wherever that action might be.[8] From the outset, whatever the motives of the crusaders, the Venetians were thinking in terms of conquest for profit. In any case, their merchant bankers were in business. The ship-builders in the arsenal expected money up front before a single keel could be laid down. Accordingly, we are told, the barons' deputies had to borrow 5,000 silver marks 'from people in the city'.

Geoffrey returned home to find his young lord, Thibaut, ill with a mysterious malady of which he died a few days later. He had rallied briefly at the news that the crusade was now practical politics. The search was on for a new leader. The choice fell, at Geoffrey's sugges-tion so he tells us, on Count Boniface of Montferrat (Italian, Monferrato), whose father had fallen prisoner to Saladin at the Battle of Hattin. Now in his early fifties Boniface, who counted leading troubadours among his friends,[9] certainly had interesting connections in the crusader world. Through his brother Conrad, the late king regent of Jerusalem, he was uncle to the heiress to that kingdom, while his younger brother Rainier, then eighteen years old, had married Maria Comnena, daughter of the Emperor Manuel I Comnenus. Honoured with the title Caesar, some compensation, perhaps, for the fact that his bride, though an imperial princess, was twelve years his senior, he died just two years later, murdered, along with Maria and hundreds of others, in the bloodbath of Latins at Constantinople in 1182, which encouraged the coup by Andronicus I Comnenus against Manuel's young son Alexius II. In the words of a twentieth-century Russian historian the massacre 'watered the seed of fanatic enmity between West and East'. It can hardly have inspired the house of Montferrat with a sympathetic understanding of the Byzantine world. Moreover, Boniface laid vague claim to honours and, he believed, land granted by Emperor Manuel to his dead brother.[10]

Boniface spent that Christmas as the guest of Philip of Swabia, a distant cousin, at Haguenau in Austria. Philip had ambitions to become emperor in the West and had reason to hate the present regime in Constantinople, since it had deposed and blinded his father-in-law. Bearing in mind that gossip rumoured Doge Dandolo had lost his sight not in an accident but as the result of a punishment blinding by the Byzantine authorities, and that the Republic was pursuing claims for compensation against the corrupt regime of Alexius III, it is apparent that top decision makers in the crusaders' councils had interests other than the service of Christ and the Holy Land.

By degrees, the various strands of crusaders made their way south-wards – but not all to Venice, the agreed port of departure. In fact, a number of leaders took ship directly from French ports or travelled by other routes so that when the muster was taken in Venice in October 1202 barely a third of the force expected reported. At about the same time news reached the army of the death of Fulk of Neuilly to the general grief of all the people, many of whom had been able to pay their way only thanks to his charitable fund-raising. For the leaders, however, a more pressing problem was the shortfall of passage money. It had been impossible to put in place a mechanism to collect money in advance from those leaders who had pledged themselves to the Venice rendezvous and now the Venetians were insisting on the full contracted payment up front before they would ship a single contingent. Since, by definition, the numbers to be transported were fewer than anticipated it should have been possible to come to a compromise. But Dandolo demanded his payment in full.

There was, it turned out, a possible deal on the table. The crusaders could discharge their debt by assisting the city in the capture of the Hungarian port of Zara (Zadar, in modern Croatia). A former Venetian dependency, the place had rebelled back in 1186 and put itself under the protection of the King of Hungary, but the Venetians were determined to recover their colony. It was a Christian city subject to a Roman Catholic monarch who himself had taken the Cross. Pope Innocent had forbidden any attack on Christians in set terms. There were even crusaders who protested they would endanger their pilgrim vows, and, truth to tell, it seemed impossible to imagine a worse offence against such vows. A small number of crusaders honourably refused to accept the revised plan and sailed direct for the Holy Land, but the main fleet set sail from its moorings on the island of St Nicholas on the Lido, its course set for Zara.

In his journal of the expedition the pilgrim knight Robert of Clari describes the spectacle as 'the finest since the beginning of the world'. The great flotilla, sails set, banners snapping on their halyards in the wind from the galley poops, seemed like a sheet of flickering fire across the sea. At the pilgrims' request the priests chanted the *Veni creator spiritus* ('Come Holy Ghost our Hearts Inspire') from the vessels' prows, while from every direction the blare and bray of ships' trumpeters and the clatter and roll of war tabor and kettle drum filled the sky with their signal calls and fanfares. Each of the leaders had a ship for himself and his entourage and his private horse transport. Most dazzling sight of all was the Doge's galley in its vermilion livery and its vermilion awning of fine silk providing a canopy for the imposing figure of the old man, his four trumpeters sounding their silver trumpets before him. The expedition arrived off Zara on 10 November. The beauty of the place, 'enclosed by its high walls and lofty towers', stirred the pilgrims' hearts with admiration and intimidated them too. Geoffrey de Villehardouin measured the challenge the town presented against the weaponry and resources stowed in the ships. He was a military commander of experience and proven ability and was well pleased with what had been assembled. Included were more than 300 pieces of siege artillery – stone throwers of various types – in addition to fine, strong warhorses, which emerged from the specially designed transports sturdy and in good health. The military mind may have been pleased with the arrangements. Pope Innocent most definitely was not. His directions had been flouted but now, rather than jeopardize the long-term objective, which he still supposed to be the Holy Land, he had sent a letter that gave a conditional absolution to the crusaders, though not to the Venetians whom he declared excommunicate. As the attack began, it was observed that the defenders had festooned the city walls with show shields,[11] displaying the sign of the cross.

After a short siege, Zara surrendered on the understanding that garrison and inhabitants were to be spared. The place was first pillaged and then razed to the ground. The Pope's demands that the demolition be halted and that the King of Hungary be compensated were ignored. The crusaders, Franks and Venetians were excommunicated and while the ban on the Franks was lifted that on the Venetians was not. However, Innocent did not forbid intercourse between them so crusaders and Venetians continued to collaborate. They passed the winter at Zara and, during this time, their leaders passed the point of no return in their collaboration with Venice. The spoils of Zara had not been sufficient either to discharge the debt owing to Venice or to meet the running expenses of the crusaders, who were for the most part penniless. It was at this point that envoys arrived from Philip of Swabia who, engrossed in his struggle with Otto of Brunswick, had remained in Germany. But he was still concerned for the fate of his father-in-law and sent this embassy to Boniface of Montferrat, leader of the crusaders in Zara with an offer of help – on condition that the army diverted to Constantinople.

In April 1195 at Constantinople, the Emperor Isaac Angelus had been deposed in a palace coup mounted by his brother who assumed the purple as Alexius III. Isaac suffered the customary cruel fate of deposed emperors, being blinded and thrown into prison. With him was his son Alexius. At some time, probably in 1202, Alexius contrived to escape and made his way to the West seeking support for the restoration of his father. The exact timing of his itinerary is unclear, but he found a sympathetic hearing at the court of Duke Philip of Swabia, possibly from Pope Innocent and more importantly from Boniface of Montferrat, who may have heard about the Byzantine's proposals from Duke Philip. In return for their military help in restoring him and his father to power in Constantinople, Alexius was prepared to fund the army's current expenses, contribute substantially to the conquest of Egypt which would follow, himself go with them to fight in Egypt and, in addition, maintain at his own expense 500 knights in the Holy Land as long as he should live. With an eye no doubt to papal support, he further pledged he would, first and foremost, enforce the submission of the Orthodox Church to Rome; it was then decided that come the spring they should sail, not for Egypt, but for Constantinople. Innocent III got wind of the plan and forbade any attack on Constantinople, but the letter arrived after the crusaders' main force had left for its revised destination. Some, among them Simon of Montfort who would achieve notoriety in the Albigensian Crusade, had withdrawn when they learnt the destination.

On 24 June 1203 the main army arrived before Constantinople. Those, the vast majority, who had never seen it before stared in disbelief when they saw the immense walls and towers which encircled the place, 'for they had never imagined there could be so rich a city . . . with so many rich palaces and great churches . . . and there was not a man who did not tremble'. The main army of the Crusades stormed Galata (the Genoese quarter) on 6 July and then marched up round the Golden Horn. The Venetians meanwhile prepared to attack the city from the sea. The two forces made a general assault on the sea wall and land wall on 17 July, broke the chain across the harbour of the Golden Horn and used fire-ships to destroy much of the Byzantine fleet. Then the attack on the world's greatest Christian city began. At the final assault, although approaching the age of one hundred, Doge Dandolo, accoutred in full armour, stationed himself in the prow of the leading Venetian war galley, the banner or gonfalon of St Mark planted before him as he urged on his men – surely, a heroic figure in an ignoble cause.

On 17 July 1203 the crusading army seized Constantinople. Alexius III fled with such treasure and jewels as he and his entourage could carry, and he was formally declared deposed. The pathetic figure of Isaac II was taken from his prison and restored to his throne with his son named co-emperor as Alexius IV. The Pope reprimanded the crusaders and ordered them to proceed forthwith to the Holy Land, but very few did. The leaders, with Dandolo to the fore, now demanded of Alexius that he fulfil his bold promises, pay them their money and prepare to sail with them to Egypt. For his part, the newly installed co-emperor begged the army to pitch camp outside the walls. The city's population was already restive under these rulers, forced upon them by a Latin army demanding swingeing taxes to pay off their accomplices and, it was rumoured, bent on the submission of the Eastern Church to the Pope in Rome. The two were soon overthrown by a revolt led by the deposed Emperor's son-in-law. Proclaimed Emperor in his turn as 'Alexius V', he had his younger rival strangled while the seventy-year-old Isaac II Angelus, broken in spirit and in health, died in prison a few days later.

The Venetians and crusaders now made a compact, 'calling upon the name of Christ, to take over the city sword in hand'. It was agreed that a Latin emperor was to be chosen by an electoral college consisting of six Venetians and six crusaders; but this emperor was to have only a quarter of the imperial domain. The other three-quarters were to be divided, the bulk going to Venice. The clergy of the party not belonging to the Emperor elect were to have Hagia Sophia and they were to chose the new, Latin, patriarch. A small amount of property was to be assigned to support the clergy, the rest to be divided as loot.

Constantinople fell on 13 April 1204. It was subjected to three days' pillage and brutal massacre, hardly the first time the place had suffered such horrors. According to T.S.R. Boase, 'Many buildings of the city, including the Great Palace, were sad ruins when the crusaders found them.' But those had been the riots of civil war; this was the work of Latin barbarians. The rank and file ran amok, but knights and men at arms, abbots and monks waded into the mayhem to plunder their full share. It was a vast booty that was taken – according to Villehardouin never had so much been taken from a single city since the creation of the world, and, of course, a mass of precious artistic treasures, sculptures and manuscripts perished. But still more flooded into Western Europe over the following years. To the modern tourist, best known are the four bronze horses which, since the mid thirteenth century, have adorned the façade of St Mark's, Venice but which up to 1204 had stood in the Hippodrome, Constantinople's great horse and chariot racing arena. They were appropriated on the orders of Doge Dandolo and sent back to the pirate city where they were first stored in the arsenal before being installed on the cathedral. Six hundred years later they were looted again, this time to Paris by Napoleon, being returned in 1815. These exquisite life-size sculptures, created by a Hellenic master some time in the early third century BC for a triumphal chariot group, and many other treasures of classical art, would have had little appeal to the average 'crusader' in comparison with the thousands of sacred relics associated with the life of Christ and the saints, stripped from the churches and sanctuaries of Christendom's metropolis – often by priests.

Such physical remnants of past holy men and women were thought to radiate, as it were, the numinous power of eternity in the mundane world of the here and now. Part of the mystic power of Rome itself resided in the fact that beneath the basilica there rested the bones of St Peter appointed by Christ as His deputy on earth. And the city was home to hundreds of other sacred relics. But not even Rome could match the sacred treasure trove, the halidom, enshrined at the New Rome founded by the Emperor Constantine – the most valued treasure known to the Christian world. Most found their way to the churches and monasteries of France where they were to be finally destroyed by mob looters during the French Revolution.[12] In addition, there were the precious manuscripts, silver and gold church plate and furniture, and numberless lesser works of art. Seven centuries later the *Exuviae Sacrae Constantinopolitanae*, a scholarly attempt to describe the sack and to enumerate the treasures known to have been pillaged by the Fourth Crusade, published at Geneva between 1877 and 1904, required three massive volumes.[13]

As some semblance of order began to return, the conquerors divided the spoils as per their agreement. The Venetian priest Thomas Morosini was appointed the first Latin Patriarch of Constantinople and Baldwin of Flanders elected 'Emperor', with Venetian support and crowned by the papal legate with great pomp and ceremony in Hagia Sophia on 16 May 1204. In announcing his elevation to the Pope, Baldwin styled himself 'by the Grace of God Emperor of Constantinople ever Augustus' and described himself as 'vassal of the pope'. Not many weeks passed before he received the Pope's official recognition. Innocent, who had lost control of his crusade from the moment Doge Dandolo had diverted it to the attack on Zara and had opposed almost every development since then, could hardly reject the outcome. In fact it must have fulfilled his subconscious agenda, an ambition of the Vatican at least since the days of the proto-crusader Pope Gregory VII. By the end of 1204 the business of replacing the Byzantine hierarchy of government with Western-style feudalism was under way, 600 'crusader' knights having been enfeoffed on lands of expropriated Greek courtiers and nobles. Some six months later Emperor Baldwin was dead. Leading a small force against an invading Bulgarian army he was defeated in March 1205 outside Adrianople, taken captive and executed by his captors.

Boniface of Montferrat had expected the imperial Crown. During the capture of the city, confident of the election, he had given protection to Margaret of Hungary, widow of Emperor Isaac Angelus and then married her. But Baldwin was young and malleable to Venetian plans, while Boniface, though the more mature and capable man, was mollified with a kingdom based on Salonicain, the Byzantine Balkans. In fact he too was dead before the end of the decade, killed in 1207 also in battle with a resurgent Bulgarian nation which had taken advantage of Byzantine troubles over the past twenty years to win independence from Constantinople. In Emperor Henry I, son of a count of Flanders, they faced a more formidable opponent. A competent and brave soldier, a conciliator and a capable ruler, in his ten-year reign he made it seem possible that this Latin continuation of the Greek rule in Constantinople might be viable. But he died, probably by poison, in 1216. The next forty-five years produced only mediocrities on the Latin throne where supermen were needed and in 1261 Byzantine rule was restored.

At no point in the partition of the Empire or the dispositions for its new government had Pope Innocent III been consulted. Six years before, he had initiated the process that had led to this sorry charade – his aim, the recovery of Jerusalem from the Infidel. His achievement, the conquest and dismemberment of the Eastern Christian empire. Just as Urban II had been horrified when the news of the sack of Jerusalem reached Europe, so the sack of Constantinople shocked Innocent. And yet, with a Roman Catholic emperor and a Roman Catholic patriarch installed in the capital of Orthodoxy, even if a Venetian, Church union of a kind had been achieved.

As for the Venetian Republic: Doge Dandolo assumed the Byzantine title of 'Despot', was excused paying homage to the new Emperor and was styled '*quartae partis et dimidiae totius Romanie dominator*

– 'Lord of the fourth part and a half [i.e. three-eighths] of the whole empire of Romania'. The designation, retained by successive doges down to the 1350s[14] followed the convention by which the rulers of Constantinople, the successors to the Roman Emperor Constantine, regarded themselves as the only true successors to the Roman Empire. A towering figure in the history of the Venetian Republic, which would remain a great power in the eastern Mediterranean for more than three centuries after his death, Enrico Dandolo, who opened his dogeship with foundational reforms of the Republic's legal system and secured the basis of its ever-expanding commercial maritime empire, ended his days directing the provision of Venetian interests in Constantinople, dying there in the year 1205, in his ninety-eighth year. His marble tomb in the great church of Hagia Sophia was left undisturbed even when the city returned to Byzantine obedience in the 1260s.

The experiment of a Latin 'Empire' had lasted just sixty years. But the wider Latin presence in the Balkans and eastern Mediterranean was much longer lived. Much of modern Greece was subject to the kingdom of Thessalonica and the Principality of Achaea, founded by the Villehardouin family and later ruled by the house of Anjou, which was a Balkan outpost of French culture for the best part of a century. The language spoken at the capital, Andravida in the Morea (today an international tourist airport in the north-western Peloponnese), was reckoned on a par with the French at Paris; the court of Andravida was recognized as a school for chivalry, and the Principality's archbishopric of Corinth a centre of Latin learning. Many of the Greek islands became dependencies of Venice or Genoa. Throughout the region, the military orders established commanderies, while from the early 1300s Rhodes provided headquarters for the Hospitallers which were absorbed into the maritime empires. The demolition of the Byzantine Empire produced three Greek successor states – the Empire of Nicaea, the rival Empire of Trebizond, at the eastern end of the Black Sea, and the Despotate of Epirus – as well as the Latin lordships of Achaea in Greece, such as the Duchy of Athens, Morea and the Duchy of Archipelago. Launched by the most powerful of all the pre-Reformation popes, preached in simplicity by a saintly evangelist, spared the politics of national leaders and planned along sound strategical principles, the Fourth Crusade failed totally in its supposed objectives of succour to the Holy Land, and its outcome shamed the very idea of Western Christendom. By contrast, its aftermath assured outposts of Latin culture in the Greek world for generations.

The consequences were mixed. These new centres of interest distracted Western knights from involvement in the recovery of the Holy Land. We learn from *The Chronicle of the Morea* that the nearest Sir Nicholas de St Omer got to Palestine were the murals he had painted on the walls of his castle in Thebes (in the Duchy of Athens) depicting how the first crusaders had conquered the land.[15] Of longer lasting importance was the fact that this early exercise in Western imperialism made the rift between the Orthodox and Roman Catholic Church establishments' worlds and the hostility between the Greek and Latin worlds permanently embittered. 'Most Greeks,' wrote Greek historian Deno Geanakoplos, 'recalling their bitter experience as a dominated people during the Latin occupation, and especially the forced conversion of the Greek clergy and people to Catholicism with the installation of the Latin patriarch in Constantinople, remained fanatically anti-Latin.'[16] As late as 1808, when a disastrous fire did extensive damage to the Church of the Holy Sepulchre, the restoration work by the Greeks wantonly destroyed the tombs of the Latin kings.

The hostility of the Latins towards their Greek contemporaries, on the other hand, was expressed not so much in hatred as in suspicion and distrust. Of course, ever since the transmission of the works of Aristotle through Latin translation, Western Christendom had venerated the ancient Greek thinkers. During the twelfth century, as more and more of ancient Greek science and philosophy became known through translation from the Arabic versions of the corpus studied in Muslim Spain, this veneration increased. With the conquest of Constantinople in 1204, most of the original Greek texts of Aristotle and other ancient writers were accessible to Western scholars in a more or less unadulterated form. And yet, such was the distrust felt for the Byzantine 'schismatics' (and also, perhaps, the institutional inertia of academic life) that for decades Western scholars continued with the familiar versions of Aristotle, derived at second or even third hand from Arabic transmissions, reworking rather than exploring the purer versions available in the Greek texts of Byzantine libraries.[17] Then, in the 1260s, at the promptings of St Thomas Aquinas, William of Moerbeke embarked on an ambitious sequence of literal Latin translations from works by Aristotle in Byzantine libraries. A brilliant career in the Latin Church in the East brought this Flemish cleric appointment as Archbishop of Corinth and prominence as a proponent of reunion between the Churches. By degrees his literal if not always literary versions from the Greek of Aristotle and other ancient writers came to be accepted, though never entirely displacing the Arabic-sourced versions. And the West was indebted to the Byzantine world for a range of everyday improvements in its lifestyle. The Italian silk industry was founded on the theft of the secret of silk making from the Byzantine industry; the use of the eating fork was a refinement learnt from the Byzantine court; and the great tourist symbol of Venice itself, the gondola, derives its name from the Byzantine–Greek word for a small boat, *kontoura*.[18]

9

Heathen, Heretics and Children

━━━━◦◦◦◦━━━━

In all, Pope Innocent III initiated five crusades. Of these the most successful was the one in which the Pope's participation was the least. In the spring of 1212 the Archbishop of Toledo persuaded Innocent to proclaim crusading indulgences for the campaign being mobilized by the Christian kingdoms of Spain against the Muslim Almohad Empire which ruled the southern half of the peninsula. The gradual recovery of the former Christian territories, the *Reconquista*, had been in progress since the original Moorish conquests some 500 years before. Urban II himself had extended the newly introduced crusading privileges to these Iberian campaigns and during the twelfth century various popes had proclaimed crusades there. For the most part, however, the Spaniards and Portuguese received little help from the rest of Europe, though the capture of Lisbon during the Second Crusade was a notable exception to the rule. In the 1160s and 1170s the military religious orders of Avis, Santiago and Alcantara were formed on the model of the Templars and Hospitallers, both of which received endowments from the various Spanish rulers. But although the church of Vera Cruz near Segovia, built by the Templars to house a portion of the True Cross, was a reminder of the Order's exertions in the Holy Land, its efforts remained directed away from the Iberian conflict. Thus when Innocent proclaimed the crusade for King Alfonso VIII of Castile, leader of the Christian coalition, the call was taken up by a few Templars and French knights, but the bulk of the army was Spanish. In July 1212 it won a crushing victory at Las Navas de Tolosa in southern central Spain, which began the break-up of Almohad power.

Of Innocent's other four crusade initiatives, he saw only one through from beginning to end and the result, although it meant the extension of Rome's authority in the lands of the Eastern Orthodox Church, was hardly the outcome which had been envisaged by the pontiff. Determined to make good the travesty of his plans contrived by the leaders of the expedition that had set out from Venice and ended up as conqueror of Constantinople, in 1213 Innocent commissioned the preaching of another, sometimes called the Fifth Crusade. He died before the campaign opened and its progress will be traced in the next chapter. The two other ventures in the 'business of the Cross' which this pope set in motion opened the crusading movement in two directions we have not explored so far – war against non-believers other than Muslims and war against misbelievers, those who might consider themselves Christians but whom Rome considered heretics or perverters of the faith. But all these enterprises, whatever the declared enemy or eventual outcomes, were crusades as the term is understood since all were under the aegis of the Pope and all, promoted by increasingly well-organized campaigns of propaganda, heightened public awareness of militant pilgrimage in the cause of Christ and His Cross.

With only slight exaggeration one could say that in early thirteenth-century Europe crusading was in vogue and crusading fever was in the air. In England, where his father King John had surrendered the Kingdom to Pope Innocent as a papal fief, the boy king Henry III could take the Cross against the rebel barons who were trying to enforce the terms of Magna Carta.

At about the same time as the Spanish triumph over the Moors, but at the very bottom of the social pyramid, a startling movement mushroomed in northern France. Stephen, a shepherd boy, appeared at St Denis in May 1212 with a letter for the King of France, which, he said, Jesus Christ himself had charged him to deliver. King Philip gave him an audience but then told him to go home. But the boy, barely in his teens, was possessed by his vision and preached at first to the street urchins; soon boys of more prosperous families, attracted by Stephen's considerable natural eloquence, joined their numbers. His message was certainly arresting. For years priests and friars had been preaching expeditions to the Holy Land, but all had failed. Now, under the direct guidance of God the children were to succeed where their elders and betters had failed. They would not need to concern themselves with food or transport, for provisions would be divinely supplied and the sea itself would open a path for them when they reached Marseille. Young helpers eagerly spread the word through northern France and by the end of June tens of thousands of boys and some girls were massed in the fields outside Vendôme, assembled for the departure.

This 'Children's Crusade' certainly had no papal authorization but local priests were happy to give their blessing and the multitude of young peasants, few older than fifteen, set off for the south accompanied by a few priests and other adults. Stephen himself, revered by some as a saint, led the way riding in a farm cart complete with canopy and accompanied by an escort of noble boys. At about the same time, a similar procession was setting off up the Rhine, under the leadership of a peasant boy named Nicholas. He too promised divine guidance and a parting of the waters, though his objective was Genoa. Both French and German groups lost many dead or strayed on the arduous journey, but for the most part they were well treated by the country people and both groups reached their destination ports. At Marseille, after days of waiting for the miracle, many turned back disillusioned; others took up the offer of free transport from merchants in the port. Years later, reports filtered back that they had sold the child soldiers of Christ in the slave markets of Algeria. At Genoa, the German children who had lost far more on their arduous route across the Alps melted away or accepted the hospitality of the city, some becoming citizens, some no doubt skivvies little better than slaves. Others followed Nicholas to Rome where, perhaps, he expected the Pope to perform the miracle. Innocent received the pitiful remnants of the glorious dream, gave them his personal blessing, and told them to return home where they might take the Cross, as grown-ups.

In the year 1226, the Emperor Frederick II, at his imperial city of Rimini, on the Adriatic coast of Italy, issued an imperial edict or Golden Bull in favour of Hermann of Salza, Master of the German crusading order known to history as the Teutonic Knights, investing him as an imperial prince for Kulmerland, an ill-defined territory situated around Kulm or Chelmno, near the River Vistula in what is today northern Poland. It reminds us that the Empire, the highest secular authority in Western Christendom, had a genuinely international reach at this time. Frederick was in the throes of preparations for a crusade to Palestine, but at the same time was able to intervene in matters that would shape the history of Europe's Baltic hinterland for centuries to come. In the 1220s Chelmno was an isolated fortress of the King of Poland's marchlands bordering the federation of pagan tribes known collectively as the Prussians. 'The Order of German Knights of the Hospital of St Mary at Jerusalem' was the creation of a body of German knights who had started off as a field hospital organization during the Third Crusade but soon, imitating the Templars and Hospitallers, adopted monastic vows. In 1199 Pope Innocent III officially recognized them as a military order of the Church dedicated to the defence of the Christian states in the Holy Land, and they soon extended their brief to the defence of endangered Christian territories on the frontiers of Catholic Europe. The Order had confirmed its military reputation in ten years of fighting for the King of Hungary against the pagan Cumans.

Its job done, the King had just expelled this ominously effective military organization from his dominions, but the Order had received an invitation from the other end of Europe to subdue the warlike Prussians on behalf of the Polish nobleman Duke Conrad of Mazovia. In return for securing his lands against heathen incursions, the Duke proposed to hand over his claims to overlordship in the Prussians' southern territories to the Knights. Before committing his brethren to the hard campaigning ahead, Hermann looked for a guarantee somewhat stronger than a nobleman's word, which he had no reason to suppose would prove more reliable than a king's.

Christian rulers had long been warring against heathen peoples in Central Europe. Early in the twelfth century the Germans of Saxony, sometimes in conjunction with Danes and Poles, mounted attack after attack on Slav peoples outside the borders of Christendom. Soon after Urban II had created the crusading concept, the same kind of indulgences began to be extended in these northern wars. In the German case colonization was their unconcealed aim. In the 1140s, Count Adolf of Holstein annexed the Wendish territory around Lübeck and developed the city as a major Baltic port. As military missionizing increasingly involved the unashamed compulsion of converts, the heathen victims proved increasingly eager to accept the Gospel so as to gain the protected status of baptized Christians. Such superficial commitment was readily accepted by the German crusaders, as baptism symbolized obedience to German rule in all things – in effect the status of a colonial serf. The bewildered Slav could hardly decide whether the physical sanctions for staying outside the community of Christendom or the spiritual sanctions for being an imperfect Christian within it (uninstructed as he remained) were likely to be the more unpleasant. At the time of the Second Crusade, Bernard of Clairvaux, mentor of Pope Eugenius, conceded that the privileges of those taking the Cross against the Muslims should also be accorded to Polish and Saxon forces at war on the heathen Wends, the inhabitants of a region of north-eastern Germany. In the years to come, such northern crusades – an important factor in that historic 'Eastwards Drive' (German, 'Drang nach Osten') of German language, culture and influence in predominantly Slav territories – were to be dominated by the Teutonic Order.

With its most reliable pool of recruitment among the Dienstknechte, 'service knights' (landless gentlemen) were rewarded by stipends as servants in the imperial administration. The Order was in search of a territorial base, preferably in Eastern Europe, almost from its inception.[1] Unlike the far older Hospitallers and Templars, it had little in the way of landed endowments, except for a few properties in Palestine, although once established it quickly became a powerful engine in the extension of German influence. In more recent times, well hated by Polish and Lithuanian historians seeing its proclaimed religious objectives as camouflage for German expansionism, in German tradition it has, not surprisingly, been equally well admired. With the emergence of pan-German patriotism in reaction to France's expansionistic militarism of the Napoleonic era, nostalgia for the German heroism of the Order was deep and in 1813, the Knights' emblem of the Black Cross provided the inspiration for the Iron Cross award for gallantry.[2]

With the imperial rescript safely in his crusader-pilgrim's wallet, Hermann von Salza eagerly took up Duke Conrad's invitation, in the engaging phrase of 1980s German historian Ferdinand Seibt, 'to missionize the Baltic coast with the sword'. For the Knights enjoyed the blessing of the Church in what, to an objective modern observer might seem a straightforward campaign of conquest against a neighbouring population – and perhaps to some thoughtful contemporary observers too. If, as Christians believed, all the peoples of the earth are the creation of God and His children, by what right and with what justification can Christians initiate aggressive war against them? St Ulfilas, the fifth-century translator of the Bible into the language of the Goths, had omitted many of the more bloodthirsty passages of the

Old Testament, considering them unnecessary incitements to his barbarian converts, already sufficiently given to such activities. Christian commentators had also to confront the parable of the Good Samaritan in which Jesus made it plain that his fellow Jews should consider even the despised Samaritans as their neighbours. For the Christian, therefore, the world was a place of neighbours, which term should include heathen and Saracen. But theological arguments were advanced to justify exceptions to this doctrine of universal love 'according to each man's condition'. Not that all consciences were happy with such formulae. In the mid twelfth century the English theologian and chronicler Ralph Niger had questioned whether Christians had the right even to make war to recover the Holy Land, and whether the shedding of human blood was a suitable way to atone for sin.[3] Pope Innocent III would not, necessarily, have agreed. In a letter from the year 1199, when his plans for the Fourth Crusade were on hold, the Pope specifically permitted those who might have vowed to go on pilgrimage to commute such a vow by participating in the war against the Livs, another pagan people on the shores of the Baltic. Western European penetration of Livonia had gathered pace during the late twelfth century, as merchants, mostly German, drawn by the wealth of raw materials such as grain, fur and wax produced by the Livs and the Letts, the region's heathen populations, opened up the valley of the River Dvina. In 1201, the port of Riga was founded at its mouth. The merchants had little interest in the locals' religion but to Hartwig, the Archbishop of Bremen, their presence in the area opened up missionary possibilities. In 1200 he had entrusted the idea to his nephew Albert (soon Bishop of Livonia) and it was he who had prompted the Pope to interest himself in the project. Soon, as we learn from the chronicler Henricus de Lettis, the Christian warriors in the region were wearing the sign of the cross.[4] To qualify as a Just War entitled to the same indulgences allowed warrior pilgrims in the Holy Land, the Livonian campaigns were claimed as defensive action against the inroads of pagan enemies into Christendom. In 1204 Pope Innocent III authorized Bishop Albert to recruit on his own initiative, which led to annual expeditions of crusaders, led by trained knights, which could offer their participants the same indulgences as those allowed crusaders to the Holy Land. The result was an extension of Roman Catholic Europe and the German sphere of influence, thanks to superior weaponry and military technology.[5] Since the, mostly German, crusaders returned to their homes at the end of the fighting season, some permanent force was needed to secure the lands conquered, and with this in mind Bishop Albert founded a new religious military order – the 'Brethren of the Sword'.

By the 1230s most of what today we know as Estonia and Latvia had been conquered (Swedish and Danish forces were active in northern Estonia) and the 'Brethren', increasingly criticized for bloodthirsty colonizing tactics, merged as junior partners in the Teutonic Order after they had suffered a heavy defeat in the lands of the heathen Lithuanians. In the same decade Pope Gregory IX adopted the Teutonic Order's lands in Prussia as a papal fief and with this Pope's blessing they extended their activities against the Russian lands of Novgorod and Pskov. Any thoughts the Knights may have had of further Eastern campaigns were, however, effectively ended by their crushing defeat at the hands of the great Prince of Novgorod, Alexander Nevsky on the frozen waters of Lake Peipus, in April 1242, forever after known as the 'Massacre on the Ice'. Alexander himself was canonized a saint of the Russian Orthodox Church in the sixteenth century, pronounced a national hero by Stalin in 1942 in the dark days of the German invasion of Russia during the Second World War and was the subject of a classic film by Sergei Eisenstein in which the 'Massacre on the Ice' sequence is one of the most dramatic battle scenes in the history of film. For the Knights it was a reverse indeed, but three years later they received a papal licence to wage permanent war against the Prussians and eventually they were to establish their own Order state in that region.

Pope Innocent largely delegated the extension of Roman Catholic Christianity in Northern Europe to German bishops and military orders. In the south he was increasingly concerned with a threat posed not by paganism but a vigorous new heresy in the French Midi, and in 1207 was seeking to recruit support of what he called 'the war against the Albigensians'.[6] Here, too, participants could expect the same 'remission of sins' as those fighting for the Holy Land.

When Pope Eugenius III had gone to France in 1147 to preach the Second Crusade, he had been dismayed to find large numbers of heretic communities in the south of the country, Provence and Aquitaine. He gave St Bernard the task of dealing with them. At that time the cultural divide between northern France, the *pays de la langue d'oeïl* and what today we would call the Midi, the *pays de la langue d'oc*, was profound and far, far wider than the differing pronunciations of the word for 'yes', *oeïl* (*'oui'*) and *oc* which provided the convenient, colloquial terms of distinction between the two. The language of Provençal culture had close affinities with the romance dialects of northern Italy; the rich and languorous aristocratic world of the south was in thrall to the cult of courtly love and the poetry of the troubadours with their *chansons d'amour* ('love songs'). Women played a dominant part in social life, above all in the conventions enlacing the lives of men and women according as they played the roles of husband or cavalier, wife or mistress. The nobility of the region, chief among them the dukes of Aquitaine and the counts of Toulouse, gave little more than courtesy acknowledgement to the overlordship of the kings at Paris, while being intensely jealous of the vast ecclesiastical estates of the bishops, their local rivals for power. Clergy were said to be fearful of going out in public and if they did so back-combed their hair so as to hide the tell-tale tonsure, while nobles used ecclesiastical appointments as a source of income for their dependants. The structure of the Church was weak, admiration for the heretics universal and the Cathar hierarchy in some regions seemed to be replacing the Church hierarchy. From Paris and Rome it looked as if a religious elite was being imposed from above by a regional aristocratic establishment as a way of ensuring its own continuing social ascendancy.[7] It was almost as if the Midi was adding a new religion to its other elements of cultural separatism.

Although he was the Pope's emissary, Bernard met with a mixed response. He found heretics strong in certain towns (at Verfeil he was even refused a hearing) and sympathy for heresy among local nobility, though this seems to have been less a matter of religious conversion than of their jealousy of the Church hierarchy. Bernard did enjoy a notable triumph at the town of Albi. In view of later developments it would also prove somewhat paradoxical. Within a few years of Bernard's mission a dramatic new surge of heresy in southern France was ringing alarm bells in Rome, a heresy to be associated by later generations particularly with that same town of Albi. In a sense statistics can be misleading. It has been estimated that at the height of the movement the total number of *perfecti*, the spiritual elite among the believers, numbered little more than 4,000; when in July 1209 almost the entire population of the city of Béziers, some 15,000 people, was massacred in a frenzy of ethnic cleansing, probably no more than 700 of them were active Cathars. But the Midi was a society where the kinship unit extended its threads of allegiance and loyalty through relatives, friends and acquaintances. It was a world where a few were committed but a majority accepted the heretical religion as their cultural heritage. It was a world where the leaders of local society, the lesser nobility and gentry not only tolerated but offered protection to the Holy Ones of the Faith. It was a world, in short, that seemed to threaten the very existence of Roman Catholic conventional religion. When attempts at missionary conversion failed, the papal curia could see only one chance of removing the threat – the counter threat of force.

The appearance and sudden growth of the heresy in southern France and northern Italy was to some extent a result of the increased contact with Eastern Christendom flowing from the pilgrimages of the eleventh century and the crusading kingdoms of the twelfth century. It derived ultimately from the teachings of a third-century mystic and teacher, probably Persian born, who always referred to himself as 'Mani apostle of Jesus Christ'. Manichaeism rejected the teachings of the Old Testament and parts of the New Testament and held, essentially, to a dualistic view of the universe according to which the perceived physical world was the creation of the Spirit of Evil, in eternal conflict with the Principle of Good. Accepting this identification of the physical world with the realm of Satan led to the ideas that the Pure or Perfect Believer should liberate himself from earthly conventions, and that the sacraments of the Church, such as Holy Communion and baptism, were to be rejected as they depended on physical attributes such as wine and water. As early as June 1119 Pope Calixtus II held a council at Toulouse to condemn certain heretics in that region who held such views and also rejected the priesthood and ecclesiastical hierarchy – with its exclusive power to administer such sacraments. Later, in the same region, a sect was found which even rejected the veneration of the Cross because it had been the instrument of Christ's suffering. Ideas like these are reminiscent of the Bogomil sect originating in Bulgaria and strong in Constantinople, and they found adherents in many parts of Europe. In twelfth-century Europe 'Manichaean' was often a term of indiscriminate abuse used to demonize political opponents, or those deemed to deviate from accepted establishment orthodoxies.

The French authorities thought that the dissident doctrines were spread among the lower classes by travelling weavers, while among the more prosperous sections of society travelling cloth merchants, bringing luxury textiles from Eastern centres, were considered the carriers. They could expect a ready welcome in the great households where the lively minds of the great ladies could be as interested in exotic ideas as they were attracted by new fashions. They were certainly among the most enthusiastic supporters of the heresy.[8] The local resident cloth merchant also maintained close business connections with northern Italy and Constantinople so that the lady's solar, her private castle apartment, another refinement more common in the south, could be a place for discussing the dangerous ideas according to which women as well as men could attain the high ranks of the Perfecti among the Cathars (from the Greek word for 'pure'). The Countess of Foix even left her husband, with his consent, to dedicate herself to the strictest vows of the Perfect. The community was divided between the ordinary members, the *credentes*, i.e. simple believers, and a small elite of *perfecti*, i.e. perfect ones, admitted to this rank in a special ceremony known as the *consolamentum*. Devoting their lives to preaching and contemplation, and faithful to vows of chastity and apostolic poverty, they were a kind of priesthood that shamed the regular clergy, notorious for its frequent laxity of morals. Pope Innocent III hoped to combat the appeal of a clergy which actually practised the simple lifestyle of Christ and his disciples when he licensed in 1206 and 1209 respectively the new bodies of travelling preachers, founded by St Francis of Assisi and St Dominic, to carry the teachings of the established Church into the heartlands of the southern heretics. Significantly both had sister orders, though Rome could not bring itself to go to the scandalous lengths of heretics of admitting women to the ranks of the lower clergy – and even the Cathars do not seem to have had women bishops or deacons.[9]

It is probably true that most people acknowledged religious belief as central to the good life, but there was a considerable diversity of private beliefs as heresy trials regularly revealed. The fact that many people were prepared to endure extreme penalty for heresy, being burnt alive, shows how strongly these private beliefs could be held. The fact that churchmen authorized such barbarity shows how fearful the hierarchy was of dissent. For the one unforgivable sin of the heretic was the rejection of the authority of the Church in matters of belief. As the twelfth century advanced diverse heresies arose in various parts of Europe, but the threat to Church authority was particularly strong in southern France. People were shocked by the often luxurious lifestyle of the ministers of God and their often shameless corruption. The Midi had its own special line in scandals, from a parish priest who refused to leave the gaming table even to celebrate the sacraments, to an abbot who ruined his abbey by selling off all its property to pay off his personal debts. The austere and puritan lives of heretic clergy seemed admirable in comparison, and by the 1190s many senior members of the Church's own hierarchy were either from heretic families or intimate friends of the heretics' great lay patron, Raymond VI, Count of Toulouse.

Paradoxically, the heresy had its own 'correct' doctrines and its own hierarchy, which claimed direct descent from the Apostles. Fundamentalist Cathars claimed theirs was the true Church and Rome an upstart. They denied that St Peter had ever been to Rome and claimed that the bones of the saint revered by the popes had been produced only 300 years after his death. In 1167, near Toulouse, the heretic bishops held a great council, presided over by one, Nicetas of Constantinople, self-styled head of the Dualist Church in the great city, who took measures to rescue the Provençal communities from certain errors and appoint new bishops. Among these the new Bishop of Albi achieved special authority among the Perfecti and believers. Soon the Cathar communities of southern France would be known from Paris to Rome as the Albigensian Church. In 1198 when Innocent III was elected to the papal throne it seemed that Rome might be in danger of losing the entire allegiance of large tracts of southern France to a popular new religion supported by the nobility.

At first the Pope tried missionaries as a way of winning back the heretics for the Church. Given the corruption and indifference of the local clergy in Languedoc he sent austere monks of the reforming Cistercian Order, chief among them Peter de Castelnau. With them went letters to the local nobility requesting they abandon their support for heretics and assist the reforms. Among the local lay authorities the neighbouring King Peter of Aragon, across the Pyrenees, had considerable influence and he agreed the need for reform – not so the local clergy! They and their noble sponsors soon relapsed into their old ways and after a brief success, by 1205 Rome's attempts to re-establish papal authority in Languedoc by persuasion seemed to have failed. However, Innocent was optimistic. Count Raymond of Toulouse seemed prepared to submit to Rome just as the Dualist heretic King Kulin of Croatia had returned to his Roman Catholic allegiance. And in the last resort, Innocent could have reflected, force might do the job. After all, only the year before the Fourth Crusade had imposed a Roman Catholic patriarch at Orthodox Constantinople and brought the schismatic Church of the city under papal domination.

Reconversion of the Albigensians by persuasion seemed to take a new lease of life when the Cistercians were joined by the Spanish monk Dominic de Guzman. He insisted that the mission only had a chance of success if they matched the heretic clergy by adopting a regime of absolute poverty. Here lay the roots of the Dominican Order of poor preachers, but despite public debates held before arbiters of lay people no real headway was made against popular hostility. The Count of Toulouse reverted to his old ways of open hostility. In January 1208, Peter of Castelnau, now the Pope's official legate, sought a meeting with the Count with a view to compromise. It ended in stormy confrontation. Preparing to quit Provence en route for Rome, Castelnau was murdered, people believed with the connivance of the Count of Toulouse. At this point Pope Innocent seems to have decided on his war against the Albigensians, to assert Rome's authority. Not having an army of his own Innocent needed military help and he could offer inducements. The papacy claimed the right to dispossess men who protected heretics and award their lands to others. King Philip Augustus of France was polite but declined to lead the war against a nobleman whose heresy had not been proved and who was, in any case, the sworn liegeman of himself, not of the Pope. In fact, the papal initiative infringed the royal sovereignty; however, a number of northern nobles, such as the counts of Blois and Champagne, were attracted by the papal promises of the same spiritual indulgences as those enjoyed by men who fought against the Infidel in the East; there was also the prospect of plundering and, with papal sanction, acquiring the rich lands of their southern neighbours. They found a leader in Simon de Montfort, a petty nobleman from the Île de France and by marriage the Earl of Leicester in England, but King Philip was loath to authorize a large expedition. The assassination of Castelnau, legate of the Holy Father, on a mission of conciliation, transformed the mood in the north. In the autumn of 1208 a motley horde of simple believers and cynical adventurers marched south under the banners of hard-faced champions of the faith bent on mayhem and conquest. It was the start of more than twenty years of warfare, defaced by heresy trials and burnings, and orgies of wanton destruction. This was the epoch which witnessed the overthrow of the sophisticated and vibrant culture of old Provence of the troubadours, which instituted the horrors of the medieval Inquisition and which deployed the torture chamber and the stake to purge the ranks of the faithful of those disobedient to Holy Mother Church; this was what later generations called the Albigensian Crusade.

Dependent upon the ruthless soldiery of the north to enforce its will, genuinely convinced that heretics must be saved despite themselves by whatever means, and in France itself led by men coldly intent on the destruction of all opposition in the south, the Roman Catholic Church was fatally compromised. Shifty and unreliable, Raymond of Toulouse at times sought rapprochement with Rome and at times sided with the heretics. Most of the secondary nobility were outright heretics, many of the towns such as Béziers, Carcassonne and Laurac were wholly for the heretic cause, as were such great fortresses as Minerve above Narbonne (today known chiefly as home of the wine classification Minervois). In the first phase of the war, while Count Raymond did a humiliating penance, for a time even joined the northern forces and with his son went on a weary journey to Rome to petition the Pope, Simon de Montfort, with the blessing of the Abbot of Citeaux, seized his lands and his titles. In July 1209 the population of Béziers was put to the sword, the town of Carcassonne pillaged by de Montfort's mercenaries and a twelvemonth later, when Minerve capitulated on terms which promised the defenders their lives, they too were butchered on de Montfort's orders.

The Pope may have been disturbed by the deeds of his bloodthirsty champions and yet the Church itself, in dealings with the Muslim Infidel, held that faith need not be kept with those who rejected the True Faith. If this was so, many churchmen argued, heretics who had heard and then betrayed the Gospel were worse malefactors than men who had never heard it. In 1211 the Council of Montpellier, dominated by Church fundamentalists, consigned the heretic south to the brutal and rapacious northern barons. Perhaps it was because they were heretics, but the southern lords refused to turn the other cheek and returned to the struggle. Once more Raymond of Toulouse was at their head and this time even King Peter of neighbouring Aragon, a good Catholic, joined their forces, horrified at the depredations of the northerners, losing his life in the Battle of Muret in 1213 in which de Montfort's veterans scattered the southern forces. Militarily a disaster, Muret in fact gave the south a breathing space. Pope Innocent was open to offers from the aristocratic establishment. At the great Council of the Western Church that he convened in the Lateran in 1215, he agreed to a reconciliation with its leaders who pledged to undertake the persecution of the heretics themselves.

Not surprisingly de Montfort was disgusted to see the spoils of his victory surrendered by others, but in July 1218 he died while besieging Toulouse and the war against the Albigenses seemed to be over. In fact, while the nine years of murder and destruction had brought southern culture to its knees, heresy was still rampant among the survivors. But Rome had not abandoned its determination for mastery. The new Pope Honorius III now supported the new French King, Louis VIII. Leading the army of northern barons in person, he forced the new young Count of Toulouse, Raymond VII, to capitulate. He committed himself to persecute the Cathar heretics, and paid a heavy indemnity and a tribute for five years while his allies such as the Viscount of Béziers also came to terms. But the Inquisition, inaugurated in 1233, provoked anger and the subdued nobility began to revert to their former sympathies and heretic preachers found friendly protectors. It was an age and a region where a friend of the family, be he heretic or no, could expect support and assistance, and the *familia* of the Midi was an extended family comprising not only relations and kin of many degrees, but also friends and dependants. Throughout these years the heretics had as a last resort their mountain-top stronghold of Montségur (literally 'Mount Security'). The pressure of the Church and its allies rarely relented. In 1234 the town of Moissac was the scene of a mass burning of Cathars; five years later Count Raymond VII failed in an attempted rebellion against the twenty-five-year-old French King, Louis IX. This time, the Count knew that if he was ever to be free of the pressure from Paris he would have to scale the craggy heights of Montségur, reduce its fortifications and effectively exterminate its defenders. Even now he was reluctant to move without provocation, but it came in 1242 when a party of Inquisitors was ambushed and massacred. Raymond had no knowledge of the ambush but was inevitably the chief suspect. To placate the vengeful government in Paris, still presided over by Louis IX's mother Queen Regent Blanche, he surrendered large numbers of heretics to the fires of the Inquisition. Noblemen and noble ladies, like Esclarmonde de Perelle, whose family were lords of Montségur, died a fearful death in company with humbler people prepared to outface the wrath of Rome. However bad the treatment European Christians accorded to their Muslim Arab enemies, it was rarely worse than that which they handed out to fellow Europeans who were deemed to have lapsed from establishment orthodoxies. The siege of Montségur, one of the grim epics of medieval history, ended in March 1244 and has become wreathed in legend. Certain it is that four of the Perfecti, leaders of the heretics, escaped over the walls with the holy books and undisclosed treasures of the Cathar sect heading for the high Pyrenees. The following day the place fell. Two hundred of the defenders who had received the *consolamentum,* the final rite of their sect, only days before were burned to death without trial; the rest were released after months of harsh imprisonment on payment of heavy fines. Even so, secret communities of Cathars lingered on, some groups making their way to the mountains of Bosnia where a dualist bishop offered them shelter. Louis IX pursued these heretics with all the fervour of a saint (he was to be canonized within thirty years of his death); nor did the Inquisition relent its ferocity. Contrary to romantic claims, persecution is usually effective – it is remarkable how many people prefer to avoid being burnt alive. The Cathar Church of southern France showed more endurance than some. But even they, after a thirty-year crusade against them and decades of brutal persecution, finally faltered and succumbed. By 1330 it seems the last of the Perfect Ones had disappeared from the lands of Provence. And in brutally practical terms the nobility who had supported and patronized them had finally been removed and replaced or bludgeoned into orthodoxy. Only then was the heresy of dualism expunged from the French Church but by that time the diverse culture of old Provence was also levelled into conformity. In the words of Sir Richard Southern, England's greatest medievalist, the medieval Europe's 'Church authorities were . . . responsible for some terrible acts of violence and cruelty, among which the Albigensian Crusade holds a position of peculiar horror'.[10] In the first half of 1244 a moratorium was called on excommunications in the diocese of Toulouse for five years, because the vast number of such sentences had brought them into disrepute.[11]

An organized church structure with a rival system of belief and an inclusive social appeal from noble to townsman, and even peasant, made Catharism a genuine threat to the Church, and we need not be really surprised at the unrelenting thoroughness with which it was harried to extinction. But much humbler opposition provoked fearful repression from the authorities. The Shepherds' Crusade that convulsed France in 1251, the crusade of the *Pastoureaux,* was such an event. Chroniclers from the Low Countries to Italy, from Germany to England refer to it and the memory lingered into the late fourteenth century. Modern commentators have seen in it the beginnings of social protest – linking the religious impulse to free Jerusalem to the social imperative to free the serf and the impoverished underclass. We catch a contemporary pre-echo of the idea in the works of the chronicler of chivalry, Jean Froissart, chronicler of the Hundred Years War, who compared the foot soldiers of England's Peasants' Revolt, of which he was a horrified spectator, with 'the *Pastoureaux* of former times'.[12]

It may have started in Picardy, for the northern French town of Amiens in that province is the first major centre of which we have knowledge of the movement, but the instigator seems to have been a certain Master Jacob of Hungary. Possibly a former monk and an educated man, he spoke French, German and Latin and proclaimed his mission at Easter 1251 to the herdsmen of animals, men whose humility and simplicity would by heaven's grace achieve the liberation of the Holy Land. Master Jacob claimed a commission from the Blessed Virgin Mary, a parchment or *cartulam et mandatum*, which he was wont to brandish as he preached. To the English chronicler he was a rank impostor and certainly did not have papal authorization. By the nature of their work, Master Jacob's target audience were among the most mobile of the regimented society of the time. Under his leadership, along with a somewhat shadowy figure, a shepherd called Roger, they were to set out to the aid of the King of France and his ill-fated mission to Outremer. By the time they reached Paris, they had managed to arm themselves with axes and knives, the weapons of the peasantry, but also swords. They numbered tens of thousands and marched behind hundreds of banners. They seem to have been favourably received by the regency government conducted in King Louis' absence by his mother Queen Blanche, who received Master Jacob with rich gifts and 'who believed, as others believed, that [he and his followers] were the good people of the Lord'.[13] But things turned sour when their leader invested himself in the regalia of a bishop, complete with mitre in the Church of Saint Eustache, while his followers, if we are to believe a monkish chronicler, conducted a bloodthirsty cull of the city's clergy.

The Queen demanded their excommunication but they were now heading south out of Paris towards Orléans where they were at first welcomed by the citizenry but continued their attacks on the clergy, and now added violence against the emblems of the faith to their outrages – desecrating the Host on the altars and the images of the saints, and even of their supposed patroness, the Virgin, cutting off her nose and gouging out the eyes. At Bourges, where despite letters from the Archbishop the citizens opened the gates, the clergy had already fled. The mob now turned its attention to the Jewish community but the citizens now seem to have had enough. The 'crusade' had long since degenerated into loosely coordinated mob violence and the prosperous Jewish community of Bourges was not only an asset to the town's commercial establishment but also under the King's special protection. Some leading citizens ordered the closing of the gates 'in order to avenge the injury to the king' caused by any attack on the Jews. Events at Bourges are confused; Master Jacob was murdered, possibly by his followers, possibly by order of the authorities and the bourgeoisie pursued and scattered his followers on horseback. At Bordeaux, where another branch of the crusade had gone, Simon de Montfort, the King of England's lieutenant there, demanded to know on what authority the crusaders marched. On being told that they owed allegiance not to the Pope but only to God and 'to the Blessed Mary, his Mother who is greater', he threatened to behead the lot if they did not disperse. According to Matthew Paris they crumbled away 'like sand without lime'. One of their leaders making good his escape to Shoreham in Kent, a major trading port with English Gascony, tried to raise a crusade following among the local herdsmen. He died a sickening death being hacked to pieces when his connections with Master Jacob become known. Eventually a few of his would-be crusaders received the Cross at the hands 'of good men' and set off to join the French King's forces.

It attracted thugs and they inevitably took over the movement, but thousands had joined in good faith. Everybody recognized the appeal of the nativity story in the Gospels, for had not the Lord 'at his nativity manifested himself to the shepherds through an angel; so they would go to the place of that nativity and overcome his enemies'? No doubt it began as a genuine appeal to humble believers. Roger, the shepherd, Jacob's lieutenant, had freely accepted women and even girls and boys to become crusaders. And it seemed that God Himself had turned against the knightly class of France in its pride, so that it was for the humble and meek of the earth to champion His cause. But of course, many saw in the whole episode a deception of the simple faithful by the Devil, and some looked back to the cruel deception practised on the children in the Children's Crusade. But there was a strong thread, probably from the very first, of anti-clericalism and as it progressed its leaders, often surrounded by armed men, preached scandalously against the clergy and 'concerning the Roman court, unmentionable shameful things'. To churchmen's dismay the audiences listened with evident approval to these 'ravings'. Monks and even the recently established order of friars were in the general condemnation, because they had preached King Louis' crusade which had failed so humiliatingly. Many, rather than blame the King, held the clergy responsible while others turned against the clergy because they had attacked Master Jacob's preaching to the humble and poor – some even considered the defeat of Christian arms proof that the cause itself was unjust. One commentator recalled that a crowd had 'hissed through their teeth at the Dominicans and Franciscans collecting arms in the name of Christ and, in their sight, calling to another poor person, they gave pennies [*denarii*] to him and said: "take these in the name of Mahomet, who is more powerful than Christ." ' Some churchmen indeed alleged that from the outset the *Pastoureaux* had been part of a Muslim plot to overthrow the established authorities in France and thus leave the 'champion of Christendom' open to subversion and defeat. Such speculations and rumours suggest that in some quarters in the middle of the thirteenth century the belief in crusading had reached an extremely low ebb. Even the recovery of Jerusalem itself by the Emperor Frederick II did little to revive enthusiasm for official crusading ventures.

10

Triumphs of an Excommunicated Emperor

In 1215, in a solemn ceremony at Aachen Cathedral, the brilliant but cruel and calculating twenty-one-year-old Frederick II, King of Sicily, King of the Romans and Holy Roman Emperor-to-be, pledged himself to take the Cross. In 1229 he signed a treaty with al-Kamil, Sultan of Egypt, which restored Jerusalem and the Holy Places, together with much of the Kingdom of Jerusalem lost to Saladin some forty years before, to Christian rule.

During those fourteen years Frederick repeatedly reneged on his pledge, was twice put under the ban of excommunication, and acquired the Crown of the Kingdom of Jerusalem by marriage to its queen. In that time, too, other crusaders from Frisia on the North Sea coast and England, France, Italy and Germany battled along the banks of the Nile in a four-year campaign intended to conquer Egypt and so open the gates for a secure reconquest of the former Christian territories in Syria. Thousands upon thousands of ordinary Christians, inspired by the call to crusade from Pope Innocent III, and trusting in strategic plans drawn up by their military leaders, gave up their lives in scorching sands and murderous Nile floods in ventures they believed to be a prelude to pilgrimage, but which never took them even on the road to Christ's Passion. Sometimes called the Fifth Crusade, this was a sorry story of lost opportunities.

It comes as something of a shock to realize that during the 1210s and 1220s the Muslim enemy offered four times to trade the Holy City itself by diplomatic treaty. When the final offer was made to Frederick he agreed, and Jerusalem fell to a stroke of the pen. It was certainly a triumph to acquire without fighting the target of so much bloodshed and sacrifice. But wiseacres said it could not last, and for once the wiseacres were right. After Frederick came others, among them his brother-in-law Richard of Cornwall, brother of King Henry III of England, and after them the saintly Louis, King of France. But his story belongs to the next chapter.

The failure of the Fourth Crusade even to reach Palestine meant that the Kingdom of Jerusalem, so-called, but now reduced to a strip of coastal territories ruled from the port city of Acre, was left undisturbed under the rule of its infant Queen, Maria, and of her uncle, the regent, John of Ibelin, lord of Beirut. Thanks to the truce struck between her stepfather King Amalric II and al-Adil, Saladin's brother and his successor as Sultan of Egypt, peace was more or less guaranteed until July 1210. With the Frankish threat effectively neutralized by the triumphs of Saladin, the Muslim world was free to return to its traditional rivalries. Al-Adil, fully occupied with fending off family and neighbours, had little to fear from the Christians unless by attacking Acre he provoked an expedition from Europe. For their part, few people in the little Kingdom saw any prospect of recovering Jerusalem without Western aid – as we shall see, few had much interest in that prospect anyway.

Moreover, it was by no means clear where such help might come from. King Philip II Augustus of France, the last surviving leader of the Third Crusade and the natural champion of the Franks of Outremer, was absorbed in a long-term struggle with King John of England, who was determined to recover his duchy of Normandy seized by Philip barely five years earlier. John himself, though the brother of Richard the Lionheart, had not the heart of a crusader and was, besides, fully stretched by his ambitions in Normandy and his rumbling dispute with a baronial opposition in England that would finally burst out in the Magna Carta rebellion. For a time it had seemed that Emperor Henry VI, son of Frederick I Barbarossa, and, through his wife, King of Sicily, might follow in his father's crusading steps. But he had died in Messina back in 1197 in the attempt to mobilize an expedition and his demise had itself contributed to the concatenation of circumstances that produced the disaster of 1204. His infant son, to be known to history as Emperor Frederick II, was the focus of civil conflicts within the Empire, and came under the watchful protection of Pope Innocent III, anxious to prevent the union of the Sicilian and imperial crowns in a single person. He would be for a time the great hope of crusaders, but was as yet a boy, when in 1208 John of Ibelin and the barons of Outremer set out in search of a husband for their Queen, now aged seventeen and well into childbearing age.

To avoid rivalries within the local aristocracy it was decided to seek a candidate among the noble families of France; envoys travelled to Paris to ask the help of King Philip. Ideally, the successful candidate would be rich and vigorous, able and willing to consolidate and revive the fortunes of the Kingdom. He would enjoy the dignity of 'king' by virtue of his marriage and much of the authority, but given the laws of succession in Outremer, Maria would remain sovereign. Moreover, the marriage itself would not advance a family's interests in the closed world of French aristocratic dynastic politics. At last, in the spring of 1210, Philip found a man willing to accept the dubious and probably hazardous honour: John of Brienne, a younger son of Erard, Count of Brienne in Champagne. He was, of course, a knight, was a capable military commander and, having spent much of his life in the service of the King of France, he knew something of international affairs. But he was sixty years old and was penniless – though the latter drawback was to some extent mitigated when King Philip and Pope Innocent III each gave him a dower of 40,000 silver pounds. As to his age, it proved less of a handicap than might have been expected. John of Brienne would have a child by his first wife, Queen Maria; a child by his second, Princess Stephanie of Armenia; and a child by his third. Having been crowned Latin Emperor of Constantinople at the ripe old age of eighty-three, he was, as we shall see, still capably directing its defence up to five years before his death.

When in July 1210 the truce with al-Adil duly expired, the Sultan proposed to renew it – a stable frontier with the Franks was as valuable as ever. Largely through the advocacy of the Grand Master of the Temple, the Council of the Kingdom, refusing to bind the king-consort by a truce agreed in his absence, rejected the proposal. Hostilities were sporadic and token. John of Brienne landed at Acre in September; the following day his marriage to Maria was celebrated by Albert, the Latin Patriarch of Jerusalem; and on 3 October the Queen and her consort were crowned at Tyre. In July 1211 King John agreed a five-year truce with al-Adil (to run from July 1212), but at the same time sent messages to Rome asking that a new crusade be prepared to be ready to come to Palestine when the truce should come to an end. Later that year Queen Maria died giving birth to a daughter, Isabella, known in Western chronicles as Yolanda. John continued to rule the Kingdom as regent on the child's behalf, his hopes set on the plans to reopen the war against the Infidel in the summer of 1217, by which time a crusading expedition from Europe might be expected to arrive.

In Rome, Pope Innocent III was as enthusiastic as the King in Acre. The recovery of the Holy City was his dearest ambition and in those days of prophecy it seemed the time was at hand. Like many of his contemporaries, Innocent believed that the world was in its last days, as foretold by St John the Divine, in the Book of Revelation. The mystic number 666, called the Number of the Beast, was held to have signified the number of years allotted to the reign of Islam, after which would come the Day of Judgement. Given that Muhammad was thought to have been born in AD 570, one should anticipate the final intervention of the Eternal Godhead in the affairs of His creation in the year 1236; and the most fitting anticipation would surely be the reconquest of the site of His Son's Passion in the world of time. Throughout the year 1213, the Pope's legate and agents were preaching the cause of the Cross, with instructions to accept all who came forward without undue concern for their fitness. Lords were angered to find their vassals being released from their vows of allegiance; some lay people doubted the ability of Christendom to defeat the enemy; many more derided the inadequate recruits being enlisted.

In the year 1215 Pope Innocent presided over the opening session of the great Council he had convened in the Lateran Palace, Rome. It was the fourth such to be held there, the twelfth Ecumenical Council in the history of the Church and it is generally considered the greatest before the Reformation; its deliberations affect the lives of Roman Catholics to this day. It was here that the eucharistic doctrine of transubstantiation was sanctioned, that the faithful were required to receive Communion during Easter Week and to make confession at least once annually. There had been years of preparation. More than 400 bishops had been assembled and twice that number of abbots and heads of religious houses; in addition there were delegations from many of Europe's crowned heads. The Council's final canon set out an elaborate crusade plan aimed at the recovery of Jerusalem. In provisions bound to affect Italian trading interests, it repeated earlier prohibition on the dealing in military materials with the Muslim world; and it also authorized the raising of money for the expedition by levies imposed on the incomes of the clergy. Finally the Council spelt out the privileges of protection and spiritual indulgences to be enjoyed by crusaders and set the date and place for the departure of the expedition, from Sicily or southern Italy, on 1 June 1217.

The following spring the roads of Europe as far afield as Scandinavia were busy with parties of clerics and monks preaching the forthcoming expedition – it was hoped that a ruling from Church lawyers at the University of Paris that to renege on a vow to take the Cross was to commit mortal sin would harden people's resolve. Mindful of the apocalyptic interpretations of the writings of St John the Divine, Pope Innocent wrote to Sultan al-Adil urging him to surrender Jerusalem back to Christendom and thus avoid the Wrath to Come.[1] The Sultan did not see the need for a reply. Surprisingly perhaps, the general response among the European public was also meagre. It is true that in the Rhineland, perhaps thanks to the inspiration of the young Emperor, there was some enthusiasm, and a fleet raised along the coast of Frisia was to play an important role; but elsewhere reactions could be hostile. Hecklers at an open-air sermon preaching the crusade in Provence jeered that Muhammad was evidently more powerful than Christ. For different reasons no doubt, Europe's Catholic rulers were also detached: the King of Norway was the one ruling monarch to take the Cross at this time but he died before he could set out.[2] King Andrew II of Hungary, who had been excused by the Pope himself from an earlier crusader's vow because baronial rebellion threatened the stability of his kingdom, now grudgingly prepared to renew his commitment, and his motives were mixed. His enthusiasm for Middle Eastern affairs had been fired by the, admittedly remote, hope of succeeding his second wife's kinsman by marriage, the childless Latin Emperor of Constantinople. The one capable and enlightened holder of that tarnished honour, Henry of Hainault, naturally made enemies when he attempted a rapprochement with his Greek subjects, seething and humiliated in the aftermath of 1204. He refused to hand over Orthodox Church lands to Rome and so angered Pope Innocent, and his generally emollient policies simply incensed the local, triumphalist Latin clergy. When he died at only forty-two in June 1216 no one was surprised by the rumours of poison. At least Andrew of Hungary was not in the frame. A rival candidate was elected emperor and Andrew was left an unwilling altruist on the crusading stage.

Pope Innocent had died in May of the same year, engaged in exhausting negotiations with the feuding maritime merchant powers, Genoa and Pisa, to settle their differences and combine to provide the shipping for the expedition to the Holy Land. Innocent was prone to bouts of fever and was struck down aged fifty-six, probably by malaria. Indefatigable in the work of the Church, magisterial in his legal enactments, humane by nature and profound of intellect, Innocent III, it is generally considered, brought the medieval Church to the pinnacle of its prestige and power. His election to the chair of St Peter eighteen years earlier had followed just two ballots on the very day of his predecessor's death. The thirty-eight-year-old, already reputed as theologian and legist, was not yet a priest – he was ordained the day following his election, which is some measure of the awe in which his contemporaries held him. Such was the man who had dedicated his best endeavours to the recovery of the Holy City. Had he lived, the outcome might, possibly, have been different. As it was, at his death, the auguries for any new crusade were hardly promising.

Among the royal delegations to the Lateran there had been one from the young Frederick of Hohenstaufen, King of Sicily, son of Emperor Henry VI, and himself Emperor elect (the Council formally confirmed the claim). In July 1215 in ceremonies at Aachen, the cathedral city of Charlemagne (in German Karl der Grosse), Frederick had been initiated in the first stage of imperial dignity when he was crowned 'King of the Romans' by the papal legate, the Archbishop of Mainz. After the service, preaching in the name of the Pope, a priest delivered a sermon appealing to the assembled lords to take the Cross. The newly crowned monarch now caused a stir among the assembly when he himself came forward, the first to answer the call. The day following, Sunday, we are told that 'the king sat in the church from early morning until mid afternoon, while the preachers [continued to preach] the word of the Cross with the result that many, not only princes but also people of the lower classes took the sign of the Cross.'[3] The compact, athletic young figure leaning forward slightly in his chair of state, with keen interest in the proceedings, was no doubt as effective a recruiting sergeant as any priestly sermonizer.

Perhaps a little under average height, Frederick was proud of his skill as a swordsman and archer, and was admired for his horsemanship – his treatise on falconry remains a classic to this day. From the sensitive and remarkable portrait head on his golden 'Augustalis' coinage it is apparent that this highly intelligent man was also capable of reflective and sensitive moods. Ruler of the multicultural realm of Sicily – where Roman Catholic Norman immigrants, Greek Orthodox local Christians and an Arab population established at the time of the Muslim invasions three centuries back lived under the rule of the Norman dynasty that had conquered in its turn – he spoke fluent Arabic, as well as German, French and Latin, had an impressive grasp of the ancient Greek philosophers and their Arabic commentators and could hold his own in discussions on mathematical questions. In middle age he was to run to fat a little and, what with this, his modest height and his balding pate he would not, according to one Arab gentleman who saw him at that time, have fetched more than a few coppers in a provincial slave market. The young Frederick, by contrast, with the sun-bronzed complexion of a southerner at home in the saddle, evidently had a charismatic presence which no doubt in part explained the good response to the crusade in the Empire – certainly he was for some years the great hope among crusaders.[4] But though Frederick had pledged himself to take the Cross he was to be repeatedly excused by the Pope on account of troubles in his vast domains, so that people came to question his motives and even his commitment to the cause.

Frederick was by no means the only one with reservations about the project being urged on by the papacy. Whatever their European-born king might wish, most of the Frankish population of Acre did not want to see their peaceful prosperity disrupted by war. It was more than twenty years since Saladin and Richard of England had agreed the terms that surrendered Jerusalem to Islam but accepted the Christian presence in the coastal territories. In that time the regent John of Ibelin had built a magnificent palace in his city of Beirut; the Latin upper classes had rapidly and cheerfully 'gone native' with a luxury of lifestyle, which to visiting Europeans seemed effete and corrupt; while the Latin clergy was absorbed with intrigue and corruption to the exploitation of Church property and the contemptuous oppression of the native Christians. For their part, the locals would almost have welcomed a Muslim regime, for this would no doubt have tolerated difference in religion in exchange for taxation and certain civil disabilities. Since they had the status of second-class citizens in the Catholic Kingdom and had to pay the heavy tithes levied by the Church, the harassment of their Orthodoxy was a gratuitous affront.

Moreover, they had little share in the prosperity derived from the revival of international trade from the Asian interior, through the ports of Acre and Tyre and so on to Mediterranean Europe. This was dominated by the ever-quarrelling Italian merchants of the colonies established by Venice, Genoa and Pisa in Egypt as well as Palestine.

The failure of even Pope Innocent III to persuade the Italians to make common cause for transporting would-be soldiers of the Cross meant that while various companies of French knights had reached Italian ports in the summer of 1217, there were still no ships to take them on. Innocent's successor Pope Honorius III had hoped to see the entire expedition en route by this time. In fact, with the Emperor excused for the moment, other participants tended to be laggard. That reluctant hero Andrew of Hungary, accompanied be it said by a respectable contingent, reached the Croatian port of Split (Latin, Spalato) only in August. Proudly sited on its peninsular site with its magnificent deep-water port to the south side, the city built within the walls of the ancient palace of Diocletian was one of the Adriatic's most prosperous merchant republics. It paid lip service to the nominal suzerainty of Hungary-Croatia but was jealous of its independence and no doubt aware of the Hungarian nobles' contempt for royal authority. The result of this independent spirit was that Andrew was still negotiating for shipping when Duke Leopold VI of Austria arrived in Split at the head of a small but dedicated body of crusaders. Son of the fractious noble who had seized King Richard of England after the Third Crusade, this Leopold was to prove one of the more serious participants in the Fifth. But there was no bad blood between him and the Spalatans. He soon found a ship sufficient for his contingent and arrived at Acre early the following month. King Andrew, humiliatingly accorded just two vessels, had to leave the bulk of his much larger force on the quayside. Nevertheless, he too disembarked at Acre later in September; within days King Hugh of Cyprus joined these European forces. Early in November 1217 the crusading force set out on campaign from Acre, to be joined later by the Military Orders.

The Sultan was alarmed, although he need not have been. It is true that the Christians outnumbered his army and that three kings headed them, and even if one of these, John of Brienne, ruled by right of his baby daughter, while the military orders operated as separate detachments, it seemed an impressive demonstration of commitment. But it was a formula for divided counsels. John, as titular King of Jerusalem and moreover an experienced military man with local knowledge, considered himself the commander-in-chief. The Cypriots, however, looked only to their King Hugh, while the Austrians and Hungarians acknowledged only Duke Leopold and King Andrew as their chiefs. The expected campaign of conquest became in fact a *chévauchée* – a glorified raiding expedition. There were some successes and much booty was won – and many holy relics. In particular, King Andrew acquired the head of St Stephen, the first Christian martyr and Hungary's patron. With this, plus an assortment of other saintly bones to add to his collection, and a number of skirmishing victories to his credit, Andrew reckoned he had fulfilled his crusading vows. Rejecting the pleas and protests of the Latin Patriarch of Jerusalem he marched his men out of Acre northwards to Armenia and, furnished with a *laissez-passer* from the Seljuk Sultan, continued on through Anatolia for Constantinople, homeward bound. Hugh of Cyprus had died meanwhile and left his strife-torn domain to his baby son Henry, under the regency of his widow, Queen Alice. In December King John suffered a military reverse and found only Leopold of Austria still in the field against the Infidel – nothing had been achieved and the initiative had been lost.

Then, on the arrival of the Frisian fleet with German crusaders aboard in late April and early May, hopes rose once more. The question was: what to do with these fresh troops? Richard the Lionheart had come to the conclusion that the basis for long-term success against Muslim Palestine lay in Egypt. The strategy was adopted. Late in May 1218, under the command of John of Brienne, the flotilla of Frisian ships with its allied troops aboard sailed out of Acre, headed for the Nile delta, its first objective the important port city of Damietta (Dumyat). With this as their supply base of operations, the invaders planned to push on to the conquest of Cairo and much of Lower Egypt. Some two miles upriver from the Mediterranean coast, and lying on the east bank of the Nile, Damietta was protected on one side by the salt-marshy lake of Manzala, and on the sea side by a heavy chain that stretched across the one navigable channel of this branch of the delta, from the east bank to an anchorage fort on an island near the west bank, backed up by a bridge or barrier of boats lashed together behind it. Led by the Austrian–Germans under Duke Leopold of Austria, and thanks to a massive floating siege engine paid for by two rich citizens of Paderborn sailing with the expedition, King John's forces finally stormed the fort late in August, despite stalwart resistance by its garrison. The tactical success was complete. The chain and boat barriers were demolished and the main expedition fleet could now sail up to the walls of Damietta. Had they done so, they would probably have been able to storm the place, but their commanders hesitated, deciding to wait for reinforcements, while numbers of the crusaders sailed for home, reckoning that by contributing to this success they had discharged their vows. For months now a large force under papal aegis had been slowly mobilizing at the Italian port of Brindisi. Now, news reached the crusaders that it was ready to depart. Pope Honorius had appointed the Spanish prelate Cardinal Pelagius his representative on the expedition; in addition, a mixed contingent of French and English had found transport at Genoa and were sailing for Egypt.

The papal force arrived at the Christian camp outside Damietta in the middle of September 1218. The Cardinal set about taking command. He seems to have seen his position as equivalent to that of Bishop Adhémar in the First Crusade – the Pope's legate to whom all the rival national contingents would naturally defer. But he lacked Adhémar's understanding of military affairs and while he was a hardworking administrator, important qualities in the commissariat department of any army, he was an arrogant man, lacking any sense of tact or feeling for army morale. John of Brienne was now accepted as commander-in-chief by the army already in place. Everyone believed that the young Emperor was planning to join the force in the near future and when he arrived, he would naturally take over command; meantime, the army would take its orders from its leading soldier. In October the Anglo-French force arrived at the lines. In November and December storms offshore whipped up floodwaters that deluged the low-lying camp and the crusaders' misery was deepened by a mystery plague that killed more than one in ten. It is worth remembering that most crusaders through most of history were volunteer recruits, aware that the way of the Cross did not always lead to profit and glory.

In February 1219 came a stroke of good fortune. Al-Kamil, Sultan of Egypt, whose forces were blocking their way to Damietta, had been warned of a plot on his life and had abandoned his camp. But still the Christians failed to take the city. Equally, al-Kamil came to the decision that it was only a matter of time before they should do so. In October he made the first of a series of unheard-of offers to induce them to withdraw from Egypt – nothing less than Jerusalem itself,

Bethlehem and Nazareth together with the True Cross still in Muslim hands since its loss by King Guy at Hattin, thirty years before. But Muslim troops would continue to garrison the great fortresses of Oultrejourdain, which had been seized from the Christians since the fall of the Kingdom. Not surprisingly, perhaps, King John and the barons of the Kingdom were eager to accept, with the knights from England, France and Germany supporting them. But Pelagius rejected the idea outright — the Holy City was not to be bartered for with the Infidel. The military orders supported him and so did the Italians who still hoped that Damietta would be taken so that they could establish their commercial interest there. In fact, the long siege of the place had weakened the garrison and citizens with sickness and in the first week of November 1219 the crusading army walked in. After much angry debate, Pelagius, who claimed that it was the trophy of the Church, had to accept that it would remain under the government of King John of Jerusalem until such time as the Emperor should join the crusade. Once again the crusaders held the initiative; once again, a bold march, though this time on Cairo, might have succeeded. Some even predicted the end of Islam itself. But if the position of Sultan al-Kamil was weak the Christian forces were in turmoil. The Italians were in open revolt and the rest of the army prepared to rest on its laurels. For twenty months they awaited the arrival of that long-expected champion of the Christian cause, Emperor Frederick II. The great mosque of Damietta was rededicated as a cathedral; the Pope confirmed Pelagius as commander-in-chief of the crusading forces and King John prepared to return to Acre.

For all its inaction, the presence of a large enemy army in his domains and occupying his chief port was perceived as a real threat by Sultan al-Kamil. In June 1221 he renewed his offer of terms. Once again Jerusalem could be the crusaders' for the asking; once again Pelagius refused. He had news that the imperial crusade was at last preparing to move and indeed a German advance force shortly arrived. Its commander had orders from Emperor Frederick to await his arrival but he did not do so. Instead, together with Pelagius he prepared for a march up the Nile before the floods season. Against his better judgement, King John of Jerusalem returned to Egypt. The combined forces were impressive, but late in July, the advance was stalled at a junction on the Nile with a waterway, and it was here that the Muslim army drew up to await events. As the waters rose, the Egyptian ships were able to sail down this canal and cut off the Christian shipping.

Pelagius saw that his army was in grave danger and agreed on a general retreat. But the time had passed, and when the Egyptians opened flood-control sluices the case was hopeless – retreat became a slow-motion panic in mud and flood waters. By 8 September 1221 it was all over and Pelagius had to admit defeat. A week of negotiations boiled down to the army's evacuation of Damietta and the guarantee of an eight-years' truce. The crusaders embarked in their ships and sailed away.

There was now an interlude in crusading. The failure of an enterprise initiated by the great Innocent III and led in the field by kings following the wisest military councils was a shock to all Christendom. At one point Francis of Assisi who had journeyed to the army on a peace mission had been granted an audience in his camp by the Sultan al-Kamil, but it had come to nothing. The legate Pelagius had made errors of military judgement; the crusaders had been divided in their intentions; above all, there were many who blamed the Emperor for not fulfilling his vows. But now Frederick could claim distractions in his Italian domains and in Sicily with the local baronage and the Muslim population. In southern Italy his architects were redrawing the landscape with new castles built to replace baronial strongholds destroyed by royal order, symbols of imperial authority as sophisticated in their domestic accommodation as in their military design. The acknowledged jewel, Castel del Monte, a mathematical and classical masterpiece in the Apulian countryside, had private rooms with bathrooms and water closets en suite supplied by water cisterns in the roof. In 1224 Frederick founded the University of Naples, Europe's first state-sponsored such institution. The following year he took two steps towards his long-promised crusade.

From the moment he succeeded Innocent III in July 1216, Pope Honorius had done all in his power to push forward the crusade. At first, the fact that Frederick had taken the Cross was a matter of joy. When still a cardinal Honorius had been his tutor and found it hard to think badly of him. In 1220 he crowned him emperor – but even he seems to have lost patience. At a great meeting held at San Germano in July 1225 in the presence of the Patriarch of Jerusalem, cardinals and bishops, King John of Jerusalem and Hermann of Salza, Grand Master of the Teutonic Order, recently inaugurated by imperial decree, Frederick once more pledged himself to both military and financial commitments, even agreeing to the remarkable proviso that if he did not lead an expedition to the east by August 1227 he would be liable to the ban of excommunication.

Four months after San Germano, Frederick had a new wife, his first having died two years before. The new Empress Isabella, the fourteen-year-old daughter of John of Brienne and his dead wife Maria, Queen of Jerusalem, brought with her the Crown of Jerusalem. Up till now John of Brienne had borne that titular honour as her father and regent. With her marriage to the Emperor in Brindisi Cathedral in November 1225 it passed to him but it was understood and agreed that John should continue as regent until his death. The day following the ceremony Frederick curtly informed his father-in-law that he had made no such pledge and formally proclaimed himself King of Jerusalem.[5] There was no formal agreement and John had no redress.

At last early in September 1227, twelve years after making his vows and more than two years after having renewed them at San Germano, Frederick prepared to embark at Brindisi, where all summer pilgrims from all over Europe, attracted by the news of the Emperor's crusades and the promises he had made of free passage to the Holy Land, had been assembling. But the plague was already abroad in the port. Many came down with the disease, others turned back rather than risk infection and then Frederick himself fell victim. He returned on shore heading for the mineral baths at Pozzuoli, near Naples. First he made arrangement for the Patriarch of Jerusalem and the Master of the Teutonic Order, together with a small force, to sail ahead of him to Syria. Next he dispatched an embassy to Rome to explain this most recent delay to his plans. But the new Pope, Gregory IX, was made of sterner stuff than the emollient Honorius. He refused to receive the imperial mission and on 29 September proclaimed the ban. Frederick pressed on with his plans for the expedition and also sent a second envoy to Rome, this time to the 'Senate and the People', with the brief to make a public reading of his justification for delay; it was apparently well received.

During the Easter services of 1228 the Pope repeated his denunciation of the Emperor and renewed the ban of excommunication with all its awful ceremonies, but this time the public was with the would-be crusader and the basilica erupted. Gregory was forced to lift up his robes and flee the building with the congregation turned mob at his heels. He found refuge at neighbouring Viterbo but he did not abandon what now began to look to some like a vindictive campaign to humiliate his rival and force him to abort his crusade.[6] The Empress Isabella/Yolanda died in April, not yet seventeen years old and just days after giving birth to a son, Conrad. The baby was the new King of Jerusalem – his father regent, subject to the agreement of the barons of the Kingdom. At Brindisi, on 28 June 1228, with a force of some 4,000 soldiers, Frederick at last embarked on his crusade. Three weeks later he arrived off the port of Limassol, Cyprus, where he claimed he had rights of a suzerain over the infant King Henry. But the regent, John of Ibelin, lord of Beirut, who had been ruling on behalf of the child's mother Queen Alice, stood firm against Frederick's demands that he reimburse the revenues of the island. When he sailed from Famagusta early in September the Emperor, who had not dared risk an armed confrontation given his small forces, had to be content with a formal recognition of himself as suzerain in the island kingdom and as regent in the Kingdom of Jerusalem.

For all his great titles and real power in Europe, Frederick's position in Acre where he arrived in mid September was perplexing. News had arrived in Palestine of Gregory's second excommunication, promulgated on the grounds that he was incompetent to lead a crusade until he had obtained absolution from the first ban. Since only the Pope could sanction a *passagium* against the Infidel it was unclear as to how the Emperor could expect to recruit an army. Hermann von Salza and the moral support of his Teutonic Order could be relied on, but who else? Would he have to rely on diplomacy and hope to reactivate the advances made by Sultan al-Kamil to his predecessors in Egypt?

Luckily for him, al-Kamil also had problems. He feared that his brother, the Sultan of Damascus, had plans for war on Egypt. At the time of the Fifth Crusade they had been allies, but in recent years his brother had been offering allegiance to a Muslim power to the north traditionally hostile to the Ayyubids, so al-Kamil looked about him for a counter-weight, and some time in 1226 sent an emissary to Frederick, 'the King of the Franks', offering to trade certain cities of Muslim Palestine if he would attack Damascus. The Emperor's preparations for his crusade were well known. Perhaps, with certain inducements, he would be willing to make common cause with Cairo. Frederick was content to explore any avenue and, at one point, seems to have conferred an honorary knighthood upon the Arab envoy.

However, by the time he reached Acre al-Kamil's brother had died, leaving Damascus to an inexperienced son. The Sultan of Egypt saw little to fear in his young nephew and moved to besiege the city.

Theoretically, Palestine was open to him, but the Christian presence at Acre could not be discounted and Damascus was proving unexpectedly determined in its resistance. Once again, to the dismay of their co-religionists, Emperor and Sultan returned to the negotiating table. Both made an occasional show of force; in one such Frederick refortified the dilapidated walls of Jaffa and eventually the port provided the venue for the final accord. At the Peace of Jaffa, signed with the Sultan of Egypt in February 1229, the excommunicate Emperor secured the return of much of the coast of Palestine, the towns of Nazareth and Bethlehem and the city of Jerusalem to Christian control. A corridor to Jaffa gave secure access to the coast. In the Holy City the Temple area, along with the Dome of the Rock and the al-Aqsa Mosque were to be retained in Muslim control. While Grand Master Hermann von Salza of the Teutonic Order, together with the bishops of Exeter and Winchester were among those who witnessed the historic agreement, the Grand Master of the Temple and of the Hospital were not. The Muslims excoriated al-Kamil for such dealings with the Infidel and for the most part despised a Christian champion who stooped to win with words what he could not win with the sword.

On the Christian side many wondered what would happen when the ten-year truce ran out, while the local great men wondered how Jerusalem could be held with virtually no hinterland to protect it from its Muslim neighbours. The Patriarch threatened a general excommunication against the inhabitants if they should welcome the infidel Emperor, and on the day Frederick received the keys of the city from the Sultan's representative and made his way in procession to the Church of the Holy Sepulchre, the streets were deserted. The next day, Sunday 18 March 1229, there was no priest to celebrate Mass and a congregation only of imperial soldiery and knights of the Teutonic Order. With no bishop to officiate, Frederick lifted the crown from the altar and crowned himself.

With this and other formalities completed Frederick shocked opinion on both sides by enthusiastically visiting the Muslim shrines, insisting that the cry of the muezzin continue to call even though the authorities as a tribute to his presence had ordered it to cease for the day. The treaty agreed not to impede the Muslim population in its commerce, the administration of its laws or the practice of its religious observances, and to prohibit any form of molestation or of discrimination against Muslims by Christians. It is difficult not to think that the man who had once said that the world had known three great impostors – Moses, Christ and Muhammad – revelled almost schoolboy-style in cocking a snook at the conventions of his day. He had certainly outraged the local great men by making a treaty to bind the Kingdom when he was only regent, and crowning himself king. The Kingdom of Jerusalem was that historical oddity, a constitutional Kingdom, and the Emperor had no time for such niceties. In fact, he stirred up general fury by his arrangements and, on learning that his Italian territories were facing an invasion army under the papal banner, decided to leave forthwith. According to later hostile reports his attempted discreet departure was transformed into public humiliation as the locals pelted him with filth and offal on his way to his ships.

Between 1239 and 1241, Count Thibauld of Champagne and Richard, Earl Richard of Cornwall, brother of the English King Henry III, led expeditions to the Holy Land. Richard, who completed the Count's unfinished business, concluded a treaty with al-Salih Ayyub Sultan of Egypt that conceded frontiers to the Kingdom of Jerusalem encompassing a larger territory than at any time since 1187. He also negotiated the release of French prisoners, captured by the Egyptians from one of Thibault's raiding parties. With evident satisfaction, the Earl was able to write back to England that the hand-over was made on St George's Day. Richard's triumph proved ephemeral, but it undoubtedly raised the morale of the settler population.

Most of the 'colonials' lived in the towns, but the ports of Acre and Tyre guaranteed a rich trade and the fact that Cyprus, despite an internecine war in 1229–33 between Emperor Frederick's Cypriot ruling council of five baillis and John of Beirut, was securely in Christian hands, and the Kingdom of Armenia had accepted the suzerainty of Rome in religious affairs, seemed to give the little state, stretching from the County of Tripoli in the north to Ascalon in the south, some security against the disintegrating state of the Ayyubid successors to Saladin. In fact, miraculous as it might have appeared, there seemed to be the possibility of the intruder state establishing a lasting *modus vivendi* with the neighbouring Muslim world. The insubstantial possibility evaporated entirely when, hoping to strengthen its position still further, the state engaged itself in an alliance with the ruler of Damascus against the Sultan of Egypt. In 1244 the army of the Kingdom was annihilated by the Egyptians in the Battle of Forbie just to the south of Ascalon, and Jerusalem lost once more, and for the last time, to the Infidel.

Events in the wider Asiatic world were soon to impact on the closed world of the Middle East. In 1211–12 Mongol armies conquered northern China; before the end of the decade they were undisputed lords of Central Asia. In the 1230s they occupied central Russia; Ukraine, Poland and Hungary were overrun in turn. Then in July 1243 a Seljuk army was annihilated and in 1258 the Abbasid caliphate at Baghdad was overthrown, the city destroyed and its 80,000 citizens slaughtered. Such seismic events necessarily sent shock waves across the neighbouring powers. In Syria and Egypt the Ayyubid Empire, chronically subject to the rivalries of Saladin's descendants, was overthrown from within by a military coup.

As early as the ninth century it had been common for Muslim rulers to protect themselves from rivals by recruiting corps of slave troops, known as mamluks from an Arabic word for slave and usually of Turkish ethnicity. The chief recruiting grounds were the southern Russian steppes and regular slave fleets brought the recruits to Egypt where their chief encampment was situated at Giza. Owing their duty solely to their commanders and with little reason to love the sultans, these Mamluk cohorts were of the highest quality as professional soldiers. Saladin had used them in conjunction with his Kurdish, Arab and Turkoman troops but the system was used by Al Malik as Salih Ayyub to its fullest extent. He recruited an entirely new and very numerous regiment and established them in an island barracks on the Nile in Cairo. Ultimately, it would cause the downfall of the dynasty. The year following his death in 1249 the Cairo Mamluks murdered his young successor and though Syria under Damascus remained loyal to the Ayyubids, their fate seemed sealed when in 1260 an invading Mongol army sacked Aleppo and seized Damascus itself. A people that had terrorized Eurasia from what we now know as Beijing, as far west as Moscow and south to Baghdad, must have seemed invincible. Then in September 1260 at Ayn Jalut, just inside the borders of the Kingdom of Acre/Jerusalem the Mongol army was annihilated by the Mamluk General Baybars, and the Mamluk dynasty which was to reign in Egypt and Syria for the next 250 years was secured.

11

The Failures of a Saint

If Emperor Frederick II, 'the marvel of the world', brilliant but unsound, astounded thirteenth-century opinion his young contemporary Louis IX of France, St Louis, was universally admired as the embodiment of the kingly ideal, the paladin of chivalry and the model crusader. The excommunicate Emperor had recovered Jerusalem for a few years by statecraft, diplomacy and the minimum of bloodshed, and yet St Louis, a far worthier knight, failed twice in the endeavour.

Louis made his vow to take the Cross in a period of lucidity during a near fatal attack of malaria in December 1244. Hovering on the brink of death, he pledged his sword to God in the service of the Holy Land if He should spare his life. Approaching the age of thirty-one he had been King since the age of twelve and, some said, had his mother Blanche of Castile, the strong-willed Queen of France who had guided his minority, to thank for his throne. She withdrew from the regency in 1234, when her son was already twenty, a comparatively late age for a monarch to assert his majority; it was she who arranged his marriage to Margaret of Provence and long continued to exercise the influence of her strong personality on him. Her fourth child, Louis had lost three siblings in childhood and was a sickly, anaemic youth, and a lifelong sufferer from a painful and recurrent skin complaint, and subject to fits of vomiting.[1] The Albigensian campaigns in the south, noble malcontents in the north (a number refused to attend Louis' coronation at Reims) and recurrent harassment from the French territories owing allegiance to Henry III of England and lord of Aquitaine, had given France domestic and foreign problems enough, even if it was at this point at peace within its borders. This commitment to an overseas expedition that was bound to be expensive and was most unlikely to succeed had critics among the King's advisers.

Louis held firm to his vows, but preparations for the crusade were protracted. It was not until 12 August 1248 that the King left Paris accompanied by an entourage that numbered many nobles such as Hugh of Lusignan, Count of La Marche and Peter, Count of Brittany, until recently in rebellion against the Crown, and his wife Queen Margaret and their children. He wanted potential troublemakers where he could keep an eye on them, and his wife by his side. Queen Blanche had arranged the marriage, certainly, but it seems the close and passionate bond between her son and his marriage partner did not best please her. She was charged once more with the government of France.

On 25 August the pilgrims embarked at the new harbour facilities at Aigues Mortes in a fleet of some 300 ships provided under contract by Marseille and Genoa, and on 17 September put in at the port of Limassol in Cyprus to be welcomed by King Henry as his guests. This had been agreed as the general rendezvous point for crusading contingents from many parts of Europe. From Acre came a number of barons from Outremer, headed by the Acting Grand Master of the Hospitallers and the Grand Master of the Templars. There was an English party under William, Earl of Salisbury and a contingent of Scots, remnant of a group organized by Patrick, Earl of Dunbar who had apparently died on the journey at Marseille; then there were a number of lesser nobles who had made their own way – for example John of Joinville from Champagne. Now in his mid twenties, he was to live to the ripe old age of ninety and, in due course, become one of Louis' close friends and confidants. His chronicle of the crusade and his biography of the King are important and surprisingly unbiased sources for the events of the period. Joinville deeply admired the saint-like simplicity of his master and his stern, sometimes puritanical devotion to religion. But he himself was simple and straightforward, a man of affairs who would follow the family tradition and become Seneschal, or senior steward, at the ducal court of Champagne. Here was a man who played the feudal game by the book and, as a liegeman of the Count of Champagne, at first refused to swear an oath of loyalty to the King over his lord's head.

The Joinvilles were a family of crusaders. John's grandfather, Geoffrey, had died at the siege of Acre in 1189; Simon his father had fought against the Cathars, but also distinguished himself in the army of John of Brienne at the capture of Damietta; while two of his uncles had also died in the service of the Cross. When he solemnly took the vows in 1248 there is little doubt that it was out of honour for his ancestors as much as to win favour with the King. And when, years later, Louis announced his intention of making a second, and quite impracticable crusade, Joinville refused to join him and bluntly told his sovereign that the scheme was a nonsense. By this time, John's own adventuring days were over, commemorated by his Uncle Geoffrey's shield hanging in place of honour in the chapel of St Laurent, at the ancestral home overlooking the River Marne.

During the winter stopover in Cyprus the crusade leaders confirmed that their objective would be Egypt in the first instance. Inevitably there were those who had reservations. Although they were not participants, the Venetians viewed the project sourly, since any Christian attack on Egypt must harm their commercial interests in trade with Alexandria. While publicly favouring the strategy – Louis' plan followed the conventional wisdom that Egypt was the principal Muslim power in the region and once it was subdued Muslim Syria would have to yield – the Templars and other great men from Outremer were secretly negotiating with the Egyptian Sultan and hoped to involve Louis in their schemes. For his part, the saint-to-be had come to fight the Infidel and had no interest in the multicultural diplomacy of the Frankish East. By the middle of May a fleet of well over one hundred vessels had been assembled in the port of Limassol and on the 14th a formidable army, swelled by recruits from Frankish Greece, set course for Egypt. Within days storms had scattered the ships but some three weeks later the royal squadron which had held together hove to off the beaches along the arm of the Nile Delta leading to Damietta (modern Damyut). Enemy troops could be seen lined up to oppose the landing and many of Louis' senior advisers urged the King to wait for the rest of the fleet to arrive – but he refused.

On 5 June 1249 the crusaders began their debarkation in the face of fierce opposition. King Louis himself was one of the first ashore planting the Oriflamme or standard of St Denis in the sand dunes.

This sacred emblem's home was the chapel of the saint guarding his relics but for a great purpose could be surrendered into the guardianship of the King of France. After heavy fighting, the Muslim forces gave ground and then fell back across a bridge of boats to Damietta which was in panic, the garrison discussing whether or not to resist. That night the army commander decided to abandon the place, the Muslim population fled, the Bedouin garrison followed without even demolishing the pontoon bridge and the next day, informed by Christian residents who had stayed on that the city was undefended, the crusaders marched in unopposed. It was a glorious success achieved against the odds thanks to the heroic leadership of King Louis in forcing the landing. The loss of the city shocked the Muslim world. The Bedouin leaders were executed, the army commanders disgraced. For the second time in twenty-five years Damietta's great mosque was recreated a cathedral, a bishop was installed and quarters assigned to the Military Orders. The Egyptian Sultan, al-Salih, in the advanced stages of tuberculosis and no longer able to lead his forces, offered to trade the city for Jerusalem. Louis, of course, holding to his policy of no deals with the enemy, refused. The next objective was obviously Cairo but it was the beginning of the Nile flood and the swollen river and overflowing feeder canals made progress impossible. The King refused to move until the waters should subside. At length, in mid December the army reached the river bank opposite the fortress town of al-Mansurah. After six weeks spent attempting to build a causeway, the army was able to make the crossing thanks to a ford revealed by a friendly Copt. The advance guard of French, led by the King's brother Robert, Count of Artois, Templars and English, led by William, Earl of Salisbury, overran the Egyptian camp two miles distant from the town. Encountering no serious resistance, the horsemen surged on into the city through the narrow gates, but it turned out to be a trap. The Mamluk troops had rallied under an able commander, Rukn al-Zahir Baybars, and they now poured out from the side streets cutting down the congested ranks of enemy cavalry. The Count of Artois and his bodyguard, all but five of the 300 Templars, the Earl of Salisbury and most of the English contingent died in the slaughter. By this time the main force had crossed the river and Louis prepared for the Mamluks to counter-attack.

Two major engagements followed over the next week, with the King always in the thick of the action. The Christian camp held firm and the Egyptian forces retired behind the fortifications of al-Mansurah. It was a stand-off. Well fortified and well provisioned by barge from Damietta, the crusader camp seemed safe from attack, the ailing Sultan had died and the Christians hoped that succession rivalries might be exploited. In fact, the new Sultan, Turanshah, quickly secured his position and reshaped Egyptian strategy. The lifeline from Damietta was cut as barge after barge was captured or sunk; with his army facing starvation and succumbing to fever, Louis had to move. He was even prepared to negotiate, but it was too late. The Sultan seems to have been prepared to do a deal, but now Jerusalem, the one thing that Louis wanted and could have had only weeks earlier, was no longer on the table. The King saw that retreat was inevitable and his advisers urged him to save himself by a dash to safety with his bodyguard. But Louis, who was not a hero in the Napoleonic mould, refused to desert his army on the sands of Egypt. Instead he ordered the sick be embarked for Damietta while he prepared to march with the rearguard of his dispirited army. On the second day of the march, he became sick and as he lay drifting in and out of delirium, the army, surrounded by the enemy, surrendered at discretion. Those too enfeebled to march into captivity were killed out of hand, but the mass of prisoners was so great that to reduce the numbers to be guarded, each day for seven days, on the Sultan's orders, 300 crusaders were marched out of the camp and executed. After long negotiations, the restoration of Damietta as ransom for himself, and the agreement of a huge ransom for the still considerable number of soldiers who had been spared, Louis was to be freed.

At first the Sultan had demanded all the Frankish lands in Syria as well as Damietta, but the King explained that that could only be granted by Emperor Frederick II, King of Jerusalem by virtue of his marriage to Queen Isabella of Brienne. At the mention of Frederick the Muslim negotiators dropped this demand and settled for the lump sum ransom and Damietta. In fact, neither term of the deal was secure. King Louis' cash reserves did not amount to even half the ransom money and the Templars, who it was known could make up the balance, were at first reluctant to disgorge. They had already lost close on 300 of their best men in the fighting which had also claimed the lives of many hundreds of knights from the lands of Outremer, as well as hundreds of French and English dead. Not only had the best part of two armies been lost, but the Christian cause in the Holy Land had suffered a terrible blow to its morale and its prestige. And lastly, there were reasons to believe that the final catastrophe had been due in part to a mismanaged surrender.

The plight of Damietta seemed almost as threatening. Because of hoarding, food shortages were threatening famine conditions and the Italian contingents, on which the defence depended, were planning to abandon the place; if the city were evacuated then the King's cause would lose a major bargaining counter, but Queen Margaret saved the situation. This remarkable lady was daily expecting a baby. Her nights were troubled by dreams that the room was filled with Saracens, so she had an old knight lie down beside her bed, hold her hand and 'when she would cry out Help! Help! He would say to her "Don't be afraid, lady, I am here."' The child, a son, was duly born, with only the old man present, and the Queen was only now informed of the Italians' plans. The next day she had their spokesmen called to her bedside 'so that the room was full'. She begged them to stay on and promised, if they did so, to buy up all the food in the city and keep their forces 'at the King's expense'.

In May 1250, Louis was once again a free man and he embarked, not for France as his advisers urged, but for Acre. Over the next four years, he showed he could learn from defeat. He had left France to fight the Infidel, rejecting diplomacy as a kind of treason to his religion. Between 1250 and 1254, holding court at Acre, he sought to smooth differences between Christian rivals but also, in a reversal of policy, made contact with the Muslim world. He even exchanged embassies with the leader of the Assassin sect. Driven from their stronghold of Alamut in the mountains of Iran by the Mongols, they were installed in Palestine, paying protection money in exchange for good behaviour to the Templars and the Hospitallers. Now Louis, who on his first coming on the Holy War had rejected Templar suggestions that he attempt to exploit the differences between Muslim Cairo and Damascus, sent the Dominican friar Yves the Breton to parley with the Muslim Assassin leader.[2] An Arabic speaker, Yves learnt something of their beliefs and was able to discuss his Holy Books with their leader, the Mountain Chief (always known in the West as 'The Old Man of the Mountains'). Traditionally, the Assassins and their leader had been regarded much as the Western world today regards Al-Qaeda and Osama bin Laden. Louis would show remarkable openness of mind to the ideas of his enemies, and came to a close understanding with the Assassin leader. But such agreements had to be strictly under his control. When the Templars went ahead and struck a deal with Damascus, the King summoned the Master to his presence and banished the Order's Marshal, the man who had overseen the negotiations, from the Holy Land.

During the four years he was there, Louis of France was, to all intents and purposes, also ruler of what could be described as 'the Second Kingdom of Jerusalem' at Acre; and it was thanks to his personal ascendancy that many local feuds were held in abeyance. Typical was the marriage treaty between Antioch and the Christian Kingdom of Lesser Armenia by the marriage of Prince Bohemond VI to the King's daughter. As Saladin had become admired in the Christian world, so Louis gained respect among his Muslim neighbours for the authority with which he ruled the alien Kingdom in their midst. But, of course, Louis could not remain in Palestine indefinitely and he took practical steps to ensure its survival after his departure. He ordered the renovation and strengthening of the fortifications at Caesarea, Jaffa, Acre and Sidon, among other towns; again like Saladin on the walls of Jerusalem, the King was wont to take his place among the labourers working on the new fortification walls. But as well as champion of Christendom and humble servant of God, Louis was a king and as such was mindful of the privileges and dignities of other sovereigns. He was disgusted with the Pope's attempts to rally Christian opinion in Holy War against the Emperor Frederick II merely because the Emperor opposed certain papal policies. When Frederick died in December 1250, Louis had insisted that the barons of Outremer respect the claims of his son Conrad to the Crown.

King Louis' European reputation attracted crusaders from all parts. We have seen that the Scots sent a contingent in 1248 and while the French King was holding court at Acre, a ship's company arrived from Norway, 'round the coast of Spain and through the straits of Morocco'. While he was living at Caesarea, John of Joinville struck up a friendship with one of their number from whom he heard for the first time of the midnight sun. He also learnt to admire the Norwegians' way with a lion hunt. Spurring his horse at the beast as fast as he could, the hunter would shoot off one or two arrows. The lion 'would spring at him to drag him down and devour him' but before it could do so another hunt rode up and threw an old garment down so that the lion turned to worrying and chewing on this, supposing it to be a man. Others would loose their arrows into the animal and others distract him, matador style, with an old cloak. 'And in this way they took several of the creatures at great risk to themselves.' No risk-taker, Joinville was content to admire.

Caesarea on the coast south of Haifa, in crusader hands since 1101, was a typical settler town. With its origins in pre-Roman times, its grid street plan essentially Roman and its walls and their square towers built by the Muslims, by Louis' time it had been the seat of a Latin archbishop for well over a century. According to the New Testament (Acts X) it was the home of the Roman centurion Cornelius, baptized by St Peter, and the first non-Jew to be admitted to the Christian community. The Muslim population had been expelled and the great mosque destroyed to make way for the Cathedral of St Peter, overlooking the harbour. Guarded by a citadel to the south and protected by a mole of reused ancient columns to the north, this was a fraction the size of its ancient Roman predecessor but still served a flourishing trade both of coastal and some long-distance shipping. A chain thrown between the mole and the headland on which the citadel was built could close it off in the event of attack from the sea. The houses, set in streets adorned with cypress trees, date palms and other trees, were mostly courtyard types dating from Muslim times and the ruins of an arched market street are still to be seen (Horbat Qesari). The lordship of Caesarea lay between the lordships of Haifa to the north, of Arsur (Arsuf) and, inland, the Principality of Galilee and the lordship of Nablus, which formed part of the royal domain of the Kingdom of Jerusalem.[3]

At last in 1254 Louis returned to France having been away from his kingdom 'on the business of the Cross' for more than six years. A contemporary attempt to assess the cost to France arrived at a figure of 1,537,570 *livres tournois* – in other words rather more than six times the King's annual income of about 250,000 *livres tournois*. The calculations took account of wages for horsemen, men at arms and crossbowmen; the purchase and replacement of camels and pack animals as well as riding mounts and war horses; the cost of ship hire and repairs; the expenses both in food and clothing for the royal household; loans and money gifts to knights; and included the immense sum paid in the King's ransom and the large sums spent on the restoration and new building of fortifications in the towns of Palestine; but it did not include other large expenditures, most notably the development and building of the embarkation port of Aigues Mortes. The buildings and facilities were for the most part of wood (the present stone structures dating from the reign of Louis' son Philip III) but the expense was clearly considerable.[4]

But despite such strains on the royal exchequer, Jerusalem was never far from Louis' mind. Councillors told him of how King Richard of England had covered his eyes rather than look upon the Holy City which God had not vouchsafed to him to deliver. With the new decade the prospects for the Christian states in Syria worsened. The new Sultan of Egypt, known to history as Baybars, was the first great ruler of the Mamluk dynasty. The commander who had rallied the panicking troops at Mansurah some ten years before, he had seized power in a coup (1260) and welded the Syrian and Egyptian territories of the former Ayyubid Empire into a formidable unity. His onslaught on the Frankish states was systematic. By 1268 most of the places refortified by Louis during his time at Acre had fallen to him and the Principality of Antioch had been reduced to a rump state around the port of Alexandretta. In that year too Conradin of Hohenstauffen, successor to Conrad as King of Jerusalem and claimant to the Italian lands of his grandfather Emperor Frederick II, had been defeated and executed by the new man of Italian politics, Charles of Anjou, since 1265 King of Sicily by grace of the Pope. The Crown of Jerusalem now passed to King Hugh of Cyprus.

Here was a world of *realpolitik* where the dreams of a crusader-saint seemed sadly out of place, but Rome was still proclaiming crusades and Louis of France formally took the Cross. As on his last expedition, he was persuaded on a strategic campaign, though this time the target was not Egypt but Tunisia – said to be the backbone of Muslim power. If it could be broken, the way to Jerusalem would be open. Few have doubted that the moving spirit behind this disastrous mistake was Louis' brother, Charles of Anjou. Harsh, cruel and uncompromising, Charles was the subject of the most revealing portrait statue of the Middle Ages, by the Italian sculptor Arnulfo di Cambio, which can be seen in the Capitoline Museum, Rome. Seated on a stark, unadorned throne, the life-sized figure, seen from the front view, shows a long face, long jaw dominated by a large nose, a face of overbearing and cruel authority. As one walks round the statue one discovers that the 'King of Sicily' as he now was, leans slightly forward almost on the edge of his seat, startlingly insecure for such a mighty potentate.

For some thirty years this Charles shaped the politics of the Mediterranean world aiming at an empire over Italy and Byzantium and the control of the North African littoral ruled by the emirs of Tunis. His ideal would have been to direct yet another crusade against the Byzantine Empire, recently restored by Michel Palaeologus; second best would be the expenditure of French treasure and manpower in a theatre of war which, if secondary, was still related to his objectives. Tunis had offended him by giving asylum to Sicilian rebels; the Emir was known to favour Christians, even if not the King of Sicily. It was moreover rumoured that he might convert to the faith if nudged by a slight show of force; however the idea was a fantasy and Joinville was not the only royal adviser to say as much. But on 1 July 1270 King Louis, with a huge expedition headed by a cavalcade of French chivalry, sailed out of Aigues Mortes once more, this time for Carthage. Some three weeks later it came to anchor and three weeks after that the great host was a stinking, disease-ridden sickbay. King Louis, one of the first to be carried off, died on 25 August just hours before his devious brother sailed into port. Charles's energy saved the remnants from total disaster but the last major crusade from the homeland of the Franks had ended as a tragic fiasco. The body of the great King, in popular eyes already a saint, was brought back to Paris for interment in the abbey of St Denis. From the tip of Italy to the Île de France, we are told, the people knelt in homage to this hero king. Before the end of the century the Church had canonized him saint.

In 1263 Pope Urban IV had begun preparations for a new expedition to liberate Jerusalem. There was little enthusiasm anywhere in Europe but in England it met with an almost neurotic response. Conspiracy theorists whispered that this call to travel oversea had been engineered with the connivance of the Pope, as a pretext for King Henry to clear England of English nobility so that he could move in alien advisers and favourites to take their places.[5] Ever since the Norman Conquest suspicion of foreigners had been endemic among England's ruling class. The adventurers (Normans, Bretons, Picards and Flemings) who had come over with Duke William of Normandy and received at his hands the plundered estates of England's dispossessed earls and thegns, soon came to look upon themselves as the true baronage of England, fearful that they in their turn would be displaced by new 'foreign' favourites of new kings. During the anarchy of Stephen's reign they resented the pretensions of his rival Matilda, wife of Count Geoffrey of Anjou, and feared Stephen's own coterie from his French county of Blois. When Matilda's son Henry succeeded as Henry II, the Anglo-Normans were resentful at being ruled

This dramatic impression of the Battle of Hattin (1187) depicts Saladin, on the left, wresting the True Cross 'crux sacra' from the contorted grasp of King Guy of Jerusalem, 'Guido rex', despite the efforts of one of Guy's companions. The True Cross apparently still bears the label with Pilate's superscription 'Jesus King of the Jews' at its top, even after a lapse of 1150 years!

The first to mobilize for the Third Crusade were the Germans under Emperor Frederick I Barbarossa. This illustration designates him 'Roman Emperor' and he bears the Cross, sign of the *crucesignati*. As befits his great power, he dwarfs the cleric presenting him with a history of the First Crusade.

The Teutonic Order, a nursing order based in the Holy Land, transferred its activities to battling the heathen populations of north central Europe and in 1309 settled at Marienburg (Malborg, Poland) on a branch of the Vistula Delta. The forbidding walls of this immense fortress-palace concealed an interior whose splendours astonished visitors.

Richard, Earl of Cornwall and al-Nasir al-Dawd, King in Transjordan, ratify the Christians' treaty of 1241 with al-Salih, Sultan of Egypt, which restored large tracts to the Kingdom of Jerusalem. The illustration shows Richard on the left; both he and al-Nasir wear chain mail and hold characteristic shields, kite-shaped for the European, and round for the Arab. Al-Nasir's helmet with fleur-de-lys type coronet rests on the ground and behind that the garrison of his chief castle look on. Behind Richard, a group of 'Christiani' lounge against the walls of a fortification.

Seals of the two women central to the life of Louis IX, France's great crusading king; Blanche of Castille, the King's mother and Margaret of Provence, the wife and companion of the King on his first crusade; an inspiration to the army following the disaster at Mansurah in 1250.

This engraving published in 1522 to illustrate 13th-century French crusaders landing at Damietta in the Nile Delta, shows knights wearing fashionable plate armour of early 16th-century design and supported by anachronistic cannon. 13th-century crusades followed the fashionable theory that the best strategy for the recovery of the Holy Land was to strike at the Muslim power bases in Egypt or Tunisia.

The fall of Acre in 1291 ended the Christian presence in Palestine. The role of the military orders, the Templars and the Hospitallers, seemed equally at an end. Wealthy, arrogant and well hated in high places, they had many enemies. The Templars, their huge assets coveted by Philip IV of France, were dissolved at his insistence by Pope Clement V, and their leaders burned as sorcerers and heretics in Paris in 1312.

In contrast, the Hospitallers transformed themselves into sea rovers and corsairs, harrying the sea lanes of the Muslim powers, and plundering their trading ships. Driven from their base in Acre in 1310-11, they established themselves as masters of Rhodes as shown here shortly before their expulsion by Sultan Suleyman the Magnificent in 1522.

The statue to Jan Hus, theologian and Czech national hero in the centre of Prague. His burning as a heretic at the Council of Constance in 1413 inflamed Czech religious and popular resistance to the Roman Catholic Church and the German Emperor. The Hussite Crusades from 1421 to 1430 ended in the defeat of the Catholic Imperial forces.

This medallion (1438) of the Byzantine Emperor John VIII Palaeologus, marked his visit to the West to supplicate aid for Constantinople against the Turks. It is considered the first example of the commemorative medal since classical times.

A medallion depicting Sultan Mehmet II the Conqueror and 'Destroyer of the Byzantine Emperor' in the year after his death, 1481. It was probably executed by one of the Italian artists summoned to Constantinople by the Sultan.

The siege of Malta, begun on 19 May, 1565. We are behind the Turkish lines looking down on the Hospitallers' on the Senglea peninsula. To our right is Dockyard Creek with the Fort St Angelo. The Great Chain anchored between it and the tip of Senglea bars the creek to Turkish galleys, the Bridge of Boats linked the Order's HQ in Birgu (modern Vittoriosa) with Senglea. In the distance is the Grand Harbour with the shoreline of Mount Sciberras. The Turks first attacked the seemingly easy target of Fort St Elmo (out of sight, top right). It held out until 23 June and Fort St Angelo was still untaken when they abandoned the campaign on 8 September. Plans for the fortress palace of Valetta, named after Grand Master, La Valette, began almost at once.

by a mere Angevin. Moreover they increasingly saw themselves as an English baronage. Rebelling against Henry's son John they appealed, with Magna Carta, to what they believed were the customs of the last great English king before 1066, Edward the Confessor. John's preferred advisers and military commanders were often chosen from his continental territories and his wife Eleanor was from Angoulême in Poitou.

Their son Henry III, who in the 1230s married Eleanor of Provence, surrounded himself with Poitevins and Provençales (the Queen's uncle Peter of Savoy built his palace on the strand of the Thames where the hotel now stands). In the 1260s a party of rebel barons led by Simon de Montfort, Earl of Leicester and Gilbert de Clare, Earl of Gloucester, took arms against what they considered the incompetent and corrupt government of the King and his 'foreign' henchmen. These were the Barons' Wars and early successes made de Montfort the most powerful man in England. At the time, Rome was preaching a new crusade and hoped for a large contingent from England. To the popes the baronial opposition, by thwarting the Holy Father's plans against the infidels, were themselves the enemies of Christ's Church. So the man charged with preaching the crusade in England, the papal legate, Cardinal Ottobuono, first preached a crusade against the rebel barons. However, years later even after the rebels' defeat at the Battle of Evesham in 1265, there was still resistance to the crusading message among certain malcontents. However, one man, and he the most important in the realm, was determined to answer the call.

Strong-willed, good-looking, immensely strong and immensely tall, Edward Longshanks, the Lord Edward, heir to the throne, had led the rout of the baronial opposition, and now effectively ruled the kingdom. In his late twenties, he was seen as a model of the chivalric ideal. There seems little doubt that his commitment to the crusade was 'a personal decision dictated by genuine if conventional piety'. King Henry, at fifty-one approaching old age in the eyes of his contemporaries, wanted his heir to remain at his side. Henry had taken the Cross in 1250 and still dreamed of fulfilling his vows. Even Pope Urban opposed Edward's ambitions – he had plans for Henry's second son Prince Edmund, more amenable to persuasion, to represent the English contingent in the papal enterprise. But Edward looked back to his great-uncle Richard the Lionheart for military inspiration, and to King Louis of France as Europe's model of knighthood, for in 1267 King Louis announced his intention for a second crusade.

As noted above, most of the places he had refortified had fallen to Baybars and in May 1268 the fabled city of Antioch itself was taken. Past the pride of its glory it yielded plunder in gold and silver ornaments and coins beyond anything seen in the campaign. Christian for more than 170 years, Antioch fell after only a few weeks' siege. Its ruler, Prince Bohemond, being away meant the defence of the city was in the hands of the Constable. Leading an ill-judged sortie beyond the city walls, he was taken prisoner. The Mamluk commander ordered him to arrange for the capitulation of the garrison, but his deputy in the city refused. On 18 May the wall was breached, the place was overrun and the gates locked. All inhabitants found in the streets were slaughtered on the spot and those who ran to cover were sold into slavery. When the news reached Europe, Prince Edward pledged himself to lead an expedition to the Holy Land.

The following summer Edward took the Cross, with his brother Edmund among many others, and Gilbert de Clare, Earl of Gloucester, former rebel leader. The core of Edward's expedition was to be members of his own household, bound by contracts defining the terms of their service and the King's contribution to their expenses, most importantly their travel costs. Edward followed the French King's example in recruiting primarily household members and contracting with them for agreed services and expenditures. In the case of independent noblemen, such as the Earl of Gloucester, upper and lower limits were set to the Lord Edward's financial commitments, depending on circumstances and securities that the money would indeed be spent on crusading expenses, wisely demanded.

In the summer of 1269 Edward visited the French court where he pledged himself to join the King at Aigues Mortes by mid August 1270. In fact his departure was delayed and he, accompanied by his wife Eleanor, did not leave England for France until the third week in August, arriving at the French Mediterranean port in late September. By then King Louis was already dead of camp fever and his brother negotiating peace terms with the Emir of Tunis. When, in the second week of November, Edward and the small force of English crusaders under his banner finally joined the main expedition at Tunis, the deal with the Emir was already done and a war indemnity agreed. Appalled, Edward refused any part in this accommodation with the Infidel;

however, he did agree to sail with the rest to winter quarters in Sicily. The avowed intention was to proceed on from there the following spring to Acre. In fact, the continental crusaders, no doubt under the suasions of Charles of Anjou, decided to postpone any further crusading for at least three years.

Early in 1271 Edward had news from England that his father had been seriously ill and was urging his return, but despite this, he held to his intention. In May the English expedition set sail from Sicily and ten days later, having paused to re-victual at Limassol, Cyprus, sailed into the harbour of Acre. Only weeks before Sultan Baybars had crowned a series of victories against the Franks with the capture of the great Hospitaller fortress, Krak des Chevaliers. News of the arrival of the English crusaders prompted him to make a ten-year truce with the ruler of Tripoli. Edward sent a three-man embassy to the Mongol. Il-Kahn Abagha, to propose an alliance against Baybars and in the same month ventured on an ineffectual raid into Muslim-held territory outside Acre. The Christian cause was divided by a dispute between King Hugh, King of Jerusalem and of Cyprus, and the barons of Cyprus as to whether they were obliged to do military service for him on the mainland. Edward was called upon to arbitrate. According to the English chronicler Walter of Guisborough the barons agreed to this since they recognized Edward as successor to the English conqueror of their island, Richard the Lionheart. This seems like a piece of pious chauvinism on Walter's part, for although a settlement was eventually agreed it came too late to be of use to Edward. In the autumn, prospects for the Christian cause seemed to brighten when a force of Mongols detached by Abagha swept down against Mamluk Syria and Edward's brother Edmund arrived with reinforcements from England. The English ventured on a forty-five-mile raid into Muslim territory against the castle of Qaqun and routed a force of Turkoman irregulars, but failed to take the place. Baybars dryly observed that the Muslim positions in Syria had little to fear from such enemies. However he was in negotiations with the Mongols and in May 1272 King Hugh agreed a ten-year truce with Baybars which guaranteed the Kingdom in its existing borders from Acre to Sidon for a period of ten years, ten months, ten days and ten hours. This, together with the truce the Sultan had already made with the County of Tripoli, meant security of a kind for the remnant of Christian possessions in the Holy Land.

That same month Edward's brother Edmund headed back for

England; Edward lingered a little longer. His wife was expecting a child (the girl would be christened Joan) and a new tower was being built at Acre destined for the guardianship of a new English Order of St Edward of Acre. This otherwise undistinguished body is nevertheless of interest for its name alone. Henry III, the patron of the rebuilding of Westminster Abbey, founded by the Old English royal St Edward, presided over a revival of the idea of Englishness. His children Edward and Edmund were the first princes since the Norman Conquest to receive names from the old Anglo-Saxon dynasties and there is little doubt that his eldest son, in choosing the name he did for the English Order at Acre, was continuing this renaissance of Englishness. In fact the Prince was delayed longer than he had intended when on 16 June an assassin penetrated the guards outside his chamber and attacked him with a poisoned dagger. Edward wrestled the weapon from the man but was seriously wounded. A charming story that historians insist we must discount as legend recounts that his wife Eleanor saved her husband's life by sucking the poison from the wound. One feature in the story rings true – few royal couples have been more deeply and faithfully in love than Edward and Eleanor. It was not until late September that Edward was in a fit state to sail for England, to find himself King.

12

Acre and After

By the 1280s it was clear that the Christian states in Palestine were under sentence. The last, remote chance of a strong and enduring military presence disappeared in 1282 when the expedition of Charles of Anjou, ruler of Sicily and titular King of Jerusalem (he had bought her rights in the succession from Mary of Antioch) had to be aborted in the wake of the rebellion against Charles, known as the Sicilian Vespers and the ensuing civil war in the island. The ruthless and hard-faced Angevin had aimed at a Mediterranean hegemony which would have subsumed the revived Orthodox Byzantine Empire under his sceptre as the champion of Rome. At the Council of Lyon in 1274, to save himself from the designs of Charles, Michael VIII, the Byzantine Emperor who had recovered Constantinople from the Latins, had agreed to submit the Orthodox Church to the authority of Rome, but had been forced to go back on the commitment by outraged public opinion in Constantinople. The French Pope, Martin IV, had excommunicated Michael and now promised crusading indulgences to all who joined the expedition against the Byzantine state, planned by Charles. In the wake of the 'Vespers' King Peter II of Aragon had himself proclaimed 'King of Sicily'. Asserting papal suzerainty of the island, and backing the embattled Charles, Pope Martin now promulgated the granting to all Christ's faithful who should join a crusade against King Peter, the same spiritual benefits customarily granted to crusaders in the Holy Land. The response to this papal politicking was feeble. Charles was unable to recover his position and died in 1285. Had he lived and succeeded against Emperor Michael, the coastal cities of the remnant Latin Kingdom of Jerusalem would have been subject to the kind of tyranny that had spurred the Sicilians to revolt. But it was no doubt only under a leader of such harsh and single-minded ambition that the lands of Outremer could hope to withstand the tides of history. With Sicilian intervention neutralized and the Byzantine Emperor occupied with questions of his own survival, the Christian garrisons from Latakiah in the north to Acre in the south were at the mercy of the Mamluk sultans of Cairo. Latakiah fell in 1287 and Tripoli two years later. The great port of Acre, for two centuries the strategic fulcrum of the Latin presence in Palestine, stood alone.

On any objective assessment the case was hopeless, but the crusading ideal was by no means dead. Popes and kings, whether for genuine piety or for more calculating reasons, still responded to it. King Edward I of England had renewed his crusader vows in 1287; Pope Nicholas IV still hoped to unite the warring factions of the Sicilian conflict; and there was an impressive body of noblemen for whom the crusading ideal was the focal point of their lives – among them Edward's courtier Odo of Grandson, and the French knight Jean de Grailly. He it was who now led a legation from Acre to the papal court to plead for immediate practical measures of military assistance. The Pope was eager, perhaps too eager, to help. In the medium term there was ambitious talk of an alliance against the Egyptian regime with the Mongol Ilkan, Arghun, the westernmost of the nomadic Asian war-lords who, for sixty years, had humiliated the Chinese Empire in the remote Orient and pillaged and conquered to the gates of Europe in the West. Was it even possible that he would convert to Latin Christianity? In the meantime, Pope Nicholas, sensing the popular mood, sent galleys and financial aid to the Holy Land, while King Edward dispatched a well-equipped contingent under the command of Grandson. Unfortunately the Pope, hoping to tap popular sentiment in a practical way, also ordered the preaching of the *passagium*. In Italy alone hundreds responded so that in the summer of 1290 Acre and its territory was deluged with bands of disorderly crusaders spoiling for a fight. There being as yet no formal hostilities in the neighbourhood, they bravely killed such infidels as they could find – peasants, farmers and merchants for the most part. The Egyptians demanded the murderers be handed over and when the request was refused prepared for war. In April the following year the citizens and garrison of Acre saw the well-drilled units of a massive army, under the command of the new Sultan, al-Ashraf Khalil, and equipped with the finest stone-throwing artillery and siege engines, deploying on the plain beyond the double line of fortifications around the city.

The Sultan was not able to blockade the sea entry to the port of Acre and on May 1291 King Henry of Cyprus sailed in with valuable reinforcements. But the main *passagium* from Europe, the only realistic hope for the city's defence, was not yet even assembled. For two weeks, the defenders led by Grailly, Grandson, the Knights of the Military Orders and King Henry, fought a heroic if desperate action until on 18 May the Muslim force launched the final, general assault. By nightfall it was plain to see the city was lost. In a panic embarkation in the harbour, the weak Mediterranean tide at treacherous low water, numbers made good their escape, among them the leaders. But many more, among these the Marshal of the Hospitallers and the Master of the Temple, lay dead among the fortifications or were to be slaughtered or captured in the last hours of the Christian city. By the end of August the whole of Palestine was in Muslim hands, a result which, at the beginning of the year, in the view of one Arab historian, would have been unimaginable.

It was a hundred years since Richard the Lionheart had abandoned the attempt to retake Jerusalem and negotiated the terms on which the Christians might continue to hold the coastal territories some called the 'Kingdom of Acre'. During that century there had been a brief return to Jerusalem under Emperor Frederick but Western Christendom's most prestigious ruler, St Louis of France, had failed in two major ventures to re-establish a permanent Kingdom of Jerusalem. Since his death in 1271, the Christian cause had suffered variable fortunes and most recently a series of major reverses; now it held not even a bridgehead. Surely the great venture was at an end. The best that could be hoped for from now on was that Christians would be able to visit the Holy Places of Christ's life as they had for centuries before the Frankish intervention in the Holy Land. To the truly devout that was all that religion demanded, but there were also many who thought the recovery of the Holy Land a solemn obligation on all Christians and especially their rulers. For a magic moment at the turn of the century God himself seemed to have overturned the judgement of Acre. In 1299 the Mongol Ilkhan Ghazan won a crushing victory over the Mamluks, broke their hold over Syria and proposed that the Christians should return to the Holy Land. Pope Boniface VIII had proclaimed 1300 a year of jubilee; now he urged the faithful to take the Cross; members of the military orders awaited mobilization; in Genoa, the Doge and council ordered preparations for a preliminary expedition ('*passagium quasi particulare*').

The moment passed. Events in Europe conspired against any would-be crusaders. Edward of England, long regarded as Europe's most committed ruler to the cause of the Holy Land,[1] faced rumbling domestic opposition, rebellion in Scotland and war against King Philip of France in Gascony. The swelling power of the monarchy in France confronted the papacy with a threat to its authority over the Church in that country, while the French Angevin rulers of Sicily were contesting papal influence in Italy. The French King's liegeman, the Count of Flanders, needed help against the burgeoning strength of commercial and industrial cities such as Ghent and Bruges; a contest between Paris and Pope Boniface VIII over clerical taxation led to an assertion of papal moral authority over lay rulers in temporal matters; and there was the scandal at the Italian town of Agnani in 1303 when French royal agents manhandled Boniface in an attempt to arrest him with a view to his deposition. An indignant citizenry rescued the seventy-eight-year-old pontiff and escorted him to Rome where he died within the month.

The new Pope, Clement V, was more pliable to French demands; he was also committed, at least in principle, to the crusade. The early fourteenth century saw the proliferation of a number of books advocating crusading theories. One, addressed to the Pope by Hetoum of Corycus, an Armenian expatriate nobleman, the prior of a monastery outside Poitiers, analysed the weaknesses of the Mamluk Sultanate of Egypt and advocated landings in 'Cilician Armenia', in southern Turkey. Others appealed to a veritable 'political theology' in vogue at the French court, according to which the 'noble and holy' kings of France were paragons of holiness and purity. Alone among the dynasties of Europe, the royal house of France, descended from Priam, King of Troy, was untainted by any bastard blood. The kings of France could, by the touch of their hands alone, miraculously heal scrofula, known as the King's Evil. The fact that Pope Boniface VIII had canonized Louis IX barely twenty years after the King's death lent force to the argument that French kings enjoyed special credit in heaven. Moreover, it was only because its enemies feared its defenders, the kings of France, that the Church could live in peace. Thus all who strove against the King and realm of France, guarantors of the peace of the Church which was a precondition for the recovery of the Holy Land, were fighting against the Church, against Catholic doctrine and against the Holy Land. So, ran the argument, the kings of France should be accorded, as of right, the leadership of all crusading ventures.

In Spain, the Catalan Franciscan Raimon Lull proposed radical changes in the strategy against Islam. Lull, who would die aged eighty from wounds suffered in a missionary venture in North Africa (1315), passionately believed that evangelism and conversion were, ideally, the right means to advance the faith. He called for the institution of monastic language colleges in Arabic, Hebrew, Greek and Tartar, to equip missionaries to Muslims, Jews, Orthodox Christians and 'pagans'. But he did not discount armed initiatives to conquer the Holy Land and advocated the merger of all the military orders – Temple, Hospital, Teutonic and Spanish – in a single *ordo militiae* to be headed by a grand master of royal blood. This provision he hoped would secure its independence of 'such Christian princes as have their eyes on crusading taxes'. Such unworldly integrity of purpose was not found among the policy makers of Europe's chancelleries.

As seen from Paris, the Holy War included a project nursed by Charles of Valois, the King's young brother, for the conquest of Byzantine Constantinople and the King's campaigns in Flanders, for the Flemings upheld injustice and the King upheld justice, so that those who died 'for king and realm' could be sure of 'the crown of martyrdom from God'. Naturally, in all crusading enterprises, the French King should be afforded lavish funding from all clerical taxation. More remarkable still was the argument, advanced in a confidential appendix to his treatise 'On the Recovery of the Holy Land' for the King's eyes only, by Pierre Dubois, a Norman lawyer, that the lands of the papacy should be placed under the control of the French King and that papal policy in general should be subordinated to the extension of French power and influence by arranging the election of more French cardinals.

Written about the year 1306, Dubois' treatise has a prophetic ring when we realize that in 1309 Pope Clement V moved the papal court to Avignon, an enclave within the Kingdom of France, where it remained for the next seventy years. During this time all the popes were French and the Palais des Papes sometimes seemed more a branch office of the Palais Royale, Paris. The move to Avignon also coincided with papal connivance in the French government's brutal suppression of the crusading order of the Knights Templar and the appropriation of its wealth – notionally in preparation for the financing of a crusade. The ideal which had first inspired men to go on armed pilgrimage to reclaim the Holy Land for Christendom had always been a matter of mixed motives. When the self-deluding piety of King Philip the Fair of France, brought on, men said, by the trauma caused by the death of his wife, combined with the remarkable doctrines of Pierre Dubois, the flawed ideal seemed little better than straightforward *realpolitik*.

But if the French King postured others acted. Under their wily Grand Master, Foulques de Villaret, the Knights Hospitallers were busying themselves to find a new military role in the new Middle Eastern theatre, transformed by the fall of Acre. Villaret seems to have seen more clearly than his brother Grand Master Jean Molay of the Knights Templars that, with the end of the crusader successor states in Palestine and with it the end of realistic crusading activity in the foreseeable future, the very *raison d'être* of both the military orders had been brought into question. Driven from Palestine and their fortress citadels, chief among them Krak des Chevaliers, the Order was without a fixed base. But the Grand Master held to his crusading vocation despite the uncertainty of the times. About 1305 he wrote a memorandum of advice to the Pope on how, in his opinion, a *passagium* should be organized. In the spring of 1306, when disturbing rumours were already abroad about papal and royal designs upon the Templars and the Order's supposed malpractices, the Hospitallers came to a secret agreement with a Genoese privateer for a joint conquest of the island of Rhodes and its dependencies. Then at Poitiers the following year, Grand Master Foulques entered into public discussions with Pope Clement to plan a limited *passagium* or expedition against the Infidel. Homeless and no longer on the front line of Christendom's war with the enemies of the faith, the Knights of the Hospital could still be seen to be on active service.

The objective was twofold: to enforce a trade embargo on the ports of Egypt, notably Alexandria, and to bring succour to the Christians of Armenia. The plan paralleled that proposed to King Philip by Prior Hetoum that same year, and the King favoured the idea as a prelude to his own more grandiose scheme. The cause attracted generous contributions from the rich while thousands of poor volunteers from southern England, northern France, the Low Countries and western Germany took the sign of the Cross. Throughout the spring and summer of 1309, loosely organized bands footslogged it southwards – the genuine pilgrims in the hope that the Pope would proclaim a general *passagium* targeted at the Holy Land; the fellow travellers in the hope of profitable looting where town authorities were not prepared for the influx of lawless vagabonds that stalked these outbursts of popular piety. Pope Clement refused to associate papal prestige with such an ill-prepared venture. The 'crusaders' dispersed, many to swell the bands of lawless vagrants that plagued the medieval countryside – 'the destitute and other wandering men and women' aiming to conceal their evil doing, 'under the appearance of piety, begging most plausibly and receiving victuals in abundance' to quote the Inquisitor of Toulouse;[2] others to face the weary trudge home, their devotion frustrated, their meagre resources exhausted in travel; and some to press on to the Mediterranean ports where an expedition was indeed assembling.

By this time King Philip had lost whatever interest he may have had in the enterprise of the limited *passagium* and was, in any case, engrossed in his process against the Templars. By contrast, Grand Master Foulques was pushing ahead with the enterprise which he saw he could turn to his own purpose. In the September of 1307 he had received the Pope's official confirmation of his Order's installation on the island of Rhodes. The grant may have been a little premature for the island, although the target of Hospitaller raids, was still in the hands of its Turkish conquerors, who had seized it some thirty years back from the Byzantines. But in the autumn of 1309, coordinating the trained men at arms financed by the contributions of the rich with the sturdy vagabonds and devotees from the northern pilgrimage, the Knights were ready to bind one thread of the fervour of the times to a practical destiny. For Grand Master Foulques, if not for King Philip, the crusading plans of 1307 were to bear fruit. The Hospitallers' capture of Rhodes was, almost coincidentally, a solid achievement of the lingering crusading impulse. And it had practical consequences. For more than two centuries, until their expulsion by the Ottoman Turks in the early sixteenth century, the Knights of St John, a company of Christian corsairs, so to speak, ensconced barely twelve miles from the southern coast of Turkish Anatolia, provided a constant harassment to the shipping of the Muslim powers in the eastern Mediterranean. On their island headquarters, the principal city and its harbour well fortified, the Knights established hostels (*auberges*) for the brethren of the various *langues* – Italy, France, Auvergne, Provence, Castile, Aragon, Germany – each with a stretch of wall assigned to their defence in case of siege. Revenues flowed in from the European commanderies and also from the Order's sugar plantation and refinery on Cyprus.

The precise details of the *passagium* whereby the Hospitallers effected the conquest of Rhodes are difficult to follow but the positive outcome is a matter of history. The crusading record of Philip IV, by contrast, is as well documented in its beginnings as it was nugatory in its results. Crusading had always been dominated by the French, in a fine blend of piety, politics and propaganda although under Philip it was complicated by the problem of the Knights Templar. Excessively rich, notorious for the independence and secrecy of their organization and with granges all over Western Europe, they were targets for the covetous greed of the kings and princes in whose lands their possessions lay, and even of the uneasy hostility of the Pope, to whom they owed their allegiance and who was, in theory, their protector. Rumour accused them of forcing new members into blasphemous initiation rites involving spitting upon the crucifix and of homosexual rituals designed to strengthen group solidarity. In his self-proclaimed role as champion of Western Christendom and protector of the Church, King Philip put pressure on the Pope to abandon his protégés and to institute a papal commission of enquiry into the charges against them. The Order's wealth in France would be a valuable resource for the King's crusading plans. Pope Clement convened a council to assemble at the ancient city of Vienne in south-central France, to consider the case of the Templars and to deliberate plans for a *passagium* to recover the Holy City. The Council opened in 1311 and in April 1312 a papal bull declared the dissolution of the Order of the Temple. The way was clear to go ahead with preparations for the crusade and the Council proclaimed the levy of taxes for the expedition.

Philip's policy requirements had dominated the Council's deliberations and when they were concluded, he announced his intention to take the Cross and to lead a *passagium generale*, a full crusading expedition to the Holy Land, in the year 1319. The cynics at court had their doubts but most people were impressed by the great ceremony in Paris with which the King formally pledged his vows at the Feast of Pentecost in 1313. Constituting one of the greatest events in the calendar of medieval chivalry, the festivities and jousting, which lasted for more than a week, were attended not only by the great nobles of France, the King's three sons and his two brothers, who joined him in taking the Cross, but also by many English knights and King Edward II of England, the King's son-in-law by his marriage to Isabella of France. The splendour of these proceedings and the lofty sentiments they encouraged masked the inadequacy of the preparations, whether military or financial, actually to implement the King's warlike vows.

In the meantime, the royal chancery had been pursuing the Templars relentlessly. Put to the torture, some senior members, among them the Grand Master Jean Molay himself, had admitted to charges of sodomy, heresy and blasphemy. Many of the members were sent to the stake as lapsed heretics, and as dusk fell on the evening of 18 March 1314 Molay, having withdrawn his confessions, was burnt to death on the personal order of King Philip. As the flames leapt on the pyre he cried out vengeance on his persecutors and a curse on the royal house. Founded by Hugh Capet in 987, when the descendants of Charlemagne finally died out, the family had reigned France, father to son, in unbroken succession for more than 320 years. That evening when he ordered the death of the seventy-six-year-old Master of the Temple, Philip IV of the house of Capet, called 'le Bel', or the Handsome, was only forty-six. He died within months of his victim.

It was a time of corruption and cynicism at court, and of rumour and superstition everywhere. The Crown took the lead. Philip IV had impaled his chamberlain Enguerrand de Marigny on trumped-up sorcery charges as cover for his own rapacious political and financial policies. His son Louis X died just two years later, his first wife Margaret having been charged with adultery and strangled in prison, his second wife Clémence giving birth to a son, John I, five months after Louis' death. The five-month regency was held by Louis' brother Philip who proclaimed the infant dead and himself King as Philip V just five days after the birth. Towards the end of his short, six-year reign, Paris was shaken by horrible events in the provinces, when only the year before, France had been in the grip of another popular mass movement called the Shepherds' Crusade – the *Pastoureaux*. Originating in Normandy in the spring of 1320, they claimed to have seen a vision of angels exhorting them to march to the aid of the Holy Land. With banners and pennants displaying scenes from the crucifixion in the lead, they marched on Paris, gathering supporters as they went.

Terrified observers spoke of a mob of some 10,000 surging round the Palais Royal calling on King Philip to lead them and his army against the Infidel. The people evidently remembered, even if the King preferred to forget, that unfulfilled crusading vow.[3] Wisely, no doubt, Philip did not appear and the mob turned their attention to a prison where some of their supporters had been incarcerated. Freeing their friends, they expected reprisals but the authorities kept a low profile. In the end the mobs, encouraged some said by 'weighty persons' and local dignitaries, left Paris. Displaying the worst kind of pre-crusade pogrom mentality they trudged south, killing Jews as they went and pillaging their property, but also, to the alarm of Pope John XXII and his court in Avignon, looting churches. The Pope issued directives deploring the savagery of the self-styled 'crusaders' and demanding they be stopped. Finally the Sénéchal of Carcassonne turned out the guard and the lawless rabble was dispersed, fugitives being hung by the score from trees or the local gibbets.[4]

Now it was rumoured that the Infidel had taken the initiative. Scores of lepers were burnt at the stake after 'confessing' that they had poisoned springs and wells hoping to infect all the Christians of France and Germany. In some places these infected men, women and children were shut up in their homes and incinerated by lynch mobs.[5] Soon Jews joined the victims, accused of inciting the lepers to wage biological war on the Christian population. At Chinon 160 Jewish men were burnt to death in a great pit – their wives, soon to be widows, threw their sons into the flames to avoid forcible baptism by the spectators who, we are told, included noblemen.[6] The head of a leper colony in Pamiers (Arièges, southern France) 'confessed' to have been party to a plot engineered by the King of Granada to place powders in various water sources. Late in June 1321 King Philip V issued orders for a nationwide arrest of lepers. A few days later documents in French were produced purporting to be translations from the Arabic of letters from the kings of Granada and of Tunis. The first of these Muslim potentates supposedly promised money to Jewish agents for inciting lepers to poison public cisterns and to supply himself a special poison to be placed in the drinking water of Philip V – the Moorish King was said to want revenge for the defeats he had suffered at the hands of the Christians of Castile. Meanwhile the ruler of Tunis confined himself to a general expression of goodwill and promises of money. The idea of an international Muslim conspiracy was not entirely new for there had been a Shepherds' movement back in 1251 and at that time the English chronicler Matthew Paris had recorded finds of money, packets of poison and letters in Arabic from the Sultan of Egypt in the baggage of one of the leaders.[7]

The troubled reign of Philip V ended in 1322 to be followed by that of his brother Charles IV. Charles was just twenty-eight when he acceded, yet only six years later, in 1328, he died childless and with him the last male in the direct line from Hugh Capet after an unbroken succession for 341 years. It was only fourteen years since the Master of the Temple had called down the judgement of heaven upon the direct descendants of Hugh Capet, so it is perhaps hardly surprising if contemporaries looked back on the last Capetians as '*les rois maudits*', 'the kings accursed'. King Charles, who had also taken the crusader's vow at Paris and had also failed to honour it, was followed by his nephew Philip of Valois: as Philip VI, the first king of the Valois dynasty.

Friends of the Templars had no doubt as to the reason for the mysteriously sudden end of the direct Capetian line, but there were those who said that its fate was the consequence of the kings' betrayal of their crusading commitments. Philip IV was absolved from such a charge by his death, but he and his successors had collected the crusading taxes granted by the Council of Vienne and they had been happy to gather the opulent legacy of the Templars into the royal treasury – and yet not one had led a crusading expedition to the relief of the Holy Land. Informed public opinion came to conclude that fund-raising for crusading expeditions was systematic establishment fraud. An embittered chronicler summed up the mood: 'the Saracens are still there in peace, and I think they may sleep on undisturbed.'[8] Now it was the turn of the new Valois dynasty to save the crusading honour of France.

King Philip, who had joined his cousins in the great oath-taking in Paris in 1313, was, like them, committed. In 1330, two years into his reign, the court was harangued by the exiled Patriarch of Jerusalem on the obligation of all Christian men to come to the aid of the Holy City. King Philip may have been sincere in his pledge to the crusading ideal; frustrated in his own plans, he looked at the possibility of crusading in Spain. In his own attempts to raise a new *passagium*, he certainly requested financial help from the cities and towns of France, but in vain. Given the cynical mood abroad we need not be surprised, for the monarchy's prestige was at a low ebb. In 1336 Philip called off yet another French crusade. Soon he would be embroiled in the early decades of the Hundred Years War against the English, which was to be an epoch of disaster. An Italian chronicler, Matteo Villani of Florence saw it as the judgement of God on France for having deceived the faithful of Christendom with its talk of crusades.

Not that Italian commentators were necessarily disinterested. The decades following the fall of Acre saw the emergence of a veritable 'recovery literature' of treatises analysing the problems of re-establishing the Latin presence in the Holy Land and offering more or less practical proposals for their solution. Probably the best was the *Liber secretorum fidelium crucis* ('The Book of Secrets') by Marino Sanudo Torsello. He did not aim to conceal 'the secrets of the faithful of the cross'. Norman Housley, the leading authority on the late crusades to whose work this chapter is indebted, has dubbed him 'a crusade propagandist'. Sanudo had a number of copies of his 'Book of Secrets' made, to be sent to the powerful men of his day, among them Pope John XXII, the King of Naples and King Charles IV of France. We may think that Sanudo's emotional commitment to the cause was not purely religious when we consider that he was a merchant of Venice, who as a young businessman had lived in the Venetian quarter of Acre during its last years as a Christian territory. The recovery of the city, and indeed of the Holy Land, could be expected to bring him commercial as well as religious satisfaction. Even so, in the short term his proposals were against the interest of his native city, for he argued that any serious campaign should be initiated with a bridgehead expedition (a *parvum passagium*, 'little passage') against Mamluk Egypt, preceded by an economic blockade of its territories. Given that trade with Alexandria and the ports of Syria, in spices, raw cotton, precious metals and other vital goods, was a staple in the commerce of the Italian city states, such a strategy would be hard to enforce.

The popes' bans on trading in war materials with Muslim power faced the same difficulties. Between 1323 and 1344, according to the Mamluk Sultan himself, no Venetian ship entered his ports – the Venetian authorities, like the governments of Pisa, Naples, Genoa and other Mediterranean states, had forbidden the trade. But of course there was sanction busting. The bans were poorly enforced, they were peppered with exemptions and loopholes, and they were temporary or partial, or trading companies simply rerouted their business through other ports – in this case, those of Cyprus and Armenia. (It comes as no surprise to learn that in the 1320s King Henry II of Cyprus was a keen advocate of the sanctions against the Mamluks and their great port of Alexandria.) And when push came to shove, the Italians could take simple, direct action. When galleys belonging to the Hospitallers' fleet arrested a Genoese merchant galley trading with Alexandria, the Council of Genoa paid Turkish pirates 50,000 florins to attack the Knights on their new base at Rhodes!

While Italian merchants protected their trade and French kings their territories with little regard to crusading platitudes – Philip VI of France spent the proceeds of a crusading tax on his wars against the English – the cause of the Cross found champions nearer home. The Lusignan family, actual kings of Cyprus, were also titular kings of Jerusalem, and in April 1359 Peter I of Cyprus, grandson of the somewhat calculating Henry II, was crowned King of Jerusalem at Famagusta. For him it was not an empty ceremonial. He had a good military track record against the Turks and his chancellor, Philip de Mézières, a capable administrator, was an obsessive propagandist for the crusading cause. Peter and his chancellor did not suppose that Cyprus could recover the Christian position in Palestine unaided, but the year after the King's accession a ray of hope glimmered on the international horizon. At the Treaty of Brétigny in July 1360, four years after the Battle of Poitiers where John II of France had been captured, England and France signed peace terms. The French exchequer was making progress collecting the huge ransom demanded for their King and though he was still a gauge for the money, John was back in his capital. Paris might be open to new foreign ventures.

In 1362 Peter notified the courts of Europe of his plans for a crusade and at Avignon the following year King John II of France took the Cross jointly with him. Of still greater practical value was a papal licence for Peter to recruit support in his own name for a preliminary expedition (*passagium particulare*). He toured Christian Europe from London to Vienna and from Toulouse to Cracow receiving everywhere lavish hospitality and still more lavish promises of assistance. Meantime, King John, known to history as John the Good, the terms of his ransom hostages having been broken, had voluntarily returned to house arrest in the Tower of London, where he died in April 1364. When, in November of that year, Peter I, titular King of Jerusalem arrived at Venice to prepare his expedition against the Infidel, it was with the realization that the only expedition realistically in prospect was the *passagium particulare*, which he himself had funded. Even so, in June 1365 he and his army estimated at some 10,000 men with perhaps 1,400 horses set course for Egypt. On 10 October following, by a feat of arms which matches any military achievement of the century, they were masters of Alexandria. An Arab observer reckoned they left the city convoying seventy shiploads of booty. For of course, there being no back-up plan and no allied support, there was little realistic hope of holding the great city against the huge forces the Mamluk authorities were bound to mobilize against it. And there was the soldiery to be considered. King Peter and his chancellor argued passionately they should hold their ground – there was a possibility that a courageous stand would have shamed the stay-at-homes to honour their promises. But it was remote – the little army had won its place in history. According to the conventions of war it was entitled to its booty; to remain in place was to invite the probability of protracted and humiliating defeat; they had shown a stirring example of what could be done. The papal court at Avignon and the royal court at Paris were again lavish, this time with praise. And did nothing.

Inevitably, people questioned Peter's motives. An Arab commentator, observing the huge profits in loot the raid had won, accused him of freebooting pure and simple. The King himself had claimed that the attack on Alexandria was the first logical stage in a campaign for the recovery of the Holy Land. Others speculated that it was just one element in a Cypriot trade war, for the popes had recently relaxed the embargo on trade with Alexandria and the commerce of Famagusta had suffered – to capture its great Egyptian rival opened the possibility of controlling its trade. In the previous two years, Cypriot forces had captured various ports on the southern coast of Turkey and after his triumph at Alexandria Peter undertook expeditions against Tripoli and other ports of the Syrian coast. Once again he sought assistance from Western powers, once again without success. His proclaimed crusading intentions chimed too neatly with his Kingdom's commercial policy. Indeed, in 1367 he was in negotiations for a treaty with the Mamluk regime. The treaty was finally sealed in 1370 and with it this episode in the West's faltering attempts to reverse the disaster of the fall of Acre came to an end.

The year before, King Peter had been assassinated by a group of nobles discontented with his increasingly autocratic rule and the growing costs of his wars.[9] It is impossible to know the true motivations of his crusading policy, but we can be sure they were mixed. As a responsible head of state, the King was obliged to take account of the interests of his Kingdom; as a pious Christian with a power base in the eastern Mediterranean he could hardly escape a sense of obligation to fight to regain the Holy Land, so recently lost; as a knight he was subject to the code of chivalry which required him to fight in the cause of Christ his liege lord. Such ideals were as inspirational to the leaders of the fourteenth-century world as is the rhetoric of universal peace and democracy to Western leaders in the twenty-first century – and were followed with equally muddled commitment.

For a few men in all ages, idealism is simple and brooks no compromise. Such a man was Peter's chancellor, Philip de Mézières. He outlived his master by several years and continued as the torchbearer of the crusading ideal which retained its hold on the imagination of fashionable society. Over the Christmas festivities of 1377–78 King Charles V of France was host to the Emperor Charles IV. At the banquet for Twelfth Night, the court was entertained to a spectacular musical, or *entremet*, of 'The Conquest of Jerusalem'. It depicted highlights of the First Crusade with sensational machinery and scenic effects. The city of Jerusalem, complete with Temple topped by a minaret, which reached almost to the roof of the great banqueting hall, was clearly in the grip of the Infidel, for a 'Saracen' *muezzin* was making the call to prayer in the Arabic language from the top of the minaret. But now the city came under attack from a company of men at arms brought to the scene of the action in a ship on wheels complete with sails and rigging. Sailing across the 'moat' the attackers raised their scaling ladders against the walls; the Saracens put up a vigorous defence fending off the ladders; many of the 'crusaders' fell back into the moat before their colleagues finally rushed the defenders and triumphantly lined the battlements. The elaborate staging would not have disgraced a Cameron Mackintosh/Lloyd Webber musical. So, what if the ships that actually took some of the crusaders to Palestine could hardly have sailed inland to Jerusalem? No matter. The dramatic spectacle delighted the spectators. Among them was the ten-year-old Dauphin Charles, the future King Charles VI. Alert and imaginative, and surely entranced, the boy had no doubt been briefed on the significance of each of the scenes by his tutor who was also the deviser of the entertainment, that ageing but still passionately committed 'crusading propagandist', Philip de Mézières.

13

Chivalry in Action and Nicopolis
'The Last Crusade'

The Battle of Nicopolis was fought under the walls of the fortress of
that name on the south bank of the River Danube on 25 September
1396 by a large Christian force commanded jointly by King
Sigismund of Hungary and John, Count of Nevers, heir to the Duke
of Burgundy, against the Ottoman Turkish army, with its Serbian
allies, commanded by Sultan Bayezid I. Two popes – Boniface at
Rome and Benedict at Avignon – had blessed the enterprise. Preparations had occupied Europe's knightly class for a twelvemonth; the
departure in April of the main Western contingent from Dijon, the
capital of Burgundy, had been a pageant of fashionable luxury in
which noblemen clothed more like kings had been escorted by heralds
and minstrelsy – an armed pilgrimage in which the pilgrims' richly
blazoned coats of arms seemed, to one observer, of greater importance to them than their vows. The result was a crushing Turkish
victory. And yet to have been present at Nicopolis became a sure
badge of Christian knighthood and valour. John of Nevers earned the
soubriquet 'John the Fearless'. Such a cavalcade in aid of the Cross
against the Infidel would never again assemble on European soil, so in
this sense at least it was 'the last crusade'.

Nicopolis came at the end of a century in which, far from slacken-
ing, the crusading impulse had in some ways quickened and diversi-
fied. In Western Europe it became something of a fashionable

diversion for the aristocracy. A favourite school of chivalry – what has been called Europe's 'forgotten Hundred Years War' – was the more or less permanent crusade prosecuted year in year out by the Teutonic Order against the non-Christian peoples of central Europe, particularly the Lithuanians. From the late thirteenth century onwards the warlike heathen Lithuanian tribes roaming the dense forests around Vilnius and the tributary waterways of the River Nemunas began to coalesce into a federation which for a time would pose a serious threat to the Christian states. Pushing southwards against Poland and northwards to the Baltic coast into territory which divided the 700-odd Teutonic Knights of Prussia from their 500 or so brethren in Livonia, they built an empire which, at its greatest extent, comprising most of modern Lithuania, much of Poland and parts of Russia, stretched from Smolensk to the Baltic.

The Lithuanians proved a more dangerous enemy than the Livs, the Prussians or the Letts, in part because they seem to have been more devoutly committed to their religion, and in part because, from the 1250s onwards, a line of capable hereditary grand princes forced the tribes into a political power structure to form the base for an aggressive expansionist state. Whereas in Christian Europe popular religion was a patchwork of folk cults and residual pagan practices camouflaged in the trappings of the official religious calendar, the system of pantheistic beliefs that made up Lithuanian heathenism was devoutly held by all sections of society, from peasant to noble. It was a homogeneous culture. It was also a militaristic culture – where Catholic Christendom burnt its heretics, the pagan Lithuanians burnt their prisoners of war on ritual pyres[1] and cremated their dead war leaders accoutred in the full regalia of war, accompanied by their warhorses.

Christian optimists and men of peace argued in favour of missionary effort. In fact, the Grand Princes found their religion a useful bargaining point too. If a Christian attack seemed imminent, then, to gain time, they might open negotiations as to the possibility of a princely conversion; on the domestic front, they discovered that the Orthodox subjects in their conquered Russian territories generally preferred cohabitation with heathen masters to the prospect of submission to Catholic Christians. Having long held a papal permission to recruit for its Prussian campaigns without the issue of special papal bulls, the Teutonic Order assured volunteers both there and in its Lithuanian wars of the indulgences and other privileges of crusaders. Of course, the word crusade was not used, instead these tours of duty were known by the German word '*Reisen*', or 'journeys', and they were immensely popular particularly in those areas of Europe where the Order had lands. That paladin of chivalry, Blind King John of Bohemia made three such journeys on Prussian campaigns, while kings of Hungary and knights at the chivalry-obsessed court of Burgundy made many a '*voyage de Prusse*'.

In England and France, lulls in the fighting in their own Hundred Years War prompted many noblemen to follow the sign of the cross as *crucesignati* and *peregrini* (pilgrims) along the Baltic rivers and in the Baltic forests. For English readers the type is idealized in the 'very perfect gentle knight' of Chaucer's *Canterbury Tales*, a worthy man with his campaigns or '*reysa*' in 'Prusse' and 'Lettow' (i.e. Lettland). In the winter of 1367–8 the chancery of Edward III granted more than ninety licences of leave for Prussia. The French Marshal Boucicaut, better known for his expeditions in North Africa, the Mediterranean and the Balkans, made three '*voyages*' as a young man; Count William IV of Holland was just one among scores of gentlemen from the Low Countries who took the Cross against the pagan Balts; noblemen from Scotland, Austria and Italy all took part, or led expeditions of their own – a duke of Austria went accompanied by no fewer than 2,000 knights. Henry, Earl of Derby, later Henry IV, led a *reysa* to Vilnius.

The *Reisen* organized by the Teutonic Order have been compared to modern luxury safari excursions and, like most medieval campaigns of any duration, they provided for leisure breaks, so to speak, lulls in the serious fighting being often filled with jousts, tournaments and ceremonial feastings. At their best, they were models for the cult of chivalry and brotherhood, which the knightly class liked to suppose was typical of their lifestyle. The participants were honoured for their conformity with that code, not according to their ranking in the hierarchy of nobility. Chaucer's model was a simple knight, neither baron nor count nor duke. And yet 'ful ofte tyme he hadde the borde bigonne' – in other words occupied the seat of honour at the banqueting table. Henry Grosmont, Duke of Lancaster who, besides *reysa* in Prussia had campaigned in Spain, Rhodes and Cyprus, would have recognized him as an equal in honour.

Perhaps part of the appeal lay in the fact that the Teutonic Order's patron was the Blessed Virgin Mary. Her cult was much in vogue in the late fourteenth-century world of International Gothic sensibility. In England the beautiful and mysterious panel painting, the Wilton

Diptych, shows King Richard II flanked by English royal saints doing homage to her while one of her angels holds a pennant with the red cross asociated with St George. At Nicopolis, as we shall see, the Burgundian contingent marched under banners depicting the Virgin. In any case a Baltic *Reise* with the German Knights became something of a fixture in the chivalric social calendar; a working holiday, so to speak, for the military man. But there was serious fighting – the chronicler Wigand of Marburg, who was also the herald of the Teutonic Order, reckoned that the capture of the major Lithuanian fortress of Kaunas would have been impossible without the aid of the pilgrims from the West. For their part, whether counts, dukes or kings, these men saw themselves as brothers in the fraternity of Christendom's knighthood when they fought with the Teutonic Order – what Pope Urban V called 'Christendom's most secure wall and marvellous propagator of the Christian Faith',[2] and who, according to that crusading enthusiast Philip de Mézières, 'put to great shame . . . all the Christian princes'.[3]

Of course, the austere and often harsh monastic soldiers of the Order were not immaculate. The capture of Danzig had been followed by a shocking massacre; faced with the hostility of a jealous Polish state they were prepared on occasion to ally with the Lithuanians (the Poles, be it said, could make similar alliances); on one occasion the Knights even diverted a Bohemian force marching to help them against the heathen to an attack on Polish troops holding a captured Teutonic fortress. In 1319 Pope John XXII set up an enquiry into the Order's actions.[4]

In the 1350s the Knights found their supremacy as the Christian champions in the region weakened when King Casimir of Poland won privileges from the papal curia. In 1364, at Cracow, Casimir assembled a congress with four other Central European monarchs to debate, among other things, the possibility of a joint contribution to the crusade planned by Peter of Cyprus. In fact, Poland was to overtake the Order as the premier crusading power in Eastern Europe against not only the heathen but also 'the schismatics', which meant the Orthodox Church in Russia. The foundation statutes of the University of Cracow (1364) allude to the need for greater activity and dedication to the teaching of the Catholic faith for the conversion of the pagans and schismatics who border the Kingdom. Twenty years after this the very reason for the existence of the Teutonic Order seemed called into question when the Lithuanian Grand Prince

Jagiello (Jogailo), having first been baptized a Roman Catholic with the Christian name Wladyslaw, married the Polish Princess Jadwiga to become King of Poland. The following year a cathedral was founded in Vilnius. To Philip de Mézières it was splendid news. In his tract of crusading propaganda, the 'Dream of the Old Pilgrim', he conjured up the heart-warming vision of the Teutonic Knights, 'the Lords of Prussia', marching with the King of Lithuania on Constantinople to crush the power of the Turks.[5] Nevertheless, the Order continued to attract 'crusader' pilgrims for years after. For one thing, they argued, Lithuanian conversions were not to be trusted – more than one Grand Prince had relapsed and one 'permitted himself to be baptized five times, alternating between the Catholic and Orthodox Churches as circumstances dictated'.[6]

In the 1340s Cyprus developed crusading initiatives in the Mediterranean. King Hugh IV and the Master of the Hospitallers approached Avignon for assistance against the growing pressure of Turkish aggression. The plan was for Pope Clement VI to finance a fleet of galleys to be manned and operated at the expense of the other partners and to be operational purely against Turkish-occupied Asia Minor – this was the birth of a pattern of anti-Turkish naval league action that would continue in various forms until the great victory over the Ottoman fleet at Lepanto in 1571. The crusading leagues in the Aegean included participants from the Papal States, the Kingdom of Naples, the islands of Crete and Rhodes as well as Cyprus, some of the Latin states in Greece and even the rump of the Byzantine Empire in the Balkans. The first league won a notable success when, in October 1344, it captured the great port of Smyrna (Izmir) from the Turks – and held it for more than half a century. In 1374 the Hospitallers took responsibility for the custody of the port and although the Christian powers did not succeed in extending their conquests from this bridgehead position, it remained a Christian enclave in Muslim territory until, in 1402, the Tatar conqueror Tamerlane ruptured the entire Muslim world.

Success at Smyrna was matched some two decades later by the fleeting triumph of the Cypriot capture of Alexandria in 1365. Listing his knight's battle honours, and his expeditions in Spain, North Africa and Asia Minor, Chaucer chose to begin with it: 'at Alisaundre he was, when it was wonne.' As always, the poet is in touch with his times. The Italian poet Petrarch, then about sixty, reckoned the triumph of King Peter of Cyprus and Prince John of Antioch in overrunning

Alexandria in October of that year could have marked a new chapter in the spread of Latin Christianity among the infidels if only the victors could have matched their valour with staying power.[7] And, he might have added, if they had been better supported.

Peter had spent some three years touring European power centres, visited the Visconti court at Milan, the papal court at Avignon and many others to rally support for his dream of the recovery of Jerusalem. In November 1363, the twenty-year-old Geoffrey Chaucer could have witnessed the Cypriot monarch's progress from Dover to London in quest of help for his crusades. In December, King Peter was in Paris. Thence he headed eastwards through Cologne, Meissen and Prague as far as Cracow, travelling through Vienna to Venice for the return journey. The King spoke of Jerusalem; the Pope conferred the status of a crusade on his proposed expedition; and a number of adventurers and some serious-minded independent crusaders like Chaucer's knight joined the colours.

They rendezvoused with Peter's main forces at Rhodes before the raid on Alexandria, but he never had the resources for Jerusalem and had to be content with the rich booty that came from the sack of Alexandria. Although the Christians could not hold the city, the sack 'administered a severe blow to Mamluk prestige'.[8] In his ten-year reign from 1359 to 1369 King Peter presided over the most brilliant epoch of the Kingdom of Cyprus, while he achieved a string of triumphs against the Muslim ports of the eastern Mediterranean. Adalia (Antalya) remained Cypriot for more than a decade; Latakia, Tortosa, Beirut, Sidon and Rosetta were just some of the rich Muslim trading ports that fell to his raids, while for a time he was in full-scale war with the Mamluk Sultanate of Egypt. Eventually Peter was murdered in a palace coup, but even so his success against Muslim targets, like the earlier capture of Smyrna, were real successes for the fading crusading impulse.

Not so the wars fought at the same time in Europe with papal blessings and crusaders' indulgences. In 1378 a split or schism had been created in the papacy when Pope Urban VI's election at Rome was challenged by a group of cardinals led by Cardinal Robert de Genève who was duly proclaimed 'Clement VII' and took up residence in the Palace of the Popes at Avignon, an imperial enclave in France which for the previous sixty years had in fact been the seat of the papacy in exile from Rome. There had been rival popes before but usually because an emperor had been dissatisfied with the incumbent and found friendly cardinals to elect a new one. In such a case few churchmen had problems in dubbing the imperial nominee the 'anti-pope'. But in 1378 the division was a gratuitous creation of the College of Cardinals. The Church itself finally decided the Roman line to be the legitimate one, but for contemporary heads of state the situation was too good to pass up. The King of England and Ireland, and his old ally the King of Portugal, like the Papal States and Catholic Eastern Europe, held to the Roman popes, while France and its old ally Scotland, together with its Spanish neighbours, of course held to Avignon. The rival pontiffs, knowing that they were the only legitimate heir to St Peter and heirs to a European tradition to which the crusade against schismatics and heretics had been integral for centuries, launched crusades against their rivals' supporters. For Rome the English led campaigns in Flanders, under Henry Dispenser, Bishop of Norwich, while John of Gaunt, Duke of Lancaster, in conjunction with the King of Portugal, warred against Castile and Leon partisans of Avignon. But there were those who still felt that the true target of crusading should be the rival faith of Islam and the advancing Turkish power in the Balkans seemed a worthy adversary.

The Nicopolis campaign may have looked like a picnic when it set out in spring of 1396. In fact, it was the outcome of a serious response to a serious threat. Since their conquest of the port of Gallipoli on the European shore of the Dardanelles about 1356, the Ottoman Turks had been systematically extending their conquests in the Balkans and in 1395 Sultan Bayezid had laid siege to Constantinople. Sigismund saw his frontier Kingdom of Hungary as the next victim of the Turks, and a confrontation on the banks of the Danube with a possible offensive to the south of it as the best answer. It made good military sense if the forces could be brought to bear. For all the extravagance of its chevaliers' wardrobes, the weaponry was of good quality, so it only needed the joint force to be well commanded, but there was no overall command and no agreed overall objective. King Sigismund saw the purpose of the expedition as the destruction of Bayezid's power to halt the advance of Islam. The Western European knights, however, dreamed of driving the Turks from the Balkans and some even fanta-sized about crossing the straits and marching on through Anatolia to Syria and the recovery of Jerusalem. For the Burgundian court, the objective, in the view of historian John Vaughan, was the expansion of the European prestige of the Burgundian state. 'The crusade was [still] of considerable importance to secular rulers, for it was one of the few undertakings which brought them prestige or renown whether it succeeded or not.'[9] This was certainly true in the case of John of Nevers and Sigismund. As for Count John's father, Duke Philip the Bold of Burgundy, the expedition 'though it ended in disastrous failure played a considerable part in the emergence of Burgundy as a European power'.[10]

Duke Philip had long been interested in the idea of crusading. It seems that he had taken the Cross along with his father King John II the Good of France back in 1363. In the 1390s he was closely involved in plans along with the Duke of Orléans and John of Gaunt, Duke of Lancaster, for a joint expedition. As late as spring 1395 it seems' he fully intended to lead the enterprise in person, but by the autumn of that year plans were completely changed; the two other noblemen withdrew their participation, as did Philip himself. Now the nominal command of the Burgundian contingent was to be in the hands of Count John, his twenty-four-year-old son and heir, under advice by five experienced senior courtiers. We don't know the reason for what seems an extraordinary decision. Perhaps it was that with a king at the head of the army, Duke Philip would lose standing. As it was, the expedition was a glittering assembly of French chivalry – among Count John's personal company and advisers was the Admiral of France; other contingents marched under the banners of famous gentlemen crusaders such as Jacques de Bourbon, Count of La Marche and Jehan de Boucicaut, Marshal of France.

The expedition was to promote the prestige of Burgundy in an age when prestige was a large component of political influence. Pope Benedict granted bulls permitting Count John to have dealings with the infidels, and assuring him of full absolution of his sins should he die on the expedition. The retinue accompanying the Count was to outshine all the other contingents on the expedition. Some 200 strong, all dressed in the Count's livery, would be accommodated on campaign in satin tents and pavilions filling no fewer than twenty-four wagons; four immense banners painted with the image of the Virgin Mary in gold were displayed on column of march; innumerable brightly coloured pennons adorned the tents in camp; twelve state trumpeters in full heraldic blazons sounded fanfares at all formal ceremonies. Most impressive of all, certainly for the participants, the members of the Count's retinue received four months advance pay before leaving Dijon.

In the first week of May, having embarked at Regensburg, the cavalcade was sailing down the Danube to Vienna where they were met by Duke Leopold of Austria, Count John's brother-in-law from whom the Count borrowed the immense sum of 100,000 ducats.[11] Finally, in late July they reached Buda where King Sigismund was waiting for them with the Hungarian army and a quite unacceptable war plan – certain that the Turks would soon invade his country he proposed that the massed armies concentrate in a defensive position on his southern frontier on the north bank of the Danube. It may have been sound strategy, but the crusaders from the West had not marched thousands of wearisome and expensive miles under the standard of the Blessed Virgin and the banners of their own liege lords to await the pleasure of the Infidel. Across the great river lay lands only recently part of Christian Bulgaria. They swung along cheerfully down the left bank of the Danube, before heading east along the great bend and past Belgrade to cross onto the right bank at the Iron Gate of Orsova in modern Romania. After cheap victories over two minor Turkish garrison towns they came up against the great fortress of Nicopolis which Bayezid had only recently captured and which was ominously well fortified. But the mood in the army was buoyant, not to say absurdly optimistic. They had done battle with the enemies of Christ and twice defeated them. Quite unknown to them, Bayezid, known to the Turks as 'the Thunderbolt', had lifted the siege of Constantinople weeks back and by 24 September was encamped within four miles of Nicopolis. Battle was joined the following day.

In the early stages the Franco-Burgundian horsemen won glory with charges that scattered their Turkish opponents, who parted to regroup. Thereafter an exact account of the leaderless battle makes any detailed account of the Christians' rout well nigh impossible. A force of *spahi* cavalry commanded by Sultan Bayezid himself played the decisive role in the Turkish victory; armed with bow, lance and sword, these were the crack horsemen of the Ottoman army. At Nicopolis they took position on a reverse slope, covered by a line of skirmishers. Against the advice of Sigismund the Western knights had insisted on charging in the grand old feudal way. Thanks to the splendid élan of their attack, the enemy front line was swept aside effortlessly and with heavy Turkish losses. But behind the skirmishers was a concealed hazard of sharpened stakes, which impaled horses and forced riders to dismount under a ceaseless hail of arrows. Few of them reached the waiting Turkish cavalry. Meantime the main Hungarian force, deserted on its flanks by its Wallachian allies and destabilized by the mayhem in the French ranks to its front, was slowly driven back by Sigismund's Serbian auxiliaries and then scattered from the field. Sigismund barely saved his life but managed to escape by boat up the Danube with a handful of followers. Virtually the entire Franco-Burgundian force that had set out so gaily from Dijon back in April lay dead or dying on the field. Scores of prisoners were killed on the Sultan's orders. Huge ransoms had to be paid for the hundreds of noble Western prisoners taken that day, among them Count John and de Boucicaut. The Admiral of France and scores of others of exalted rank were dead.

When news began to reach Paris it was not believed and the survivors with their harrowing stories were thrown into prison as rumour-mongers. The arrival, the day before Christmas, of a herald bearing Bayezid's detailed requirements in the matter of ransom payments left no room for any kind of doubt. After nine months in captivity at Gallipoli and Bursa, Count John and his companions began a leisurely return home, staying for a time with the Hospitallers at Rhodes. Meantime, the Chancellor of Burgundy, with the aid of the textile-rich towns of Flanders, the estates of Artois and of Burgundy itself, and all the Duke's numerous other territories and clients, by pawning the ducal jewels and by raising loans – all of which would be duly repaid – had been raising vast sums of money. Finally, on 22 February 1392, Count John and his companions made their formal entry into Dijon to scenes of jubilant exaltation. In the coming weeks he and his father made triumphal progress through city after city, to be greeted by fanfares, trumpeters and minstrels, and by burgomasters and town dignitaries.

> Thus ended the disaster of Nicopolis, in a blaze of glory which somehow conjured up triumph out of defeat and tragedy. The fame and prestige of the house of Burgundy had been successfully promoted, and it was now linked forever with the proud and almost magic tradition of the crusades.[12]

Bayezid's triumph was short-lived. Having secured the Ottoman position in the Balkans, he turned his attention to the Turkoman emirates in Anatolia which his Ottoman predecessors had tended to ally with while they extended their conquests in Christian Europe. By attacking Muslim rulers Bayezid betrayed the spirit of the *ghazi*, warriors against the Infidel, which had been the inspiration of Ottoman conquests up to this time. He found resentment amongst friends and former allies while his victims found a ready welcome at the court of Tamerlane, the Mongol tyrant of North India, Persia and Russian Asia and destroyer of Baghdad, who regarded Anatolia as his sphere of influence. In July 1402 he crushed the forces of Bayezid at the Battle of Ankara and the victor of Nicopolis died in captivity the following year.

14

The Lingering Decline of a Flawed Ideal

From the times of the First Crusade, the movement had been flawed by mixed motives. Emperor Alexius hoped he would received a disciplined body of fighting men to recover lands of the Empire in Anatolia, but whereas Pope Urban recruited an immense force for the capture of Jerusalem with the consequent prestige to the papal office, some of the lay participants had straightforward personal agendas of personal aggrandisement and the founding of new political units. As the centuries advanced, this politicization of the ideal tended to come to the fore. In Spain it had always been difficult to disentangle the politics of national expansion from the pieties of Holy War so that when the final expulsion of the Moors from the Kingdom of Granada coincided with the discovery of the New World by Columbus, a contemporary was moved to remark the following year, 1493, that 'the conquest of the Indies began when that of the Moors was over, for the Spanish have always fought against the Infidels.'[1]

But perhaps the crusades' deepest impact on Western Europe's Christian community was caused by the concept of the indulgence. Probably the most attractive inducement to participation was Pope Urban's Clermont promise that this would be a sufficient substitute for other acts of penance. To the ordinary Christian this meant that provided he went into battle in a state of repentance and had made confession, he could be assured of immediate entry into Paradise. As Joinville wrote of Louis IX's crusades, while 'they caused great mourning in this world, [they caused] much rejoicing in Paradise, for such as died true crusaders in these pilgrimages'.[2] When Pope Innocent III extended the plenary indulgence for fighting crusaders to those who contributed money or advice to the crusade[3] a dangerous new idea was introduced. Over the centuries, the idea that Christians could shorten the time of sufferings in Purgatory before entering Paradise by the purchase of an official papal indulgence became regularized into a commodity trade like any other. In fact it became scandalous and attacks on abuses of the system by a cash-hungry Church proved a powerful ingredient in the ferment of criticism of the Roman Catholic Church which would produce the Protestant Reformation in the sixteenth century.

This chapter examines a number of cases where, to an outside observer, it seems obvious that politics predominated over religion in expeditions blessed by popes as crusades, or aspects of the movement were perverted by political considerations. The conquest of Spain's colonial empire in the Americas was a classic instance. A fundamental question of natural law had been raised by the campaigns of the Canary Islands. The inhabitants were clearly heathen, but did not even infidels, God's children if awaiting enlightenment, have the right to govern themselves, and if they did, by what right could Christians invade them? Fortunately, the Pope found the correct answer: yes, they did have that right, ruled the pontiff, but it was overridden by papal responsibility for their souls.[4] Therefore, by inference, conquest by crusade could be viewed as a form of missionary activity. Such cynical rationalizations were common among the population at large, for Spain's crusades of conquest were financed by the sale of indulgences. However, as early as 1500 most purchasers were more interested in the fringe exemptions they might carry, such as the permission to eat eggs and milk during Lent, than any supposed spiritual benefits.[5]

Set against such trivia a giant step in politicization would be taken in 1520 when its Grand Master dissolved the Teutonic Order and its territory of East Prussia was established as a nascent secular state. Some twenty years later, Thomas Cranmer, King Henry VIII's saintly Archbishop of Canterbury, faced a dilemma when his master and the Emperor Charles V were hoping to present their aggressive pact against King Francis I of France and his ally Sultan Suleyman the Magnificent as a crusade on behalf of Christendom. Cranmer's orders were to have the appeal read from the pulpits of England's churches in what, in fact, amounted to the last proclamation of a crusade in English history. But as Cranmer's biographer Diarmaid MacCulloch observes, this required that the Archbishop, a reformer by inclination, 'sanitize an aspect of the world of traditional religion that he now abhorred. Crusades were, after all, intimately connected with the origin of papal indulgences.' To make it plain that there was no question of a straight commercial transaction in which, as in former times, people 'departed with their money . . . for counterfeit pardons', the exhortation assured its listeners that a charitably intended cash gift would be rewarded by a 'true pardon granted by him that hath purchased pardon for all penitent sinners, our Saviour Jesus Christ'.[6] Another forty years on, and cynics were bound to see the crusade of the Spanish Armada in 1588 as a cloak for Spanish imperialism. But the identification of national interest with religious virtue took an unexpected turn in 1898 when the Bishop of Segovia called for a national crusade against the US following the loss of Cuba.[7] There was a steady decline in the flawed ideal from the 1400s onwards, but there were, too, moments of glory.

In 1530 the Knights Hospitaller of St John, having been driven from Rhodes by Sultan Suleyman the Magnificent, were given the island of Malta as their new home by Emperor Charles V. In 1565 the ageing Sultan launched a huge naval and military force determined to extirpate the Christian troublemakers and their galleys from the Mediterranean sealanes. This time, however, under their heroic septuagenarian Grand Master, Jean Parisot de la Valette, the Knights, loyally helped by the people of Malta, withstood the pounding of a four-month siege by a vastly superior enemy, which was forced to retire in humiliating disarray. Six years later, at the Battle of Lepanto the Ottoman fleet suffered another crushing defeat at Christian hands. But the crusading Knights' triumph at the Great Siege of Malta will remain one of the majestic episodes in the history of Europe so long as that history is remembered.

In the twenty-first century, the tradition of the Hospitallers is continued by the Order of the Knights of Malta with its HQ in the Palazzo Malta, in the via Condotti, Rome and Associations in most European countries as well as in America and Australia.

With his defeat of Bayezid I, the first Ottoman to bear the title Sultan, at the battle at Ankara, it seemed that Tamerlane (Timur Lenk) had finished Turkish power. Bayezid died the following year and the Ottoman domains in Europe as well as Asia lay open to the

Mongol conqueror. John VII, Byzantine co-emperor, hastened to make his submission, but it was only casually acknowledged, for Tamerlane's interests lay in the East. A divided Ottoman state, at war between the dead Sultan's sons and tributary princes, seemed to safeguard his rear while he embarked on an expedition against China. Then, in February 1405, he too died. With the Islamic Middle East in utter confusion there was, perhaps, a decade of opportunity for Western Christendom to attempt to recoup the catastrophe at Nicopolis and reverse the Turkish advance in the Balkans. Instead, the wars fought in the name of religion became increasingly embroiled in politics and the rhetoric of crusade became part of the vocabulary of international diplomacy. Sigismund of Hungary, after Nicopolis, returned to his interests in Central Europe, where he hoped to displace his older half-brother Wenceslas (Czech, Waclav; German, Wenzel) on the Bohemian throne, held by their family for three generations. Failing in this he began to canvas the cause of a new expedition against the Islamic powers, hoping at the same time to boost his own precarious standing as potentate of high pretensions.

Sigismund, with his long face and long, curly, spade-cut beard, toque headgear, somewhat watery eyes, notoriously spendthrift ways (more than once he had to pawn the imperial crown jewels), his cruelty and his deep unpopularity in Hungary, might seem a somewhat uncharismatic icon of authority. The Hungarian Crown had come to him by right of marriage to its queen, Maria, but as the son of the Holy Roman Emperor Charles IV (d. 1378), he also laid claim to the imperial title against Wenceslas. He had himself crowned King of the Romans at Aachen in November 1414, the preliminary ceremony to the full imperial title (achieved only twenty years later). Maybe he calculated that to champion the cause of the Holy Land would add weight to his imperial pretensions. Maybe he was disinterestedly devout. He certainly stirred up the chancelleries of Europe as he travelled far and wide to promote a united Christendom under his 'imperial' leadership, and he startled Paris by asserting his right 'as Emperor' to create a Frenchman knight while assisting at the adjudication of a case in a French court.[8] The gesture was noted in London where King Henry V hoped to reach an Anglo-Imperial accord in the line-up of diplomatic forces at the international Council of Constance, convened under pressure from Sigismund himself to examine religious dissidence in Bohemia and to resolve the scandal of the Great Schism in the papacy. The French found Sigismund's manners disgusting, his debauchery excessive and his imperial pretensions an affront, yet they paid handsomely for his entertainment in Paris, in part to distract him from any entente with Burgundy, now an independent player on the international scene, or England.

In April 1416, the year after Agincourt, with great pomp and splendour the Earl of Warwick, Captain of the place, received the 'imperial' cavalcade in the English town of Calais. On the last day of the month, in a fleet of 300 ships provided by King Henry V, Sigismund and his entourage crossed the narrow sea for Dover. There, the next day, the imperial barge hove to, some yards from the shore, to be met by a noble reception committee advancing through waves waist high, their swords drawn, demanding the Emperor renounce all rights he or his successors might claim over the realm of England as the result of the homage performed two years before by King Richard the Lionheart to his predecessor, Emperor Henry VI. Perhaps the Paris 'knighting' made this seem advisable. From Dover it was a triumphal progress through Canterbury, to be received by the Archbishop, Rochester, by Henry's elder brother the Duke of Bedford, Blackheath, by the Lord Mayor of London, and for the last mile into the city by an escort of 5,000 noblemen and knights led by the King himself. Throughout his stay, funded by the English exchequer, the Emperor lodged in the Palace of Westminster, the King at Lambeth Palace. At a ceremony in Westminster, the Emperor, as he styled himself, was invested with the Order of the Knight of the Garter and, we are told, presented the King with the relic of the Heart of St George, Patron of the Order and of Christian Knighthood. At the Treaty of Canterbury agreed on 15 August 1416, the two brothers in arms made a complete offensive and defensive alliance and the Emperor made public recognition of the English King's claim to be rightful King of France.

Both signatories benefited. Sigismund's assumed imperial status was flattered by endorsement from Europe's most powerful monarch; Henry won legitimacy for the fact established by the slaughter on the field of Agincourt. To both, crusading rhetoric was integral to the event. Henry had spoken of his French wars as a pious duty to unite the greatest powers of the Christian West preparatory to leading their combined forces against the Turk. His victory at Agincourt over the full might of the French army against impossible odds seemed (and not only to him) to vindicate the rhetoric by an act of God. Canterbury gave it the blessing of Christendom's secular overlord. Henry of

England's designation as the French King's heir by the international Treaty of Troyes in 1420 was another massive diplomatic fact. Had he outlived his feeble father-in-law, King Henry III and V of France and England would have been the incontestable candidate to lead a united Christendom. (Henry himself always accorded the priority of honour to his French realm.) And there can be little doubt that he would have done so – after all, there were many at the time who saw the Agincourt campaign itself as a calculating foreign venture undertaken to distract conspirators at home. There were many voices appealing for Christian princes to help the embattled Byzantine state while its chief enemy was weak and divided. The leader of a successful campaign would win golden opinions in Christendom while participation in the joint venture might well reconcile the French nobility to their new monarch. In fact Henry died in August 1422 leaving a baby boy as his heir to the two kingdoms.

With the death of Wenceslas in 1419 Sigismund returned to the situation in the Kingdom of Bohemia. A constituent part of the Empire, Bohemia (roughly equivalent to the modern Czech Republic) was also one of the most prosperous regions of Central Europe (German, *Mitteleuropa*) – much of Europe's silver came from the mines at Kutna Hora, populated by a people with a strong sense of what can only be called national identity. Emperor Charles IV (who ruled Bohemia 1347–78), builder of the Charles Bridge and the other glories of medieval Prague, founded the city's university and instituted Czech as a medium of instruction there. The charismatic theologian and professor and from 1409 rector of Prague University, Jan Hus, whose pre-Reformation theology owed much to the Oxford theologian John Wyclif, opened up teachings which the Church rejected. For refusing to submit to the rulings of the Church he was burnt alive as a condemned heretic at the Council of Constance on 6 July 1415, having submitted himself to trial there only on the assurance of a safe conduct from Sigismund that he would be able to return to Prague whatever the verdict. Bohemian nobles present at Constance protested the judgement and Sigismund's reputation in Bohemia was blackened. Resistance, led by the Hussites, combined Czech national objections to Sigismund as champion of German culture and religious objections to him as a supporter of Roman Catholic orthodoxy.

Hussite objections to the Church were to its corruption, typified by indulgences being levied for a proposed crusade; and also to the privileged position of the priesthood symbolized at the service of

Communion by the fact that they only could drink the wine symbolizing Christ's blood. These heretics believed that all Christians had the right to take Communion in both kinds and to conduct the services of the Church in their own language – they used a Czech liturgy, which affronted German as well as papal ideas. For some fifteen years Central Europe witnessed a series of campaigns, now known as the Hussite Crusades, in which an army of peasants, at first armed with farm implements such as pitchforks and flails, and gentry, marching under banners which displayed the emblem of the Communion chalice, destroyed one army after another of mounted knights and professional men at arms sent against them by the German King and blessed by the Church. The Hussites established themselves in military encampments in the vicinity of Prague to which they gave the Biblical names of Mount Tabor and Horeb.

The movement had moderate and extremist wings but also many influential supporters: the widowed Queen Sophia, for a time regent, favoured Hussite pastors. The new Pope, Martin V, sponsored Sigismund in a crusade against the Hussites which would also justify the Emperor's own agenda, the suppression of Bohemian political opposition. Shortly after his election in November 1417 he had made a provocative offer of reconciliation, though it was surely intended to incite rejection – for example, it insisted that the Hussites should publicly approve the condemnation and burning of Hus. Now, at Sigismund's request, he produced a crusading bull, which was publicly read out in the city of Breslau (Wroclaw) in what is now Polish Silesia. It called for the extermination of Wyclifites, Hussites and other heretics, without mention of the Kingdom of Bohemia. The crusade was proclaimed at Breslau in March 1420. Sigismund crossed the frontier with a force of some 25,000 crusaders in April 1420 and marched via Kutna Hora, the centre of the silver mining district in the valley of the Elbe River, to Prague where his supporters, holed up in their fortress Hradčany Castle, held his coronation as King of Bohemia on 28 July. But the Hussites under their inspiring leader Jan Žižka the Blind, a member of the lesser gentry and a professional soldier, twice defeated Sigismund's forces. His coronation unrecognized by the vast majority of his Bohemian subjects, his German army routed, the new 'king' had to abandon his crusade and retire humiliated in March 1421. In June the Hradčany Castle surrendered to the Hussite army.

In August northern Bohemia came under attack from an army led by Margrave Frederick of Meissen, which was defeated outside the Catholic town of Most, a few miles inside the Bohemian border, and another led by a cardinal, the Archbishop of Magdeburg, the Duke of Saxony and a Count Palatine, although it was forced to withdraw from the country in October. That same month, Sigismund was back, attacking through Moravia, Catholic country, and marching up through Brno towards Kutna Hora, where his army was routed, so that he had to leave his kingdom a loser once more in January 1422. From October to December 1422, Frederick of Brandenburg tried his luck, attacking from Bavaria in the west but hardly encroaching on Bohemian territory before abandoning the project. The crusade of July–August 1427 led by Frederick of Brandenburg and the fifty-three-year-old Cardinal Henry Beaufort, great-uncle of King Henry VI of England, Bishop of Winchester and Archbishop elect of Trier, who was pleased to designate the stalwart Czech Protestants 'infidels',[9] lasted barely a month and when the Brandenburger tried again, in August 1431, this time with the Elector of Saxony and Cardinal Julian Cesarini, this enterprise was even less long lived. Thus it was that for more than a decade the Roman Catholic establishment of southern Central Europe was outfought and outgunned by professional armies of Protestant dissidents led first by Jan Žižka, and, after his death in 1424, by Prokop the 'Bald', or the 'Shaven'.

They were literally outgunned, in fact, since these men and their lieutenants were the first commanders in Europe to deploy the developing arm of gunpowder artillery in mobile warfare. In its most advanced form, the Hussite war wagon has been compared to the tank; certainly it carried medium light field pieces that could be fired on the move but were more commonly deployed in virtually impregnable laager fortresses complemented by handguns and crossbows. The germ of the idea seems to have originated with Žižka's experience of the Russian *goliaigorod*, a formation of transport wagons that could be rapidly thrown into a defensive laager.[10] At first, the Hussites used ordinary farm wagons, but later built specialized vehicles of sturdier construction, with grappling hooks at each end and with high sides of thick boarding pierced with loopholes for light field artillery weapons and handguns. Each wagon carried a score of men, half of them armed with pikes and flails being placed between the wagons, the other half, armed with handguns and crossbows, pouring a rain of missiles from the gun ports in the wagon sides.

A Hussite army normally marched in five columns with the cavalry and field artillery in the middle and the wagons on the flanks. The system relied on the skill of the highly trained wagon drivers who could throw their cumbersome vehicles into varied formations with a discipline that astonished contemporaries. It was found possible to manoeuvre the war wagons into the standard oblong laager so rapidly that a Hussite force could drive between the columns of an opposing army, establish its defensive formation and, before the enemy could redeploy, charge out from the laager with such force that the enemy often fled without a fight. Other manoeuvres included loading wagons with rocks and stones and setting them rolling downhill like battering rams, and on at least one occasion firing off the light artillery pieces mounted in the wagons while on the move. From 1427 onwards defence moved to offence as Hussite forces sallied out across neigh-bouring German Catholic territories in destructive raids. The Catholic enemy were unable either to learn to use the innovative techniques or find any effective response to the Czech military superiority, so although the Hussite cause was itself divided between moderates and extremists Sigismund was obliged to call off his crusading allies and in 1436 come to terms with his rebellious subjects.

None of Sigismund's activity had done anything to ease what many, even in the West, were beginning to see as the real menace to Christendom – the threat to Constantinople, now surrounded by the resurgent power of the Ottoman Turks under Sultan Murad II. For its part, the Byzantine establishment, realizing that it could expect no help from the West until it admitted subjection to the Roman Cath-olic Church and the claims of papal supremacy, made formal submis-sion to Pope Eugenius IV in 1439. Agreed at a Council at Florence, though never accepted by the Byzantine public, it produced rewards. The Pope preached a crusade and himself helped mobilize consider-able funds and the intervention of a Venetian fleet designed to block the passage of Turkish forces across the Dardanelles. Polish-Hungarian forces under their young King and John Hunyadi, gover-nor of Transylvania and a fine soldier, had achieved considerable successes against the Ottomans and in July 1444 even forced a ten-year truce which among other things bound Murad not to cross the Danube. It was a major blow against the Ottomans, but it was wasted. Almost at once, persuaded by the papal legate that no undertaking to the Infidel need be honoured, the Catholic forces broke the truce. The Venetian fleet failed to prevent Murad returning from Anatolia with a force which vastly outnumbered his opponents, destroying their army at the Battle of Varna, killing the young King and driving Hunyadi into flight.

Obsessed with fears that the Turks might conquer Rome itself, in Italy humanists like Biondo Flavio of Forli, author of a *History from the Decline of the Roman Emperors* and Aeneas Silvius Piccolomini, later Pope Pius II, called for action from the Emperor Frederick III and King Alfonso of Aragon and Naples. Biondo reminded Frederick of the warlike ventures of his predecessors Frederick I and Frederick II in a speech he gave before the two monarchs in 1452.

The very next year, on Monday, 28 May 1453, Constantinople fell to the young Turkish Sultan, Mehmet II. The last Emperor, Constantine XI Palaeologus, was last seen dashing towards the mass of Turkish Janissaries pouring through the defences. The city was lost, the Roman Empire at last finished. Hours of massacre followed: 'blood ran in rivers down the steep streets . . . towards the Golden Horn'[11] – then came the statutory three days of looting.

For fifty years, Byzantine emperors had made sporadic begging trips round the courts of Europe seeking aid against the Ottoman menace, but the price of a papal crusade was always submission by the Orthodox Church to the supremacy of Rome. The Union of the Churches agreed at Florence in 1439 was opposed by public opinion and by many leading Orthodox clergy, although Pope Nicholas V still insisted on total commitment. As late as 1452 a cardinal had arrived with troops, not to help against the Turks but to protect the Latin delegation. Finally, in December that year, at a solemn service held in the Cathedral of Hagia Sophia (Holy Wisdom), the Union was formally read before the Emperor and his court, and the Pope's name honoured in the prayers. The citizenry continued to attend only those churches whose priests had refused to accept the Union. Had the betrayal of the faith been followed by Western troopships sailing into the Golden Horn and the possibility of saving the Christian Empire been in prospect, the people could, perhaps, have swallowed the bitter humiliation. As it was, apart from the residents in the Venetian quarter and a force of some 700 well-armed Genoese,[12] together with a few score Western well-wishers, the Orthodox population of Christendom's greatest metropolis were left to fight their last battle alone.

The Christian West had failed to save Constantinople while it was still occupied by a Christian emperor and a Christian population. Now, dreamers believed it could be recovered, the Ottomans driven out of the Balkans and even Jerusalem could be recaptured. Pope Nicholas V called for a crusade and Aeneas Sylvius (later Pope Pius II), the Emperor Frederick III's ambassador, urged action and an army was actually raised in the Balkans, as we shall see. In Western Europe Philip the Good, Duke of Burgundy, was said to be fervent to fight in the cause and at Lille on 17 February 1454, he hosted the Feast of the Pheasant – so called from the live pheasant adorned with a jewelled collar which was the emblem of the banquet – to proclaim his intention and recruit his knights and courtiers to make their vows. The grand banquet, watched by a large audience from the galleries of the hall, was punctuated by elaborate tableaux, designed and decorated by no fewer than thirty-five artists, and ended with a solemn ceremony of vow taking. The Duke swore to go on crusade, and should the occasion arise, even to do battle in single combat with the Grand Turk. Courtiers, more or less sober, followed him with extravagant promises of how they would follow the Duke. All these texts were incorporated in the official report of the event, which was widely distributed. Observant readers would have noticed that the Duke's vow, on which all the others were dependent, was carefully hedged about with conditions that were most unlikely to be fulfilled.[13] But the political prestige of Burgundy was raised another notch.

Others did take action. Also in 1454, setting out from Frankfurt, the Franciscan friar John of Capistrano, with papal blessing, embarked on a preaching tour in southern Germany and Hungary, where John Hunyadi was recruiting for a campaign against a Turkish advance threatening Belgrade. Many thousands were inspired to take the Cross by Capistrano's charismatic presence. In July 1456 the Christian forces before Belgrade, under Hunyadi's command and chanting the battle cry 'Jesu! Jesu! Jesu!' drove off the far larger Ottoman army under Mehmet II. It was a notable triumph over the brilliant young conqueror of Constantinople, although it was sadly not to be a prelude to greater things. Soon after the victory, an epidemic raged in the Christian camp and both Hunyadi and Capistrano were among the thousands who died.

Humanist scholars, to whom ancient Rome and Greece represented a lost ideal culture, lamented the fall of Constantinople as a blow to the tradition of Plato. The centuries between the fall of Rome and their own day, which they were to dub 'the middle ages', they despised as lost time between the glorious classical past and its revival, under their supervision, in the modern world. For this reason, the doings of the crusaders met with their approval as much because they were seen as wars *'contra barbaros'*, against the barbarians, as for any religious consideration. Biondo had nothing but praise for the First Crusade, which he considered the greatest undertaking by any pope. Following the publication of a revised edition of his book in 1463, the emphasis was to be taken up by other Italians, notably Benedetto Accolti. His Latin *Historia Gotefridi*, i.e. 'Godfrey of Bouillon', would go through numerous translations in German and French as well as Italian and provide the material for Torquato Tasso's *Jerusalem Liberated*. However, the efforts by Pope Pius II (d. 1464) to mobilize a great crusade for the recovery of Constantinople ended in fiasco – Europe was too busy with its own concerns.

Insofar as most of the North African littoral had once been subject either to ancient Rome or to the empire of Constantine and his Byzantine Christian successors, the fifteenth-century campaigns there by the Iberian powers could presumably have been seen by humanists as wars against the barbarians or justified by the religiously inclined as crusades of recovery of Christian territory. Certainly, when they took the North African port of Ceuta in 1415, the Portuguese boasted they had seized 'the door and the key' to all Africa on behalf of Christendom.[14] To the royal treasury, of greater interest was the fact that whatever the spiritual gain for Christendom they represented, the seizure of Ceuta and a string of other North African coastal towns gave the Portuguese control of the routes by which gold from sub-Saharan Africa, notably the empire of Mali, reached the coast. The rulers of Castile were jealous, the more so as Portugal was able to persuade successive popes to dignify its commercial conquests with the privileges attaching to crusades. Not that these awards were entirely disinterested as the papal curia, in return, imposed financial levies towards the costs of its own wars against rivals in Italy.

As the fifteenth century opened Spain witnessed the rise of a new form of popular literature, the *romances frontizeros*, 'frontier romances', in which the frontier was the border with Granada and the fighting there a chivalric holy war. Like the *Reisen* in Lithuania there was little noble about these expeditions, but then brutality and destruction were often the reality behind the tapestry of chivalry. Moreover, the early fifteenth century in Iberia also witnessed the beginnings of pogroms against the Jews, the traditional accompaniment of Europe's earlier crusades, and the first discriminatory legislation against both Jews and Muslims. It was a far cry from the days of

Ramon Lull's preaching tours in the Arabic language in the thirteenth century. Tolerance was less and less acceptable. King Henry IV of Castile attracted criticism for 'eating and drinking, dressing in the heathen manner' which made him an enemy to Christians.

As the fifteenth century progressed, the popes granted the privileges of crusaders to men fighting in expeditions organized by local nobles or town authorities against the Moors.[15] The conquest of Granada seems to have been almost completely financed by the sale of indulgences and the thought police of the Spanish Inquisition were closely linked with it. In the popular mind it was very definitely part of the general crusading picture. A song of the 1480s expresses the pious and politically correct hope that the Catholic monarchs will carry their conquests 'as far as Jerusalem'.[16] Ferdinand of Aragon claimed to be heir to the Crown of Jerusalem and years later wrote that the conquest of Jerusalem belonged to him. The fact that Charles VIII of France also claimed that title and also voiced pious ambitions of liberating the Holy City is proof to the longevity of the crusading dream, however debased it might become by political calculations.

For the Spanish monarchs the financial revenue from the papal crusade bulls, the *bula de la crusada*, were to become an essential element in the national finances. A scale of charges offered even the poorest consumers access to valuable spiritual privileges and exemptions. The introduction of the receipt, or *buleta*, proof of the purchaser's entitlement to these benefits brought an attractive new product onto the market. With the invention of printing all output was magically increased.

From the start of the Granada war the *cruzada* was granted to the Spanish Crown on a regular basis. During Emperor Charles V's reign, the annual yield was not much less than proceeds from America so that, inevitably, abuse became integral to the system. The Crown farmed out the collection of revenue for each *bula* to the highest bidder who then recouped his investment and maximized his profits by hiring preachers, who were not necessarily even clerics, to hawk the *buletas* on a commission basis. When a new papal bull was pending, privileges itemized on existing *buletas* were nullified until the purchase of a new *buleta*, or some stopgap to tide the sinner over until the next preaching.

Pope Paul III tried to suspend the *cruzada* in 1536 but only to replace it with the *fabrica*, indulgences sold to pay for the fabric of St Peters. In the 1560s, the Council of Trent ruled against the sale of all indulgences, but Philip II of Spain protested and the governmental post of *Comisario general de la cruzada* was not abolished until 1851.

In Europe's sixteenth-century Wars of Religion, the popes of the Counter Reformation and the Roman Catholic rulers had no doubt that they were involved in a Holy War to defend the Church against Protestant heretics, just as their predecessors had warred against Hussites and Albigensians. King Philip II of Spain never sought papal blessing for his decades of war against Dutch Calvinism as a crusade because, among other reasons, this would make it impossible to hire Protestant mercenaries. But there can be little doubt he would have received such a blessing. Pope Gregory XIII celebrated the Massacre of St Bartholomew's Day of French Huguenots in 1572, with a solemn *Te deum*. Three years later he granted indulgences for an invasion of Ireland as a first step to removing Queen Elizabeth.

The Spanish Armada against England of 1588 marked the culmination of papal and Spanish plans for the destruction of Protestant England by force, though it could equally well be seen as an extension of Spanish imperialism. Pope Sixtus V sanctioned Philip II's collecting Spain's traditional crusading taxes for the campaign. Soldiers and sailors of the Spanish fleet enjoyed crusade indulgences; at least one of the commanders, Don Alonso de Leira, wore a gold pendant in the form of the lily-sword, the emblem of the crusading Order of St James of Santiago da Compostella.[17] There were traditional crusade ceremonies: the dedication of the Armada's banner at Lisbon on 25 April 1588 mimicked the ceremony of dedication for the banner of the fleet setting out to fight the Turks at Lepanto in 1571. It would seem that not only the English saw the storm that scattered the Armada as the wind of God – a Roman Church dignitary in Madrid noted that everybody was dismayed 'to see the hand of God so openly against us'.[18]

It is surely one of the more bizarre paradoxes of European history that the crusading order dedicated to the gentle cult of the Blessed Virgin Mary should have provided the origins of the state that became a byword for regimented, aggressive militarism. But when, in 1525, Albert of Hohenzollern, the Teutonic Order's last Grand Master in East Prussia, converted to Lutheranism, proclaimed the dissolution of the Order and the secularization of its territories as a duchy under his hereditary rule, this is what happened. In fact, the lands of the Knights had been organized as a political entity, in German the *Ordenstaat* ('Order State') – a theocratic state based on and governed by the military monastic order. In fact, it seems that the Grand Master, Hermann von Salza, may have envisioned such an outcome from the moment he received Emperor Frederick II's imperial bull back in 1221. Tensions developed between the German-based membership and those garrisoning its fortresses in Palestine over which they had priority. At the siege of Acre in 1291 there had been bitter controversy between those who held priority that they should be given to resourcing the struggle against the rebellious Prussian tribes in their Baltic territories, and those led by the then Grand Master, who said the Order's first loyalty was to the defence of the Holy Land. Astonishingly the Grand Master had transferred his personal allegiance to the Knights Templar, so strong was his conviction.

From the start then, there was a conflict inherent within the idea of the *Ordenstaat* and its commitment to the Holy War as such. After 1291 the Order's headquarters were for a time in Venice, before being established at Marienburg (Malbork, Poland) in 1309. The Knights had been called in by the Polish King to help him defend the port of Danzig (Gdansk) against aggression from neighbouring Brandenburg, but, claiming that the King had failed to pay the sum agreed for their help, they seized the port and, in addition, occupied the province of Pomorze or eastern Pomerelia. From Marienburg the Grand Masters presided over the Order's golden age. In the last chapter we saw how their yearly *Reisen* against their heathen neighbours became part of the calendar of European chivalry, but the internal development of the *Ordenstaat* was equally important in the history of Central Europe. From the start the Order had been overwhelmingly German in membership; now the process was completed. During the fourteenth century non-German lands and possessions, from Castile to Greece, were sold off and membership restricted to the Empire. In addition, the Grand Masters achieved total independence of action. Both the Emperor Frederick II and Pope Gregory IX had made grants to the first Grand Master, but though both Empire and papacy thus had claims to claimed suzerainty in Prussia neither could enforce them.

The castle-palace complex that grew up at Marienburg comprised monastic buildings, an arsenal and 'parliament house' and astounded visitors with its size, opulence and impregnability. It was the administrative capital of a highly centralized state, with a rapid twenty-four-hour post-horse network, unique in contemporary Europe, to assure the rapid communication between the centre and regional commands. It developed a flourishing economy (in 1392 some 300 English ships loaded up with grain in Danzig alone), with the Grand Master a member of the powerful and far-flung German commercial Hanseatic League. It won the compliance of the old Prussian nobility by concessionary measures and encouraged German peasant and merchant immigration with generous terms. By 1500 Prussia was thoroughly Germanized. But the Order, celibate and disdainful of the local population, never integrated into that society. Worse still, as the kings of Poland grew in power and respect, so it found its position under threat. In July 1410 the Knights suffered a crushing defeat by a joint Polish and Lithuanian force at the Battle of Tannenberg (Polish, Stebark) in East Prussia. Invading in support of a rebellion of Samogitian tribes, the allies' target had been Marienburg. The fortress was not taken but the ten-hour battle saw the death of the Grand Master and most of the high command along with more than 200 of the Knights; the surrender of Samogitia followed.

Four years later the Order and its Polish enemies met in diplomatic encounter at the Council of Constance in 1414 to argue their claims to be sole champions of Christendom in the region. The Order, which challenged Lithuania's Christian credentials, wanted a crusade against the Poles for obstructing their work. The Poles wanted nothing less than the Order's dissolution. Among other things they charged that the Knights had not even managed the conversion of the peoples they had conquered – after more than a century heathenism still thrived in many parts of Prussia, while witnesses from Samogitia complained that the Order's brutal methods actually hindered conversions. The Council assigned the Samogitian mission field to the Poles and Lithuanians but left the Order intact; however it was losing the PR war. By the 1430s Germans from the Empire were refusing to join up for campaigns against the Lithuanians saying that they were Christians. By 1500 Poland had re-annexed Pomerze and while the Order retained Königsberg (today Kaliningrad, Russia) and East Prussia it was as fiefs of the Polish Crown: Polish noblemen were admitted to membership of the Order and the Grand Masters had to do homage and render military assistance – in 1497, under the Grand Master it took the field under the command of John Albert, King of Poland against the Turks.

In the context of their history as champions of Roman Catholic Christianity against the heathen peoples of Central Europe, the end of the Knights' rule in Prussia came through an act of shameful betrayal. In 1525 Albert of Hohenzollern, Grand Master of the Order, following the advice of Martin Luther having converted to Protestantism, dissolved the Order in East Prussia and converted the territory into a hereditary dukedom, subject to the overlordship of the King of Poland. In the generations to come this Ducal Prussia, as it was known, would provide the foundation for the Kingdom of Prussia.

Outside Prussia commanderies of the Order continued both their military and hospital activities in the nineteenth century, when it seemed moribund, enjoyed a revival under the sponsorship of the Habsburgs. In the twentieth century, under the Austrian Republic, it was reorganized yet again as a brotherhood of priests with its head-quarters in Vienna. The historic castle-palace of Marienburg, demol-ished by Red Army artillery in 1944 in the Second World War, was rebuilt and restored after the war by the Polish authorities. It is a strange quirk of history that thanks to the developments in Ducal Prussia centuries before that an order of crusading monks dedicated to the Blessed Virgin Mary proved the nursery for the state that became Europe's byword for aggressive militarism.

There remained one further sacrifice of the crusading ideal on the altar of political expediency. In 1839, Louis Philippe, King of the French, France's fourth monarch since the overthrow of the Republic by Napoleon, embarked on the renovation of the Palace of Versailles. A new wing was added with rooms dedicated to the era of the crusades, seen as one of the epochs of France's national *gloire*. The King ruled that those whose ancestors had fought in the crusades might have their coats of arms displayed in the rooms. Many families of ancient lineage could show just title to do so, but others of less venerable ancestry turned to the mushrooming market in forged charters and managed to convince the authorities with their fake crusading ancestry.[19] It is to be feared that some of the heraldic achievements proudly displayed on these bombastic walls never appeared on battlefield or route of march in any *passagium generale*, *iter* or *voyage* of the crusading era. It is, perhaps, a fitting irony with which to conclude a story that had moments of true glory and gestures of hypocrisy, but was above all inspired by that confusion of motives and ideals which tends to be inherent in the human condition.

Epilogue: The Aftermath

With the Frankish evacuation of Acre in 1291, after close on two centuries the Western European presence in Palestine came to an end. Despite the numerous crusading expeditions that were to follow, it was not re-established. It was not until the late seventeenth century, with the failure of the second Turkish siege of Vienna in 1683, and the Peace of Karlowitz in 1699, whereby the Ottoman Empire was obliged to cede Hungary and other territories back to Western powers such as Austria, that the tide was seen to turn. The classic age of the crusades, Europe's first military venture beyond its borders, some would say its first venture into colonialism, ended in defeat.

Today it is fashionable among liberal opinion both in Christian and Muslim circles to regard the crusades as an episode of unwarranted aggression by the West. Indeed, one Muslim commentator has written that 'the Crusades [are] deeply felt by Arabs, even today, as an act of rape.'[1] This has not always been the Arab view. During the Peace Treaty negotiations that followed the First World War in 1920, confronted by a French delegate who excitedly traced his country's claims on Syria back to the crusades, King Faysal, as he became, dryly responded, 'And would you be so good as to remind me just which one of us won that war?'[2] Recently, the crusades have even been the subject of a formal apology by the Pope. Exactly why is not clear. As yet the world awaits an apology from the Arab world for the aggression of the *jihad* wars of the seventh and eighth centuries which conquered the Christian lands from Syria to Egypt, and the North

African coast from the Christian Roman Empire and the Christian king-doms of Spain; or from Istanbul for the aggressive conquest of the Greek Orthodox Byzantine Empire. After all, the armies of the Prophet had no doubt that they were doing the will of Allah by winning these territories from their infidel rulers for the True Religion – just as the Christian crusaders were to believe that they were fulfilling the will of their God. The crusades, then, in Arab eyes ended in a second victory for Islam over Christendom. In 1993, the 700th anniversary of the death of Saladin, Syria's President, Hafiz al-Asad, unveiled a bronze equestrian statue of the hero of Islam as victor at the Battle of Hattin with his Frankish prisoners in chains around him.

In her Nash Memorial 'Lecture on the Legacy of the Crusades', delivered at the University of Regina in Saskatchewan in the year 2000, Penny J. Cole recalled how recitation of the deeds of another Islamic hero, the Mamluk Sultan Baybars, victor over both Christians and Mongols, is still a favourite entertainment in the popular cafés of Egypt and Syria. Following the humiliating withdrawal of the Anglo-French expedition after the Suez debacle of 1956, the Egyptian leader, Colonel Gamal Abdel Nasser, likened the struggle to Saladin's triumph over the Third Crusade with the French under King Philip II and the English under Richard the Lionheart.

In the 1960s, Professor S. Aziz Atiya saw the study of crusading history merging into the Pan-Arab movement.[3] For centuries, it would seem, the elimination of the barbarian crusader states from Palestine, followed by the triumphant advance of Islam into Europe under the banners of the Ottoman Empire, relegated Islam's clash with medieval Europe, what Gibbon dubbed in his *Decline and Fall of the Roman Empire* the 'World's Debate', to the status of an unfortunate interlude. Today, many Muslims would argue that in fact the crusades never ended but are continued in the twenty-first century in the confrontation between the Western world and the world of Islam. In 2002 it was reported that murals in one of the palaces of Saddam Hussein of Iraq depict him presiding over a column of tanks and, adjacent, the great Kurdish hero of the crusades, Saladin, presid-ing over columns of Muslim horsemen of an earlier age. And yet, it appears that it was not until the mid nineteenth century that the Arabic language felt the need for a special term (*Hurub al-Salibayya*) to designate the wars against the crusaders.[4]

But through those same centuries, the defeat rankled as much in the West as it was taken for granted in the Arab world. Within a few years of the death of Saladin, romance and rumour in the West were claiming that there were great men in Europe who could trace their descent back to some illicit amour of the great Sultan. We have seen how, in the south of France in the early 1200s, crowds heckled open-air preachers with the jibe that the fall of Jerusalem showed that Muhammad was evidently more powerful than Christ. In the early 1300s, missionary ventures by well-meaning Christians were met with hostility or derision. His listeners contemptuously heckled Ramon Lull, the doughty Catalan missionary who laboured to convert the Moors of North Africa, because of his faulty command of Arabic.

Nothing could better illustrate the Church's unshakeable conviction in its own moral rectitude, and the self-evident superiority of the Christian message it was called upon to proclaim in the world, than the reaction of Pope Pius II, as a churchman, to the fall of Constantinople to Mehmet II in 1453. As a humanist, he had lamented the event as the passing of the Greek tradition of Homer and Plato; when he ascended the papal throne in 1458 as head of the Roman Catholic Church he was among those who almost welcomed the catastrophe as the ending of the division in Christendom by the amputation of a 'schismatical patriarchate'; as a Christian he apparently perceived the possibility of a conversion. Almost his first act as Pope was to approach the Conqueror, not with a challenge of defiance but with an offer of the now vacant imperial Byzantine throne! 'Be baptized,' he urged 'and we will call you Emperor of the Greeks and of the Orient . . . And will love you like any Christian king.'[5] Ethnocentric self-absorption could hardly go further. It is on the authority of Sir Richard Southern, that great medievalist, that we learn the head of Western Christendom seriously imagined that the fiery young hero of Islam, who had conquered the Christian bastion of the Eastern world in the name of Allah, would desert the faith of Islam for the meaningless approval of an infidel potentate.

Even the most liberal-minded Christians took it as axiomatic that Christendom had a duty to win the whole world to the Gospel, just as few devout Muslims today doubt that Islam is the only true way to eternal life and proselytize for their faith. Writing in the 1530s on the theme of war against the Turks, Erasmus of Rotterdam, the great Roman Catholic humanist, while he opposed reckless warmongering which was likely to exasperate the enemy and make him more 'vicious', regretfully conceded that force would probably prove the only effective means of conversion and that 'conquest of Turkish dominions was unlikely to be achieved by the way the Apostles brought people into the empire of Christ'.

In the sixteenth century, the sultans Selim I and Suleyman I the Magnificent brought the Islamic eastern Mediterranean into the Ottoman Empire, but from the 1700s onwards that empire entered upon a slow decline with respect to the surging power of Western Europe so that in the nineteenth century it became common to refer to Turkey as the 'sick man' of the international scene. At the same time, the epoch of the crusades was enjoying something of a cult in Romantic art and literature with the novel *Ivanhoe*, by Sir Walter Scott, the painting *The Entry of the Crusaders into Constantinople* by Delacroix and the decorations for King Louis Philippe's *Salles des Croisades* at Versailles. Verdi's opera *I Lombardi*, a somewhat romanticized treatment of Italian participation, was rapturously received by Italian nationalist sentiment which seems to have identified Italy as the Holy Land and the Austrian forces occupying northern Italy as an imperial province as the Saracens. Adapted in a French version as *Jérusalem*, it received a command performance before Louis Philippe who awarded the composer the *Légion d'Honneur*.

There were few European countries that did not see operas or plays on crusading themes. In Norway in 1872 the nationalist poet Bjørnstjerne Bjørnson produced *Sigurd Jorsalfare* ('Sigurd the Jerusalem Farer'), a play based on the sagas of Norway's twelfth-century king, Sigurd I Magnusson, formerly Earl of Orkney. Distinguished as being the first reigning European monarch to visit the Kingdom of Jerusalem, where King Baldwin I received him with great pomp and ceremony, Sigurd was a considerable figure in the history of the Scandinavian Middle Ages.

Leaving Norway in 1107 with a fleet of some sixty longships, he visited England, France, Spain, Portugal and Sicily en route for Palestine. There, Sigurd assisted at the capture of the port of Sidon. Heading for home via Constantinople, he presented his fleet with its entire complement to Emperor Alexius I, himself continuing overland and arriving back in Norway in the year 1111. For Bjørnson and his public, Sigurd was not simply a glamorous figure from the pages of medieval romances – he was also a heroic emblem of the glorious days of a once independent Norwegian nation whose last great king, Haakon VI, had died in 1387. Subject to first Danish and then Swedish rule since the 1390s, Norway in the late nineteenth century was beginning to stir with nationalist sentiment. Edvard Grieg provided the incidental music to Bjørnson's drama and subsequently adapted it for piano solo and piano duet and as an orchestral suite. When in 1905 the country finally won full independence from the Swedish Crown, Grieg's *Sigurd Suite* accompanied the ceremony of welcome for the young Danish prince who had been elected to accede to the restored throne, as King Haakon VII. Perhaps young National-ist hotheads had cast the staid outgoing Swedish bureaucrats as the Saracens to Haakon's Sigurd. Certainly, Norway's chivalrous crusader king seemed a benign figure to preside over the idealist dreams of newly revived nationhood.

The crusading metaphor seized the European imagination as the continent entered upon the murderous struggle we call the First World War. In Germany, the self-dramatizing Kaiser Wilhelm II sol-emnly vaunted himself the champion of Catholic Christendom against the Slav hordes of schismatic Orthodox Russia. For their part Ger-many's Western enemies saw themselves as the champions of Christian values against the revived forces of heathen barbarism embodied in the German Reich – the Huns of the twentieth century.

Given that the Ottoman Empire was allied with Germany, General Edmund Allenby's British army advancing through Mesopotamia and the Turkish provinces in Syria was operating in the theatre of war of their crusading predecessors. Like them, both sides in the modern European conflict had Muslim allies – while the Germans had the Turks, the British had the Arab nationalist guerrillas under the leader-ship of Faysal ibn Husayn ibn Ali, son of the grand sharif of Mecca in conjunction with Britain's military liaison officer, Colonel T.E. Lawrence, 'Lawrence of Arabia' (he had first lived in Palestine as a student, writing a pioneering thesis on crusader castles).

Finally, on 9 December 1917, Allenby's force captured Jerusalem from the Turks. Some years later, Major Vivian Gilbert, one of his officers, published a book recounting his own experiences with the army in Palestine entitled *The Romance of the Last Crusade – with Allenby to Jerusalem* (London, 1923). In it Major Gilbert compared him with Godfrey of Bouillon. Allenby himself is said to have invoked the memory of Richard the Lionheart on the day of his entry to the city with the words, 'Now the crusades have ended.'

In 1920 at the international conference of San Remo, Syria was awarded as a mandated territory of the League of Nations to France. Penny Cole notes that virtually the first visit of the French governor on his arrival at Damascus (Faysal being forced into temporary exile) was to the tomb of Saladin where he placed his gun on the sarco-phagus with the words 'Saladin, we have returned.'[6]

For their part, many Arabs saw the Anglo-French Suez venture of 1956 as yet another Western attempt to redress the balance tipped so decisively against them by the armies of Islam in the thirteenth century. When, in 1958, President Nasser proclaimed the union of Egypt and Syria in the United Arab Republic, he was lauded as a second Saladin, who had brought the two countries under his sole rule. In fact Nasser's new united state was short-lived and the Arab world has drawn other less happy parallels with the crusading era.

According to Penny Cole, the Egyptian President, Anwar Sadat, who signed the Camp David Accords of 1978 with the then Israeli Prime Minister Menachem Begin and the subsequent Peace Treaty of 1979, the first such by an Arab country to recognize the State of Israel, compared his role as peacemaker with that of Saladin's nephew al-Malik al-Kamil, the Egyptian ruler who came to terms without a blow being struck with the Emperor Frederick II in 1229. But for devout Muslims in the twentieth century, as in the thirteenth, he was a rank traitor to the faith. This view, quite opposed to Sadat's Western liberalism, was succinctly put in 1984 by Amin Maalouf in his book *The Crusades through Arab Eyes*. 'It is difficult,' he wrote as translated by Jon Rothschild, 'not to think of President Sadat when we read the words of Sibt Ibn al-Jawzi speaking to the people of Damascus and denouncing the "betrayal" [of Islam] by al-Kamil, ruler of Cairo.' At least al-Kamil survived his own audacity. Sadat, by contrast, paid the price, for in October 1981 he was shot dead at a military parade by fundamentalist troopers in the army tank corps. Before his failed attempt on the life of Pope Paul John II in May the same year, the Turkish gunman Mehmet Ali Agca recorded in a letter that his intention was to kill 'the supreme commander of the Crusades'.

Today, the State of Israel occupies much the same territories as the twelfth-century Kingdom of Jerusalem, and is regarded by the Muslim world as much of a client state to the Western world as was its medieval forerunner to Western Christendom. In his book, written in the 1980s, Amin Maalouf tells us that one of the three divisions of the Palestine Liberation Army bore the name of Hattin after the battle in which Saladin won his decisive victory over the crusader state. And in the final paragraph of that book the author offered this chilling reflection: 'it seems clear that the Arab East still sees the West as a natural enemy. Against that enemy, any hostile action – be it political, military or based on oil – is considered no more than legitimate vengeance.'[7]

Appendix I:
The Popes, from Gregory VII to Sixtus V

The dates show the regnal years, calculated from the time of election. POPES particularly associated with crusading history indicated in capitals. From time to time, sometimes because emperors appointed their own popes, sometimes because of political rivalries between the great families of Rome, sometimes because of divided elections among the cardinals, there were rival claimants to the papal office – most notably at the time of the Great Schism 1378–1417. Certain 'anti-popes' are indicated thus (*Clement III 1084–1100*).*

(Capital letters denote pivotal events or key personalities.)

GREGORY VII 1073–1085
Gregory's plan for a military campaign against Constantinople to enforce the authority of Rome over the Eastern Orthodox Church, a campaign that he himself would lead, has been described as 'the precursor of the fully-fledged crusading movement some twenty years later'. But his pontificate was dominated by other issues, notably the great contest with Emperor Henry IV over the rival claims of Empire and papacy to supreme authority in Western Christendom.

(*Clement III 1084–1100, papal candidate of Emperor Henry IV. The great*

---

* Occasionally, the election of a pope among rival candidates could be so protracted as to produce an interregnum of months, even years.

conflict between Empire and papacy was still active at the time of the First Crusade and in part explains why the Emperor did not participate in the expedition.)

Victor III 1086–1087

URBAN II 1088–29 July 1099
He inaugurated the crusading movement.

Paschal II 1099–1118
He authorized the preaching of a crusade against the Byzantine Empire in support of Bohemond of Antioch's campaign against Emperor Alexius I.

Gelasius II 1118–1119

CALIXTUS II 1119–1124
He confirmed the same remission of sins to wars against the Muslims in Spain as those offered to crusaders in the Holy Land. By 1123 the three essential elements constituting a crusade – the vow, the symbol of the Cross and rewards of penitential remissions – were established for the Spanish theatre.

Honorius II 1124–1130

Innocent II 1130–1143

(Anacletus II 1130–1138, candidate of rival Roman faction.)

Celestine II 1143–1144

Lucius II 1144–1145

EUGENIUS III 1145–1153
A pupil of St Bernard of Clairvaux, he proclaimed the Second Crusade and recruited St Bernard to preach it. In December 1145 he addressed a bull to King Louis VII and the nobles of France urging they participate.

Anastasius IV 1153–1154

Adrian IV 1154–1159

Alexander III 1159–1181

(1159–1180 four anti-popes sponsored by Emperor Frederick I Barbarossa.)

Lucius III 1181–1185

Urban III 1185–1187
He died of grief on hearing news of Saladin's capture of Jerusalem.

GREGORY VIII Oct–Dec 1187
It was he who effectively initiated the Third Crusade, writing to Europe's leaders urging a campaign for the recovery of Jerusalem and assuring crusaders of plenary indulgence and the protection of their property while on crusade, by the Church.

Clement III 1187–1191

Celestine III 1191–1198

INNOCENT III 1198–16 July 1216
After Urban II the most important pope in crusading history.

HONORIUS III 1216–1227
He equipped the fleet to transport troops to Egypt for the Fifth Crusade at his own expense and appointed Cardinal Pelagius his legate, as commander.

GREGORY IX 1227–1241
He excommunicated Emperor Frederick II for tardiness in departing on crusade, and again for departing without papal authorization. Later he attacked Frederick's lands in Sicily and Italy. He founded the papal Inquisition to purge the Albigensian heresies.

Celestine IV Oct–Nov 1241

INNOCENT IV 1243–1254
In 1245 he granted the Teutonic Order the privilege of recruiting crusading forces without waiting for the formal papal proclamation of a crusade.

Alexander IV 1254–1261

Urban IV 1261–1264
In 1261, in support of the ambitions of Charles of Anjou, he proclaimed a crusade against the restored Byzantine Emperor Michael VIII – to no effect.

Clement IV 1265–1268

GREGORY X 1271–Jan 1276
He achieved the temporary submission of the Orthodox Church to Rome, conceded by Byzantine envoys to the Council of Lyon. Outrage in Constantinople.

Innocent V Jan 1276–June 1276
As a cardinal at the Council of Lyon, 1274, he baptized two Mongol envoys seeking possible Western allies against the Mamluks.

Adrian V July 1276–Aug 1276

John XXI 1276–1277

Nicholas III 1277–1280

MARTIN IV 1281–1285
He excommunicated Byzantine Emperor Michael VIII and promised crusading indulgences to all who joined the attack planned by Charles of Anjou,

King of Sicily, against Constantinople. When Charles was ousted by rebellion in Sicily and Peter II of Aragon had himself proclaimed king of the island in Sept 1282, Martin proclaimed a crusade against *him*.

Honorius IV 1285–1287

Nicholas IV 1288–1292

Celestine V July–Dec 1294 (resigned, d. 1296)

Boniface VIII 1294–1303

Benedict XI 1303–1304
He too proclaimed a crusade in favour of the French claim to Constantinople.

CLEMENT V 1305–1314
He presided over the suppression of the Templars, and granted Templar property to the Hospitallers. It was also during his pontificate that the seat of papal government was moved from Rome to Avignon, then a semi-autonomous enclave in French territory.

From 1309 to 1378 AVIGNON was the seat of the papacy.

John XXII 1316–1334
He promoted missionary activity in Asia. John was unusual among popes for being condemned as a heretic by a committee of theologians. He proclaimed the deposition of Emperor Ludwig IV who occupied Rome for a time.

(*Nicholas V 1328–1330, appointee of the Emperor Ludwig IV, but he resigned when the imperial army was forced to leave Rome.*)

Benedict XII 1334–1342

Clement VI 1342–1352

Innocent VI 1352–1362

Urban V 1362–1370
He urged support for the crusading expedition of Peter I of Cyprus.

Gregory XI 1370–1378

The return to ROME and the beginning of the GREAT SCHISM.

Roman Popes	*Avignon Anti-Popes*
Urban VI 1378–1389	
Urban moved the papal seat back to Rome. However, a rival body of cardinals declared the election invalid because made under duress from the Roman mob and elected	*Clement VII 1378–1394 who continued at Avignon. Benedict XIII 1394–1423*

Boniface IX 1389–1404
He, like *Clement VII* supported the Nicopolis Crusade.

Innocent VII 1404–1406

Gregory XII 1406–1415

The Council of *Pisa* in 1409 attempted to end the Schism. Gregory declared he was willing to resign but Clement refused, Gregory retracted and the Council declared both rivals deposed and elected *Alexander V (1409–1410)*. Western Christendom now had three popes since neither Gregory nor Benedict acknowledged the Pisan Line. On Alexander's early death this was continued in the person of John XXIII (1410–1415) who, as Baldassare Cossa, had been a successful mercenary commander of papal troops. At his request the Emperor designate Sigismund convoked a Council of the Church which opened at Constance in November 1414 under an edict of John's. Pope Gregory XII tendered his formal resignation and the Council having deposed *Benedict XIII* the twenty-three cardinals present elected as Pope, Cardinal Otto Colonna who thus ended the Schism and took office as Martin V.

Martin V 1417–1431
He sponsored the German crusade against the Hussites.

EUGENIUS IV 1431–1447
Forced through nominal submission of the Eastern Orthodox Church to Rome. Supported the failed crusade to Varna.

Nicholas V 1447–1455

Calixtus III 1455–1458

PIUS II 1458–1464
He worked in vain for a crusade to recover Constantinople. Weeks before his death he himself took the Cross at a ceremony in St Peter's having ordered the muster of a fleet to assemble at Ancona at his own expense. He died before he could reach the port. His cardinals did not tell him that no king or prince had responded to the call.

Paul II 1464–1471

Sixtus IV 1471–1484

Innocent VIII 1484–1492

Alexander VI 1492–1503

Pius III Sept 1503–Oct 1503

Julius II 1503–1513

Leo X 1513–1521

Adrian VI 1522–1523

Clement VII 1523–1534

Paul III 1534–1549

Julius III 1550–1555

Marcellus II April–May 1555

Paul IV 1555–1559

Pius IV 1559–1565

Pius V 1566–1572

Gregory XIII 1572–1585
He ordered celebrations of the mass killings of Huguenot Protestants in France on the Feast of St Bartholomew's Day, 24 August 1572.

SIXTUS V 1585–1590
He blessed the Spanish Armada as a crusade against Protestant England.

Appendix II:
Rulers of the Kingdom of Jerusalem

(Their regnal dates are given)

GODFREY of BOUILLON 1099–1100, with the title 'Advocate of the Holy Sepulchre'.

BALDWIN I 1100–1118, brother of the above. He took the title 'king'; it was he who secured the territory of the Kingdom.

BALDWIN II 1118–1131, cousin of the above.

MELISENDE 1131–1152, daughter of the above, Queen of Jerusalem (d. 1161).

FULK of Anjou 1131–d. 1143, husband of the above and co-ruler.

BALDWIN III 1143–1152, son of Queen Melisende and Fulk. Co-ruler with his widowed mother whom he deposed; sole ruler 1152–1162. Took Ascalon 1153. Forced Egypt to agree the payment of an annual tribute, though this in fact was never paid.

AMALRIC I 1162–1174, brother of the above, he was an able ruler and general. He failed in his attempts to conquer Egypt, but the Kingdom reached its high point in his reign. He allied with the Byzantine Emperor Manuel I.

BALDWIN IV, 'the Leper' 1174–1185, when he died aged twenty-four, son of the above. Courageous and able, his death was a heavy blow to the Kingdom.

BALDWIN V 1183–1185, co-ruler with his uncle Baldwin IV. He died, aged nine, in 1186 and was succeeded by his mother.

SIBYL 1186–1190, daughter of Amalric I, Queen of Jerusalem and wife of

GUY of LUSIGNAN 1186–1192, co-ruler through right of his wife. He led the army of the Kingdom to defeat in the Battle of Hattin and surrendered Ascalon to Saladin who conquered Jerusalem in Oct 1187. Sole ruler 1190–1192 when he was deposed. After the loss of Jerusalem, the coastal strip of Palestine that remained in Christian hands would retain the name 'Kingdom of Jerusalem' but the royal court and centre of administration was moved to Acre. With the deposition of King Guy, the Crown passed to Sybil's sister.

ISABELLA I 1192–1205 Queen of Jerusalem, three of her husbands were considered joint rulers by virtue of their marriage to her:

CONRAD I of Montferrat 5–28 April 1192, when he was assassinated, second husband of the above.

HENRY I of Champagne 1192–(d.) 1197, third husband of Isabella.

AMALRIC II 1198–1205, fourth husband of Isabella and, before his marriage to her, King of Cyprus. In 1204 he concluded a six-year treaty with al-Adil, Sultan of Egypt. With the death of both Amalric and Isabella in 1205 the throne passed to:

MARY of Montferrat, daughter of Isabella I and Conrad I, Queen of Jerusalem and sole ruler 1205–1210, and co-ruler with her husband John of Brienne, 1210–1212.

JOHN I of Brienne, co-ruler by virtue of his marriage to Mary, 1210–1212 when she died leaving their one-year-old daughter Yolande who became Queen of Jerusalem as:

ISABELLA II, sole ruler 1212–1225, with her father as regent; co-ruler 1225–(d.) May 1228 with her husband Emperor Frederick II.

FREDERICK 1225–1228 who after his wife's death illegally crowned himself King of Jerusalem, in the Holy City, in Mar 1229. As Emperor Frederick II, he recovered the city for Christendom by treaty with al-Malik al-Kadil, ruler of Egypt. Technically, however, with the death of his wife the Crown had passed by right of the boy's mother to their son, b. April 1228.

CONRAD II May 1228–1254. Neither the absentee boy King, nor his father Emperor Frederick (whom he was to succeed as Emperor in 1250) could prevent the Muslim recapture of Jerusalem in 1244.

(CONRAD III, known in European history as Conradin, b. 1252, reigned 1254–1268. An absentee monarch in conflict with Charles of Anjou in Italy, he was executed after defeat by Charles.)

In the remaining twenty-three years of its existence after 1268, the 'Kingdom of Jerusalem', in territorial terms an ever-diminishing strip on the coast of Palestine, became a titular counter in the turmoil of Mediterranean politics.

From 1277 to his death in 1282, Charles of Anjou, King of Sicily, claimed the title. Through the agency of the Pope he had bought her rights from Mary of Antioch, a granddaughter of Queen Isabella I and her fourth husband Amalric II. But the barons of the High Court of Jerusalem recognized instead King Hugh of Cyprus, descended from Isabella and her third husband and it was his son, Henry II of Cyprus and I of Jerusalem, who was on the throne, though an absentee monarch, when Acre, the last Latin foothold in Palestine, fell and the Kingdom, as such, ceased to exist.

But this did not prevent the title 'King of Jerusalem' being bandied about the chancelleries of Europe for generations to come. Thus, in the late fifteenth century King Charles VIII of France, a descendant of Charles of Anjou, and King Ferdinand II of Aragon, who could also trace his descent from the House of Jerusalem, both laid claim to it when vaunting their intention for a crusade.

Appendix III:
Ayyubid Dynasty – Rulers of Egypt

From 973 Egypt was ruled from Cairo, a city that they founded, by a line of Shi'ite caliphs known as the Fatimids. At its height their empire embraced not only Egypt but also much of North Africa, Sicily, the Yemen and Palestine. From about 1100 the caliphs were increasingly excluded from government which was conducted by chief ministers or viziers. These were often foreigners, especially Armenians. In 1171 the Caliphate was abolished and the Sunni caliphs of Baghdad acknowledged by Saladin who inaugurated the Ayyubid dynasty of rulers.

SALADIN 1171–1193, son of Ayyub (d. 1173). In 1176 he took the title King of Egypt and Syria and had coins struck in his name alone. In 1187 he destroyed the army of the Kingdom of Jerusalem at the Battle of Hattin and recovered Jerusalem for Islam.

Al-Adil 1193–1218, brother of above.

Al-Kamil, al-Malik 1218–1238, son of above. He was successful against the Fifth Crusade. In 1221 St Francis of Assisi crossed battle lines for an audience with him in an attempt to convert him to Christianity. In 1229, al-Kamil ceded Jerusalem to the Emperor Frederick II by treaty. Both rulers were excoriated as traitors by their respective co-religionists.

Al-Adil II 1238–1240, younger son of above. Deposed in favour of:

Al-Salih Ayyub 1240–1249, elder brother of the above. Jerusalem was recaptured for Islam under him.

Turanshah 1249–1250, son of above. He contributed to defeat of Louis IX's army at al-Mansurah. Murdered in a rising by the Mamluk corps under

Baybars. A confused decade followed his death, presided over by three Mamluk sultans. He was murdered by:

Baybars I, the fourth MAMLUK Sultan 1260–1277. In 1260 he won the decisive Battle of Ayn Jalut (the 'Spring of Goliath') against the Mongols. In 1261 established a remote descendant of the Abbassid caliphs as Sunni caliph at Cairo to legitimate his rule. He reunited Syria and Egypt under a single rule and waged constant war against the crusader states. In 1265 the Hospitallers surrendered their stronghold of Arsuf to him. In 1268 he took Antioch. In 1273 he destroyed the Syrian Assassins and in 1276 he defeated a Seljuk/Mongol army.

Appendix IV:
Byzantine Emperors at the Time of the First Crusades

The term 'Byzantine' is a coinage of historians to distinguish the Roman Empire in the East established by Constantine I the Great in the early fourth century from the Roman Empire in the West, which collapsed in the late fifth century. The Emperors at Constantinople rightly considered themselves the true successors to Augustus and their state the Roman Empire.

ALEXIUS I Comnenus 1081–1118. His appeal to Pope Urban II for help in the recruiting of Western cavalry to help the imperial army recover lands lost to Turkish incursions in Anatolia led to the First Crusade. He gave valuable help to the crusaders, despite mutual suspicion and mistrust. He made large commercial concessions to Venice.

John II Comnenus, son of the above, 1118–1143. He failed to rescind his father's concessions to Venice but successfully resisted Roger II of Sicily's designs on the Empire, allying with Conrad III of Germany.

MANUEL I Comnenus, son of the above, 1143–1180. He favoured westerners at his court and seems to have envisaged a reunion of the Eastern and Western Empires and Churches. The Italian cities won increased trading and extra-territorial privileges in his reign and resulting unpopularity with public opinion at Constantinople. In 1176 his army was crushingly defeated by the Seljuk Turk, Kilij Arslan of Konya at the Battle of Myriocephalum. After him, the Empire was riven with faction fighting between rivals for the throne.

Alexius II Comnenus (b. 1169), son of the above, 1180–1183. He was murdered by order of:

Andronicus I Comnenus 1183–1185, his uncle. Killed in a mob riot.

Isaac II Angelus, cousin of the above, his first reign 1185–1195 ended when he was deposed and blinded on the orders of his brother:

Alexius III Angelus 1195–1203, who in his turn was driven from power by the Fourth Crusade.

Isaac II was restored for a brief second reign (deposed 1204) as co-ruler with ALEXIUS IV Angelus, his son (brother-in-law of Philip of Swabia), 1203–1204. Overthrown and strangled on the orders of the usurper:

Alexius V Ducas Jan–April 1204, executed as regicide by order of the crusaders. From its capture by the Fourth Crusade in 1204 to 1261, Constantinople was the seat of the LATIN EMPIRE.

The governor of Trebizond (Trabzon), a Byzantine province on the Black Sea coast, proclaimed his independence with the title of 'emperor' and the state maintained its independence until conquered by Sultan Mehmet II in 1461. An Eastern Roman Empire in exile was established at NICAEA under the Lascarid dynasty – Theodore I (1206–1222); John III Ducas Vatatzes (1222–1254); Theodore II (1254–1258); and John IV (1258–1261), who was deposed by his co-ruler.

MICHAEL VIII Palaeologos 1258–1282. In July 1261 Michael drove the last Latin 'emperor' from the city and re-established the Empire at CONSTANTINOPLE where he was crowned in August of that year. Apart from a few years in the mid fourteenth century the PALAEOLOGI ruled at Constantinople until its capture by the Ottoman Turks in 1453 from the last Emperor, Constantine XI Palaeologus.

Appendix V:
Ottoman Princes and Sultans 1300–1566

Othman or Osman c. 1300–c. 1326. Dynastic founder. The chief of a tribe of Turkish nomads, dedicated *ghazis*, i.e. 'warriors of Islam'. He established them in NW Anatolia on the frontier of the shrinking Byzantine state.

Orkhan c. 1326–c. 1360. Son of the above, he took Bursa from the Byzantines in 1320 and made it his capital. He led the first major Ottoman expedition into Europe.

MURAD I c. 1360–1389, son of the above. He established the Ottomans' permanent presence in Europe, making large conquests against the Serbs and the Bulgars and seizing Edirne (formerly Adrianople), his new capital. He and his son Bayezid defeated the Serbs at the Battle of Kossovo in 1389, but Murad was killed.

BAYEZID I 1389–1402, the first Ottoman sultan, son of the above. Nicknamed the Thunderbolt, he crushed the Christian crusaders at Nicopolis, 1396. He extended Ottoman territory in Anatolia against the local Muslim rulers, but was defeated near Ankara by the Mongol conqueror Tamerlane and died in capitivity.

1402–1413 were years of anarchy in the Ottoman world as Bayezid's four sons fought for his inheritance and defended themselves against the neighbouring Muslim rulers. A well-organized and determined crusading expedition from the West might just have ended the Turkish threat to Constantinople – the opportunity was missed.

Mehmet I 1413–1421. The son of Bayezid who emerged triumphant from the decade of interregnum.

MURAD II 1421–1444; 1444–1451. Son of the above and restorer of Ottoman power in the Balkans, victor at the Battle of Varna, Nov 1444, against the Hungarians. He had abdicated in favour of his twelve-year-old son, but returned to deal with the threat from the West. Murad founded the Janissaries, the Ottomans' famous elite corps of mercenary troops, recruited as children from Christian familics.

MEHMET II (Feb–Oct 1444) 1451–1481, called 'the Conqueror'. Born in 1432 he captured Constantinople in May 1453. He also added many conquests in the Balkans as well as the Christian Empire of Trebizond (Trabzon).

Bayezid II, 1481–1512, son of the above. Deposed by a Janissary rebellion.

SELIM I, 1512–1520, brother of the above, called 'the Grim'. He ordered the killing of all his close male relations, and all his sons except one, to secure his position. He added Syria, Palestine and Egypt to Ottoman domains as well as the Holy City of Mecca and was acknowledged leader of the Muslim world.

SULEYMAN I, 1520–1566, son of the above, called 'The Magnificent'. He drove the Knights Hospitaller from the island of Rhodes; brought the Empire to its greatest extent in Europe, annexing Hungary, and in 1529 laid siege to Vienna, before being driven back. In 1565 he ordered the capture of the island of Malta from the Knights Hospitaller but heroic resistance defeated the combined might of the Turkish fleet and army. For many years, Suleyman was in alliance with Francis I of France against the Habsburg Empire.

Appendix VI:
Western Emperors 1056–1555

When the Emperor Constantine I founded his new city of Constantinople as the administrative capital of the Eastern provinces of the Roman Empire that empire was already divided between two emperors, one based in Rome itself – the Western Empire – and the other at Constantinople. The last emperor in the West was deposed in 478, and Europe was divided among barbarian kingdoms with the popes at Rome the sole international authority. On Christmas Day 800 the Frankish King, Charles the Great, Charlemagne, received a form of imperial coronation at the hands of Pope Leo which came to be seen as the revival of the line of the Western Roman Empire. With the coronation of Otto I in 962 this empire, later to be known as the Holy Roman Empire, was effectively a German institution. The ruler, or German King, was elected by the leading magnates of the German duchies and the convention arose whereby he bore the title 'King of the Romans'. Only when he received imperial coronation by the Pope at Rome did he become 'Emperor'.

By the late tenth century the prestige of the papacy was at a low ebb thanks to corrupt politicking at elections and the dubious morals of many popes. The prestige of the Empire was by contrast high and Emperor Henry III (1039; 1046–56) in particular presided over the deposition of bad popes and the election of reforming popes. But the reformed papacy soon began to contest the imperial ascendancy. A major point at issue arose from the fact that high churchmen were also great landowners – should they be invested with their office by Pope or Emperor? At a higher level, which was the supreme authority in Western Christendom – the religious or secular power? Emperors claimed they were ordained by God, the popes claimed it was they who gave the imperial power its legitimacy. The first great clash came between Emperor Henry IV and Pope Gregory VII, but the struggle rumbled on for generations. Emperor Frederick I installed a number of anti-popes (one of whom canonized the Emperor Charlemagne, or in German *Karl der Grosse*). Under his grandson, Frederick II, Pope and Emperor came to armed hostilities. Popes came to claim the power to depose emperors; for example, in the fourteenth century, Pope John XXII deposed Emperor Ludwig IV.

It is a supreme irony that from 1095 onwards the one area where the Pope's authority was not contested was in the military field, surely the secular province *par excellence*, in the summoning and control of crusades. Pope Urban II's initiative at Clermont can be seen without undue cynicism as a masterstroke in the contest with the emperors over the issue of ultimate authority.

The list shows regnal dates from accession as German king and imperial coronation where relevant – many of the rulers listed never received coronation at the hands of the Pope and so remained emperor elect.

HENRY IV son of Henry III, 1056; 1084–1105
  His reign was dominated by a titanic struggle with the papacy, notably with Pope Gregory VII.
HENRY V, son of above 1105; 1106–25
LOTHAIR II 1125; 1133–7
  No relation to above, chosen by electors to counteract power of Hohenstaufen dynasty. Crowned emperor by Pope Innocent V, rival of anti-pope *Anacletus*. Lothair allied with Byzantine Emperor John Comnenus against Roger of Sicily.
CONRAD III of Hohenstauffen 1138–52
  Nephew of Henry V. On SECOND CRUSADE 1147–8. Allied with Byzantine Emperor Manuel Comnenus against Roger II of Sicily. Unable to visit Rome for formal coronation as emperor.
FREDERICK I, Barbarossa, 1152; 1155–90
  Nephew of above. Led major crusade out of Germany but died before reaching the Holy Land.
HENRY VI 1190; 1191–7
  Second son of the above, his elder brother Frederick having died on their father's crusade. Henry married the heiress to the Kingdom of Sicily so that the lands of the Empire threatened to encircle Rome and the Papal States. He died preparing a crusade with Constantinople as its probable target.

Philip of Swabia 1198–1208

Brother of the above, his claim was contested by Otto of Brunswick. Philip's marriage to the Byzantine Princess Irene led to his involvement with the preliminaries of the Fourth Crusade. He seemed to be making headway in his struggle with Otto when he was murdered by a German nobleman whom he had offended.

OTTO IV 1198; 1209–15

Otto of Brunswick elected king by the German nobles opposed to the Hohenstauffen. When Philip died Pope Innocent III switched his support to Otto.

FREDERICK II (1198) 1215–50

The son of Henry VI and Constance of Sicily, and consequently King of that realm. Only three when his father died, Frederick's German claims were opposed by German factions. However he was crowned emperor in 1215. He claimed the Crown of Jerusalem by right of marriage. He led a crusade, despite papal excommunication, and in 1229 negotiated the cession of Jerusalem by the Egyptian Sultan.

CONRAD IV 1250–54

Son of the above, by his wife Isabella of Jerusalem and hence, technically, King of Jerusalem. He was succeeded by his son 'Conradin' (b. 1252) who was unable to make good his titles as King of Sicily and Emperor Conrad V before his defeat and death, on charges of treason to the Church, at the hands of Charles of Anjou. Charles was the papal candidate for the Kingdom of Sicily and with ambitions on Jerusalem himself.

From 1254 to 1273 the rivalries for the imperial titles amount to an:

INTERREGNUM

Conrad V 'Conradin' 1254–5

In theory the Empire, though dominated by German kings and candidates, was a European-wide dominion. Men with money to bribe the electors could look for election from whatever nationality they might be. Thus both Alfonso X of Castile and Richard of Cornwall, brother of Henry III King of England won election as King of the Romans during these years. In fact, Richard had led a successful expedition to the Holy Land in 1240–2, where he secured a good treaty to extend the territory of the Kingdom of Jerusalem. In 1252–3, he turned down Pope Innocent IV's offer of the Crown of Sicily against Conrad IV and instead accepted nomination as King of the Romans, buying four of the electoral votes and being crowned at Aachen in 1257. The Interregnum is reckoned to have to come to an end with the election of:

RUDOLF I of Habsburg as King of the Romans, in 1273.

He had crusaded with the Teutonic Order in the 1250s. He was elected to counteract the growing power of King Otakar of Bohemia whom he defeated and killed (1278). Rudolf, the first Habsburg ruler of the German lands, acquired territory in Austria, formerly Otakar's, which became the nucleus of the Habsburg family lands. He was crowned king at Aachen in 1273. He was recognized as Emperor elect by Pope Gregory X on condition he renounced imperial claims to authority in Rome and, also, that he lead a crusade. In fact French influence at the papal court ensured that Rudolf was never crowned emperor, while electoral fear of Habsburg dynastic ambitions prevented him securing the succession of his son, Albert.

ADOLF OF NASSAU 1292–8

Elected in preference to Albert of Habsburg, to check growth of Habsburg power. In fact defeated and killed by Albert of Habsburg who succeeded him as German King.

ALBERT I 1298–1308

Son of Rudolf of Habsburg. He extended Habsburg power and seemed to be on the verge of a real curb of electoral power when he was assassinated.

HENRY VII of the House of Luxembourg 1308; 1312–13

Elected as a check on Habsburg ambitions. In fact he built a power base for himself and had his son John created King of Bohemia. Crowned emperor in 1312, he was threatening to re-establish real imperial power when he died unexpectedly.

LUDWIG IV of the Wittelsbach dynasty of Bavaria 1314; 1338–47

He asserted the independence of the secular power in a long contest with Pope John XXI.

CHARLES IV of the house of Luxembourg 1347; 1355–78

Grandson of Henry VII and son of King John of Bohemia, and himself its king from 1347. He was the builder of the glories of medieval Prague and, by fostering Czech identity, indirectly responsible for the strongly nationalistic Hussite heresy. Charles lessened the likelihood of contested imperial elections and papal interference by regularizing the number of electors and legislating for majority voting in the famous Golden Bull of 1356.

WENZEL 1378–1400; d. 1419

Son of the above, King of Bohemia but not crowned emperor. Deposed in favour of:

RUPERT d. 1410, Emperor elect

SIGISMUND 1410; 1433–7

Rival for the Empire to his half-brother Wenzel. He convened the Council of Constance to end the Great Schism in the papacy. Titular King of Bohemia, he was principal instigator of the crusade against the Hussites.

ALBERT II of the house of Habsburg 1438–9, Emperor elect
FREDERICK III of the House of Habsburg 1440; 1452–93
  A remote cousin of the above.
MAXIMILIAN 1493–1519
  Son of the above.
CHARLES V 1519–55
  Grandson of the above. He won election as Emperor from Francis I of
  France, by bribing the electors. He was also King of Spain, ruler of the
  Low Countries and of Spanish America.

Notes

Introduction (pages 1–8)

1 Riley-Smith, Jonathan (ed.), *The Oxford Illustrated History of the Crusades* (Oxford, 1997), p. 10.
2 Bull, Marcus, *Knightly Piety and the Lay Response to the First Crusade* (Oxford, 1993), p. 204.
3 Ibid., p. 113.
4 Frend, W.H.C., *The Early Church* (London, 1956), p. 250.
5 Bull, op. cit., p. 286.
6 France, John, *Victory in the East: A Military History of the First Crusade* (Cambridge, 1994), p. 1.
7 Ibid., p. 50.
8 Ibid., p. 13.
9 Ibid., p. 16.
10 Bradford, Ernle, *The Great Betrayal 1204* (London, 1967), p. 66.
11 Cited in France, op. cit., p. 42.
12 Ibid., p. 81.

Chapter 1: Beginnings 632–1095 (pages 9–23)

1 Ullman, Walter, *A Short History of the Papacy in the Middle Ages* (London, 1972), p. 150.
2 Bull, op. cit., p. 32.
3 Runciman, Steven, *A History of the Crusades*, vol. I (Cambridge, 1951, reprinted 1957), p. 104.
4 Brown, Peter, *The World of Late Antiquity from Marcus Aurelius to Muhammad* (London, 1971), p. 191.
5 Ibid., p. 169–70.
6 Ibid., p. 192.

7   Housley, Norman (ed. and trans.), *Documents on the Later Crusades, 1274–1580* (Basingstoke, 1996), p. 41.
8   Riley-Smith, Jonathan, *What were the Crusades?* (Basingstoke, 1977), p. 35.
9   Barber, Richard, *Henry Plantagenet* (London, 1964), p. 223.
10 Brundage, James, *The Crusades, Holy War and Canon Law* (Aldershot, 1991), VII, 291.
11 Ibid., IX, 177.
12 Ibid., VI, 93.
13 Ibid., VIII, 234.
14 Bull, op. cit., p. 108.
15 Ibid., pp. 62, 66–7.
16 Parkes, James, *A History of the Jewish People* (Harmondsworth, 1964), p. 68.

Chapter 2: The First Crusade 1095–1099 (pages 25–49)

1   Eidelberg, Shlomo (ed. and trans.), *The Jews and the Crusaders: The Hebrew Chronicles of the First and Second Crusades* (London, 1977), p. 35.
2   Runciman, op. cit., p. 140.
3   France, op. cit., p. 44.
4   Bull, op. cit., pp. 83–5.
5   France, op. cit., p. 14.
6   McLennan, Graham, *Women Crusaders: Women and the Holy Land 1095–1195* (Hawker, 1997), p. 4.
7   France, op. cit., p. 84.
8   Runciman, op. cit., p. 168.
9   Comnena, The Princess Anna, *The Alexiad: Being the History of the Reign of her Father, Alexius I, Emperor of the Romans 1081–1118 AD*, trans. Elizabeth A.S. Dawes (London, 1928, reissued 1967), pp. 261 & 265.
10 Ibid.
11 France, op. cit., p. 111.
12 This account of the campaign against Nicaea relies on France, op. cit., pp. 143–62.
13 Ibid., p. 175.
14 Ibid., p. 184.
15 Ibid., p. 193.
16 Ibid., p. 206.
17 Ibid., p. 227.
18 Boas, Adrian J., *Crusader Archaeology: The Material Culture of the Latin East* (London and New York, 1999), p. 42.
19 France, op. cit., p. 212.
20 Ibid., pp. 239–41.
21 Ibid., p. 263.
22 Ibid., p. 269.
23 Ibid., p. 270.
24 Ibid., p. 280.
25 Ibid., p. 283.
26 Cited ibid., p. 284.

27 Barnet, Corelli, *Marlborough* (London, 1974, reissued Ware, 1999), p. 107.
28 France, op. cit., p. 295.
29 Ibid., p. 112.

Chapter 3: Life and Politics in a Multicultural World (pages 51–69)

1 Bull, op. cit., p. 25.
2 Runciman, Steven, *A History of the Crusades*, vol. II (Cambridge, 1952, reprinted 1957), p. 151.
3 Riley-Smith, Jonathan (ed.), *Atlas of the Crusades* (London, 1991), pp. 40–1.
4 Boas, op. cit., p. 24.
5 Riley-Smith, (ed.) *The Oxford Illustrated History of the Crusades*, pp. 198–9.
6 Boas, op. cit., p. 26.
7 Ibid., p. 22.
8 Ibid., p. 23.
9 France, op. cit., p. 15 and note.
10 Boas, op. cit., pp. 60–5.
11 This account of the sugar industry in Cyprus and Outremer is based on Boas, op. cit., p. 81.
12 Ibid., p. 143.
13 Riley-Smith, (ed.), *Atlas of the Crusades*, pp. 42–3.
14 Hindley, Geoffrey, *Saladin: A Biography* (London, 1976), p. 165.
15 Ibid., p. 166.

Chapter 4: The Second Crusade: Disaster on the Road to Damascus (pages 71–85)

1 Weir, Alison, *Eleanor of Aquitaine: By the Wrath of God* (Harmondsworth, 1999), p. 35.
2 Owen, D.D.R., *Eleanor of Aquitaine: Queen and Legend* (Oxford, 1996), p. 149.
3 Runciman, op. cit., vol. II, p. 254.
4 Bull, op. cit., p. 77.
5 Constable, Giles, 'The Second Crusade as seen by Contemporaries', *Traditio IX* (New York 1953), p. 53.
6 Hindley, op. cit., p. 16.
7 Weir, op. cit., p. 56.
8 Runciman, op. cit., vol. II, p. 279.
9 Hindley, op. cit., p. 42.
10 Runciman, op. cit., vol. II, p. 286.

Chapter 5: Turk and Kurd: Heroes of Islam (pages 87–105)

1 Hindley, op. cit., p. 49.
2 Warren, W.L., *Henry II* (London, 1973), p. 604.
3 Hassal, W.O., *Who's Who in History*, Vol. I (Oxford, 1960), p. 96.
4 Cochrane, Louise, *Adelard of Bath: The First British Scientist* (London, 1994),

gives the best recent account of this important figure in Europe's 'twelfth century renaissance'.

5 Warren, loc. cit.
6 Ibid.
7 Gabrieli, Francesco, (ed.) *Arab Historians of the Crusades*, trans. E.J. Costello (London, 1969), p. 123.
8 Ibid, p. 146.

Chapter 6: Women and an Alternative Feudalism (pages 107–119)

1 Miller, William, *The Latins in the Levant: A History of Frankish Greece (1204–1566)* (London, 1908), pp. 35 & 55.
2 See Owen, op. cit., p. 150.
3 Gabriel, op. cit., pp. 189–207.
4 Aldington, Richard (trans.), *The Decameron* (London, 1959), p. 153.
5 Gabrieli, op. cit., pp. 204–5.
6 Brundage, op. cit., XIX, 58.
7 Ibid., XV, 429.
8 Ibid., XV, 431.
9 Ibid., XV, 435.
10 Ibid., XVII, 260.
11 Ibid., XVII, 271.
12 Ibid., XVII, 260.
13 Ibid., XVII, 263.
14 McLennan, op. cit., p. 7.
15 Boase, T.S.R., *Kingdoms and Strongholds of the Crusaders* (London, 1971), p. 108.

Chapter 7: Loss of Jerusalem and the Third Crusade 1187–1192 (pages 121–142)

1 Munz, Peter, *Frederick Barbarossa: A Study in Medieval Politics* (London, 1969), p. 242.
2 Ibid., p. 371.
3 Ibid., p. 372.
4 Ibid., p. 377.
5 Ibid., p. 383.
6 Hindley, op. cit., p. 145.
7 Lane-Poole, Stanley, *Saladin and the Fall of the Kingdom of Jerusalem* (New York and London, 1906), p. 245.
8 Hindley, op. cit., p. 163.
9 France, op. cit., p. 170.
10 Munz, op. cit., note on p. 371.
11 Hindley, op. cit., p. 142.
12 Riley-Smith, *Atlas of the Crusades*, p. 63.
13 Munz, op. cit., p. 397.
14 Schmugge, Ludwig, *Der Kreuzfahrer aus der Sicht humanistischer Geschichtsschreiber* (Basel, c. 1987), p. 15.

15 Lloyd, Sir John Edward, *A History of Wales*, 2 vols, 3rd ed. (London, 1948), p. 562.

16 Thorpe, Lewis, (trans.) Gerald of Wales: *The Journey Through Wales* (Harmondsworth, 1978).

17 Appleby, John T., *England without Richard 1189–1190* (London, 1965), pp. 11–12.

18 Tyerman, William, *England and the Crusades 1095–1588* (Chicago and London, 1978), pp. 69–71.

19 Ibid., pp. 45–7.

20 Brundage, op. cit., IV, p. 67.

21 Ibid., IV, p. 68.

Chapter 8: The Fourth Crusade: The Latin Conquest of Constantinople and the Scandal of Christendom (pages 143–158)

1 Runciman, op. cit., vol. II, pp. 109 & 112.

2 Vasiliev, A.A., *History of the Byzantine Empire 324–1453*, vol. II, 2nd ed. (Madison, 1964), p. 452.

3 Ibid., p. 451.

4 Shaw, M.R.B. (trans.), *Joinville & Villehardouin. Chronicles of the Crusades* (Harmondsworth, 1965), p. 29.

5 Vasiliev, op. cit., p. 425.

6 Shaw, op. cit., p. 35.

7 loc. cit.

8 Shaw, op. cit., p. 33.

9 Boase, op. cit., p. 153.

10 Ibid., p. 154.

11 Vasiliev, op. cit., p. 454.

12 Ibid., p. 462.

13 Geanakopolos, Deno J., *Byzantine East and West: Two Worlds of Christendom in the Middle Ages and Renaissance* (Oxford, 1966), p. 18.

14 Vasiliev, op. cit., p. 463.

15 Riley-Smith, (ed.) *Atlas of the Crusades*, p. 86.

16 Geanakopolos, op. cit., p. 3.

17 Ibid., p. 22.

18 Ibid., p. 39.

Chapter 9: Heathen, Heretics and Children (pages 159–176)

1 Based on Housley, Norman, *The Later Crusades: From Lyons to Alcazar 1274–1580* (Oxford, 1992), pp. 324–5.

2 Seibt, Ferdinand, *Glanz und Elend des Mittelalters* (Berlin, 1987), p. 321.

3 Brundage, op. cit., X, 120.

4 Ibid., XIV, 3.

5 Ibid., XIV, 5.

6 Riley-Smith, Jonathan, *What were the Crusades?* (Basingstoke, 1977), p. 14.

7 Based on Barber, Malcolm, *Crusaders and Heretics* (Aldershot, 1995), XI, 14.

8 Based on Runciman, Steven, *The Medieval Manichee* (Cambridge, 1947), pp. 131–3.
9 Barber, op. cit., III, 51.
10 Southern, Richard, *Western Society and the Church in the Middle Ages* (Harmondsworth, 1970), p. 19.
11 Ibid., p. 122.
12 Barber, op. cit., IX, 1.
13 Ibid., IX, 3.

Chapter 10: Triumphs of an Excommunicated Emperor (pages 177–193)

1 Runciman, *A History of the Crusades*, vol. III, p. 145.
2 Ibid., p. 146.
3 Van Cleve, Thomas Curtis, *The Emperor Frederick II of Hohenstaufen: Immutator Mundi* (Oxford, 1972), p. 96, to which this chapter is much indebted.
4 Hindley, Geoffrey, *Castles of Europe*, (Feltham, 1968), pp. 154–5.
5 Ibid., p. 165.
6 Ibid., p. 204.

Chapter 11: The Failures of a Saint (pages 195–208)

1 Runciman, *A History of the Crusades*, vol. II, p. 255.
2 Boase, op. cit., p. 186.
3 Riley-Smith, (ed.) *Atlas of the Crusades*, pp. 36–9.
4 Riley-Smith, (ed.) *Oxford Illustrated History of the Crusades*.
5 Prestwich, Michael, *Edward I* (London, 1988), p. 67.

Chapter 12: Acre and After (pages 209–223)

1 Housley, op. cit., p. 24.
2 Barber, op. cit., IV, 145.
3 Ibid., IV, 12.
4 Ibid., V, 148.
5 Ibid., IV, 4.
6 Ibid., IV, 5.
7 Ibid., IV, 17.
8 Cited in Housley, op. cit., p. 30.
9 Edbury, Peter W., *The Kingdom of Cyprus and the Crusades, 1191–1374* (Cambridge, 1991), pp. 173–6.

Chapter 13: Chivalry in Action and Nicopolis 'The Last Crusade' (pages 225–235)

1 Housley, op. cit., p. 338.
2 Ibid., p. 347.
3 Ibid., p. 350.
4 Ibid., p. 345.
5 Ibid., p. 354.

6   Ibid., p. 352.
7   Riley-Smith, *Atlas of the Crusades*, p. 142.
8   Riley-Smith, *The Oxford History of the Crusades* (Oxford, 1999), p. 247.
9   Vaughan, Richard, *Philip the Bold: The Formation of the Burgundian State* (London, 1962), p. 59.
10   Ibid.
11   Tuchman, Barbara, *A Distant Mirror* (Harmondsworth, 1979), p. 552.
12   Vaughan, op. cit., p. 76.

Chapter 14: The Lingering Decline of a Flawed Ideal (pages 237–253)

1   Housley, op. cit., p. 308.
2   Shaw, M.R.B., op. cit., p. 181.
3   Southern, op. cit., pp. 136–7.
4   Housley, op. cit., p. 309.
5   Ibid.
6   MacCulloch, Diarmaid, *Thomas Cranmer* (New Haven and London, 1996), p. 313.
7   Housley, op. cit., p. 317.
8   Hutchinson, Harold, *Henry V* (London, 1967), p. 266.
9   Riley-Smith, *Atlas of the Crusades*, p. 131.
10   Hindley, Geoffrey, *Medieval Warfare* (London, 1971), p. 120.
11   Runciman, Steven, *The Fall of Constantinople 1453* (Cambridge, 1965), p. 145.
12   Ibid., p. 83.
13   Vaughan, Richard, *Philip the Good: The Apogee of Burgundy* (London, 1970), pp. 144–5 & 297.
14   Housley, op. cit., p. 288.
15   Ibid., p. 290.
16   Ibid., p. 301.
17   Riley-Smith, op. cit., p. 160.
18   Housley, op. cit., p. 20.
19   Riley-Smith, *Oxford Illustrated History of the Crusades*, p. 7.

Epilogue: The Aftermath (pages 255–260)

1   Maalouf, Amin, *The Crusades through Arab Eyes* (London, 1983), p. 266.
2   Riley-Smith, op. cit., p. 384.
3   Atiya, Aziz S., *The Crusade: Historiography and Bibliography* (Bloomington & London, 1962), p. 11.
4   Riley-Smith, op. cit., p. 89.
5   Southern, op. cit., p. 89.
6   Cole, Penny, 'The Legacy of the Crusades', Nash Memorial Lecture in the University of Saskatchewan, 2000.
7   Maalouf, op. cit., p. 266.

Select Bibliography

Aldington, Richard (trans.) *The Decameron* (London, 1959).

Appleby, John T., *England without Richard 1189–1190* (London, 1965).

Asthor-Strauss, E., 'Saladin and the Jews', in *The Hebrew Union College Annual Journal* (Cincinnati, 1956).

Atiya, Aziz Suryal, *The Crusade: Historiography and Bibliography* (Bloomington and London, 1934).

——, *The Crusade of Nicopolis* (London, 1934).

Barber, Malcolm, *Crusaders and Heretics 12th–14th Centuries* (Aldershot, 1995).

Barber, Richard, *Henry Plantagenet* (London, 1974).

Barnett, Corelli, *Marlborough* (London, 1974).

Bienvenu, Jean-Marc, 'Aliénor d'Aquitaine et Fontevraud', *Cahiers de Civ. Med XXIX* (1986).

Boas, Adrian, *Crusader Archaeology: The Material Culture of the Latin East* (London and New York, 1999).

Boase, T.S.R., *Kingdoms and Strongholds of the Crusaders* (London, 1971).

Boxer, C.R., *The Portuguese Seaborne Empire 1415–1825* (London, 1969).

Bradford, Ernle, *The Great Betrayal: Constantinople 1204* (Harmondsworth, 1976).

——, *The Great Siege: Malta 1565* (London, 1967).

Brand, Charles M., 'The Byzantines and Saladin 1185–1192. Opponents of the Third Crusade', in *Speculum XXXVII* (Cambridge, Mass., 1962).

Brown, Peter, *The World of Late Antiquity from Marcus Aurelius to Muhammad* (London, 1971).

Brundage, James A., *The Crusade, Holy War and Canon Law* (Aldershot, 1991).

Bull, Marcus, *Knightly Piety and the Lay Response to the First Crusade* (Oxford, 1993).

Cahen, Claude, *Orient et Occident au temps des Croisades* (Paris, 1983).

Cochrane, Louise, *Adelard of Bath: The First English Scientist* (London, 1994).

Cohn, Norman, *The Pursuit of the Millennium* (London, 1970).

Comnena, the Princess Anna, *The Alexiad: Being the History of the Reign of her Father, Alexius I, Emperor of the Romans 1081–1118 AD*, trans. Elizabeth A.S. Dawes (London, 1928, reissued 1967).

Constable, Giles, 'The Second Crusade as seen by Contemporaries', *Traditio IX* (1953).

Daniel, Norman, *Islam and the West* (Edinburgh, 1960).

Davis, R.H.C., *King Stephen 1135–1154* (London, 1967).

De Sismondi, Simon J.C.L., *History of the Crusades against the Albigenses* (London, 1826).

Edbury, Peter W., *The Kingdom of Cyprus and the Crusades, 1191–1374* (Cambridge, 1991).

Ehrenkreuz, Andrew S., *Saladin* (Albany, 1972).

Eidelberg, Shlomo (ed. and trans.), *The Jews and the Crusaders: The Hebrew Chronicles of the First and Second Crusades* (London, 1977).

Elliott, J.H., *Imperial Spain 1469–1716* (London, 1965).

Fox Davies, Arthur Charles, *A Complete Guide to Heraldry* (1929, reprinted London, 1993).

France, John, *Victory in the East: A Military History of the First Crusade* (Cambridge, 1994).

Frend, W.H.C., *The Early Church* (London, 1965).

Gabrieli, Francesco (ed.), *Storici Arabi delle Crociate* (Torino, 1957).

——, *Arab Historians of the Crusades*, translated from the Italian by E.J. Costello (London, 1969).

Geanakopolos, Deno J., *Byzantine East and Latin West: Two Worlds of Christendom in the Middle Ages and Renaissance* (Oxford, 1966).

Grousset, R., *Histoire des croisades et du royaume latin de Jerusalem*, 3 vols (Paris, 1933–38).

Hamilton, Bernard, 'Women in the Crusader States: The Queens of Jerusalem 1100–90', in Derek Baker (ed.), *Medieval Women* (Oxford, 1978).

Hassall, W.O., *Who's Who in History, Vol. I British Isles* (Oxford, 1960).

Hindley, Geoffrey, *Castles of Europe* (Feltham, 1968).

——, *Medieval Warfare* (London, 1971).

——, *Saladin: a Biography* (London, 1976).

——, *Under Siege* (London, 1979).

Housley, Norman, *The Later Crusades: From Lyons to Alcazar 1274–1580* (Oxford, 1992).

—— (ed. and trans.), *Documents on the Later Crusades, 1274–1580* (Basingstoke, 1996).

Hussey, J.M., *Church & Learning in the Byzantine Empire 867–1185* (London, 1937).

Hutchinson, Harold F., *Henry V* (London, 1967).

Hyland, Ann, *The Medieval Warhorse* (Stroud, 1994).

Kaminsky, Howard, *A History of the Hussite Revolution* (Berkerley and Los Angeles, 1967).

Kinglake, Alexander William, *Eothen* (London, 1952).

Kirkby, J.L., *Henry IV of England* (London, 1970).

Lane-Poole, Stanley, *Saladin and the Fall of the Kingdom of Jerusalem* (New York and London, 1906).

Lloyd, Sir John Edward, *A History of Wales*, 2 vols, 3rd ed. (London, 1948).

Lloyd, Simon, *English Society and the Crusades* (Oxford, 1988).

Lyons, Malcolm Cameron and Jackson, D.E.P., *Saladin: The Politics of Holy War* (Cambridge, 1982).

Maalouf, Amia, *The Crusades through Arab Eyes*, trans. John Rothschild (London, 1983).

MacCulloch, Diarmaid, *Thomas Cranmer* (New Haven and London, 1996).

McGinty, Martha Evelyn, *Fulcher of Chartres, Chronicle of the First Crusade* (Philadelphia, 1941).

McLennan, Graham, *Women Crusaders: Women and the Holy Land 1095–1195* (Hawker, 1997).

Miller, William, *The Latins in the Levant: A History of Frankish Greece (1204–1566)* (London, 1908).

Morgan, M.R., *The Chronicle of Ernoul and the Continuations of William of Tyre* (Oxford, 1973).

Müller-Wiener, *Castles of the Crusaders* (London, 1976).

Munz, Peter, *Frederick Barbarossa: A Study in Medieval Politics* (London, 1969).

Owen, D.D.R., *Eleanor of Aquitaine: Queen and Legend* (Oxford, 1996).

Parkes, James, *A History of the Jewish People* (Harmondsworth, 1964).

Pernoud, Regine, *La Femme au temps des Croisades* (Paris, 1990).

Powicke, F.M., *King Henry III and the Lord Edward* (Oxford, 1947).

Prawer, J., *Crusader Institutions* (Oxford, 1980).

——, *The History of the Jews in the Latin Kingdom of Jerusalem* (Oxford, 1988).

Prestwich, Michael, *Edward I* (London, 1988).

Queller, Donald E., *The Latin Conquest of Constantinople* (New York, 1971).

Renouard, Yves, *The Avignon Papacy 1305–1403*, trans. Denis Bethell (London, 1970).

Riley-Smith, Jonathan, *What were the Crusades?* (Basingstoke, 1977).

—— (ed.), *Atlas of the Crusades* (London, 1991).

Robinson, John J., *Dungeon Fire and Sword: The Knights Templar in the Crusades* (London, 1994).

Roche, T.W.E., *The King of Almayne* (London, 1966).

Runciman, Steven, *The Medieval Manichee* (Cambridge, 1947).

——, *A History of the Crusades*, vol. I, *The First Crusade* (Cambridge, 1951, reprinted 1957).

——, *A History of the Crusades*, vol. II, *The Kingdom of Jerusalem* (Cambridge, 1952, reprinted 1957).

——, *A History of the Crusades*, vol. III, *The Kingdom of Acre* (Cambridge, 1954, reprinted 1955).

——, *The Sicilian Vespers* (Harmondsworth, 1960).

——, *The Fall of Constantinople 1453* (Cambridge, 1965).

Scarisbrick, J.J., *Henry VIII* (London, 1968).

Schmugge, Ludwig, *Der Kreuzfahrer aus der Sicht humanistischer Geschichtsschreiber* (Basel, c. 1987).

Seibt, Ferdinand, *Glanz und Elend des Mittelalters: Eine endliche Geschichte* (Berlin, 1987).

Setton, K.M. (editor-in-chief) *A History of the Crusades*, 2nd ed., 6 vols (Madison, Wis., 1969–89).

Shaw, M.R.B. (trans.), *Joinville & Villehardouin, Chronicles of the Crusades* (Harmondsworth, 1965).

Sivan, Emmanuel, *L'Islam et la Croisade* (Paris, 1968).

Smail, R.C., *The Crusaders in Syria and the Holy Land* (London, 1973).

——, *Crusading Warfare, 1097–1193* (Cambridge, 1956).

Southern, R.W., *Western Society and the Church in the Middle Ages* (Harmondsworth, 1970).

Thorpe, Lewis (trans.), *Gerald of Wales: The Journey Through Wales* (Harmondsworth, 1978).

Tydeman, William, *The Theatre in the Middle Ages* (Cambridge, 1978).

Tyerman, Christopher, *England the Crusades 1095–1588* (Chicago and London, 1988).

Tyre, William of, *A History of Deeds Done Beyond the Sea*, 2 vols, E.A. Babcock and A.C. Kay (eds) (New York, 1976).

Ullmann, Walter, *A History of Political Thought: The Middle Ages* (Harmondsworth, 1965).

——, *A Short History of the Papacy in the Middle Ages* (London, 1972).

Van Cleve, Thomas Curtis, *The Emperor Frederick II of Hohenstaufen: Immutator Mundi* (Oxford, 1972).

Vasiliev, A.A., *History of the Byzantine Empire 324–1453*, vol. II, 2nd ed. (Madison, 1964).

——, *John the Fearless: The Growth of Burgundian Power* (London, 1966).

Vaughan, Richard, *Philip the Bold: The Formation of the Burgundian State* (London, 1962).

Vlasto, A.P., *The Entry of the Slavs into Christendom* (Cambridge, 1970).

Vryonis, Speros, *Byzantium and Europe* (London, 1967).

Warren, Raoul de, et Lestrange, Aymon de, *Les Prétendants au trône de France* (Paris, 1990).

Warren, W.L., *Henry II* (London, 1973).

Weir, Alison, *Eleanor of Aquitaine* (London, 1999).

Index

INDEX